Susan Brownmiller

Against Our Will

Men, Women and Rape

Penguin Books

Penguin Books Ltd, Harmondsworth, Middlesex, England
Penguin Books, 625 Madison Avenue, New York, New York 10022, U.S.A.
Penguin Books Australia Ltd, Ringwood, Victoria, Australia
Penguin Books Canada Ltd, 41 Steelcase Road West, Markham, Ontario, Canada
Penguin Books (N.Z.) Ltd, 182–190 Wairau Road, Auckland 10, New Zealand

First published by Martin Secker & Warburg, 1975
Published in Penguin Books 1976
Reprinted 1976, 1977

The author gratefully acknowledges permission to reprint material from the
following sources:
    ABKCO Music, Inc., for material from 'Midnight Rambler' by Mick Jagger and
Keith Richard; copyright © 1969. All rights reserved.
    Beacon Press for material from *The Winter Soldier Investigation: An Inquiry
Into American War Crimes* by the Vietnam Veterans Against the War, copyright
© 1972 by Vietnam Veterans Against the War, Inc.
    The Belknap Press of Harvard University for material from *Bracton on the Laws
and Customs of England*, Vol. II, Samuel E. Thorne, translator and editor;
copyright © 1968 by the President and Fellows of Harvard College.
    Grune and Stratton, Inc., and Dr. Helene Deutsch for material from *The
Psychology of Women*, Vols. I and II, by Dr. Helene Deutsch; copyright 1944, 1945;
copyright renewed © 1971 by Helen Deutsch.
    The Journal Press and W. H. Blanchard for material from 'The Group Process
in Gang Rape,' by W. H. Blanchard, from *The Journal of Social Psychology*, 1959,
49, 259–66.
    Random House, Inc., for material from *I Know Why the Caged Bird Sings* by
Maya Angelou, copyright © 1969 by Maya Angelou.

Made and printed in Great Britain by
Richard Clay (The Chaucer Press) Ltd, Bungay, Suffolk

Penguin Books
Against Our Will

Susan Brownmiller is a graduate of Cornell University.
She has worked as a television news writer and reporter
and has contributed to the *New York Times* Book
Review. In 1973 she won the journalistic award, the
Alicia Patterson Foundation Fellowship. Her previous
works include a biography of Shirley Chisholm.

CONTENTS

A PERSONAL STATEMENT

The question most often asked of me while I was writing this book was short, direct and irritating: "Have you ever been raped?"

My answer was equally direct: "No."

This exchange, repeated many times in many places, seemed to satisfy neither the questioner nor me. When I thought about it, I decided that there were differing motivations on the part of my interlocutors. For some, I concluded, the question was a double-edged credentials challenge: If you're not a criminologist or a victim, then who are you? (Why wasn't it enough that I was a writer onto an interesting subject, I wonder.) For others, I suspected, a curious twist of logic lay behind the question. A woman who chooses to write about rape probably has a dark personal reason, a lurid secret, a history of real or imagined abuse, a trauma back there somewhere, a fixation, a Bad Experience that has permanently warped her or instilled in her the compulsion to Tell the World.

I hate to disappoint, but the answer is still "No." I may have been shortchanged here and there, but I have never been coerced. Yet there did come a time when I knew with certainty that I had to write a book about rape, and I proceeded to do it with more tenacity and grueling methodical effort than I have ever applied to any other project in my life.

The matching up of author with subject matter is a mysterious process. I could point with professional detachment to the fact that rape has been a theme of mine in print since 1968 when I wrote a piece for a magazine about an interracial rape case with political ramifications. I could argue forcefully that years ago, before the current interest, I had staked out the territory. But this would be more than slightly disingenuous. For when I wrote about rape for that magazine, a magazine that prides itself, incidentally, on being "the magazine for men," and one which at the time I was proud to be writing for, I wrote the story from the perspective of a woman who viewed a rape case with suspicion. And I would have to say today that this suspicion, this harsh "objectivity," was what made my story printable. Although I conducted scores of interviews for that article, I did not seek out nor did I attempt to speak with the victim. I felt no kinship with her, nor did I admit, publicly or privately, that what had happened to her could on *any level* happen to me.

I have always considered myself a strong woman, although I understand that the strength I possess is a matter of style and, secretly, of theatrical bravura. I am combative, wary and verbally aggressive. I like to think I know my own mind, and I like to think I act on my principles. This has led me, at times, to work harder at politics than at writing. Knowing my own mind, I also know that a good mind must be flexible and open to change. The older I get the more I realize that there are few absolutes and many perspectives.

The views I used to hold about rape were compatible with the kinds of causes, people and ideas I identified with generally: the civil rights movement, defense lawyer heroics, and psychologic sympathy for the accused. I saw no need to re-examine my views since people I respected espoused them, and since they were sufficiently intricate and conspiratorial to appeal to my sense of radical drama. That these attitudes might be anti-female never occurred to me. It also did not occur to me that acceptance of these attitudes gave me a feeling of security I needed: it can't happen *here*.

And so, when a group of my women friends discussed rape one evening in the fall of 1970, I fairly shrieked in dismay. *I* knew what rape was, and what it wasn't. Rape was a sex crime, a product of a diseased, deranged mind. Rape wasn't a feminist issue, rape was . . . well, what was it? At any rate, I certainly knew something about rape victims! The women's movement had nothing in common with rape victims. Victims of rape were . . . well, what were they? Who were they?

I learned that evening, and on many other evenings and long afternoons, that victims of rape could be women I knew—women who, when their turn came to speak, quietly articulated their own experiences. Women who understood their victimization whereas I understood only that it had not happened to me—and resisted the idea that it could. I learned that in ways I preferred to deny the threat of rape had profoundly affected my life.

I didn't learn easily. I argued, confronted, scoffed and denied. To placate some of the others, I went along with the idea of a public rape speak-out. Will we really get women to stand up and testify, I wondered, and what will they come up with? (What they came up with blew my mind.) Out of a sense of "let's get on with it," I proposed a rape conference. Conferences are not like personal speak-outs. Conferences require objective information, statistics, research and study. What will we be able to come up with, I wondered. The conference, which I had proposed out of restlessness and participated in only marginally, as a sort of senior planning consultant, proved to be my moment of revelation. There, in a high school auditorium, I finally confronted my own fears, my own past, my own intellectual defenses. Something important and frightening to contemplate had been left out of my education—a way of looking at male-female relations, at sex, at strength, and at power. Never one to acknowledge my vulnerability, I found myself forced by my sisters in feminism to look it squarely in the eye.

I wrote this book because I am a woman who changed her mind about rape.

SUSAN BROWNMILLER

New York City
February 1975

1

The Mass Psychology of Rape: An Introduction

Krafft-Ebing, who pioneered in the study of sexual disorders, had little to say about rape. His famous *Psychopathia Sexualis* gives amazingly short shrift to the act and its doers. He had it on good authority, he informed his readers, that most rapists were degenerate, imbecilic men. Having made that sweeping generalization, Krafft-Ebing washed his hands of the whole affair and turned with relish to the frotteurs and fetishists of normal intelligence who tickled his fancy.

Sigmund Freud, whose major works followed Krafft-Ebing's by twenty to forty years, was also struck dumb by the subject of rape. We can search his writings in vain for a quotable quote, an analysis, a perception. The father of psychoanalysis, who invented the concept of the primacy of the penis, was never motivated, as far as we know, to explore the real-life deployment of the penis as weapon. What the master ignored, the disciples tended to ignore as well. Alfred Adler does not mention rape, despite his full awareness of the historic power struggle between men and women. Jung refers to rape only in the most obscure manner, a glancing reference in some of his mythological interpretations. Helene Deutsch and Karen Horney, each from a differing perspective, grasped at the female fear of rape, and at the feminine fantasy, but as women who did not dare to presume, they turned a blind eye to the male and female reality.

And the great socialist theoreticians Marx and Engels and

their many confreres and disciples who developed the theory of class oppression and put words like "exploitation" into the everyday vocabulary, they, too, were strangely silent about rape, unable to fit it into their economic constructs. Among them only August Bebel tried to grasp at its historic importance, its role in the very formulation of class, private property and the means of production. In *Woman Under Socialism* Bebel used his imagination to speculate briefly about the prehistoric tribal fights for land, cattle and labor power within an acceptable Marxist analysis: "There arose the need of labor power to cultivate the ground. The more numerous these powers, all the greater was the wealth in products and herds. These struggles led first to the rape of women, later to the enslaving of conquered men. The women became laborers and objects of pleasure for the conqueror; their males became slaves." He didn't get it quite right, making the rape of women secondary to man's search for labor, but it was a flash of revelation and one that Engels did not achieve in his *Origin of the Family*. But Bebel was more at ease researching the wages and conditions of working-women in German factories, and that is where his energies went.

It was the half-crazed genius Wilhelm Reich, consumed with rage in equal parts toward Hitler, Marx and Freud, who briefly entertained the vision of a "masculine ideology of rape." The phrase hangs there in the opening chapter of *The Sexual Revolution*, begging for further interpretation. But it was not forthcoming. The anguished mind was in too great a state of disarray. A political analysis of rape would have required more treachery toward his own immutable gender than even Wilhelm Reich could muster.

And so it remained for the latter-day feminists, free at last from the strictures that forbade us to look at male sexuality, to discover the truth and meaning in our own victimization. Critical to our study is the recognition that rape has a history, and that through the tools of historical analysis we may learn what we need to know about our current condition.

No zoologist, as far as I know, has ever observed that animals rape in their natural habitat, the wild. Sex in the animal world, including those species that are our closest relations, the primates, is more properly called "mating," and it is cyclical activity set off by biologic signals the female puts out. Mating is initiated and "controlled," it would seem, by the female estrous cycle. When the female of the species periodically goes into heat, giving off obvious physical signs, she is ready and eager for copulation and the male becomes interested. At other times there is simply no interest, and no mating.

Jane Goodall, studying her wild chimpanzees at the Gombe Stream reserve, noted that the chimps, male and female, were "very promiscuous, but this does not mean that every female will accept every male that courts her." She recorded her observations of one female in heat, who showed the telltale pink swelling of her genital area, who nevertheless displayed an aversion to one particular male who pursued her. "Though he once shook her out of the tree in which she had sought refuge, we never saw him actually 'rape' her," Goodall wrote, adding, however, "Nonetheless, quite often he managed to get his way through dogged persistence." Another student of animal behavior, Leonard Williams, has stated categorically, "The male monkey cannot in fact mate with the female without her invitation and willingness to cooperate. In monkey society there is no such thing as rape, prostitution, or even passive consent."

Zoologists for the most part have been reticent on the subject of rape. It has not been, for them, an important scientific question. But we do know that human beings are different. Copulation in our species can occur 365 days of the year; it is not controlled by the female estrous cycle. We females of the human species do not "go pink." The call of estrus and the telltale signs, both visual and olfactory, are absent from our mating procedures, lost perhaps in the evolutionary shuffle. In their place, as a mark of our civilization, we have evolved a complex system of psychological signs and urges, and a complex structure of pleasure. Our call to sex occurs in the head, and the act is not necessarily linked, as it is with animals, to Mother Nature's pattern of procreation. Without a biologically determined mating season, a human male can evince sexual interest in a human female at any time he pleases, and his psychologic urge is not dependent in the slightest on her biologic readiness or receptivity. What it all boils down to is that the human male can rape.

Man's structural capacity to rape and woman's corresponding structural vulnerability are as basic to the physiology of both our sexes as the primal act of sex itself. Had it not been for this accident of biology, an accommodation requiring the locking together of two separate parts, penis into vagina, there would be neither copulation nor rape as we know it. Anatomically one might want to improve on the design of nature, but such speculation appears to my mind as unrealistic. The human sex act accomplishes its historic purpose of generation of the species and it also affords some intimacy and pleasure. I have no basic quarrel with the procedure. But, nevertheless, we cannot work around the fact that in terms of human anatomy the possibility of forcible intercourse incontrovertibly exists. This single factor may have been sufficient to have caused the creation of a male ideology of rape. When men discovered that they could rape, they proceeded to do it. Later, much later, under certain circumstances they even came to consider rape a crime.

In the violent landscape inhabited by primitive woman and man, some woman somewhere had a prescient vision of her right to her own physical integrity, and in my mind's eye I can picture her fighting like hell to preserve it. After a thunderbolt of recognition that this particular incarnation of hairy, two-legged hominid was not the Homo sapiens with whom she would like to freely join parts, it might have been she, and not some man, who picked up the first stone and hurled it. How surprised he must have been, and what an unexpected battle must have taken place. Fleet of foot and spirited, she would have kicked, bitten, pushed and run, but she could not retaliate in kind.

The dim perception that had entered prehistoric woman's consciousness must have had an equal but opposite reaction in the mind of her male assailant. For if the first rape was an unexpected battle founded on the first woman's refusal, the second rape was indubitably planned. Indeed, one of the earliest forms of male bonding must have been the gang rape of one woman by a band of marauding men. This accomplished, rape became not only a male prerogative, but man's basic weapon of force against woman, the principal agent of his will and her fear. His forcible entry into her body, despite her physical protestations and struggle, became the vehicle of his victorious conquest over her being, the ultimate test of his superior strength, the triumph of his manhood.

Man's discovery that his genitalia could serve as a weapon to generate fear must rank as one of the most important discoveries of prehistoric times, along with the use of fire and the first crude stone axe. From prehistoric times to the present, I believe, rape has played a critical function. It is nothing more or less than a conscious process of intimidation by which *all men* keep *all women* in a state of fear.

2

In the Beginning
Was the Law

From the humblest beginnings of the social order based on a primitive system of retaliatory force—the *lex talionis*: an eye for an eye—woman was unequal before the law. By anatomical fiat—the inescapable construction of their genital organs—the human male was a natural predator and the human female served as his natural prey. Not only might the female be subjected at will to a thoroughly detestable physical conquest from which there could be no retaliation in kind—a rape for a rape—but the consequences of such a brutal struggle might be death or injury, not to mention impregnation and the birth of a dependent child.

One possibility, and one possibility alone, was available to woman. Those of her own sex whom she might call to her aid were more often than not smaller and weaker than her male attackers. More critical, they lacked the basic physical wherewithal for punitive vengeance; at best they could maintain only a limited defensive action. But among those creatures who were her predators, some might serve as her chosen protectors. Perhaps it was thus that the risky bargain was struck. Female fear of an open season of rape, and not a natural inclination toward monogamy, motherhood or love, was probably the single causative factor in the original subjugation of woman by man, the most important key to her historic dependence, her domestication by protective mating.

Once the male took title to a specific female body, and surely for him this was a great sexual convenience as well as a testament to his warring stature, he had to assume the burden of fighting off all other potential attackers, or scare them off by the retaliatory threat of raping their women. But the price of woman's protection by some men against an abuse by others was steep. Disappointed and disillusioned by the inherent female incapacity to protect, she became estranged in a very real sense from other females, a problem that haunts the social organization of women to this very day. And those who did assume the historic burden of her protection—later formalized as husband, father, brother, clan—extracted more than a pound of flesh. They reduced her status to that of chattel. The historic price of woman's protection by man against man was the imposition of chastity and monogamy. A crime committed against her body became a crime against the male estate.

The earliest form of permanent, protective conjugal relationship, the accommodation called mating that we now know as marriage, appears to have been institutionalized by the male's forcible abduction and rape of the female. No quaint formality, bride capture, as it came to be known, was a very real struggle: a male took title to a female, staked a claim to her body, as it were, by an act of violence. Forcible seizure was a perfectly acceptable way—to men—of acquiring women, and it existed in England as late as the fifteenth century. Eleanor of Aquitaine, according to a biographer, lived her early life in terror of being "rapt" by a vassal who might through appropriation of her body gain title to her considerable property. Bride capture exists to this day in the rain forests of the Philippines, where the Tasadays were recently discovered to be plying their Stone Age civilization. Remnants of the philosophy of forcible abduction and marriage still influence the social mores of rural Sicily and parts of Africa. A proverb of the exogamous Bantu-speaking Gusiis of southwest Kenya goes "Those whom we marry are those whom we fight."

It seems eminently sensible to hypothesize that man's violent capture and rape of the female led first to the establishment of a rudimentary mate-protectorate and then sometime later to the full-blown male solidification of power, the patriarchy. As the first permanent acquisition of man, his first piece of real property, woman was, in fact, the original building block, the cornerstone, of the "house of the father." Man's forcible extension of his boundaries to his mate and later to their offspring was the beginning of his concept of ownership. Concepts of hierarchy, slavery and private property flowed from, and could only be predicated upon, the initial subjugation of woman.

A female definition of rape can be contained in a single sentence. If a woman chooses not to have intercourse with a specific man and the man chooses to proceed against her will, that is a criminal act of rape. Through no fault of woman, this is not and never has been the legal definition. The ancient patriarchs who came together to write their early covenants had used the rape of women to forge their own male power—how then could they see rape as a crime of man against woman? Women were wholly owned subsidiaries and not independent beings. Rape could not be envisioned as a matter of female consent or refusal; nor could a definition acceptable to males be based on a male-female understanding of a female's right to her bodily integrity. Rape entered the law through the back door, as it were, as a property crime of man against man. Woman, of course, was viewed as the property.

Ancient Babylonian and Mosaic law was codified on tablets centuries after the rise of formal tribal hierarchies and the permanent settlements known as city-states. Slavery, private property and the subjugation of women were facts of life, and the earliest written law that has come down to us reflects this stratified life. Written law in its origin was a solemn compact among men of property, designed to protect their own male interests by a civilized exchange of goods or silver in place of force wherever possible. The capture of females by force remained perfectly acceptable outside the tribe or city as one of the ready fruits of warfare, but clearly within the social order such a happenstance would lead to chaos. A payment of money to the father of the house was a much more civilized and less dangerous way of acquiring a wife. And so the bride price was codified, at fifty pieces of silver. By this circuitous route the first concept of criminal rape sneaked its tortuous way into man's definition of law. Criminal rape, as a patriarchal father saw it, was a violation of the new way of doing business. It was, in a phrase, the theft of virginity, an embezzlement of his daughter's fair price on the market.

About four thousand years ago the Code of Hammurabi, chipped on a seven-foot column of diorite stone, made plain by its omissions that a female was allowed no independent status under Babylonian law. She was either a betrothed virgin, living in the house of her father, or else she was somebody's lawfully wedded wife and lived in the house of her husband. According to Hammurabi, a man was to be seized and slain if he raped a betrothed virgin, but the victimized girl was considered guiltless. As an interesting indication of the powers and rights of patriarchs over their female dependents, Hammurabi decreed that a man who "knew" his own daughter (i.e., committed incest) was merely banished from the walls of the city. A married woman who had the misfortune to get raped in Babylon had to share the blame equally with her attacker. Regardless of how the incident occurred, the crime was labeled adultery and both participants were bound and thrown into the river. Appeal from such stern justice is revealing. A husband was permitted to pull his wife from the water if he so desired; the king, if he wished, could let his errant male subject go free.

Influenced by Hammurabi's code but lacking the glorious Tigris and Euphrates, the ancient Hebrews substituted death by stoning for a watery grave. When Moses received his tablets from God on the top of Mount Sinai, "Thou shalt not rape" was conspicuously missing from the Ten Commandments, although Moses received a distinct commandment against adultery and another, for good measure, against the coveting of thy neighbor's wife, bracketed this second time around with thy neighbor's house, his field, his servant, ox and ass. Like her Babylonian sister, a married woman within the Hebrew culture who was victimized by rape was considered culpable, adulterous and irrevocably defiled. She was stoned to death along with her attacker at the gates to the city. But unlike the woman of Babylon, who before her last gasp might be rescued by her grief-stricken husband, for the women of Israel there was no reprieve. Reprieve from adultery, real or imagined, had to wait till the Gospel of St. John, in which appears Jesus' famous statement, "He that is without sin among you, let him first cast a stone at her."

We must cut through the thicket of some minor passages in Deuteronomy, written long after the original Ten Commandments, to arrive at the true Hebraic concept of a criminal act of rape, one in which the violator, and not the violated, bore full responsibility for his unlawful act.

In the Hebrew social order, which differed only in its exquisite precision from the simpler Babylonian codes, virgin maidens were bought and sold in marriage for fifty pieces of silver. To use plain language, what a father sold to a prospective bridegroom or his family was title to his daughter's unruptured hymen, a piece of property he wholly owned and controlled. With a clearly marked price tag attached to her hymen, a daughter of Israel was kept under watch to make sure she remained in a pristine state, for a piece of damaged goods could hardly command an advantageous match and might have to be sold as a concubine.

Like the Hebrew wife who was held responsible for her own defilement, a Hebrew daughter was given the task of guarding her own untouched flesh. If a man raped a virgin within the walls of the city both shared the same fate of death by stoning, for the elders reasoned that if the girl had screamed she would have been rescued. Patriarchal wisdom allowed that if the act of rape took place outside the city or while the girl was laboring in the field, for all her screaming, no one might hear, so a judicious solution was put into effect. The rapist was ordered to pay the girl's father fifty silver shekels in compensation for what would have been her bride price and the pair was simply commanded to wed. But if the maiden who was raped in a field was already betrothed to someone else, and betrothals in infancy were common, Hebraic wrath descended with unilateral vengeance on the rapist's head. No civil exchange of money and goods could be countenanced, for not only was the original betrothal null and void, but the house of the father had suffered an irreparable blow to its honor. In this singular instance the incautious rapist was stoned to death while the girl went unpunished, to be sold at a markdown to one who might have her.

One authority on the blood-vengeance justice of the early Assyrians has noted that under the lex talionis the father of a raped virgin was permitted to seize the wife of the rapist and violate her in turn. Before the codification of Mosaic law, Hebrew retribution for rape was even deadlier than this, particularly if the offender came from outside the tribe. The story of Dinah stands as a warning to any who might violate a Hebrew daughter. It is also a serious warning to young women of what might befall them if they stray too far from their father's house.

As told in Genesis, Dinah was a virgin daughter of Jacob by Leah. She was raped by a gentile when she left the house one day to go to visit some female friends. Dinah's attacker, who was not without his own tribal code, then applied to Jacob's family for permission to marry the woman he had violated. Pretending agreement, Jacob's sons suggested to the eager young man that he and all the male members of his uncivilized tribe undergo the ritual of circumcision. Three days later, the Bible tells us, when the gentile tribe was still sore from the painful operation, Jacob's sons descended on their encampment, slaughtered the weakened men and made captives of their women and oxen. Thus was the house of Jacob vindicated, but what benefit accrued to Dinah is questionable.

Protecting wellborn daughters of Israel from rape by the threat of massive retribution was obviously serious business, but as the story of Dinah shows, men of the Hebrew tribes, like their neighbors, had no compunctions against freely raping women of tribes they had conquered, for in this way they prospered and grew. Captured slave women were lawfully employed as servants, field hands, concubines and breeders of future slaves in much the same manner that the eighteenth-century American slaveholder made use of his black female slaves, and indeed, this Biblical parallel was often cited as religious justification by upholders of American slavery.

The unfortunate lot of women caught in the middle of intertribal warfare *within* the confederated twelve tribes of Israel is demonstrated by a series of swiftly moving events reported in the Book of Judges. A Levite, accompanied by his unfaithful concubine, seeks rest and shelter for the night with an old man in Benjamite territory. Hearing that a stranger has come to town, some men of Benjamin approach the house with the intention of committing homosexual abuse. The Levite's protector offers up his own virgin daughter and the Levite's concubine to deflect the energy of the eager young bloods. They graciously decline the use of the daughter but they rape the concubine through the night. When the Levite discovers her dead on the doorstep in the morning, he calls on the other tribes of Israel to defend his honor. In the ensuing battle most of the Benjamite men and all of the Benjamite women are slaughtered. Now the Hebrew elders become seriously concerned, for without women the tribe of Benjamin will cease to exist. They arrange for the defeated Benjamites to catch and rape four hundred young virgins of neighboring Shiloh, and thus secure for them legal wives.

With all this lawful rape as the order of the day, it comes as no surprise that the Bible's major rape parable is not concerned with the plight of an unfortunate female or even with the efforts of her father and brothers to avenge their house. The famous story of Potiphar's wife is an important morality lesson in Hebrew, Christian and Moslem folklore, and it expresses the true, historic concern and abiding fear of egocentric, rapacious man: what can happen to a fine, upstanding fellow if a vengeful female lies and cries that she has been assaulted.

Joseph the Israelite was a highly placed slave in the household of Potiphar the Egyptian. As recorded in Genesis, Potiphar's wife—she is not identified by a first name—cast a lecherous eye upon the Hebrew slave. She was always pestering this unwilling sex object to "lie with me," and the virtuous Joseph was forever reminding her of their master in common. One day Joseph and Potiphar's wife found themselves alone in the house. Seizing her opportunity, Potiphar's wife caught Joseph "by his garment" and commanded, "Lie with me." At this point, supposedly, Joseph fled—and Potiphar's wife began crying rape or its Biblical equivalent.

This is the Hebrew male side of the story, I must stress. When Potiphar came home his wife showed him Joseph's torn cloak and wailed, "The Hebrew . . . came in unto me to mock me!" Potiphar had no choice but to throw his favorite slave into prison. But God, as would be expected, remained on the side of the Israelite. Once in jail Joseph became quite the prison leader, and by correctly interpreting the Pharaoh's dreams he won a full pardon and rose to become prime minister. The moral of the story of Potiphar's wife is that a woman scorned—especially if she is gentile—can get a good man into a hell of a lot of trouble by crying rape.

The legend of Potiphar's wife, in some form or other, is a familiar staple in many ancient cultures. Joseph's misfortune occupies a place of importance in the teachings of the Koran and a similar tale has been traced to Egyptian folklore of 1300 B.C. A variation appears in Celtic myths. One historian of sexual attitudes has noted the frequent recurrence of the theme in romantic histories of the Crusades, where "very often the rapacious maiden is a Saracen who jumps into the bed of a crusader," all the more significant when we remember that the Crusades were marked by Christian rape and pillage of Moslems as the crusaders pursued the Holy Grail. The universal promulgation of a parable of rape that places the full burden of blame squarely on a lascivious female of another race or nation can hardly be accidental. Aggressive warlike peoples must have found it highly expeditious to promote this sort of legend as they went about their routine business of conquering others. What better way, after all, to absolve themselves from guilt as they plucked the fruits of victory?

As the centuries rolled by and Jewish women began to win a measure of independence, the learned men who interpreted the Bible became increasingly concerned about an act that was not quite rape but had some elements of mutual seduction. The emergence of an independent female, one whose father had died or one who did not marry, began to affect the ground rules governing criminal-rape prosecutions for "she herself became a litigant," writes a modern rabbinical authority, and "her consent to the act had great bearing on the payments due." Talmudic theorists of the Middle Ages, the Jewish intellectual elite, manfully sought to cover all the new contingencies. Virginity remained the *sine qua non* of individual rape prosecutions, but maidens who displayed "sexual eagerness" were added to the official list of statutory nonvirgins, along with gentile women, captives and slaves.

Under Talmudic interpretation, a raped virgin was no longer required to marry her rapist. If she had acquired a semi-independent status and her age fell between three and twelve and a half— the rabbis were real sticklers about the age of *bona fide* virgins— she was permitted to receive the fine of fifty coins herself. Allowing a female to keep the money tampered with the hallowed concept of rape as the theft of virginity. In time the award came to be seen as punitive damage for *injury to a female's body*, as well as payment for enjoying sexual intercourse with a virgin. This was real progress for women, hard won. The great Jewish theologian Maimonides was forever arguing that in his view a raped virgin had no right to receive monetary compensation. He did not prevail.*

Concepts of rape and punishment in early English law are a

---

* Maimonides dominated Jewish philosophic thought in the twelfth century and beyond, but on matters pertaining to women this strict constructionist was often overruled by other rabbis. It is a little-known fact that in addition to his other accomplishments, the great Maimonides was the author of a slender sex manual that had quite a vogue in its day. Women figure hardly at all in his little book, which is mainly about food. Not to put too fine a point on it, Maimonides' manual is a collection of recipes guaranteed by the author to sustain an erection.

wondrous maze of contradictory approaches reflecting a gradual humanization of jurisprudence in general, and in particular, man's eternal confusion, never quite resolved, as to whether the crime was a crime against a woman's body or a crime against his own estate.

Before the Norman Conquest of 1066 the penalty for rape was death and dismemberment, but this stern justice pertained exclusively to the man who raped a highborn, propertied virgin who lived under the protection of a powerful lord. Feudalism took root in the early Middle Ages as ownership of land became an inherited right, "the lands passing by immemorial custom from father to son . . . maintained, among other ways by the system of wardship and marriage." Since females were allowed to inherit property, a matter of necessity if there were no extant male heirs, "trading in marriages," to borrow a telling phrase from G. G. Coulton, was a lucrative enterprise among the nobility, practiced in much the same manner "as men trade in shares and investments today." For obvious economic reasons a landed heiress could not marry without permission of her overlord, under penalty of losing her inherited fortune. Yet once the nuptials had taken place, their legal and churchly sanctity could not be challenged, and so the custom of "stealing an heiress" by forcible abduction and marriage became a routine method of acquiring property by adventurous, upward-mobile knights. As a matter of record, not until a fifteenth-century edict of Henry VII was heiress-stealing ruled a felony unto itself.

Gothic literature has made heiress-stealing a subject of great romance, replete with midnight assignations, loyal maidservants and a great thundering of horses' hooves, but in actuality it was predicated on the desire for land, not love. If a captured virgin managed to escape before her forced marriage, or if an errant knave had merely taken her on the spot, she could attempt to seek redress in the court of her lord's manor. Trial for capital crime in those days was by physical ordeal, and grueling tests by water and hot irons were probably employed to arrive at the "truth."

Henry of Bratton (Bracton), who lived and wrote in the thirteenth century, is our best authority for these ancient Saxon times, accepted by Coke, Hale and Blackstone, the later giants of English jurisprudence. Bracton informs us that during the tenth-century rule of King Athelstan, if a man were to throw a virgin to the ground against her will, "he forfeits the King's grace; if he shamelessly disrobes her and places himself upon her, he incurs the loss of all his possessions; and if he lies with her, he incurs the loss of his life and members." Vengeance did not stop at death, for, Bracton continued, "even his horse shall to his ignomy be put to shame upon its scrotum and tail, which shall be cut off as close as possible to the buttocks." A similar fate awaited the rapist's dog, and if he happened to own a hawk, "Let it lose its beak, its claws and its tail."

After his animals were cropped and his own human life was taken, a rapist's land and money were supposed to be given to the ravished virgin. But one manner of redemption was possible. As a benevolent way of saving him from terrible death, a raped virgin might be permitted by King and Church to accept her ravisher in marriage. Since consolidation of property was uppermost in the minds of men, we may assume that a violated virgin was encouraged or not encouraged toward matrimony depending on which arrangement of the land was most beneficial, or least inconvenient, to the domain of Church and King.

Punishment for raping a virgin of property was thoughtfully reduced to castration and the loss of both eyes by William the Conqueror. The mode of trial under William also switched from ordeal to combat, so we may assume that unless the stakes were high, few virgins were actually championed by their chivalrous kin. Speaking to this point, the English legal historians Pollock and Maitland remark, "In one respect a woman's capacity of suing was curtailed by her inability to fight."

Castration and blinding was still the appropriate penalty for raping a virgin in Bracton's day and he explained the law's intent—"member for member"—with these words: "Let him lose his eyes which gave him sight of the virgin's beauty for which he coveted her. And let him lose as well the testicles which excited his hot lust."

King Henry II, the Plantagenet who married Eleanor of Aquitaine, brought the principles of Frankish law to England during his twelfth-century reign. If a raped virgin filed a civil suit or "appeal" and an indictment was obtained, the resulting trial was by jury in the king's assize instead of by combat or duel. This was clearly an advance in procedures. Bracton was most meticulous as to the proper form the suit should take. He entitled his instructions "An appeal concerning the rape of virgins." An appeal concerning the rape of nonvirgins does not appear anywhere in his compendium, for Bracton was describing the king's jurisdiction, which by this time included murder, mayhem and major theft. "Minor" offenses were still being handled by the manorial courts. In fact, Bracton tells us that a raped virgin's appeal and a wife's appeal in the matter of a husband "slain within her arms" were the only suits a woman could bring to the courts of the king. The procedure a raped virgin was to follow went like this:

> She must go at once and while the deed is newly done, with the hue and cry, to the neighboring townships and there show the injury done to her to men of good repute, the blood and her clothing stained with blood, and her torn garments. And in the same way she ought to go to the reeve of the hundred, the king's serjeant, the coroners and the sheriff. And let her make her appeal at the first county court, unless she can at once make her complaint directly to the lord king or his justices, where she will be told to sue at the county court. Let her appeal be enrolled in the coroners' rolls, every word of the appeal, exactly as she makes it, and the year and day on which she makes it. A day will be given her at the coming of the justices, at which let her again put forward her appeal before them, in the same words as she made it in the county court, from which she is not permitted to depart lest the appeal fall because of the variance . . .

If the man whom our raped virgin accused protested his innocence, "Let the truth be ascertained by an examination of her body, made by four law-abiding women sworn to tell the truth as to whether she is a virgin or defiled." If she proved to be defiled, the trial might continue; if she proved a virgin still, the case was dismissed and the false accuser was thrown into custody.

The man accused, Bracton writes, had several possible defenses. He might say

> that he had her as his concubine and amica before the day and the year mentioned in the appeal . . . or that he had her and defiled her with her consent and not against her will, and that if she now appeals him it is in hatred of another woman whom he has as his concubine, or whom he has married, or that it is at the instigation of one of her kinsmen. He may also except that on the year and day the deed was supposed to be done he was elsewhere, outside the realm.

. . . Or he may also except on the ground of an omission made in the appeal. . . . Many other matters may constitute exceptions though I do not now call them to mind.

Despite a spirited defense, the male justices who heard the case might sometimes decide they had to convict, and then our victim-prosecutrix* would be given her old option of marrying her rapist as a benevolent way of saving him from gruesome mutilation.

Bracton allowed that this time-honored custom of redeeming a rapist through marriage could cause considerable mischief to the social structure, for "a common person might bring perpetual disgrace upon a woman of nobility and good family by a single act of defilement and take her to wife to the disgrace of her family." On the other hand, "But suppose that the ravisher is a nobleman and the woman raped a common person; will it be for the defiled person to exercise a choice and decide whether she will marry the nobleman or not?"

Apparently this was to be—if the nobleman valued his sight and his testicles—but the chance that a man of nobility might be convicted of raping a commoner would have been slight. "As a rule," Sidney Painter writes in his *History of the Middle Ages,* "the nobleman's crime was blamed on his men." Painter reports on one case in which a young girl was abducted on the highway, taken to a knight's house, and raped by the knight and his men: "The court solemnly accepted the statement of the knight that he was horrified to hear that she had not been in his house of her own free will. . . . Even in England," he continues, "if a member of the feudal class committed his crimes against anyone other than the king or a great lord, he was fairly safe from prosecution, or at least from punishment."

("Even in England" is an important qualifying phrase, for while the Middle Ages was a time of savage wife beating, Court

---

* The term "prosecutrix" stems from this time in English history when a female had the burden of instituting a civil suit in order for a rape trial to take place. Today, of course, it is the state, not the woman, that prosecutes for rape, yet "prosecutrix" continues to appear with regularity in appellate briefs that are written by rapists' defense attorneys, where it is used interchangeably with "complainant" and "alleged victim." Much of legal language is archaic, but in this instance it is hard not to conclude that the word is favored for the harsh, vindictive quality of personal prosecution that it plainly connotes.

prostitution, and general all around lawlessness and feudal oppression, things seemed to be far worse for women on the Continent.
The *jus primae noctis*, right of the first night or *droit du seigneur*,
the custom of giving the manorial lord the right to take the virginity
of the bride of any one of his vassals or serfs unless the bride and
bridegroom paid a specific amount of produce in redemption dues
—certainly a form of rape—appears to have been enforced irregu-
larly in certain parts of Germany, France, Italy and Poland but not,
however, in England. Still, it cannot be overstressed that "even in
England" the law that evolved was feudal class law, designed to
protect the nobleman's interest. Although it took place much later,
the celebrated eighteenth century trial and acquittal of Frederick
Calvert, the seventh and last Lord Baltimore, for a rape upon the
body of Sarah Woodcock, a milliner, is a case in point. Baltimore
had the twenty-nine-year-old virgin hat-maker abducted and he kept
her a virtual prisoner for more than a week. At the trial he claimed
consent and pleaded, "Libertine as I am represented, I am sure I
have sufficiently atoned for every indiscretion, which a weak attachment to this unworthy woman may have led me into, by having
suffered the disgrace of being exposed as a criminal at the bar."
Apparently the judge and jury agreed. The wonder of Lord Baltimore's case is that it came to trial at all.)

How was justice secured for raped women who were not propertied virgins, that is, as Bracton himself was careful to enumerate,
for "matrons, nuns, widows, concubines and even prostitutes"?
The legal scholar who so minutely described the procedures and
punishments in regard to "an appeal concerning the rape of virgins" hurriedly passed by the rest of womankind's rapists with the
comment, "Punishment of this kind does not follow . . ." although he did report that it might be "severe." What precise
punishment *did* follow he never records, and probably for good,
practical reason. Either he had few convictions to go by, or the
penalties were not uniform, or he and his fellow men did not
consider the matter of any great legal concern. All three of these
possibilities are highly likely in concert. Pollock and Maitland, the
law historians, write, "Concerning these matters we find little case-
law. Appeals of rape were often brought in the thirteenth century;
but they were often quashed, abandoned or compromised." But
what is significant is that by Bracton's time, the thirteenth century,
the legal concept of criminal rape had clearly, if haphazardly, been

broadened by the manorial courts to include at least in principle the rape of "matrons, nuns, widows, concubines and even prostitutes." Bracton's glancing reference may be the first in written history.

The comprehensive Statutes of Westminster put forward by Edward I at the close of the thirteenth century showed a gigantic advance in legal thinking as the Crown, and by "Crown" Americans should read "state," began to take an active interest in all kinds of rape prosecutions, not just those concerning violated virgins. Our modern principle of *statutory* rape—felonious carnal knowledge of a child in which her "consent" is altogether immaterial—dates from this time and these statutes.

Of critical significance, Westminster extended the king's jurisdiction to cover the forcible rape of married women as well as virgins, with no difference in punishment to offending males. To further erase the distinction between the rape of a virgin and the rape of a wife, the old, ignoble custom of redemption through marriage was permanently banned under suits by the king. In concession to the proprietary rights of husbands—for the Crown had ventured into an area it had never ventured into before—Westminster also saw fit to legislate a definition of lesser ravishment, a sort of misdemeanor, applicable in cases where it could be argued that a wife did not object strenuously enough to her own "defilement." The aggrieved party in these cases was the husband, and the wife was peremptorily stripped of her dower. *Within* a marriage, the theory went—and still goes—that there could be no such crime as rape by a husband since a wife's "consent" to her husband was a permanent part of the marriage vows and could not be withdrawn.

To give the new law teeth, Edward I decreed that if a raped woman or her kin failed to institute a private suit within forty days, the right to prosecute automatically passed to the Crown. This bold concept, applicable only to virgins in previous reigns, was a giant step for the law and for women. It meant that rape was no longer just a family misfortune and a threat to land and property, but an issue of public safety and state concern.

The First Statute of Westminster, enacted in 1275, set the Crown's penalty for rape at a paltry two years' imprisonment plus a fine at the king's pleasure, no doubt to ease the effect of a major transition, for what had occurred at the Parliament of Westminster was only tangentially and in retrospect a recognition of women's rights; its inexorable, historic purpose had been to consolidate political power in the hands of the king. But within a decade an emboldened Second Statute of Westminster amended the timorous First. By a new act of Parliament, any man who ravished "a married woman, dame or damsel" without her consent was guilty of a full-blown felony under the law of the Crown, and the penalty was death.*

It read better on parchment than it worked in real life, but the concept of rape as a public wrong had been firmly established.

From the thirteenth to the twentieth century, little changed. The later giants of jurisprudence, Hale, Blackstone, Wigmore and the rest, continued to point a suspicious finger at the female victim and worry about her motivations and "good fame."

"If she be of evil fame and stand unsupported by others," Blackstone commented, "if she concealed the injury for any considerable time after she had the opportunity to complain, if the place where the act was alleged to be committed was where it was possible she might have been heard and she made no outcry, these and the like circumstances carry a strong but not conclusive presumption that her testimony is false or feigned."

---

* Under modern English law the maximum penalty for rape is life imprisonment.

3

War

This is my weapon, this is my gun
This is for business, this is for fun

—DRILL SERGEANT'S DITTY

I then told him that, in spite of my most diligent efforts, there would unquestionably be some raping, and that I should like to have the details as early as possible so that the offenders could be properly hanged.

—GENERAL GEORGE S. PATTON, JR.
War As I Knew It

It's funny about *man's* attitude toward rape in war. *Unquestionably* there shall be some raping. Unconscionable, but nevertheless inevitable. When men are men, slugging it out among themselves, conquering new land, subjugating new people, driving on toward victory, *unquestionably* there shall be some raping.

And so it has been. Rape has accompanied wars of religion: knights and pilgrims took time off for sexual assault as they marched toward Constantinople in the First Crusade. Rape has accompanied wars of revolution: George Washington's papers for July 22, 1780, record that one Thomas Brown of the Seventh Pennsylvania Regiment was sentenced to death for rape at Paramus, and it was Brown's second conviction at that. Rape in warfare is not bound by definitions of which wars are "just" or "unjust." Rape was a weapon of terror as the German Hun marched through Belgium in World War I. Rape was a weapon of revenge as the Russian Army marched to Berlin in World War II. Rape flourishes in warfare irrespective of nationality or geographic location. Rape got out of hand—"regrettably," as the foreign minister was later to say—when the Pakistani Army battled Bangladesh. Rape reared its head as a way to relieve boredom as American GI's searched and destroyed in the highlands of Vietnam.

In modern times, rape is outlawed as a criminal act under the international rules of war. Rape is punishable by death or imprisonment under Article 120 of the American Uniform Code of Military Justice. Yet rape persists as a common act of war.

It has been argued that when killing is viewed as not only permissible but heroic behavior sanctioned by one's government or cause, the distinction between taking a human life and other forms of impermissible violence gets lost, and rape becomes an unfortunate but inevitable by-product of the necessary game called war. Women, by this reasoning, are simply regrettable victims—incidental, unavoidable casualties—like civilian victims of bombing, lumped together with children, homes, personal belongings, a church, a dike, a water buffalo or next year's crop. But rape in war is qualitatively different from a bomb that misses its military target, different from impersonal looting and burning, different from deliberate ambush, mass murder or torture during interrogation, although it contains elements of all of the above. Rape is more than a symptom of war or evidence of its violent excess. Rape in war is a familiar act with a familiar excuse.

War provides men with the perfect psychologic backdrop to give vent to their contempt for women. The very maleness of the military—the brute power of weaponry exclusive to their hands, the spiritual bonding of men at arms, the manly discipline of orders given and orders obeyed, the simple logic of the hierarchical command—confirms for men what they long suspect, that women are peripheral, irrelevant to the world that counts, passive spectators to the action in the center ring.

Men who rape in war are ordinary Joes, made unordinary by entry into the most exclusive male-only club in the world. Victory in arms brings group power undreamed of in civilian life. Power for men alone. The unreal situation of a world without women becomes the prime reality. To take a life looms more significant than to make a life, and the gun in the hand is power. The sickness of warfare feeds on itself. A certain number of soldiers must prove their newly won superiority—prove it to a woman, to themselves, to other men. In the name of victory and the power of the gun, war provides men with a tacit license to rape. In the act and in the excuse, rape in war reveals the male psyche in its boldest form, without the veneer of "chivalry" or civilization.

Fighting to secure women was on a par with fighting to secure food among ancient primitive tribes, an activity that still survives in certain parts of the world. The practical Hebrews, anxious to get a law on the books for all contingencies, made no bones about the status of women who were captured in war. Female captives were allowable as slaves and concubines, according to Deuteronomy, but Hebrew men were discouraged from marrying them. If a Hebrew male did marry a captive woman, unlike a Hebrew woman she could be divorced without cause or complicated rigmarole.

Among the ancient Greeks, rape was also socially acceptable behavior well within the rules of warfare, an act without stigma for warriors who viewed the women they conquered as legitimate booty, useful as wives, concubines, slave labor or battle-camp trophy. Homer's Iliad describes the Trojan War as the attempt by Menelaus of Sparta to recapture Helen, who had been stolen by Paris along with her treasure. The face that launched a thousand ships was the ultimate prize. Since Helen was a queen, she lived as wife of Paris during her stay in Troy. Lesser women fared less advantageously during the war. The Trojan Chryseis was captured by the Spartans and allotted to Agamemnon as his concubine of the battle camp, and her father had to enlist the god Apollo to help reclaim her. Agamemnon angrily sought compensation for the loss of Chryseis by seizing Briseis, a slave-concubine that his warrior Achilles had won. Achilles responded by sulking in his tent and refusing to fight, and the Spartan cause began to suffer. Agamemnon was forced to make a delicate settlement for unity. He ceremoniously returned Briseis to Achilles, along with the following carefully enumerated loot from his treasure hut: seven tripods, twenty cauldrons, twelve horses, ten talents of gold and seven craftswomen. Briseis held out hope that Achilles might marry her after this elaborate negotiated settlement, but the warrior didn't. The battle-camp arrangements suited him fine.

The rape of the Sabine women, which supposedly led to the founding of Rome, is another famous example of woman-stealing in war, an event that captured the imagination of artists in later centuries who invariably painted the captured Sabines as full-fleshed and luscious and having a good time. In a curious bit of moralizing, Saint Augustine chose to quibble with the sneaky manner in which the Sabine women were raped.

> Even if the Sabines were unfair to refuse to give their daughters [he argued in City of God], it was surely much more unfair to take them by force after this refusal. It would have been more just to have waged war against a people that refused a request for marriage with its daughters on the part of close neighbors, than against those who asked for the restoration of daughters who had been carried off. . . . It might have been in accordance with some sort of law of war, had the victor justly won the women who had been unjustly refused him; it was contrary to every law of peace that he seized those who had been denied him and then waged unjust war with their indignant parents.

Because the Sabine women had been carried off and raped *before* the war, Augustine called the operation a "shady trick."

There is no precise moment in history when bells clanged and rape in war universally came to be considered a criminal act, outside the province of a proper warrior. The historic development of the rights of women, like the development of nations, proceeded at an uneven pace. Totila, the Ostrogoth who captured Rome in 546 A.D., forbade his troops to rape the Roman women, but the source from which I rescued this obscure bit of history warned that "Totila stands out as a bright chivalrous knightly figure in an age of savagery." Nonetheless, Totila deserves a nod as a man ahead of his time.

One of the earliest surviving Articles of War was proclaimed by Richard II of England in 1385. Among the twenty-four articles governing the conduct of his soldiers, King Richard decreed "That none be so hardy as to . . . force any woman, upon pain of being hanged." An equal penalty was applied to the hardy who pillaged a church. Yet as late as the seventeenth century, the Dutch jurist Grotius, who wrote at length on international military law, was forced to muse that some countries held that the dishonoring of women in war was allowable while other countries held to the contrary. Grotius asserted that the more civilized of nations disallowed rape. The outlawing of rape in warfare, at least on the books, was an important advance for women, but despite the penalties, and whether or not they were rigorously applied, rape in warfare continued to flourish.

A simple rule of thumb in war is that the winning side is the side that does the raping. There are two specific reasons for this, one pragmatic and one psychologic, and neither has much to do with the nobility of losers or with the moral superiority of an heroic defense. First, a victorious army marches through the defeated people's territory, and thus it is obvious that if there is any raping to be done, it will be done on the bodies of the defeated enemy's women. Second, rape is the act of a conqueror. This is more than a truism. It helps explain why men continue to rape in war.

Long after the enemy's women had lost their utilitarian value as slave labor or battle-camp trophy, and long after rape was frowned upon by the more civilized kings and generals, rape remained a hallmark of success in battle. In medieval times, opportunities to rape and loot were among the few advantages open to common foot soldiers, who were paid with great irregularity by their leaders. The Byzantine emperor Alexius is supposed to have extolled the beauty of Greek women in his appeals for recruits for the First Crusade. When the city of Constantinople was sacked in 1204, rape and plunder went hand in hand, as in the sack of almost every ancient city, Totila's Ostrogoths notwithstanding. "To the victor belong the spoils" has applied to women since Helen of Troy, but the sheer property worth of women was replaced in time by a far more subtle system of values. Down through the ages, triumph over women by rape became a way to measure victory, part of a soldier's proof of masculinity and success, a tangible reward for services rendered. Stemming from the days when women were property, access to a woman's body has been considered an actual reward of war.* "Booty and beauty" General

---

* Because access to women after a battle has been a traditional reward of war, it is impossible to discuss rape in warfare without touching also on prostitution, since the two have been linked in history. Not that if prostitutes are not readily available men will turn to rape "to satisfy their needs," but that the two acts—raping an unwilling woman and buying the body and services of a more or less cooperating woman—go hand in hand with a soldier's concept of

Andrew Jackson supposedly named it in New Orleans during the
War of 1812. He was commenting, naturally, on the *English*
attitude.

Of course, the soldier-rapist may not see his act in these terms.
In the thick of his cause, the rape for him may assume heroic
proportions, justified by ideology or even by God. Sexual violence
against women was fervently committed in the name of God,
although not, we may believe, with His blessing, during the Wars
of Religion in France. A remarkable description of one such religious rape, which occurred on December 18, 1567, near Provins,
was recorded by Claude Haton, a local Catholic priest and a meticulous diarist. The victim was a Huguenot woman.

> It so happened that this LeBlanc and his wife fell into the hands
> of some soldiers. The soldiers who held the woman did not hold her
> husband, but others did, and during this time they were not per-
> mitted to see or talk to each other. The woman was finally delivered
> from the hands of these soldiers and put at liberty but only after they
> had used and enjoyed her at their pleasure and led her through the
> streets with her feet and legs and head all bare. The only clothing
> she had on was an undergarment and an apron . . . made of red
> material all covered with blood. This happened on the 18th day of
> December. When they passed by the church of St.-Ayoul the poor
> Huguenot was brought inside. This was between eight and nine
> o'clock in the morning. At the entrance to the church she was forced
> to take holy water and sprinkle her face with it and then she was
> brought before the main altar where a priest was saying mass. Here
> she was forced to both knees and given a lighted candle to hold dur-
> ing the elevation of the mass. . . . She was told to ask mercy of
> God . . . for the terrible sin she had committed in straying from
> the true Catholic religion and adhering to the false Huguenot faith.

---

his rights and pleasures. Prostitution near a battle camp has been linked historically with the phenomenon of the camp follower, but this is a misrepre-
sentation of history. Up to and including the American Revolution, camp
following was an occupation based on necessity, practically built into the
conduct of war. Female camp followers—many of them were wives of the
soldiers—cooked, washed laundry and functioned as nurses for their men, in
addition to their obvious sexual function. When the army and Florence
Nightingale took over the first-named activities, camp following lost its nonsexual functions. Interestingly, while marriage to a foreign woman is made
difficult for a soldier by complicated military regulations, access to prostitutes
has generally been encouraged.

Then, too, there is mention in history of those chivalrous souls, those knights and squires, who took it upon themselves to protect women of rank, though not of the lower classes, from assault by common soldiers. Froissart's chronicles of the Hundred Years' War between England and France are filled with romantic incidents such as the moment when Edward III occupied the castle of Pois and found it deserted except for two noblewomen "who would have been raped by the low-born archers had not two noted knights . . . rescued them." Sidney Painter observed in his book on French chivalry, "Froissart took great delight in describing the courteous treatment accorded by French and English knights to any ladies whom the fortunes of war had placed at their mercy. When a nunnery was pillaged and the nuns were raped, he was careful to point out that it had been done by the Germans." Knights, however, did not always respect the class system. The chronicler Monstrelet reported with shock that when the French Army captured Soissons in 1414, noblemen joined the ordinary soldiers in "indiscriminately raping women of all ranks."

When a victorious army rapes, the sheer intoxication of the triumph is only part of the act. After the fact, the rape may be viewed as part of a recognizable pattern of national terror and subjugation. I say "after the fact" because the original impulse to rape does not need a sophisticated political motivation beyond a general disregard for the bodily integrity of women. But rape in warfare has a military effect as well as an impulse. And the effect is indubitably one of intimidation and demoralization for the victims' side.

An aggressor nation rarely admits to rape.* Documentation of rape in warfare is something the *other side* totals up, analyzes and

---

* An exception to this rule has been the United States. Individual cases of rape by American soldiers have received considerable attention in this country. Sometimes a case comes to light because of a strong court-martial defense of mistaken identity. There were some highly publicized U.S. courts-martial for rape involving a defense of mistaken identity in Japan and Okinawa during World War II and also during the Korean War. The defendants were black. A similar case and defense, involving two American GI's stationed with the army of occupation in Germany, surfaced in 1971. As a sign of the changing times, cases of rape by American soldiers in Vietnam have come to light as part of the many journalistic exposés documenting the horrors of the Southeast Asian war.

propagandizes when the smoke has cleared after defeat. Men of a conquered nation traditionally view the rape of "their women" as the ultimate humiliation, a sexual coup de grace. Rape is considered by the people of a defeated nation to be part of the enemy's conscious effort to destroy them. In fact, by tradition, men appropriate the rape of "their women" as part of their own male anguish of defeat. This egocentric view does have a partial validity. Apart from a genuine, human concern for wives and daughters near and dear to them, rape by a conqueror is compelling evidence of the conquered's status of masculine impotence. Defense of women has long been a hallmark of masculine pride, as possession of women has been a hallmark of masculine success. Rape by a conquering soldier destroys all remaining illusions of power and property for men of the defeated side. The body of a raped woman becomes a ceremonial battlefield, a parade ground for the victor's trooping of the colors. The act that is played out upon her is a message passed between men—vivid proof of victory for one and loss and defeat for the other.

In April, 1746, King George's army led by the Duke of Cumberland put down an insurrection in the Scottish Highlands. The Highland clans that rallied to the banner of Bonnie Prince Charlie were thoroughly decimated in the Battle of Culloden. That battle, and the brutal pacification program that followed, marked the end of organized clan life in Scotland. The modern British historian John Prebble collected the story of Culloden and its aftermath from records kept by the proud old clans. In the clansmen's view, rape of their women was a deliberate act of tyranny by the English invader, and Prebble wrote the story as he found it.

Sexual mutilation of women on Culloden Moor during the battle proper was only the beginning. Lord George Sackville led a command of infantrymen to Moidart, where Clan Macdonald rebels "showed no enthusiasm for surrendering." A few screaming clansmen raided the rear of his column and captured some horses and provisions. Sackville "allowed his men to take revenge at the next hamlet, where the women were first raped and then held to watch the shooting and bayonetting of their husbands, fathers, brothers and sons."

Major Lockhart's platoons pushed through the glen at In-verwick:

Where the River Doe meets the Moriston in a black waterfall, Isobel Macdonald was raped by five soldiers, and her husband, skulking high in the heather, watched this in agony. There were other women raped, too, and always before the doors of their burning homes. . . . The women who had been ravished made pacts not to lie with their husbands until nine months were passed. "Which resolution," said the Laird of Glenmoriston, thinking of Isobel Macdonald and one other, "the husbands agreed to. But they happened luckily not to fall with child by the ravishing, nor to contract any bad disease."

Lockhart's next stop was at Strathglass, the land of the Chisholms and Frasers, where his soldiers raped a pregnant woman.

In July of that year, Captain Scott led an expedition to the Outer Hebrides in search of the fugitive Prince Charles. He was ferried from island to island by Captain John Fergusson of the H.M.S. *Furnace.* "The Laird of Raasay, John MacLeod, said that Scott's men raped a blind girl on Rona. . . . On the island of Raasay . . . they ravished two women whose names were Kristie Montgomery and Marion MacLeod."

Captain Fergusson had been cruising the Western Isles since March, raiding the islands for fresh beef and mutton, and, said one of the Macdonalds of Canna, "to make ane attack upon all the girls and young women in all the Isle, marryed or otherwise." The women of Canna took shelter in the caves.

In the cottage of Evan Mor MacIsaacs, where there had been two young girls, the sailors found only the mother. . . . Evan Mor was put under guard of drawn swords, and the sailors made ready to rape his wife, but she escaped from them into the darkness. They pursued her drunkenly, shouting and waving their cutlasses, and passing by her where she had hidden in a bog. The Macdonald of Canna who told this story to Robert Forbes said that Mrs. MacIsaacs was pregnant, and that she died of a miscarriage before morning.

The *Furnace* went next to the isle of Eigg, where the sailors went ashore and slaughtered cattle, pillaged houses and "ravished a girl or two."

At least one Highland woman got her revenge, Prebble records: "In Appin a young girl, whose cow had been shot by a soldier, killed him with a stone when he attempted to rape her. The body was buried secretly at Airds . . ."

An act of rape in war that a husband or father is forced to watch is quite common. Sometimes it is simply a matter of proximity, as when Isobel Macdonald's husband skulked in the heather, but more often it is part of the plan, as in the house of Evan Mor MacIsaacs. Rape of a woman in war may be as much an act against her husband or father, for the rapist, as it is an act against the woman's body. The attitude of husbands after a rape is equally interesting. The ravished women of Inverwick did not sleep with their husbands for nine months after their assault. Although it appears from the Laird of Glenmoriston that this was a pact that the husbands agreed to, the more common experience is for the husbands to turn from their raped wives in revulsion—as witness the recent mass rejection of the raped women of Bangladesh. In war as in peace, the husbands of raped women place a major burden of blame for the awful event on their wives. The hallowed rights of property have been abused, and the property herself is held culpable.

A casual reader of history quickly learns that rape remains unmentionable, even in war. Serious historians have rarely bothered to document specific acts of rape in warfare, for reasons of their own scale of values and taste, as well as for lack of hard-and-fast surviving proof. Thus the story of Culloden is exceptional for its wealth of detail. Systematic rape of Highland women by English forces during the occupation of Scotland fitted perfectly into a bold pattern of national subjugation. It also fitted logically into a retrospective analysis of the ultimate destruction of the proud and tightly knit hierarchical clans. Perhaps for these reasons the Highland lairds of Scotland understood, as few have, the military importance of rape, and kept their painful records.

Not until World War I was documentation of rape in warfare ever again preserved so faithfully.

World War I

When the Germans invaded Belgium in August, 1914, rape was suddenly catapulted into prominence as the international metaphor of Belgian humiliation. This unprecedented attention had little to do with an understanding of the rights of women. It had a lot to do with the evolution of a new form of battle—the scientific use of propaganda.

We are indebted for our most complete and factual knowledge of rape in World War I to the distinguished British historian Arnold Joseph Toynbee, who was a young Thucydides scholar at Oxford when the war broke out. Toynbee published two small volumes in 1917, one devoted to the early months of the war in Belgium and a second to the war in France. Both books were basically compendiums of German Army atrocities, gathered by Allied commissions of investigation and cross-checked against available German documents. As Toynbee and his contemporaries saw it, the German General Staff deliberately mounted a campaign of terror in the first three months of the war.*

From Liège to Louvain, as Toynbee wrote it, the German Army cut a swath of horror. Houses were burned, villages were plundered, civilians were bayonetted, and women were raped. "A number of women" were raped at Tremeloo. At Rotselaer "a girl who was raped by five Germans went out of her mind." In Capelle-au-Bois a woman told how "the German soldiers had held her down by force while other soldiers had violated her daughter successively in an adjoining room." At Corbeek-Loo "a girl of sixteen was violated by six soldiers and bayonetted in five places for offering resistance." An eyewitness who survived the siege of Louvain reported, "The women and children were separated. . . . Some German soldiers came up to me sniggering and said that all the women were going to be raped. . . . They explained themselves by gestures."

That was a sample of August in Belgium. The pattern held for September in France. Jouy-sur-Morin: "Two Germans came into a house carrying looted bottles of champagne, and violated a girl of eighteen—the mother was kept off with the bayonet by each sol-

---

* In *The Guns of August* Barbara Tuchman attributes the German campaign of terror to the influence of Clausewitz, the nineteenth-century military theorist. She may have taken Clausewitz too literally, but then again, so may have the Germans. More to the point, Tuchman does not bother to include rape among her many examples of terror. In this omission I believe she was unduly influenced by those who sought to unravel and debunk Allied propaganda after the war.

dier in turn." Le Ferte-Gaucher: "The Germans broke into a house and violated a woman in the presence of her four-year-old child." Amillis: "They violated a woman, attacking her with bayonets drawn and revolver in hand." Beton-Bazoches: "They violated a woman . . . with her child three years old in the room." Sancy-les-Provins: "A woman whose husband was with the colours and who was alone in the house with four children was violated by a Germany cyclist quartered on her for the night." On the road from Fosse to Vitrival, an eyewitness recounted, "A soldier approached one of the women, intending to violate her, and she pushed him away. He at once struck the woman in the breast with his bayonet. I saw her fall."

Château-Thierry . . . Charmel . . . Gerbeviller . . . a tale of rape in each town. The terror continued in northern France through the month of October, broken briefly by the Battle of the Marne. It was the same story in Flanders and along the Franco-Belgian border. A British professor of constitutional law named J. H. Morgan examined the sworn statements of thirty women who were raped at Bailleul during eight days of occupation. Because he was a cautious lawyer he also demanded and received their medical certificates of injury. Professor Morgan later published his findings.

> Outrages upon the honour of women by German soldiers have been so frequent that it is impossible to escape the conviction that they have been condoned and indeed encouraged by German officers. . . . At least five officers were guilty of such offences, and where the officers set the example the men followed. . . . In one case, the facts of which are proved by evidence that would satisfy any court of law, a young girl of nineteen was violated by one officer while the other held her mother by the throat and pointed a revolver, after which the two officers exchanged their respective roles. The officers and soldiers usually hunted in couples, either entering the houses under pretense of seeking billets or forcing the doors by open violence. Frequently the victims were beaten and kicked, and invariably threatened with a loaded revolver.

Nieppe . . . Laventie . . . Lorgies . . . Armentières . . . Estaires . . .

Toward the end of 1914 the strategy of warfare underwent a revolutionary change. Historians agree that war was "modernized": stationary trenches, barbed wire, machine guns, gas and gas masks replaced the concept of the maneuvering, marching army. From the best information available it appears that the incidence of rape and other weapons of terror employed by the German Army dramatically dropped off at approximately the same moment in time.

Interestingly, the young Arnold Toynbee was at great pains in 1917 to deny that the two events were related. He was convinced that the German Army abandoned rape and other terror tactics independent of their adoption of stationary trench warfare, and that the commission of atrocities on a grand scale during the first three months of the war was deliberate in its limits.

> This has not been due to the immobility of the fronts [he argued], for although it is certainly true that the Germans have been unable to overrun fresh territories on the west, they have carried out greater invasions than ever in Russia and the Balkans, which have not been marked by outrages of the same specific kind. This seems to show that the systematic warfare against the civilian population in the campaigns of 1914 was the result of policy, deliberately tried and deliberately given up. This hypothesis would account for the peculiar features in the German Army's conduct . . .

The imposition of a Machiavellian scheme on German Army rape is tantalizing, but I fear when Toynbee wrote those sentences he was serving the cause of propaganda more than the cause of history. It is logical to believe that rape may have been a deliberate tactic of the German Army during the first few months of the war, or if not deliberate, certainly not discouraged, but it seems more rational to conclude that the *opportunity* to rape was effectively cut down by the new system of stationary trench warfare, the *frequency* curtailed by military stalemate, and the *horror* of it superseded by the staggering loss of life as the war went on.

After the first three months of the war, the Allied countries no longer bothered to tally rape reports or tried to verify the rumors. There was no need. The war had given birth to a new and highly effective tool of battle: the scientific use of international propaganda. The German Army may have temporarily seized the military initiative, but in the vivid war of propaganda it was the Allied nations that swarmed the field and moved decisively. In the hands of skilled Allied manipulators, rape was successfully launched in world opinion, almost overnight, as a characteristic German crime, evidence of the "depraved Boche" penchant for warfare by atrocity.

Never before in history had rape in war—the privilege of territorial conquest—boomeranged quite so spectacularly. Neutral America was the chief target of the propaganda technicians from both sides of the fence, but the unimaginative Germans never stood a chance. "The Rape of the Hun" became an instant byword in this country. It came to symbolize the criminal violation of innocent Belgium. It dramatized the plight of La Belle France. It charged up national patriotism and spurred the drive for Liberty Loans by adding needed authenticity to the manufactured *persona* of an unprincipled barbarian with pointed helmet and syphilitic lust who gleefully destroyed cathedrals, set fire to libraries, and hacked and maimed and spitted babies on the tip of his bayonet. As propaganda, rape was remarkably effective, more effective than the original German terror. It helped to lay the emotional groundwork that led us into the war.

In his 1927 study, *Propaganda Technique in the World War*, the pioneer work in propaganda analysis, Harold D. Lasswell wrote, "A handy rule for arousing hate is, if at first they do not enrage, use an atrocity." As for the propaganda value of rape, Lasswell speculated, "These stories yield a crop of indignation against the fiendish perpetrators . . . and satisfy certain powerful, hidden impulses. A young woman, ravished by the enemy, yields a secret satisfaction to a host of vicarious ravishers on the other side of the border."

Lasswell's Freudian analysis is a revealing glimpse of the male mentality. (It could hardly apply to the reactions of women.) It is even more revealing when we realize that he wrote those lines to leave the reader with doubt as to whether or not women *actually were raped* in any great number in Belgium and France. His next and final words on the subject were "Hence, perhaps, the popularity and ubiquity of such stories." But Lasswell's theory certainly does apply to the lustful, rape-mongering prose that was cheerily ground out by Allied propaganda mills once they moved into full swing.

German Atrocities: Their Nature and Philosophy by one Newell Dwight Hillis, a volume that was simultaneously published in Great Britain, the United States and Canada in 1918, is a vintage example. The author, a popular Brooklyn clergyman in his day, lovingly built his own amazing construct as to why German soldiers committed rape. None of it had anything to do with hostility toward women, naturally.

> Should the average American return home at night to find that his wife and children had been massacred and mutilated in his absence, he would not go to the office on the following morning . . . and weeks would pass before he could steel his hand to the accustomed task. Now the German war staff fully realized the true value of the atrocity as a military instrument. Their soldiers ran no risk in . . . raping young girls, but they hoped that when the news of their crimes reached the armed opponent, the atrocity committed upon his wife or child would break his nerve and leave him helpless to fight.

The Reverend Hillis reported the desperate cry of a French soldier:

> "The Germans have been in my land for a year. . . . My little house is gone, and gone my little shop! My wife is still a young woman! My little girl—she is just a little, little girl! Why, I never thought of her as a woman! And now our priest writes me that my young wife and my little girl will have babes in two months by these brutes!"

After which the author intoned,

> Such devastations of the soul are why there must be no inconclusive peace. Unconditional surrender is the only word.

Hillis was adept at painting a graphic picture:

> When the Germans ruined a village near Ham, they carried away some fifty-four girls and women between the ages of fourteen and forty. These girls were held behind the lines among the camp women, kept for the Huns. One chilly morning last April a French boy, lying on a board on the bottom of his trench, heard the wild shrieks of a girl. Standing on tiptoe he peeped over the top. . . . One week of cruelty had driven the girl insane. The German soldiers had lifted her out of the trench, and with their bayonets had pushed her in the direction of the French lines. . . . What the French soldiers saw was a young woman, clothed in a dark blue skirt, her waist torn, her bosom exposed, her hair loose upon her shoulders. She was standing bewildered in No Man's Land. Now she

poured forth the pealing laughter of a maniac. . . . So terrible was the scene that for the moment the Frenchman and German alike forgot all warfare! Finally a German lifted his rifle to the shoulder, and as the girl, rising to her feet . . . screamed, "The Boche! the Boche!" his rifle cracked, and the young woman sank slowly down.

And then the clincher:

That is why the fire sparkles in the eyes of the Allied soldiers whenever you suggest peace by negotiation, or a peace without victory.

But the masterpiece of *German Atrocities: Their Nature and Philosophy* was this convoluted paragraph:

THE FOUL CRIME AGAINST WOMEN

Many Americans have looked with horror upon the photograph of the mutilated bodies of women. Sacred forever the bosom of his mother, and not less sacred the body of every woman. Not content with mutilating the bodies of Allied officers, of Belgian boys, they lifted the knife upon the loveliness of woman. . . . When the Hun joins the army . . . a few drops of blood are taken from the left arm, and the Wassermann blood culture is developed. If free from disease, the soldier receives a card giving him access to camp women, who are kept in the rear for the convenience of the German soldier. If, however, the Wassermann test shows that the German has syphilis . . . he must stay away from the camp women upon peril of his life . . . he will be shot like a dog. Having syphilis himself, the German will hand it on to the camp girl, and she in turn will contaminate all the other soldiers, and that means the Kaiser would soon have no army. Therefore, the soldier that has this foul disease . . . has but one chance, namely to capture a Belgian or French girl; but using her means contaminating her, and she in turn will contaminate the next German using her. To save his own life, therefore, when the syphilitic German has used a French or Belgian girl, he cuts off her breast as warning to the next German soldier. The girl's life weighs less than nothing against lust or the possibility of losing his life by being charged with the contamination of his brother German.

After reading this kind of emotional propaganda it might be said quite seriously that the raped women of France and Belgium, by the way in which their violation was cleverly turned to Allied advantage, played a real role in the ultimate defense of their countries. But if a reader believes that this unusual contribution far beyond the line of duty has been duly recognized in history, please be disabused of that notion. There was one further way to play with rape in World War I, and of course that happened, too. The final step was to deny that rape occurred at all.

When the war was over, a wholly predictable reaction set in. Scholars of the newly refined art of propaganda set about to unravel its mysteries by trying to separate fact from fiction. It was inevitable that a deep bias against women (particularly against women who say they have been raped) would show in their endeavor. There had been some gross lies in the manufacturing of Allied propaganda and these were readily brought to light by the experts. Among the most famous of the fabricated wartime stories was the tale of German soldiers who spitefully cut the hands off Belgian children to render them unfit for fighting when they grew up. A few widely circulated atrocity photographs were shown to have been lifted from other theaters of war. Some German Army excesses were indisputable, even if they had been blown out of proportion for propaganda purposes. Yes, the cathedral at Rheims had been burned, and yes, the library at Louvain had truly been vandalized. But what about the rape of all those women? The crime that is by reputation "the easiest to charge and the hardest to prove" has traditionally been the *easiest to disprove* as well. The rational experts found it laughably easy to debunk accounts of rape, and laughably was the way they did it.

One lengthy study, *Atrocity Propaganda, 1914–1919*, published by the Yale University Press in 1941, expended no more than a few skimpy sentences to construct a witty dismissal of rape. They are worth examining as a perfect example of between-us-men logic in a serious work that ironically purports to explore the nature of propaganda. The author, James M. Read, reported that in French accounts of the German terror the phrase *des viols et des vols* (translation: rapes and thefts) cropped up with frequency. (A police detective in any American city would hardly find such a combination startling since rape and theft are often committed together if an opportunity arises.) Read jumped on *des viols et des vols* as something suspicious if not downright sinister—a "euphonious concatenation"—and left the reader to speculate that if any crime had been committed, it was probably the French sin of alliterative exaggeration!

Having thus delivered a mortal blow to rape, Read finished it off in another half paragraph. Addressing himself to the validity of 427 depositions of atrocity taken in northern France during October and November of the first year of the war, after the German forces had retreated, he wrote, "Three hundred were sworn statements; approximately 100 were not attested, while the remainder lacked even names. The latter cases were those of women who had been attacked. One or two of these were almost ludicrous in the paucity of facts, such as the declaration of 'Dame X, 38 years old, at Compiègne.'" Professor Read then availed himself of the opportunity to reprint Dame X's testimony, which even he admitted was atypical: "I swear to tell the truth, and I consent to make a declaration to you of the facts of which I have been a victim, but I would be crushed if my deposition were made public . . ." To hammer home the point, Read wrote, "After this somewhat noncommittal statement followed four rows of dots."

The reluctance of Dame X to have the story of her humiliation set in type and publicized is far from an unusual attitude, even for our present day. After all, she had to live in Compiègne for the rest of her life. The dots do not refute her credibility; they merely deny authentic details to history. Other depositions, as we can see from Toynbee and Morgan, were obviously more specific. But the declaration of Dame X of Compiègne represents the sum total of factual information on rape that Read presented in his otherwise heavily annotated study of fact and propaganda in World War I. To the professor the case of Dame X was enough ammunition to make his point that rape reports could hardly be taken seriously by a scholar of his most estimable stature.

WORLD WAR II

As interpreted by the loyal philosopher-servants of the Third Reich, fascism's very nature was an exaggeration of the values that normal society held to be masculine. Goebbels himself had said as much, and before him Nietzsche, that fount of inspiration, had instructed, "Man should be trained for war and woman for the recreation of the warrior." Therefore, it was not surprising that the ideology of rape burst into perfect flower as Hitler's armies goose-stepped over the face of Europe in the early days of World War II.

> Hitler always said that the masses are essentially feminine, and his aggressiveness and charisma elicited an almost masochistic surrender and submission in his audience—a form of psychic rape. . . . He didn't convince his audiences; he conquered them.

We owe this vivid image of a Hitler speech to Albert Speer, but the metaphor is clearly Hitler's. The Nazi aim was to conquer, not merely to win or convince, and that, of course, was the heart of the matter. A mind that perceived—and then set about to institutionalize—the masses as weak and feminine, and the Jewish masses as especially weak and feminine, and the Bolshevik masses as equally weak and feminine (and strangely susceptible to the feminist notion that women are the equals of men), was a mind that naturally turned to rape as a means of suppression.

The analogy between Jews and women—and between Aryan supremacy and male supremacy—that the Third Reich promulgated has been discussed by Eva Figes and Kate Millett. The point I want to make here is that as rape is the quintessential act by which a male demonstrates to a female that she is conquered—vanquished—by his superior strength and power, it was perfectly logical within the framework of fascism that rape would be employed by the German soldier as he strove to prove himself a worthy Superman. In fact, it would have been highly *illogical* if rape were not in the German soldier's kit bag of weapons. Rape for the Germans, and to a similar extent for the Japanese, played a serious and logical role in the achievement of what they saw as their ultimate objective: the total humiliation and destruction of "inferior peoples" and the establishment of their own master race.

Reports of mob rape directed against Jewish women made their first appearance during the secretly ordered "spontaneous" riots of November, 1938, the *Kristallnacht* that began in Munich and spread throughout Germany in planned response to the assassination, by a Jew, of a minor German Embassy official in Paris. The *Kristallnacht* became the model for a pattern that was to be repeated in many towns in many places once the official war began.

When the advancing German Army approached a Polish or a

Russian village, the pattern of first-phase violence was almost invariable. Homes were looted, but first and especially the Jewish homes, and Jewish girls were singled out for torture and rape, often in front of their parents. Days, weeks or months later, depending on the timetable, the second, or "serious," phase began: the round-ups of the Jewish population, the mass shootings, the herding into ghettos, and the eventual dispatch in boxcars to the concentration camps and the Final Solution. A Russian-Jewish woman named Sophia Glushkina gave this eyewitness account of the pattern of German terror in the city of Krasny, preserved for us in the unemotional form of a war-crimes trial deposition.

Before the war I lived in Minsk. On June 24, 1941, I saw my husband off to the front. I walked out of the town with my eight-year-old child, heading east. I decided to go to my birthplace—the city of Krasny—to get to my father and brothers. In Krasny the Germans caught up with me, on July 13th.

On July 25th a notice was posted ordering a meeting of all residents of the town. At the meeting the Germans said that anybody may move into the houses of Jews. The Germans also announced that the Jews must obey all orders of German soldiers.

They began to raid apartments, to undress people, to beat them with sticks and whips.

On August 8th, SS men invaded my house. They grabbed my brother, Boris Semenovich Glushkin. He was 38 years old. They began to beat him; then they threw him out onto the street, tormented him and finally threw him into a cellar. The next morning they posted notices: "All inhabitants are invited to the public execution of a sheeny." My brother was brought out, he had an inscription on his chest saying that he was to be executed. He was undressed, tied to the tail of a horse and dragged off. When the moment of execution came, he was already half dead.

The next night at 2 o'clock they knocked on the door again. The commandant entered and demanded the wife of the executed Jew. She wept, being shaken by the dreadful death of her husband; the three children wept. She was taken away. We thought that she would be killed, but the Germans acted more beastly than that; they raped her right here in the yard.

On August 27th a special detachment arrived. The Jews were driven together and were told to bring all of their belongings immediately and turn them over to the Germans. Then they moved to the ghetto. The Germans fenced a plot of land in with barbed wire and hung up a sign—"Ghetto, Entrance forbidden." All Jews, even children, had to wear six-pointed stars made of yellow cloth on their chests and on their backs.

In February one night the SS men dashed into the barracks. Their choice was an eighteen-year-old girl, Etta Kuznetsova. She was ordered to take her skirt off. She refused. She was beaten for some time. Her mother, fearing that they would kill her, whispered: "Do not resist." She undressed. Then she was placed on a chair, spot-lighted with a flashlight, tortured and assaulted. It is difficult to describe it all . . .

After witnessing this second rape, Sophia Glushkina escaped to the forest with her young son and joined the partisans. Within hours of her flight, the remaining Jews of Krasny were herded into the town square and shot. She concludes her terse narrative, "For two years we fought, and then the day came when I saw the Red Army . . ."

Technically it was *verboten* for a German to rape a Jew under the stern prohibition against "race defilement"—the injunction against contaminating Aryan "blood" contained in the Nuremberg race laws of 1935 that extended under its own twisted logic to forcible intercourse as well as to marriage or extramarital liaison.* The fear of being caught at race defilement apparently created an arena of acute conflict for some of the *Soldaten*. In her published memoirs Sala Pawlowicz, a survivor of Bergen-Belsen, tells of a terrifying visit to the police station in Lask, her German-occupied Polish village. She was called in on a minor pretext, forced to strip before the assembled Gestapo men, slapped about and then dragged by one of them into an adjoining room.

I was in a small office and the German had a long heavy whip in his hand. "You don't know how to obey . . . I'll show you. But I can't have you, scum, because you're Jewish, and filthy. What a shame!" He swung the whip across my breasts. "Here's what you can have for being a dirty Jew—instead of me—this!" He lashed the whip again and again and I fainted.

---

* Race defilement was similar to the prohibition against "the mixture of the races" that was part of the legal code in the American South before and after slavery, and which hardly affected the rape of black women by white men. See subchapter on rape in slavery.

When Sala Pawlowicz regained consciousness she found herself lying naked and bloody in the street. According to her memoirs, the Nazis made nightly swoops through the ghetto in search of young Jewish girls, and despite her mother's attempts to hide her, she did not escape this attention. It was, she felt, part of a general sado-sexual humiliation that the Germans inflicted on the Jewish population. During daylight, the Germans would stage mass disrobings of men, women and children "for diversion": "They forced us to undress and lie on the ground as they walked by, laughing and making lewd comments. Then we were beaten with whips on our bare backs and chased through the ghetto Their actions shamed me."

Sexual humiliation had a part to play as the Germans tightened their grip on the Warsaw ghetto. A series of depositions collected by members of the Warsaw Judenrat, the Nazi-established Jewish governing council, dwells on the German Army's attempt in late 1939 and early 1940 to cajole the Judenrat into setting up a brothel stocked with Jewish girls that would be divided into two sections, one for officers and one for ordinary soldiers. The Jewish brothel in the Warsaw ghetto was apparently never established. According to the Judenrat, this was where it drew the line; the German soldiers had to make do with mass forays into the ghetto in search of young women.

Surgeon-gynecologists of the ghetto methodically administered antitetanus shots to victims of German rape—"of course keeping secret the names," reported one Jewish doctor of Warsaw. His deposition goes on to say, "In one mirror shop in Swietokerska Street there was a mass raping of Jewish girls. The Germans seized the most beautiful and most healthy girls in the streets and brought them in to pack mirrors. After the work the girls were raped." Another affidavit tells of a similar incident on Franciszkanska Street, where "40 Jewish girls were dragged into the house which was occupied by German officers. There, after being forced to drink, the girls were ordered to undress and to dance for the amusement of their tormentors. Beaten, abused and raped, the girls were not released till 3 A.M."

These depositions appear in The Black Book of Polish Jewry, a mid-war volume that was published in New York in 1943, before the final liquidation of the ghetto. Curiously, no full-length account of the Warsaw ghetto that I have ever examined, either fact or fiction, details any incident of rape. It is possible that this failure has been a mere historic oversight, or that the awful destruction of the ghetto and the last bit of heroic resistance on the part of the Jews has overshadowed early stories of the rape of women, but I am inclined to a more cynical interpretation. *The Black Book of Polish Jewry* was published as a propaganda volume, a cry for help. After the war was over perhaps it was no longer politically necessary to believe the word of women, or to consider the special fate of females a matter of importance or significance.

Captured German documents presented at the Nuremberg war-crimes tribunal in 1946 corroborate the routine use of rape as a weapon of terror. The reason for the existence of these documents is fascinating. Sometimes German authorities in an occupied city made a straight-faced stab at collecting reports of informal atrocities under the pretext of a concern for legality. The official German position was that "uncontrollable elements" were responsible for the ugly excesses, an excellent excuse for the formal repressive measures that followed, which required cooperation from the ghetto leadership. Sometimes the gathering of information was inspired by more complex motivation, such as the desire of a German Army commander to build up a case against his SS competitor. In February, 1940, a German Army commander in Poland compiled a long list of complaints against the SS. Last on the list, Item 33, discussed the case of two policemen who had dragged two teen-age Jewish girls out of bed. One of the girls was raped in a Polish cemetery; the other, who got violently ill, was told they would "get her next time and pay her five zlotys." The Army commander who wrote up the report was outraged over the *amateurish* way in which the SS was attempting to deal with the problem of two million Jews.

What remained of Orthodox Jewry during the Final Solution, the remnants of the religious leadership, tried to stretch old doctrines to accommodate the new reality. Rape had to be dealt with because it raised unsettling philosophic and practical questions that required rabbinical interpretation.

A rabbi from the Kovno ghetto in Lithuania sought to formulate answers to many difficult situations as they arose for his dwindling flock. Jewish slave laborers were fed a bowl of soup that wasn't kosher. Were they permitted to eat the soup? Yes, they were. Could one purchase a certificate of baptism to save one's life?

No. Could circumcision be performed by a nonpracticing doctor since there were no pious circumcisers left alive in Kovno? Yes. Since the Germans published an edict ordering death for any Jewish woman who became pregnant, were abortion and contraception permitted? Yes. Suicide? No.

And, wrote the rabbi,

Immediately after we were liberated from the ghetto I was asked an important question which touched not only on the person who came before me but many other Jewish women as well who had survived humiliation and physical abuse by German officers. The specific question was this: A young woman of good family came to me crying that she was one of our poor sisters who had been humiliated by the Germans. Besides abusing her body, the Germans had tattooed on her arm the legend, *Whore for Hitler's Troops*. After liberation she had succeeded in finding her husband, and they hoped to resume their marriage and set up a proper Jewish home. They had lost all their children at the hands of the Germans. But, seeing the fearful tattoo on her arm, the husband was taken aback . . . Before living together as man and wife they had first to clarify whether she was permitted to him.

The rabbi responded,

Far be it from any man to cast aspersions on pious Jewish women in such a plight as this. Rather, it is our duty to proclaim the reward they will receive for their suffering. We must avoid causing them any unnecessary anguish. Certainly husbands who have divorced their wives under similar circumstances have acted reprehensibly. Nor, in my opinion, need husband and wife in this case make any effort to remove the cursed legend on the wife's arm. Rather, let it be preserved and exhibited—not as a sign of disgrace and humiliation, but as the symbol of honor and courage, in behalf of those who were slaughtered. Let it be a reminder to us and to the world that God has taken and will take His revenge on His people's oppressors.

Jewish women alone did not suffer rape as the German Army advanced into Russia. All women were prey. From evidence presented to the Nuremberg tribunal the pattern becomes clear.

The people who came to Nuremberg armed with the bitterest memories and the best-kept records were the Soviet prosecutors, for the Soviets, who sustained the worst numerical losses of any of the Allies, had been collecting their data and gathering their depositions throughout the long war. A distillation of atrocities committed by the Nazi invader during the dark days of 1941 was submitted as U.S.S.R. Exhibit No. 51. Prepared by the Russian foreign minister, V. M. Molotov, in January, 1942, as an interim war report directed to the Allied governments, it was entered into evidence at Nuremberg as "The Molotov Note." "Women and girls are vilely outraged in all the occupied areas," the diplomat had written.

• In the Ukrainian village of Borodayevka, in the Dniepropetrovsk region, the fascists violated every one of the women and girls.
• In the village of Berezovka, in the region of Smolensk, drunken German soldiers assaulted and carried off all the women and girls between the ages of 16 and 30.
• In the city of Smolensk the German command opened a brothel for officers in one of the hotels into which hundreds of women and girls were driven; they were mercilessly dragged down the street by their arms and hair.
• Everywhere the lust-maddened German gangsters break into the houses, they rape the women and girls under the very eyes of their kinfolk and children, jeer at the women they have violated, and then brutally murder their victims.
• In the city of Lvov, 32 women working in a garment factory were first violated and then murdered by German storm troopers. Drunken German soldiers dragged the girls and young women of Lvov into Kesciuszko Park, where they savagely raped them . . .
• Near the town of Borissov in Bielorussia, 75 women and girls attempting to flee at the approach of the German troops fell into their hands. The Germans first raped and then savagely murdered 36 of their number. By order of a German officer named Hummer, the soldiers marched L. I. Melchukova, a 16-year-old girl, into the forest, where they raped her. A little later some other women who had also been dragged into the forest saw some boards near the trees and the dying Melchukova nailed to the boards. The Germans had cut off her breasts in the presence of these women, among whom were V. I. Alperenko and V. H. Bereznikova.
• On retreating from the village of Borovka, in the Zvenigorod district of the Moscow region, the fascists forcibly abducted several women, tearing them away from their little children in spite of their protests and prayers.

• In the town of Tikhvin, in the Leningrad region, a 15-year-old girl named H. Koledetskaya who had been wounded by shell splinters was taken to a hospital (a former monastery) where there were wounded German soldiers. Despite her injuries the girl was raped by a group of German soldiers and died as a result of the assault.

All of this occurred in the first flush of the German invasion.

Yet another aspect of wartime rape—rape as a method of military retaliation or reprisal—was briefly illuminated at the Nuremberg tribunal when it came the turn of the French prosecution.

Accounts of punitive measures taken by the Germans in occupied France during the summer of 1944 in response to the active presence of the Maquis (resistance fighters) were marked as evidence and read into the trial record. One Maquis stronghold was the region of Vecours. On June 15, 1944, the Germans staged a "surprise" raid on the village of St. Donat: "The Maquis had evacuated the town several days earlier . . . 54 women or young girls from 13 to 50 years of age were raped by the maddened soldiers." A raid at Nice on July 20, 1944, had a similar conclusion:

. . . having been attacked at Presles by several groups of Maquis in the region, by way of reprisal this Mongolian detachment, as usual commanded by the SS, went to a farm where two French members of the resistance had been hidden. Being unable to take them prisoners, these soldiers then arrested the proprietors of that farm (the husband and wife), and after subjecting them to numerous atrocities, rape, et cetera, they shot them with machine guns.

As the French prosecutor sifted through his documents, the standard censoring mechanism that men employ when dealing with the rape of women was put into effect. "The Tribunal will forgive me if I avoid citing the atrocious details," he said with gallantry. "A medical certificate from Doctor Nicolaides who examined the women who were raped in this region—I will pass on."

The Far East equivalent of the Nuremberg International Military Tribunal was held in Tokyo in 1946. Now it was the Japanese war machine that was held under scrutiny, and now it was the master-race theory of the Land of the Rising Sun—with the Chinese nation forced to play the role of "inferior people"—that the ultimate victors of World War II had cause to examine and pass judgment upon. At the Tokyo tribunal the full story of the Rape of Nanking, almost ten years after the fact, was finally made known.

Hard news out of Nanking was slow in coming when the Japanese Army took China's capital city in December, 1937. General Chiang Kai-shek had pulled out his Nationalist forces prior to the invasion, moving his capital westward to Hankow. Any Chinese civilian with the wherewithal had also fled, leaving the defenseless city to the poorer classes and a handful of foreign missionaries, including some Americans, who elected to stay. What happened next when the Japanese conqueror entered Nanking can only be described as an orgy of wholesale assault against the remaining civilian population.

Reports of unchecked violence, including terrifying accounts of mass rape, filtered out of the captured city despite an official news blanket ordered by Generalissimo Chiang. But when the silence was finally broken in January, a curious thing happened. Nanking had clearly been the victim of unlawful atrocity. As the Western press jumped into the breach, accounts of wanton murder and looting were gravely brought to the world's attention, but stories of rape were handled gingerly—almost reluctantly—by international reporters. "A few uninvestigated cases of rape were reported" was the way Life magazine cautiously chose to inform its readers.

Despite the cynicism brought to bear by the Western press, stories of systematic mass rape in Nanking were unusually persistent, so much so that the "Rape of Nanking" soon passed into common usage as the world-wide metaphor for that city's invasion. In June of 1938 the Nanking International Relief Committee, the missionary group that remained in the city, completed a survey of damage in the Nanking area. Its sixty-page report was a model of the detailed minutiae of devastation. Injury and death to the Chinese population was reported on a percentile basis, broken down by age, sex, previous employment and mode of death. Property loss from fire and looting by Japanese soldiers was estimated in neat, round sums from street to street. Loss of labor animals and damage to winter crops found permanent validation in separate columns marked water buffalo, oxen, donkeys, wheat, barley, broad beans, field peas, and, irony of ironies, rapeseed. As for the act that gave its name to the Rape of Nanking, the compilers of the official report had only this to say: "Among the injured females, 65 percent were between the ages of 15 and 29, although the terms and method of inquiry excluded rape *per se*."

Rape in Nanking might have passed out of history then and there, relegated in typical fashion to the dubious area of unsupported wartime rumor. But as it turned out, the Allied Powers elected to hold an International Military Tribunal for the Far East once the global war was finished. In order to prove the awesome crimes against humanity, facts that a few years before had been inaccessible—"excluded" from the ever-so-proper "terms and method of inquiry"—suddenly loomed important. One of the defendants in the docket at Tokyo was General Iwane Matsui, the man in charge of the Nanking invasion.

No raped women were called to testify at the Tokyo tribunal, but there were witnesses enough. The star witnesses, by and large, were the very same missionaries who had chosen to exclude rape from their official report of war damage. As it turned out, they had not been unmindful of the crime. Rather, the enormity of it apparently had paralyzed them. A page from the Nanking diary of American missionary James McCallum was entered into evidence:

> Never have I heard or read of such brutality. Rape! Rape! Rape! We estimate at least 1,000 cases a night, and many by day. In case of resistance . . . there is a bayonet stab or a bullet. We could write up hundreds of cases a day.

Mrs. Shui Fang Tsen, director of dormitories at Ginling College, a missionary institution, submitted a lengthy deposition. At the start of the invasion the missionaries proclaimed Ginling an international safety zone, and the college grounds became a refuge for more than ten thousand frightened women and children. The "safety zone" hardly proved safe for women. According to Mrs. Shui, "Japanese soldiers would enter the grounds on the pretext of looking for soldiers, but were in fact looking for our girls." On the night of December 17, 1937, a gang of soldiers forcibly entered the college and carried off eleven young women. Nine later made their way back to the grounds, "horribly raped and abused." "We never heard any more of the other two girls," Mrs. Shui reported. This was a typical incident.

Witness after witness told similar stories—girls dragged off by gangs of four or five men in uniform; abducted women forced to wash clothes for the Army units by day and to "service" as many as fifteen to forty men at night; women forced to perform sex shows for troops at play; fathers forced at gunpoint to rape their own daughters. Many of the stories had similar endings. When a group of soldiers was finished with a captured woman, a stick was sometimes pushed up into her vagina; in some cases the woman's head was severed. A statement from Mrs. Chang Kia Sze was read into the record:

> The first day the Japanese entered Nanking they fired and burnt our home and we were proceeding to the refugee camp. There were the following in the party, my mother, my brother and his wife, two children of mine, and my brother's two children, aged 5 and 2 years of age.
> As we were proceeding and came to a place called Lao Wong Fou in Nanking City, we were met by twelve Japanese soldiers, including some officers who wore swords. One of the soldiers wearing a sword, whom I thought was an officer, grasped my sister-in-law and raped and then killed her in the presence of her husband and children, who were killed at the same time. The husband was killed for trying to defend his wife and the two children were killed because they wept when their mother was being raped. The five-year-old girl was suffocated by having her clothing stuffed in her mouth and the boy was bayoneted. Their father and mother were both bayoneted and thereby killed. My mother was also bayoneted and died twelve days later. I fell to the ground and escaped later with my two children.
> This all happened about 10 o'clock in the morning and in broad daylight on the streets of Nanking. I was an eyewitness to all of this. I went to the refugee camp and on the way saw many corpses, women and civilian men. The women had their apparel pulled up and looked like they had been raped. I saw about twenty, mostly women.

Wong Pan Sze, who was fifteen years old at the time of the Nanking invasion, submitted the following affidavit:

> At the time the Japanese entered the city on December 13, 1937, I and my father and my sister had already been removed to live in a house on Shanghai Road No. 100 which was in the refugee

zone. There were about 500 persons living in that house, and I often saw the Japs come to the house asking and searching for women. On one occasion one woman was raped in the open yard. This happened in the night, and all of us could hear her cry while she was being raped. But when the Japs left we could not find her, they had taken her away with them. Twice I saw the Japs' truck come to the house and round up women living at the house. These women were taken away by the Japs and none of them returned with the exception of one girl who managed to get back home after having been raped by the Japs, and she told me that all the girls who had been taken in the trucks had been raped many times by the Japs, one after the other. This one girl who managed to get back to the house told me that she had seen one of the girls raped, and after being raped the Japs stuck weeds into her vagina, and the girl died from this treatment. At this time I was about 15 years of age. I hid every time a Jap came near the house and this is why the Japs never caught me . . .

Nanking was a totally defenseless city. The twenty or so foreign missionaries were totally unable to stem the tide. Reading through the pages of their testimony, one can't help thinking how woefully inadequate and ludicrous their efforts were as they literally ran about and tried to shoo away the Japanese soldiers they found assaulting Chinese women within their self-declared neutrality zone. For a time they made a stab at reporting a daily list of atrocities to the Japanese authorities. The reports averaged at least ten gang rapes a day—"sample cases" they called them. Chinese names were rarely recorded. The report filed on December 16, 1937, duly entered into evidence, is pathetic, both in its sense of outrage and priority. Items No. 12 and 13 were as follows:

12. At 10 P.M. on the night of December 14, a Chinese home on Chien Ying Hsiang was entered by 11 Japanese soldiers who raped four Chinese women.

13. On December 14, Japanese soldiers entered the home of Miss Grace Bauer, an American missionary, and took a pair of fur-lined gloves, drank up all the milk on the table, and scooped up sugar with their hands.

The pathetic evidence submitted to the military tribunal was conclusive enough. The judgment at Tokyo found that "approximately 20,000 cases of rape occurred within the city during the first month of occupation."* In its summation the tribunal stated:

> Death was a frequent penalty for the slightest resistance on the part of a victim or the members of her family who sought to protect her. Even girls of tender years and old women were raped in large numbers throughout the city, and many cases of abnormal or sadistic behavior in connection with the rapings occurred. Many women were killed after the act and their bodies mutilated. . . . The barbarous behavior of the Japanese army cannot be excused as the acts of a soldiery which had temporarily gotten out of hand when at last a stubbornly defended position had capitulated—rape, arson and murder continued to be committed on a large scale for at least six weeks after the city had been taken.

One month before the Nanking invasion General Matsui had crowed that his mission was "to chastise the Nanking Government and the outrageous Chinese." He wanted, he proclaimed, "to dazzle China with Japan's military glory." Ten years later it was the considered opinion of the Tokyo tribunal that the sack of the city had been "either secretly ordered or willfully committed." For his part in the Rape of Nanking General Matsui was sentenced to be hanged.

Matsui's defense had been to deny all charges of illegal atrocities, particularly the accounts of rape, which he called mere "rumors, Chinese passing on the information, perhaps in fun." On cross-examination he repeated in exasperation, "I am only trying to tell you that I am not directly responsible for the discipline and morals of the troops under the respective armies under my command." His intelligence officer, Major Yasuto Nakayama, was a trifle more humble, correctly polite. Concerning cases of rape and assaults against women and girls, Nakayama testified, "I believe there were several cases of this to a limited extent, and I regret that such cases occurred. It is very improper for me to state an opinion before this Tribunal—however, I hope that such incidents will not in the future occur."

Had it not been for the Tokyo war-crimes tribunal, who would

---

* Given the size of the city and the concentration of assault, the Rape of Nanking was on a par with an event that occurred thirty-four years later, the Rape of Bangladesh.

have believed the full dimensions of the Rape of Nanking? The Japanese, like all warring governments, were mindful that rape in war was an unconscionable crime under the Hague Convention, and they did their best to cover their unfortunate traces. The attempted cover-up was duly entered into evidence at the postwar trials.

In February, 1939, the Japanese War Ministry issued a set of top-secret instructions to commanders in the field regarding the explicit stifling of certain kinds of conversation heard among men returning home on furlough. This was after the occupation of Nanking and Hankow, and the soldiers of the Rising Sun had been rather loose-tongued about where they had been and what they had done. The orders gave examples of the sort of remarks to be avoided in the future, citing quotes that had appeared in foreign newspaper stories:

> —"One company commander unofficially gave [us] instructions for raping as follows: 'In order that we will not have problems, either pay them money or kill them in some obscure place after you have finished.' "
> —"If the army men who participated in the war were investigated individually, they would probably all be guilty of murder, robbery or rape."
> —"At ——— we captured a family of four. We played with the daughter as we would with a harlot. But as the parents insisted that the daughter be returned to them we killed them. We played with the daughter as before until the unit's departure and then killed her."
> —"In the half year of battle about the only things I learned are rape and burglary."

America had not yet entered the war, and the secret orders were an effort to avoid unfavorable criticism at home and abroad.

Agnes Newton Keith, an American who spent World War II in a Japanese prisoner-of-war camp on Borneo and later wrote *Three Came Home*, a spunky narrative of her adventures, was the victim of an attempted rape in her detention camp, and of retaliatory violence when she tried to report it. Mrs. Keith was of the opinion that her Japanese guards were under orders not to molest their Western detainees. Yet early one morning as she sat on the steps of her barracks, a prison guard approached and threw her a pack of cigarettes.

> The guard hesitated, giggled, and . . . then bent quickly over me, ran his two hands roughly down my breasts, over my thighs, and forced them violently up between my legs. The gesture so astounded me that I was paralyzed. I could think of nothing but, Well, it's fortunate I have on slacks.
>
> What followed then was unpleasant, a kind of unpleasantness that a woman resents more than any other, and which hurts her as much psychologically as physically. The soldier was strong and rough and crude and nasty, and he enjoyed humiliating me; his ideas of pleasure were new ones to me; had they been familiar I still could not have liked them.

In the ensuing scuffle Mrs. Keith managed to kick her assailant in the stomach. "He stumbled backwards down the stairs, and there hesitated as to what to do: whether to kiss, or to kill, or to pull up his pants and go." By this time several other women in the barracks had rallied to her cries and the thwarted guard "picked up his fallen rifle and went sourly down the path."

The indomitable Agnes Keith reported this attempted rape to the prison-camp authorities, who rewarded her with several fractured ribs and a dislocated shoulder for her "lies."

Concentration-camp rape and institutionalized camp brothels in which women were held against their will for the pleasure of the soldiery were a most sinister aspect of the abuse of women in World War II, since acceptance of continuous rape without protest was held out as a possible chance for survival. According to a document in the Vatican archives, as early as March, 1942, the papal envoy in Bratislava, Archbishop Giuseppe Burzio, informed Pope Pius XII that the Nazis were taking young Jewish women from their families to make them prostitutes for German soldiers on the eastern front and were preparing for the total deportation of all other Jews.

House of Dolls, the nightmare novel by Ka-Tzetnik, describes a day's routine in a nameless forcible brothel in which Jewish females under threat of death prepared their cots for the precise arrival at 2 P.M. of the German soldiers. The daily routine was bitterly called Enjoyment Duty and the soldiers, when finished, were expected to file reports on the performance of their Dolls. Three negative reports meant death. Ka-Tzetnik 135633 was the Auschwitz camp number of the pseudonymous author, and despite his use of the novel form—some things are still too horrible for nonfiction—there is not much reason to doubt that the House of Dolls existed.

Dr. Alina Brewda, a Jewish woman from the Warsaw ghetto who was permitted to practice medicine at Auschwitz, devoted a chapter in her wartime memoirs to an Auschwitz brothel of Aryan women prisoners, some of whom she covertly treated and aborted. A deposition taken by the Jewish Anti-Fascist Committee of the U.S.S.R. gave testimony concerning a concentration camp in Tulchin, Rumania, "under the rule of the infamous Petekau who asked each night for two Jewish virgins." A New York Times front-page account in 1944 of the liberation of Vught, a Nazi concentration camp in Holland, reported, "Violation of young Jewish women by prison wardens was a common occurrence." A German brothel in the captured city of Smolensk "into which hundreds of [Russian] women and girls were driven" was mentioned at the Nuremberg tribunal. Similarly it was entered into evidence at the Tokyo tribunal that during the Japanese occupation of the Chinese city of Kweilin, in Kwangsi Province, "They recruited women labor on the pretext of establishing factories; they forced the women thus recruited into prostitution with the Japanese troops."

I would like to say with conviction that a noticeable difference in attitude and behavior toward women existed on the part of the armies of liberation as opposed to the armies of conquest and subjugation in World War II, and that the weight of evidence presented at Nuremberg and Tokyo conclusively proves it. Patterns of German and Japanese aggression clearly included overt expression of contempt for women as part of an overall philosophy of the master race, as well as a most pragmatic means of terror. Rape fit well, was conceptualized even, as a fascist act of domination. Yet it is in the nature of any institution in which men are set apart from women and given the extra power of the gun that the accruing power may be used against all women, for a female victim of rape in war is chosen not because she is a representative of the enemy, but precisely because she is a woman, and therefore an enemy. An all-male army cannot help but become imbued with a sense of its own male mastery, and in the last analysis, the Axis war machine merely carried the male ideology to a further degree, to an unacceptable exaggeration.

As it happened, the right side won in 1945, and the evil that was brought forward for judgment was undeniably the ultimate evil; no one who has ever examined the holocaust literature of World War II can walk away from it without the knowledge that she or he has peered directly into the pit of hell. But those who judged at Nuremberg and Tokyo were those who had emerged from the war victorious. It was *the other side* that was held accountable. No international tribunals were called to expose and condemn Allied atrocity, no war-crimes depositions were taken from "enemy" women, no incriminating top-secret documents from our side of the war were held up to merciless light. A theorist of rape must admit that the evidence has been unfairly weighted.

I am not suggesting that an equality of rape existed in World War II. I doubt that it did. But Allied soldiers did commit rape, with gusto. The sexual assault may not have been a logical weapon within a total concept of "destruction of inferior peoples," but it was just as real a humiliation for the female victims. Instead of a motive of out-and-out conquest we may substitute a motivation (or excuse) of retaliation and revenge. Logic of a sort pertains here as well. I rather suspect that Allied rape, for the rapists, was often joyous—a sporadic, hearty spilling over and acting out of anti-female sentiment disguised within the glorious, vengeful struggle, an exuberant manifestation of the heroic fighting man who is fighting the good fight.

When Ilya Ehrenburg, the flinty Soviet novelist-turned-war correspondent, larded his front-line dispatches in 1942 with tales of German rape, the accounts he wrote set his ideological juices flowing.

> These filthy lechers have now come to Russia. They are polluting our houses. They are violating and infecting our women. Red Army men, in the name of our girls' honour, in the name of our women, in the name of human purity, smash these fornicating Fritzes!

Ehrenburg's job was to light a patriotic fire, and what better kindling was there than the tried-and-true "protection of our women"? These were the dark days for the Russians, before Stalingrad, and Ehrenburg may be pardoned, I suppose, for creating the simplistic slogan, "To gain an hour is to save a Russian man from the rope and a Russian girl from dishonour." His call to arms and human purity became faintly ridiculous three years later when the glorious Red Army, risen at last like a great bear from slumber, turned around and raped German women on the road to Berlin with a ferociousness that matched those "fornicating Fritzes."

The German actress Hildegard Knef described the fall of Berlin from a woman's perspective in her fiercely written autobiography, *The Gift Horse*. As Knef stood in a doorway watching truckloads of women and children rattle past, refugees from Frankfurt-on-Oder, Strausberg and Spindlersfeld, the women shouted, "Clear out, the Russians'll rape you." Knef dressed herself in a German Army uniform, she tells us, to *avoid assault*. Later, crouched in a makeshift bunker with her male comrades she heard

> screams, dreadful heartrending screams, high thin shrill. I call out softly to the next hole: Are you there?
> Yes.
> What's that screaming?
> Russians are in that house over there started on the women shitshitohshitohshit.

When the actress was eventually captured, she had a remarkable exchange with her Russian interrogator. "What you do in German army?" he asked repeatedly in halting German. She coolly answered, "I didn't want to be raped." Furious with her response, the Soviet officer could only bellow, "Russian soldiers not rape! German swine rape!"

But Russian soldiers did rape. Cornelius Ryan, author of *The Last Battle*, a well-researched narrative of the fall of Berlin, was one of the few historians to write of rape in war in its proper perspective. "The fear of sexual attack lay over the city like a pall," Ryan wrote at the start of his story, for six years into World War II Berlin was very nearly a city of women. Refugees who fled the advancing Soviet troops knowledgeably told Berliners what to expect: front-line Red Army men were disciplined and well behaved; they did not rape—but the second wave was close to a disorganized rabble, and it was they who committed the atrocities. (This makes supreme sense. The front-line troops, some of whom were veterans of Stalingrad, had an important, heroic job of retribution to do for their country. Those bringing up the rear had missed out on the most emotional and satisfying moment of the war—to be among the first Russians to march on German soil—and they would thus have been more inclined to take out their vengeance on persons and property.)

Rumor turned to reality when, in Ryan's words, "hordes of Russian troops coming up behind the disciplined front-line veterans . . . demanded the rights due the conquerors: the women of the conquered." Ryan conducted his research in Berlin in the early sixties, aided by a team of interviewers. Although no functioning administration capable of documenting the extent of the rampage existed in Berlin in 1945, the trail was not quite cold and the historian managed to obtain firsthand accounts.

Ursula Köster was sleeping in a basement shelter with her parents and her three children when four Russian soldiers beat in the door with their rifles. They searched the cellar, confiscated some canned goods and watches, and then held her parents and children at gunpoint while, one after another, all four assaulted her. At dawn two more soldiers found their way to the cellar; they, too, raped her.

Anneliese Antz was dragged screaming out of a bed she shared with her mother and was raped by a Soviet officer. When he was finished he stroked her hair, murmured, "Good German," and asked her not to tell anyone an officer had raped her. A food parcel for her was dropped off the following day. Anneliese's older sister, Ilse, was raped by a trooper who entered their cellar with a pistol in each hand. As he ripped off her sweaters and ski pants he stopped to inquire, "Are you a German *soldier?*" Ilse told her interviewer, "I was not surprised. I was so thin from hunger I hardly looked like a woman." After the act her attacker told Ilse, "That's what the Germans did in Russia." He left, but returned to spend the rest of the night with her—to guard her from other soldiers. Ilse Antz's protection lasted just so long; she was later raped by another soldier.

Hannelore von Cmuda, seventeen years old, was raped by a mob of drunken soldiers. When they were finished they fired three shots into her body; she survived.

Margarete Promeist, warden of an air-raid shelter, watched for two days and nights as "wave after wave of Russians came into my shelter plundering and raping. Women were killed if they refused. Some were shot and killed anyway. . . . I found the bodies of six or seven women, all lying in the position in which they were raped, their heads battered in." Frau Promeist herself was assaulted despite her appeals that "I am much too old for you."

Mother Superior Cunegundes of Haus Dahlem, an orphanage and maternity hospital run by the Mission Sisters of the Sacred Heart, was shot at by a soldier when she tried to interfere with the rape of the mission's Ukrainian cook, Lena. The mission was overrun with soldiers who entered the maternity wards and raped pregnant women and those who had given birth.

Some women of Berlin committed suicide, either in fear of rape or in shame after the act. Some avoided assault by making themselves appear diseased or as unattractive as possible with the aid of coal dust, iodine and bandages. Others found ingenious places to hide and remained in cellars and holes until the danger had passed. And some, Ryan wrote, "saved themselves from rape simply by fighting back so fiercely that the Soviet soldiers stopped trying and looked elsewhere." Jolenta Koch was one such fighter. Tricked into entering an empty house by a soldier who had a buddy waiting inside, Frau Koch "put up such resistance that both men were glad to see her go."

Dora Janssen avoided assault by claiming she had tuberculosis. Her servant, Inge, was less lucky and was injured so badly she could not walk. Frau Janssen ran into the street and told a man who looked like an officer what had happened. He responded, "The Germans were worse than this in Russia."

Klaus Küster, a member of the Hitler Youth, saw three Russians grab a woman on the street and take her into a hallway. He followed. One soldier trained his pistol on Klaus. The second held the screaming woman while the third raped her. Klaus watched the Russian who had done the raping emerge from the doorway. Tears were streaming down the soldier's face as he wailed, "Ya bolshoi svinya"—"I am a big pig."

In 1951 a committee of anti-Communist German scholars directed by Dr. Theodor Schieder of the University of Cologne set about to document the flight and expulsion of German nationals from Eastern and Central Europe in the wake of the Red Army victories of 1944–1945. Volume I of the compendium they produced concerned itself with the fate of German refugees east of the

Oder-Neisse Line, in what is now Poland. In the abridged selection of personal testimonies available in English there are close to thirty separate depositions from women regarding mass rape by Russian and Polish soldiers. The testaments have a certain sameness about them, a sameness not of fabrication but of the universality of a woman's experience in war.

E.L. was trapped in Posen (now Poznań) when the Russians entered the city. She attested:

> When we were lying in bed at night we kept hearing steps coming up the stairs; these were always Russians, who were sent by the Poles into the dwellings of the Germans. They beat on the door with their rifle-butts until it was opened. Without any consideration for my mother and aunt, who had to get out of bed, we were raped by the Russians, who always held a machine pistol in one hand. They lay in bed with their dirty boots on, until the next lot came. As there was no light, everything was done by pocket torches and we did not even know what the beasts looked like. During the day we had to work hard, and at night the Russians left us no peace. . . . One could hardly any longer call it raping, for the women were passive instruments, for one could not protect one's self or refuse, and one therefore suffered it.

"Where could one lodge a complaint?" echoed a schoolteacher from Breslau (now Wroclaw). "Everywhere one was chased away like a stray dog."

And so it went for German women at the close of the war. At Nuremberg the Soviet prosecutors had tried to show that the rape of Russian women had been part of a systematic Nazi campaign of terror and genocide. At the Tokyo tribunal the Allies had made a similar case against the Japanese. Jewish pleas for help from the Warsaw ghetto had used the mass rape of Jewish women to demonstrate *their* systematic annihilation. Arnold Toynbee, among World War I propagandists, had sought to use rape as evidence of the bestial campaign of terror by the Hun, and the lairds of the Scottish Highlands, we may recall, used evidence of rape by English soldiers as proof of their enemy's efforts to destroy *them* as a national people. And so it was not surprising that when the anti-Communist German professors compiled their documents, they, too, attempted to make nationalistic sense out of what they had found.

The raping of German women and children by Soviet officers and men was systematic in the truest sense of the word [they wrote]. Apart from the physical and spiritual suffering inflicted upon the huge numbers of women raped, the brutality and shamelessness with which this was done increased the fear and terror of the German population. It is clear that these rapings were the result of a manner of conduct and mentality which are inconceivable and repulsive to the European mind. One must partially attribute them to the traditions and notions in the Asiatic parts of Russia, according to which women are just as much the booty of the victors as jewelry, valuables, and property in dwellings and shops. The nature and the huge numbers of rapings would be inconceivable if there had not been a fundamental motive of such a kind at the back of the minds of the Soviet troops.

The German professors went further. Ilya Ehrenburg, they said, had incited the Russian troops to rape by his front-line dispatches and patriotic leaflets.

Ehrenburg's role as whipping boy for Russian rape crops up in such odd places that it is worth some study. The memoirs of Admiral Doenitz, published in English in 1959, quote a purported Ehrenburg leaflet as follows:

Kill! Kill! In the German race there is nothing but evil! . . . Follow the precepts of Comrade Stalin. Stamp out the fascist beast once and for all in its lair! Use force and break the racial pride of these Germanic women. Take them as your lawful booty . . . you gallant soldiers of the Red Army!

Karl Bednarik, the contemporary Viennese sociologist, takes the Ehrenburg leaflet at face value and writes, "The offer of the defeated enemy's women as a safety valve to the ravening troops here wears only the most transparent veil of ideology."

In fairness to Ehrenburg, I must admit that I could not find this particular exhortation to "break the racial pride of these Germanic women" and "take them as your lawful booty" among the hundreds of Ehrenburg war dispatches I examined. Neither could Cornelius Ryan, who quotes the Doenitz version in *his* book and remarks that many Germans he interviewed did claim to have seen it. Ryan pursued the matter to Moscow, where Soviet newspaper editors and historians, he found, were "defensive" about the entire matter of rape. Most Moscow historians he spoke with attributed the worst of the atrocities to vengeance-minded ex-prisoners of war who were released as the Russian troops advanced to the Oder. A newspaper editor told him, "We were naturally not one hundred percent gentlemen; we had seen too much."

Ryan discovered that Ehrenburg had once been publicly reprimanded for propaganda excesses by the military newspaper *Red Star*. That clinched it for Ryan, I think, and he came away believing that the leaflet was not a fake. I am not as certain, imbued as I am with the history of faked propaganda leaflets. Bearing in mind that Ehrenburg was Jewish, the wicked exhortation makes too much of a neat package for the defeated Nazis and smacks of the scurrilous *Protocols of the Elders of Zion.*

Bednarik's suggestion (he gives no source for *his* use of the leaflet) that Ehrenburg was consciously trading off women's bodies against a more fearful, wanton destruction by an avenging Red Army is an interesting extrapolation. He, too, like the German professors, needed to pin the blame on *someone*. Milovan Djilas, the renegade Yugoslav Communist turned fierce anti-Communist, also discusses Red Army rape in his overly emotional and not altogether trustworthy *Conversations with Stalin*. Djilas reports that according to complaints filed by the local populace, the Soviet Army committed 121 rapes and many rape-murders in his country—"figures that are hardly insignificant if it is borne in mind that the Red Army crossed only the northeastern corner of Yugoslavia." Djilas claims to have taken up the matter with Stalin himself.

"Djilas, Djilas!" he says the Russian dictator answered him. "Does Djilas, who is himself a writer, not know what human suffering and the human heart are? Can't he understand it if a soldier who has crossed thousands of kilometers through blood and fire and death has fun with a woman or takes some trifle?"

Not all Russian soldiers were rapists, and individual instances of kindness toward women are sprinkled throughout the German accounts of Red Army atrocity. But there is no point, it seems to me, in trying to pin the blame for the Soviet troops' behavior on an Ehrenburg leaflet, a Stalin attitude of "boys will be boys" or, laughably, on certain national characteristics. In war or peace men do not need orders or permission or a particular national heritage to commit an act of rape. Soviet rape was especially ironic because the Russians themselves had made so much of the New Soviet Man—

who in war turned out to be the old, familiar man. The misuse of ideology was not that the political commissars consciously traded off women's bodies against a worse destruction by their embittered men, but that whatever socialist ideology the Red Army men were exposed to in their indoctrination, sexual oppression of women was evidently not part of the course. The hard political truth is that the Red Army behaved no differently from any conquering army when it came to women's bodies or wristwatches in Germany and Eastern Europe in 1945.

A passage in Solzhenitsyn's *Gulag Archipelago* reveals that Russian writer's own ideological confusion. Stripped of his rank and thrown into a punishment cell for writing anti-Stalinist letters from the front he discovers that his three cellmates, "tankmen in soft black helmets; honest, openhearted soldiers," have been charged with breaking into a bathhouse and attempting to rape two German peasant women, whom Solzhenitsyn takes it upon himself to characterize as "raunchy broads." To Solzhenitsyn, the stern, uncompromising judge of Communist ethics, this rape rap is a vindicative, deliberate miscarriage of justice, for one of the women, he believes, "was the property of the army Chief of Counterintelligence, no less."

Never pausing to contemplate the problem or the meaning of rape in war, or a workable system of deterrence and punishment, Solzhenitsyn plainly considers the offense in question no offense at all, attributable to overenthusiastic drunkenness. This he must do because his only concern is to demonstrate the horrors of a cowardly police state, and so he tells us with casuistic logic,

> Yes! For three weeks the war had been going on inside Germany and all of us knew very well that if the girls were German they could be raped and then shot. This was almost a combat distinction. Had they been Polish girls or our own displaced Russian girls, they could have been chased naked around the garden and slapped on the behind—an amusement, no more. But just because this one was the "campaign wife" of the Chief of Counterintelligence, some deep-in-the-rear sergeant had viciously torn from three front-line officers the shoulder boards awarded them by the front-headquarters . . .*

---

* Solzhenitsyn is not the only Soviet dissident whose *politik* of anguish left him sublimely insensitive to the rights of women. When the physicist Valery

General George S. Patton, Jr., unintentionally gave us some insights into the nature of rape in his memoirs of World War II. During the North African campaign in Morocco in 1942, Patton conducted a delicate discussion with an aide to the Sultan in which he advised that "in spite of my most diligent efforts, there would unquestionably be some raping" by American soldiers under his command. Patton's promise that the American miscreants would be hanged brought the response that this would "bring great joy to all Moroccans." A year later, when Patton was on hand for the invasion of Sicily, the very same Moroccans were on the giving, instead of the receiving, end, and Italian women had become the victims. It was all something of a joke to Patton.

> One funny thing happened in connection with the Moroccan troops [he wrote in the same volume of memoirs]. A Sicilian came to me and said he had a complaint to make about the conduct of the Moroccans, or Goums, as they are called. He said he well knew that all Goums were thieves, also that they were murderers, and sometimes indulged in rape—these things he could understand and make allowances for, but when they came to his house, killed his rabbits, and then skinned them in the parlor, it was going too far.

A different view of rape in Italy was presented in the powerful De Sica movie *Two Women*. A mother (played by Sophia Loren) and her virgin daughter survive the war only to be gang-raped by celebrating Moroccan soldiers in a bombed-out church. The rape of the two women is the movie's ultimate ironic comment on the nature of war and survival. I once attended a lecture by the Hollywood screenwriter John Howard Lawson, one of the Hollywood Ten, who took violent exception to De Sica's casting of the soldier-

---

Chalidze came to this country, *New York Times* editor Harrison Salisbury tried to draw from him what he knew or thought about the movement for women's liberation. Bewildered by the question but eager to provide an informative answer, Chalidze went into a rambling discourse on "the right of women to participate in polygamous marriage contracts" and the "right" of women to be abducted into marriage, which he linked up with the glorious heritage of the Caucasus and Central Asia and the principle of ethnic self-determination: "For example, very often the ritual kidnapping of the bride was looked upon by Soviet authorities as forcible abduction. Soviet law, in this instance based on European law, violates national tradition and insults the national tradition of various people."

rapists as Africans. As I recall, Lawson felt that this amounted to overt racism, and that by right the movie rapists should have been Germans, since everybody knows that the Germans were the villains of the war. Lawson's commentary is a pristine example of the old left mentality as regards rape; when their side does it, it's exquisite proof of the bestiality of the enemy; when our side does it, it's bad politics to bring it up. De Sica stuck with the truth.

Lawson's suspicion of racism was utterly unfounded as far as the movie Two Women is concerned, but in the curious case of the Stuttgart subway incident, racism, or a strong propensity to believe the worst of the dark-skinned peoples, seems to have been an operating factor.

In June of 1945, during a filibuster against the Fair Employment Practices Act, the junior senator from Mississippi, James O. Eastland, announced that he was privy to information from the highest military sources that "a good many Negro soldiers" had committed rape during the invasion of Normandy and afterward, and had to have their weapons taken from them. Out of 33 rape cases on the Normandy peninsula that came to the military's attention, Eastland charged, 26 assaults were committed by blacks. As further proof that "all races have certain racial characteristics," Eastland informed his colleagues, "in the city of Stuttgart, when the French Army moved in, several thousand Christian German girls from good families were rounded up and placed in the subway, and for four or five days they were kept there and criminally assaulted by Senegalese soldiers from Africa. It was one of the most horrible occurrences of modern times. White soldiers would not have been guilty of such a thing."

The NAACP, other civil-rights organizations and the French consulate immediately filed a protest, and a week later Allied Supreme Headquarters issued a short formal reply. It had "no comment" on the Normandy charge, except for the rather disingenuous remark that there were "no Negro combat troops in the Normandy campaign. The only Negroes used there were service troops."* But as for Stuttgart, the Allied command had "no

---

* Segregated black troops may not have played a combat role in the Normandy invasion, but they provided most of the manpower for the major supply route that operated out of the Normandy beachhead, the famous Red Ball Express.

knowledge" of that event whatsoever; in fact, Stuttgart did not even have a subway.

It would be nice to leave the Stuttgart subway incident right there, as a jokey figment of the racist imagination of one of the South's leading anti-integrationists. But one month later, the German police chief of Stuttgart, one Karl Weber, issued his own report. Stuttgart did not have a subway, but it did have a central station for streetcars and trains and it did have a famous big tunnel for auto traffic, the Wagenburg. The soldiers who occupied Stuttgart that April had not been Senegalese, they had been Moroccan. According to the German report, local police had managed to verify 1,198 rape cases—"women whose ages ranged from 14 to 74." Most of the women in the verified cases "were attacked in their homes by turbaned Moroccans who broke down the doors in looting forays. Four women were killed and four others committed suicide after being raped. In one case, a husband killed his wife who had been attacked, and then committed suicide."

How much rape did American soldiers commit in World War II? Certainly they did not share the unenviable reputation of the Germans, the Russians or the Moroccans. American GI's viewed themselves, and were viewed by the local populace, as liberators in much of the European territory they fought for and occupied. In the time-honored tradition of the conquering hero, liberators are often presented with the bodies of women, from a female sense of "just reward" or adventure, but more realistically and more typically, out of urgent economic need. Writing of the desperate conditions that existed in Rome after the Italian capitulation, a pair of historians said succinctly, "Italian women would perform any service for a can of food."

"You should have seen the streams of women," an old woman from Palermo told the sociologist Danilo Dolci. "Business boomed when the Yanks—the whites and the blacks—were here. . . . The American troops set up their camps in the parks. Husbands brought their wives to them, and took the money. As soon as one man came out, another went in; they waited in line. *Ol rait. God foc. Uon dollar.* The park keepers provided the mattresses so that the Yanks would be comfortable."

Free enterprise, the murky line that divides wartime rape from wartime prostitution, cannot be cleanly delineated. When the SS policemen told the Jewish girl that they would "get her next time and pay her five zlotys," they were trying to turn an act of rape into an act of whoring in which the victim shared responsibility. Similarly, when the Japanese commander told his men in the field that to avoid any problems of rape, "either pay them money or kill them," he was utilizing the same principle. German and Japanese military brothels, into which conquered women were forcibly placed, were considered examples of Axis war crimes at the Nuremberg and Tokyo tribunals, but the American military never rounded up women for purposes of prostitution during World War II, as far as I know. The lure of the dollar to starving women in wartorn, liberated countries was coercion enough.

But the difference between prostitution and rape in war is real, for there are always those men who choose, or prefer, to rape.

"Rape has nothing to do with the availability of willing women or prostitutes," a member of the U.S. Army Court of Military Review told me in Washington. "Wherever there are soldiers, there are prostitutes in a war."

"Then what makes men rape in war?" I asked rhetorically.

"I don't know," he answered. My reluctant conversation partner was a retired colonel who preferred that I not use his name.

I had gone to Washington to see what figures might be available on the number of U.S. Army courts-martial for rape in World War II. Not that the lump sum of men brought to trial and conviction by the military would be an accurate reflection of the actual number of rapes committed by our armies—far from it—but a set of statistics would at least be a beginning, and might offer some sort of perspective, especially since I doubted that these statistics had ever before seen the light of day.

The office of the Judge Advocate General complied with my request to the best of its ability. It was able to give me the number of convictions stemming from general courts-martial for rape from January, 1942, to June, 1947, broken down by six-month periods.

These Army figures include Air Force convictions (information from the Navy and the Marine Corps was not available for World War II). They were culled from the ledgers of general courts-martial since rape is a capital offense under military jurisprudence. As in civilian law, cases of rape have a way of getting knocked down to lesser charges before trial. The military may try its rapists on lesser charges, such as assault with intent to commit rape, sodomy, assault with intent to commit sodomy, carnal knowl-

U.S. ARMY GENERAL COURTS-MARTIAL FOR RAPE, WORLD WAR II

Convictions

Jan.–June, 1942	1
July–Dec., 1942	10
Jan.–June, 1943	25
July–Dec., 1943	43
Jan.–June, 1944	52
July–Dec., 1944	82
Jan.–June, 1945	60
July–Dec., 1945	247
Jan.–June, 1946	355
July–Dec., 1946	50
Jan.–June, 1947	46
Total	971

edge (the equivalent of statutory rape, involving a minor), or under a utilitarian catchall known as lewd, lascivious and indecent acts. Sodomy, for example, carries a maximum sentence of ten years.

The Army Judiciary could give me no statistics on the number of convictions for these lesser charges, nor could it give me the number of reported rapes, arrests, and rape cases brought to trial, to compare with the number of convictions. If the records available for Vietnam (see pages 98–99) may be used as a gauge, the number of military convictions for rape is approximately 60 percent of the number of cases tried, slightly higher than the civilian conviction rate.

To the detriment of history, the Army Judiciary could shed no light on the median sentence given to those GI's convicted of rape, nor could it give me a theater-by-theater breakdown. It did have available the information that out of the 971 rape convictions, 52 soldiers were executed. An additional 18 men (not included among the 971) were executed after a combined conviction for rape and murder. (The military has executed no one for a capital offense since 1962.)

One obvious fact emerges from the record of the Army's World War II convictions for rape. More than two-thirds of the convictions took place not during the war itself but during the occupation. This, I was assured by the Clerk of the Court, was not the result of a backlog of courts-martial. "In the Second World War," he told me, "courts-martial were held right in the locus. A man was tried shortly after the offense; there was no delay. In those days the theater commander could take affirming action without a Washington review."

It was the Clerk of the Court's opinion that the geometric progression of convictions from 1942 into 1946 represented not only an increase in troop strength—by 1945 the United States had mobilized twelve million persons, overall, as compared to two million in 1941—but demonstrated a fact of war. In his words, "There is more rape during an occupation because soldiers have more time on their hands during an occupation."

This observation, coming from a retired Army colonel who has spent the last twenty years reviewing courts-martial, must carry a certain amount of weight. However, one can speculate that a preponderant number of courts-martial took place during the occupation because the military judges also had more time on their hands during the occupation. It seems logical to assume that during a time of heavy fighting a military tribunal would be reluctant to convene over a case of rape involving an enemy woman, if indeed the woman or a member of her family had been able to step forward, find the proper authority, and make the complaint. During the years of occupation, when some semblance of cooperation between the military and the local civilian authority would be established, a case of rape would stand a better chance of being processed to justice.

BANGLADESH

Indira Gandhi's Indian Army had successfully routed the West Pakistanis and had abruptly concluded the war in Bangladesh when small stories hinting at the mass rape of Bengali women began to appear in American newspapers. The first account I read, from the Los Angeles Times syndicated service, appeared in the New York Post a few days before Christmas, 1971. It reported that the Bangladesh government of Sheik Mujibur Rahman, in recognition of the particular suffering of Bengali women at the hands of Pakistani soldiers, had proclaimed all raped women "heroines" of the war for independence. Farther on in the story came this ominous sentence: "In traditional Bengali village society, where women lead cloistered lives, rape victims often are ostracized."

Two days after Christmas a more explicit story, by war correspondent Joseph Fried, appeared in the New York Daily News,
datelined Jessore. Fried described the reappearance of young Bengali women on the city streets after an absence of nine months.
Some had been packed off to live with relatives in the countryside
and others had gone into hiding. "The precautions," he wrote,
"proved wise, if not always effective."

> A stream of victims and eyewitnesses tell how truckloads of
> Pakistani soldiers and their hireling razakars swooped down on
> villages in the night, rounding up women by force. Some were
> raped on the spot. Others were carried off to military compounds.
> Some women were still there when Indian troops battled their way
> into Pakistani strongholds. Weeping survivors of villages razed
> because they were suspected of siding with the Mukti Bahini free-
> dom fighters told of how wives were raped before the eyes of their
> bound husbands, who were then put to death. Just how much of
> it was the work of Pakistani "regulars" is not clear. Pakistani officers
> maintain that their men were too disciplined "for that sort of
> thing."

Fearing I had missed the story in other papers, I put in a call
to a friend on the foreign desk of The New York Times. "Rape of
Bengali women?" He laughed. "I don't think so. It doesn't sound
like a Times story." A friend at Newsweek was similarly skeptical.
Both said they'd keep a lookout for whatever copy passed their
way. I got the distinct impression that both men, good journalists,
thought I was barking up an odd tree.*

In the middle of January the story gained sudden credence. An
Asian relief secretary for the World Council of Churches called a
press conference in Geneva to discuss his two-week mission to
Bangladesh. The Reverend Kentaro Buma reported that more than
200,000 Bengali women had been raped by Pakistani soldiers during the nine-month conflict, a figure that had been supplied to him
by Bangladesh authorities in Dacca. Thousands of the raped
women had become pregnant, he said. And by tradition, no Moslem husband would take back a wife who had been touched by

---

* NBC's Liz Trotta was one of the few American reporters to investigate the
Bangladesh rape story at this time. She filed a TV report for the weekend
news.

another man, even if she had been subdued by force. "The new authorities of Bangladesh are trying their best to break that tradition," Buma informed the newsmen. "They tell the husbands the women were victims and must be considered national heroines. Some men have taken their spouses back home, but these are very, very few."

A story that most reporters couldn't find in Bangladesh was carried by AP and UPI under a Geneva dateline. Boiled down to four paragraphs, it even made *The New York Times*.

Organized response from humanitarian and feminist groups was immediate in London, New York, Los Angeles, Stockholm and elsewhere. "It is unthinkable that innocent wives whose lives were virtually destroyed by war are now being totally destroyed by their own husbands," a group of eleven women wrote to *The New York Times* that January. "This . . . vividly demonstrates the blindness of men to injustices they practice against their own women even while struggling for liberation." Galvanized for the first time in history over the issue of rape in war, international aid for Bengali victims was coordinated by alert officials in the London office of the International Planned Parenthood Federation. The Bangladesh government, at first, was most cooperative. In the months to come, the extent of the aggravated plight of the women of Bangladesh during the war for independence would be slowly revealed.

Bengal was a state of 75 million people, officially East Pakistan, when the Bangladesh government declared its independence in March of 1971 with the support of India. Troops from West Pakistan were flown to the East to put down the rebellion. During the nine-month terror, terminated by the two-week armed intervention of India, a possible three million persons lost their lives, ten million fled across the border to India, and 200,000, 300,000 or possibly 400,000 women (three sets of statistics have been variously quoted) were raped. Eighty percent of the raped women were Moslems, reflecting the population of Bangladesh, but Hindu and Christian women were not exempt. As Moslems, most Bengali women were used to living in purdah, strict, veiled isolation that includes separate, secluded shelter arrangements apart from men, even in their own homes. The Pakistanis were also Moslem, but there the similarity stopped. Despite a shared religious heritage, Punjabi Pakistanis are taller, lighter-skinned and "rawboned" compared to dark, small-boned Bengalis. This racial difference would provide added anguish to those Bengali women who found them-selves pregnant after their physical ordeal.

Hit-and-run rape of large numbers of Bengali women was brutally simple in terms of logistics as the Pakistani regulars swept through and occupied the tiny, populous land, an area little larger than the state of New York. (Bangladesh is the most overcrowded country in the world.) The Mukti Bahini "freedom fighters" were hardly an effective counterforce. According to victims, Moslem Biharis who collaborated with the Pakistani Army—the hireling razakars—were most enthusiastic rapists. In the general breakdown of law and order, Mukti Bahini themselves committed rape, a situation reminiscent of World War II when Greek and Italian peasant women became victims of whatever soldiers happened to pass through their village.

Aubrey Menen, sent on a reporting assignment to Bangladesh, reconstructed the modus operandi of one hit-and-run rape. With more than a touch of romance the Indian Catholic novelist chose as his archetypal subject a seventeen-year-old Hindu bride of one month whom he called "the belle of the village." Since she was, after all, a ravished woman, Menen employed his artistic license to paint a sensual picture of her "classical buttocks": ". . . they were shaped, that is, as the great Sanskrit poet Kalidasa had pre-scribed, like two halves of a perfect melon."

Menen got his information from the victim's father. Pakistani soldiers had come to the little village by truck one day in October. Politely and thoroughly they searched the houses—"for pam-phlets," they said. Little talk was exchanged since the soldiers spoke a language no one in the village could understand. The bride of one month gave a soldier a drink of coconut juice, "in peace."

At ten o'clock that night the truckload of soldiers returned, waking the family by kicking down the door of their corrugated iron house. There were six soldiers in all, and the father said that none of them was drunk. I will let Menen tell it:

> Two went into the room that had been built for the bridal couple. The others stayed behind with the family, one of them covering them with his gun. They heard a barked order, and the bridegroom's voice protesting. Then there was silence until the bride screamed. Then there was silence again, except for some muffled cries that soon subsided.

In a few minutes one of the soldiers came out, his uniform in disarray. He grinned to his companions. Another soldier took his place in the extra room. And so on, until all the six had raped the belle of the village. Then all six left, hurriedly. The father found his daughter lying on the string cot unconscious and bleeding. Her husband was crouched on the floor, kneeling over his vomit.

After interviewing the father, Menen tracked down the young woman herself in a shelter for rape victims in Dacca. She was, he reported, "truly beautiful," but he found her mouth "strange." It was hard and tense. The young woman doubted that she would ever return to her tiny village. Her husband of one month had refused to see her and her father, she said, was "ashamed." The villagers, too, "did not want me." The conversation, Menen wrote, proceeded with embarrassing pauses, but it was not without high tension.

> I took my leave. I was at the door when she called me back.
> "Huzoor," a title of honour.
> "Yes?"
> "You will see that those men are punished," she said.
> "Punished. Punished. *Punished*."

Menen's report on the belle of the village was artfully drawn, but it did dramatize the plight of thousands of raped and rejected Bengali women. Other observers with a less romantic eye provided more realistic case studies. Rape in Bangladesh had hardly been restricted to beauty. Girls of eight and grandmothers of seventy-five had been sexually assaulted during the nine-month repression. Pakistani soldiers had not only violated Bengali women on the spot; they abducted tens of hundreds and held them by force in their military barracks for nightly use. The women were kept naked to prevent their escape. In some of the camps, pornographic movies were shown to the soldiers, "in an obvious attempt to work the men up," one Indian writer reported.

Khadiga, thirteen years old, was interviewed by a photojournalist in Dacca. She was walking to school with four other girls when they were kidnapped by a gang of Pakistani soldiers. All five were put in a military brothel in Mohammedpur and held captive for six months until the end of the war. Khadiga was regularly abused by two men a day; others, she said, had to service seven to ten men daily. (Some accounts have mentioned as many as eighty assaults in a single night, a bodily abuse that is beyond my ability to fully comprehend, even as I write these words.) At first, Khadiga said, the soldiers tied a gag around her mouth to keep her from screaming. As the months wore on and the captives' spirit was broken, the soldiers devised a simple quid pro quo. They withheld the daily ration of food until the girls had submitted to the full quota.

Kamala Begum, a wealthy widow, lived in a Dacca suburb. When the fighting started she sent her two daughters into the countryside to hide. She felt she could afford to stay behind, secure in her belief that she was "too old" to attract attention. She was assaulted by three men, two Pakistanis and one razakar, in her home.

Khadiga and Kamala Begum were interviewed by Bérengère d'Aragon, a woman photographer, in a Dacca abortion clinic.

Rape, abduction and forcible prostitution during the nine-month war proved to be only the first round of humiliation for the Bengali women. Prime Minister Mujibur Rahman's declaration that victims of rape were national heroines was the opening shot of an ill-starred campaign to reintegrate them into society—by smoothing the way for a return to their reluctant husbands or by finding bridegrooms for the unmarried ones from among his Mukti Bahini freedom fighters. Imaginative in concept for a country in which female chastity and purdah isolation are cardinal principles, the "marry them off" campaign never got off the ground. Few prospective bridegrooms stepped forward, and those who did made it plain that they expected the government, as father figure, to present them with handsome dowries.

"The demands of the men have ranged from the latest model of Japanese car, painted red, to the publication of unpublished poems," a government official bitterly complained. Another stumbling block, perhaps unexpected by the Bangladeshis, was the attitude of the raped women. "Many won't be able to tolerate the presence of a man for some time," the same official admitted.

But more pressing concerns than marriage had to be faced. Doctors sent to Bangladesh by International Planned Parenthood discovered that gynecological infection was rampant. "Almost every rape victim tested had a venereal disease," an Australian physician told *The New York Times*.

The most serious crisis was pregnancy. Accurate statistics on the number of raped women who found themselves with child were difficult to determine but 25,000 is the generally accepted figure. Less speculative was the attitude of the raped, pregnant women. Few cared to bear their babies. Those close to birth expressed little interest in the fate of the child. In addition to an understandable horror of rearing a child of forcible rape, it was freely acknowledged in Bangladesh that the bastard children with their fair Punjabi features would never be accepted into Bengali culture—and neither would their mothers.

Families with money were able to send their daughters to expert abortionists in Calcutta, but shame and self-loathing and lack of alternatives led to fearsome, irrational solutions in the rural villages. Dr. Geoffrey Davis of the London-based International Abortion Research and Training Center who worked for months in the remote countryside of Bangladesh reported that he had heard of "countless" incidents of suicide and infanticide during his travels. Rat poison and drowning were the available means. Davis also estimated that five thousand women had managed to abort themselves by various indigenous methods, with attendant medical complications.

A Catholic convent in Calcutta, Mother Theresa's, opened its doors in Dacca to women who were willing to offer their babies for overseas adoption, but despite the publicity accorded to Mother Theresa, few rape victims actually came to her shelter. Those who learned of the option chose to have an abortion. Planned Parenthood, in cooperation with the newly created Bangladesh Central Organization for Women's Rehabilitation, set up clinics in Dacca and seventeen outlying areas to cope with the unwanted pregnancies. In its first month of operation the Dacca clinic alone reported doing more than one hundred terminations.

The Bangladesh Central Organization for Women's Rehabilitation, created by Bengali women themselves, proved to be an heroic moving force. In a country with few women professionals, those who had the skills stepped forward to help their victimized sisters. One, a doctor, Helena Pasha, who admitted that prior to the war she had thoroughly disapproved of abortion, gave freely of her

time and services with little monetary compensation. Women social workers like Tahera Shafiq took over the organizational work
and gave aid and comfort that the traumatized rape victims could
not accept from men. Tahera Shafiq was adamant on one point.
Rape or forcible prostitution were false, inadequate words to describe what the Bengali women had gone through. She preferred in
conversation to use the word "torture."

Rehabilitation meant more than comfort, tenderness and
abortion. The women's organization sought to train the homeless,
rejected women in working skills. Handicrafts, shorthand and typing were the obvious choices—small steps until one remembers
that most of the women had never been outside their rural villages
before. The hoped-for long-range goal of "rehabilitation" still remained marriage. "An earning woman has better prospects of marriage than others," one social worker said dryly. But for many of
the tortured women, aid and succor arrived too late, or not at all.
"Alas, we have reports of some who have landed in brothels," a
male government official acknowledged. "It is a terrible tragedy."

As the full dimensions of the horror became known, those
who looked for rational, military explanations returned again and
again to the puzzle of why the mass rapes had taken place. "And a
campaign of terror includes rape?" Aubrey Menen prodded a Bengali politician. He got a reflective answer. "What do soldiers talk
about in barracks? Women and sex," the politician mused. "Put a
gun in their hands and tell them to go out and frighten the wits
out of a population and what will be the first thing that leaps to
their mind?" Fearing the magnitude of his own answer, the politician concluded, "Remember, some of our Bengali women are very
beautiful." Mulk Raj Anand, an Indian novelist, was convinced of
conspiracy. The rapes were so systematic and pervasive that they
had to be conscious Army policy, "planned by the West Pakistanis
in a deliberate effort to create a new race" or to dilute Bengali
nationalism, Anand passionately told reporters.

Theory and conjecture abounded, all of it based on the erroneous assumption that the massive rape of Bangladesh had been a
crime without precedent in modern history.

But the mass rape of Bangladesh had not been unique. The
number of rapes per capita during the nine-month occupation of
Bangladesh had been no greater than the incidence of rape during
one month of occupation in the city of Nanking in 1937, no greater

than the per capita incidence of rape in Belgium and France as the German Army marched unchecked during the first three months of World War I, no greater than the violation of women in every village in Soviet Russia in World War II. A "campaign of terror" and a charge of "conscious Army policy" had been offered up in explanation by seekers of rational answers in those wars as well, and later forgotten.

The story of Bangladesh was unique in one respect. For the first time in history the rape of women in war, and the complex aftermath of mass assault, received serious international attention. The desperate need of Sheik Mujibur Rahman's government for international sympathy and financial aid was part of the reason; a new feminist consciousness that encompassed rape as a political issue and a growing, practical acceptance of abortion as a solution to unwanted pregnancy were contributing factors of critical importance. And so an obscure war in an obscure corner of the globe, to Western eyes, provided the setting for an examination of the "unspeakable" crime. For once, the particular terror of unarmed women facing armed men had full hearing.

VIETNAM

Among the secret documents concerning American involvement in Vietnam that came to light with the publication of *The Pentagon Papers* was a report on a covert mission headed by U.S. Air Force Colonel Edward G. Lansdale in 1954–1955. Set into motion right after the fall of Dienbienphu while the French met with the Vietminh at Geneva, the broad purpose of the Lansdale mission was "to assist the Vietnamese in unconventional warfare" by undertaking paramilitary operations and by waging political-psychological warfare—"psywar" for short in Pentagon terminology.

"Psywar" consisted of carefully planted rumor campaigns designed to confound the forces of Ho Chi Minh and undermine Hanoi's relationship with the Chinese Communists. The first rumor campaign concerned rape. Mindful of Nationalist Chinese troop behavior in 1945 and seeking to play on Vietnamese fears of Chinese occupation under Vietminh rule, an American-trained

Vietnamese Psywar Company was instructed to dress in civilian clothes, infiltrate Hanoi and spread the rumor that a Chinese Communist regiment had raped the women of a North Vietnamese village. According to the Lansdale Team's report as printed in *The Pentagon Papers*, "The troops received their instructions silently, dressed in civilian clothes, went on their mission, and failed to return. They had deserted to the Vietminh."

The Vietnam war, not just America's twenty-year involvement but beginning with the original struggle for independence against the colonial French, has been a sociological crucible of rape in which certain groups of people have been observed to behave differently from other groups of people, and for this reason it sheds valuable light on the rape mentality. In one respect, of course, this war was no different from others—rarely, if ever, was rape considered newsworthy enough to find its way into the dispatches of a foreign correspondent.

In December, 1972, when the Paris "peace" talks had finally reached an intensive phase, I had several long interviews in New York with Peter Arnett, Associated Press correspondent in Vietnam for eight years. Like the rest of the Saigon press corps, this Pulitzer Prize winner had never filed a rape story from Vietnam, but like the rest of the press corps he had certainly been aware of its incidence. When he began to think about it, Arnett was able to delineate rape in Vietnam on many levels.

Before 1954 the foreign presence in Vietnam had been French, and it was Arnett's reading of history that the French paratroopers maintained a stricter discipline than their mercenary legionnaires who were permitted to rape and loot, or so he had heard from South Vietnamese for whom life "before the Americans" was already folklore.

It was Arnett's impression that the South Vietnamese Army, the ARVN, had participated in little raping at the beginning of the long war, but with the escalation of the conflict, concomitant with a growing brutalization, the incidence of ARVN rape increased. Disciplinary machinery within the South Vietnamese Army was always lax but other factors militated against ARVN rape. In the government-controlled areas, the larger cities, an illegal act was always punishable and therefore dangerous: a raped woman might turn out to be a wife or daughter of a well-connected family. "The

ARVN could not go through Saigon and rape, obviously," he told me, but the situation was different during military operations. "When the government-controlled areas came under pressure—remember the Tet offensive—anything could happen. There could be little redress by the population. Nongovernment-controlled areas, the free-fire zones, were always fair game."

South Vietnamese soldiers were allowed to keep their families with them at their base camps. Arnett believed that the presence of the wives and a general availability of sex (the brothel system has been a traditional part of Vietnamese society) gave ARVN soldiers less cause to rape. Another possibility is that the presence of wives and children on the campgrounds would exert a moral force against the rape of other women. Also, the ARVN's military operations were always in the neighboring vicinity and of short duration. Not only did the men understand that they were to soon return to their wives and/or brothels, there was also a strong probability that they might actually know, or even be related to, the girls in the villages they passed through. "A lot of casual rape was avoided because of family relations," Arnett had concluded.

That family relations served as a deterrent is a point to give one pause. The American Civil War, like Vietnam, in some respects a struggle of brother against brother, is considered a low-rape war by those few historians who have thought about it. Injunctions against assaulting one's sister or one's buddy's sister are part of the code of honor among men; furthermore, anonymity between rapist and victim is an important factor in rape since an unknown woman is more easily stripped of her humanity.

In contrast to the ARVN, the South Vietnamese Rangers—elite fighting troops who were transported from one part of Vietnam to another—were commonly credited with a higher incidence of rape by the foreign press. Set down in an unfamiliar area, the Rangers were without family ties and less likely to know or care about the feelings of the local women. As the elite corps of the South Vietnamese, I might add, they may also have been influenced by a swaggering, swashbuckling self-image.

Similarly, when the regular South Vietnamese forces were sent into Cambodia during the brief invasion of May, 1970 they freely looted and raped in every village they passed through—to such an extent that the Lon Nol government ("our" Cambodian government) officially protested. "It must be harder to rape your own nationality" was Arnett's sudden insight when he put his own facts together.

Regarding this Cambodian invasion, the pro-Communist Prince Sihanouk later remarked in black humor that President Thieu actually had been "very useful" to him: "Yes, indeed," he told Italian journalist Oriana Fallaci, "Sirik Matak used to say that the North Vietnamese and Vietcong behaved badly in Cambodia. But when he saw Thieu's soldiers—those wild beasts who murdered children, raped women, burned houses, destroyed temples, he had to admit: 'Sihanouk's Vietnamese were better.' In short, if Thieu had not sent his wild beasts, there wouldn't be so many Khmer Rouge; young Cambodians would not have flocked into the resistance groups in tens of thousands."

As the war dragged on, geographic and nationality considerations diminished. "After being in a war and seeing your buddies killed, your intent becomes evil," Arnett believes. "It was true for all troops—all they'd think about was eating, drinking and screwing." And so the South Vietnamese Army, which raped little at the beginning of the war, stepped up its activity. The "main molesting"—Arnett's phrase—was done at the special interrogation centers. "Under the pretext of finding out Vietcong information they would pick out an attractive young girl in a village and march her along in their column to take her to the interrogation center. Sometimes the unit might lead her into the forest, and then we, the reporters, would hear screams. She could be raped down the line at stages before she was finally released. When she was brought before the commander even then it might turn out that he knew her family and then she'd be let go."

Arnett was among those reporters who heard screams when interrogation units led a woman into the forest, and like the others, he never investigated further. "The South Vietnamese are a private people and it was always done quietly. They were much less likely to have a public gang-rape scene than the Americans," he offered by way of sociological explanation. He also used the typical reporter's stand-by that rape was "hard to verify," although he admitted that "at the end of the war all women who came out of Army jails would say they had been raped." *Time* magazine, in a wrap-up on Saigon's political prisoners that appeared in December,

1972, stated with caution, "Horror stories abound and most Saigonese accept them as true. One woman recently released from central police headquarters reported that her interrogators shoved a rubber stick up her vagina."

Torture of female political prisoners traditionally includes rape or variations of genital abuse. Whether sadistic torture leads by its own logic to the infliction of sexual pain, or whether the motive of eliciting political information is merely a pretext for the commission of hostile sexual acts, the end result for a woman is almost inevitable. As German soldiers in 1944 tortured and raped Maquis supporters, and as French paratroopers tortured and raped Algerian resistance leaders a decade later, so in the year 1972 beyond the horrors of the interrogation centers in South Vietnam one heard of electric shocks and rape applied to female political prisoners in Argentina and severe beating and electric shocks administered to the sexual organs of male and female prisoners in Brazil, including the doubly vengeful act, "a woman raped in front of her husband by one of his torturers." Six months later the pattern was repeated by the Portuguese in the colonies of Angola and Mozambique, and a year after that by the military government of Chile. Throughout much of the world the pretext of securing political information has led, in a woman's case, to rape.

With political objectivity Peter Arnett, a New Zealander, told me that it was common knowledge among the Saigon press corps that the Vietcong and the North Vietnamese Army rarely committed rape. "The VC used terror as a daily weapon," he said bluntly. "They would line up and behead the leaders of a village as a matter of course, but rape was not part of their system of punishment. They were prohibited from looting, stealing food or rape, and we were always surprised when they did it. We heard very little of VC rape."

The Vietcong prohibition against rape went further than moral suasion. American military intelligence routinely made available to reporters captured documents taken from dead Vietcong in the field. Among these documents Arnett had several times seen papers referring to Vietcong soldiers who were reprimanded, sent to the rear or even shot for rape. "The VC would publicize an execution for rape," he said. "Rape was a serious crime for them. It was considered a serious political blunder to rape and loot. It just wasn't done. At the same time they made women who were raped by the other side into heroines, examples of enemy atrocity."*

Arnett's analysis of why the Vietcong didn't rape went beyond their efficient system of reprimands. He was aware that Vietcong women played a major role in military operations and that the presence of women fighting as equals among their men acted against the sexual humiliation or mistreatment of other women, and he understood that a guerrilla force depends for its survival upon the good will of the people, men and women alike. He was also mindful of what he called the Vietcong's "sense of dedication" to their revolutionary mission. To elaborate on this point he employed an interesting comparison. "I knew American officers," he said, "who did not use the brothels during all the time they were in Vietnam. These men were so involved with their dedication to winning the war that they literally did not need sex, while it was a different story, of course, for the American enlisted men. I think the Vietcong could control their lust from a similar sense of dedication."

The AP correspondent and I differed strongly during our several interviews over whether "lust" or a powerful male need for sex had anything to do with the incidence of wartime rape, or, for that matter, the use of Army brothels, and I am at great pains to quote him fairly, although I disagree with this part of his analysis. Observers in Vietnam, and 99 and 9/10ths of them were men, were usually confounded by the lack of Vietcong rape (if they thought about it at all).† The experience of Kate Webb, United Press

---

* The concept that a revolutionary guerrilla army of peasants does not rape was laid down with simple eloquence in 1928 by the great Chinese general Chu Teh, whose motto was "Take not even a needle or thread from the people." Chu Teh's rules, a far cry from the practices of his enemy, the Kuomintang, included, "return all straw on which you sleep before leaving a house; speak courteously to the people and help them whenever possible; return all borrowed articles; pay for everything damaged; be honest in all business transactions; be sanitary—dig latrines a safe distance from homes and fill them up with earth before leaving; never molest women; do not mistreat prisoners."

† CBS correspondent Dan Rather, who was assigned to Vietnam in 1965–1966, told me that he, for one, remained unaware of any political distinctions in rape habits during his one-year tour. "Rape was not something that was foremost in my mind when I talked to people," Rather admitted. "My average story was shooting, shelling and bombing. The pattern was to jump on a helicopter, shoot a story very quickly and ship the film back to Saigon. I

International's bureau chief in Cambodia, bears this out. Webb, like Arnett a New Zealander, was captured and kept prisoner by the Vietcong for twenty-three days. Months after her release she said, "Everybody wants to know if I was raped. And when I tell them no, most people seem to be disappointed. They don't understand the Vietnamese code of very strict behavior."

An American, Dr. Marjorie Nelson, who worked in a medical rehabilitation center for Vietnamese civilians from 1967 to 1969 and was captured along with another American woman by Vietcong in Hué during the Tet offensive, also needed to protest her chastity after her release. She said, "This is a question that I know comes up in the minds of, well, certainly of any GI who's been in Vietnam, and many other people. Certainly this thing could have occurred, and I think on a couple of occasions we were simply lucky that it didn't. However, once we were in the camp it was quite clear that the cadre also were concerned about this, and they made sure that our privacy was respected."

And so we come to the Americans—where first we must look at institutionalized prostitution, for as the American presence in Vietnam multiplied, the unspoken military theory of women's bodies as not only a reward of war but as a necessary provision like soda pop and ice cream, to keep our boys healthy and happy, turned into routine practice. And if monetary access to women's bodies did not promote an ideology of rape in Vietnam, neither did it thwart it.

General George S. Patton, who had been so pragmatic about expectations of rape, is credited with the desire to experiment with military brothels during his World War II command, an idea he abandoned when he became convinced that the uproar they would create among wives and mothers back in the States might hurt the

---

never did a rape story, and if you had been doing my job I don't think you would have, either. Everywhere you looked there was a horror and a brutality. Rape may have been mentioned to me several dozen times while I was in Vietnam. When you see women crying, and you see that universal look of bitterness and anger, you find out about rape. My own limited experience led me to conclude that everybody who passed through a village did it—steal a chicken and grab a quick piece of ass, that sort of thing. Based on my own experience I would have to say that the Americans and the Korean troops were probably the worst—they had the least to lose—but I wouldn't build any case for the other side's superior morality. Vietnam was a loosely organized gang war, and the women caught it from all sides."

war effort. Patton did not have his way in World War II but his ghost must have approved of Vietnam.

The tradition of military brothels had been established in Vietnam long before the American presence. The late Bernard Fall, who wrote so vividly of the war in its early years, detailed with enthusiasm the French Army's particular contribution to the use of women in war—the mobile field brothel, or *Bordel Mobile de Campagne*, stocked with girls imported from Algeria. "The B.M.C.'s would travel with units in the combat zones," Fall wrote, "and in general, the French Army in Indochina kept them pretty much out of sight of American newsmen and officials. 'You can just imagine the howl if some blabbermouth comes out with a statement to the effect that American funds are used to maintain bordellos for the French Army,' said one colonel." A mobile field brothel, Fall reported, was inside the famous fortress of Dienbienphu when the French surrendered.

By the time the Americans had fully replaced the French in Indochina the war had sufficiently disrupted South Vietnamese society to a point where it was no longer necessary to import foreign women for the purpose of military prostitution. I do not mean to imply that prostitution was unknown in Vietnam before the long war. As Peter Arnett told me, "Prostitution was a time-honored tradition. Certain heads of families would not think twice before routinely selling their daughters if they needed the money." But as the long war progressed, prostitution increasingly became the only viable economic solution for thousands of South Vietnamese women. By 1966 the problem had reached such proportions that a Committee for the Defense of the Vietnamese Woman's Human Dignity and Rights was organized in Saigon by several hundred women educators, writers and social workers, according to an AP dispatch. The wire service reported that "bitter words" were expressed at the first meeting. "The miserable conditions of war have forced our people to sell everything—their wives, children, relatives and friends—for the American dollar," a woman educator was quoted. The Committee for the Defense of the Vietnamese Woman, overwhelmed by the reality of the Vietnam war, was never heard from again.

The American military got into the prostitution business by degrees, an escalation process linked to the escalation of the war. Underlying the escalation was the assumption that men at war required the sexual use of women's bodies. Reporter Arnett saw the gradual acceptance of U.S. military-controlled and -regulated brothels as a natural outgrowth of what he called "the McNamara theory": "In 1965 the main idea was to keep the troops contented and satisfied. Ice cream, movies, swimming pools, pizza, hot dogs, laundry service and hootch maids. The hootch maids were brought in as maids, not as prostitutes. Sex with a hootch maid was a private arrangement, a relationship of convenience. A lot of hootch maids did become prostitutes, however, but in the early days if they were discovered at it, they were fired."

The hootch maids were the first step toward accommodation; bar girls and massage parlors soon followed. According to Arnett, the rear-area troops caused the most "problems": "There was a lot of discontent and boredom. The men were aware that they were soldiers who weren't fighting, who weren't getting any medals. They might drive into town to the illegal brothels, but for reasons of VD and security the brothels were off limits." (Massage parlors, that vague gray area of sexual action from Saigon to New York City, were always considered legal.)

In 1965 the Marine Corps base at Danang began experimenting with organized battalion trips to town on a once-a-month basis, but according to Arnett it was a disaster: "The men would hit town like animals, they couldn't cope, it was pure chaos." After this early experience the Marine command decided to confine their men to the base camp, but the inviolate law of supply and demand went into operation. A shantytown of brothels, massage parlors and dope dealers, known as Dogpatch, soon ringed the base. "The marines would bust through the wire at night—the Marine command could live with that," the reporter told me.

It was Arnett's opinion (not shared by me) that the U.S. Army was "more enlightened" than the Marine Corps when it came to sexual accommodation. By 1966 the 1st Cavalry Division at An Khe, in the Central Highlands, the 1st Infantry Division at Lai Khe, twenty-five miles north of Saigon, and the 4th Infantry Division at Pleiku had established official military brothels within the perimeter of their base camps.

The Lai Khe "recreation area" belonging to the base camp of the 3rd Brigade, 1st Infantry Division was a one-acre compound surrounded by barbed wire with American MP's standing guard at the gate. It was opened only during daylight hours for security reasons. Inside the compound there were shops that sold hot dogs, hamburgers and souvenirs, but the main attraction was two concrete barracks, each about one hundred feet long—the military whorehouses that serviced the four-thousand-man brigade. Each building was outfitted with two bars, a bandstand, and sixty curtained cubicles in which the Vietnamese women lived and worked.

An individual cubicle contained little more than a table with a thin mattress on it and a peg on one wall for the girl's change of clothing. On the opposite wall a *Playboy* nude centerfold provided decoration and stimulation for the visiting soldier. The women who lived in the Lai Khe recreation-center cubicles were garishly made up with elaborate, sprayed bouffant hairdos and many had enlarged their breasts with silicone injections as a concession to Western fetish. The sexual service, as Arnett described it, was "quick, straight and routine," and the women were paid five hundred piasters (the equivalent of two dollars in American money) for each turn by their GI clients. Americans always paid in piasters. For each trick she turned, a girl would get to keep two hundred piasters (seventy-five cents), the rest going to various levels of payoffs. By turning eight to ten tricks a day a typical prostitute in the Lai Khe compound earned more per month than her GI clients, Arnett advised me—a curious sidelight to a not-so-free enterprise system.

Refugees who had lost their homes and families during the war and veterans of the earlier Saigon bar trade formed the stock of the brothel. They were recruited by the province chief, who took his payoff, and were channeled into town by the mayor of Lai Khe, who also got his cut. The American military, which kept its hands partially clean by leaving the procurement and price arrangement to Vietnamese civilians, controlled and regulated the health and security features of the trade. "The girls were checked and swabbed every week for VD by Army medics," my informed source told me approvingly.

Military brothels on Army base camps ("Sin Cities," "Disneylands" or "boom-boom parlors") were built by decision of a division commander, a two-star general, and were under the direct operational control of a brigade commander with the rank of colonel. Clearly, Army brothels in Vietnam existed by the grace of Army Chief of Staff William C. Westmoreland, the United States Embassy in Saigon, and the Pentagon.

Venereal disease, mostly gonorrhea, was a major preoccupation of the military in Vietnam. One official brothel outside Saigon had a sign on the wall of the bar that read "GIRLS WITH TAGS ARE CLEAN." Lest the declaration failed to make its point, a sign on the opposite wall spelled out "GIRLS WITHOUT TAGS ARE DISEASED." It was mandatory for all units to report their incidence of VD to the higher-ups, since it reflected on military discipline as well as on the health of the soldiery, and a high VD count was charged against the merit rating of a battalion. "Most units lied about their VD count," Arnett believed. It was also his understanding that the reported VD rate "was high from the beginning" in relation to other wars and to a normal civilian population. (In 1969 GI's contracted venereal disease in Vietnam at a reported rate of 200 cases per 1,000 persons; the United States rate at the time was 32 per 1,000.) Company commanders often went to ingenious lengths to lower their counts. One commander, Arnett told me, boasted that there was no VD at all in his company. His method of protecting his men was highly enterprising: "He didn't allow them to use the official brothel, he didn't trust it. It turned out he kept six girls sequestered on his part of the base and had them shot full of penicillin every day."

I am sorry that it is not within the scope of this book to explore the lives of Vietnamese women who became "Occupation: prostitute" as a direct result of the foreign military presence in their country. It is a story that should be told in detail, from the tremendous source of revenue that prostitution provided their beleaguered country, to accounts of Saigon brothels filled with ten-year-old girls, to the incidence of work-related deaths from tuberculosis and venereal disease, and with a special nod of recognition to those who survived. I have dwelt on official U.S. military prostitution, and the concomitant concern for control of venereal disease, because it is necessary to understand the military mind before proceeding to an examination of GI rape.

Except for the Marine Corps, which attempted to enforce a relatively strict moral code, the use of women's bodies on the base camps was seen as a way to "keep the boys happy." Officers were not expected to engage in whoring; the institution was made available for the foot soldier, or "grunt," the fellow with the least to gain from being in Vietnam, the one who needed to be mollified and pacified—perhaps because he was fighting a war he did not understand and because he daily faced the possibility that he might be killed. As Arnett cautioned me to remember, "These guys were always thinking, 'I'm gonna get screwed tonight—this may be my last.'"

It was this mollification aspect, and not a belief that soldiers *required* the use of a woman's body out of some intrinsic male urge, that motivated the U.S. Army to get into the prostitution business. A regular tour of duty in Vietnam consisted of a one-year stretch, not an unconscionably long period of time to be without a woman, and relief from sexual tension could be, and I presume routinely was, accomplished by masturbation. As one GI prisoner of war remarked upon his repatriation in February, 1973, "This stuff about not being able to live without sex is nonsense. What I dreamed about was food and medicine." And while the military's emphasis on avoidance of venereal disease is certainly commendable, for all the anti-VD training films and for all the concern about merit ratings, there was no comparable cautionary training against committing rape.

At peak strength the United States had slightly under 550,000 men in South Vietnam, twelve divisions of infantry and marines. Nine men were required to back up and service one man in the field, so there were never more than sixty or seventy thousand men available for combat at any given time and only one-fifth of these men were operating in highly populated areas. From what we already know about the rape of women in war, we can say that no more than fourteen thousand GI's in Vietnam at any given time had the two prerequisites: access and opportunity. It stands to reason that there would be fewer incidents of rape, overall, in the highlands because there were fewer Vietnamese people in this forbidding terrain. In contrast, the two divisions that worked in the heart of the population—the 9th Division in the Mekong Delta and the Americal Division (to which Lieutenant William Calley belonged), which operated along the central coast—had particularly bad reputations for atrocity.

Despite the intense propaganda throughout the long war, our American soldiers did not believe that they were "liberating" anyone, nor were they perceived as liberators. Men in the field were perpetually in a tenuous, frustrating semicombat situation. As

Arnett described it, "There were no fixed targets, no objectives, no highways to take—it was patrol and repatrol, search and destroy. Anything outside the perimeter of the base camp or the nearest government-controlled village was enemy territory, and all civilians were treated as enemy. It was so easy to rape on a squad level. Soldiers would enter a village without an interpreter. Nobody spoke Vietnamese. It was an anonymous situation. Any American could grab any woman as a suspect and there was little or no recourse to the law by the people."

Raping and looting go hand in hand in warfare but there was little to loot in the villages of South Vietnam. Arnett believed that the juxtaposition of fragile, small-boned Vietnamese women against tall, strong American men created an exaggerated masculine-feminine dynamic that lent itself readily to rape (a similar situation had occurred in Bangladesh). He thought that the Americans participated more in gang rape than in individual assault, the style of the South Vietnamese Army, "because the Americans were trained in the buddy system, for security. They were warned against the dangers of individual fraternizing on operations." The likelihood of sexual assault diminished, he believed, "if the company commander was present—a career officer, a captain or a lieutenant. The noncoms and soldiers had less at stake." His final observation, shared by his Vietnamese wife, his wife's family and others he knew, was that whatever the incidence of atrocity from 1965 on, "the Americans' personal conduct was far better historically than the French, their mercenaries, or the Japanese."

U.S. Army court-martial statistics for rape and related charges in Vietnam from January 1, 1965, to January 31, 1973, are as follows:

RAPE
    tried   38
    convicted   24

RAPE AND ASSAULT (Combined Charge)
    tried   5
    convicted   3

ASSAULT WITH INTENT TO COMMIT RAPE
    tried   8
    convicted   4

ATTEMPTED RAPE
    tried   18
    convicted   10

SODOMY
    tried   11
    convicted   5

ATTEMPTED SODOMY
    tried   5
    convicted   3

CARNAL KNOWLEDGE (Statutory Rape)
    tried   1
    convicted   1

Total tried: 86. Total convicted: 50. Conviction rate: 58 percent.

To avoid redundancy and overkill I have spared my readers a stopover in Korea during this long march through the history of rape in war. However, partial figures for Army court-martial convictions from May 31, 1951, to May 30, 1953, are available. Rape: 23; assault with intent to commit rape: 9. Thus, in a two-year period in Korea there were more convictions in these two categories than there were during eight years of U.S. involvement in Vietnam. It also should be kept in mind that the United States had a peak troop strength in Korea of 394,000 men while the peak troop strength in Vietnam reached 543,400. It is possible to conclude from this limited comparison that the rape rate was higher per soldier in Korea (unlikely) or that investigatory and court-martial procedures for rape-related charges were more lax in Vietnam.

Court-martial statistics for other branches of the service in Vietnam were more difficult to obtain. In my many inquiries to the different branches of the military I found the Army Judiciary to be the most open and most cooperative of all, and this despite the Army's recognition that in a sense there was little to gain from cooperation. As a retired colonel in the Judge Advocate General's office told me, "Whatever we give you, some people will say the Army is a bunch of criminals and the rest will say we run kangaroo courts."

Air Force court-martial statistics for rape and related charges in Vietnam, Thailand and the Philippines from 1965 to 1973 were:

RAPE

tried	2
convicted	1 rape; 1 lesser offense

ARTICLE 134 ("lewd, lascivious and indecent acts")*

tried	12
convicted	8

The Air Force also released to me their world-wide figures for this time span, including offenses traceable to base camps in the continental United States:

Convictions for Rape	58
Additional convictions, men charged with rape but convicted of a lesser offense	11
Convictions under Art. 134	554

Because of a conversion to computerized information retrieval, I was told, court-martial statistics for the Navy and the Marine

---

* Article 134 of the Uniform Code of Military Justice is a general catchall charge that includes the following specifications: indecent assault; assault with intent to commit sodomy; assault with intent to commit rape; indecent acts with a child under sixteen; indecent exposure; indecent, obscene language; and indecent, lewd acts, in addition to many nonsexual specifications including nonpayment of debts; tampering with the mail; drunk and disorderly; driving infractions; and straggling. Article 120 of the UCMJ is the rape and carnal knowledge statute. Article 125 defines sodomy and Article 128 defines assault. On the books, a conviction for rape under Article 120 could bring a death sentence (the military has executed no one under court-martial law since 1962) or any number of years at hard labor. Carnal knowledge carries a maximum sentence of fifteen years. A conviction for forcible sodomy under Article 125 carries a maximum of ten years; if committed on a person under sixteen the maximum is twenty years. The heaviest specification under Article 134 is assault with intent to commit rape, carrying a maximum of twenty years. Indecent assault under Article 134 (which would include all "attempts") carries a maximum of five years. The growing popularity of Article 134 as the vehicle for trying sex offenses deserves comment; clearly it is preferred because it carries lesser maximum penalties. Under pressure from watchdog liberals inside and outside the Armed Forces, since the days of World War II the military has grown cautious about its court-martial procedures for all offenses, not just those of a sexual nature. In 1954, for example, 8.2 percent of all servicemen faced a court-martial proceeding; in 1971 the percentage had dropped to 3.5.

Corps in Vietnam were available only for the period from 1970 to 1973 and were limited to convictions for rape, carnal knowledge and "lesser offenses." The Navy man explained the paucity of figures from his branch with the astute comment, "Remember, we didn't live there."

VIETNAM COURT-MARTIAL CONVICTIONS, 1970–1973

	Navy	Marine Corps
1970	Carnal Knowledge: 1	Rape: 1
1971	0	Rape: 2; lesser offense: 2
1972	Rape: 0; lesser offense: 1	Rape: 8; lesser offense: 2
1973	Rape: 1; lesser offense: 1	Rape: 2

What meaning can be read into all of these figures? As an indicator of the actual number of rapes committed by the American military in Vietnam they are practically worthless. If in the United States a mere one in five rapes is reported, what percentage might have been reported in Vietnam, where a victim who survived the assault knew no English, had little or no recourse to the law, and was considered an enemy, a gook, a slope, a slant, or a "female Oriental" in the legal language of the courts-martial briefs?

A Clerk of the Court in the U.S. Army Judiciary could provide me with no raw arrest figures to compare with actual courts-martial, nor could he give me an official breakdown on the length of sentence imposed. My cursory examination of a handful of convictions led me to believe that a sentence of two to eight years at hard labor might be typical for rape, even in cases in which the victim had been murdered; that sodomy, attempted rape and attempted sodomy were preferred as charges because they carried lesser penalties; and that sentences were routinely cut in half by a board of review.

New Yorker writer Daniel Lang detailed one specific incident of GI gang rape in Vietnam. In November, 1966, a squad of five men on reconnaissance patrol approached the tiny hamlet of Cat Tuong, in the Central Highlands. Their five-day mission was to have been a general search for VC in the area, but when they entered the village they searched instead for a young girl to take along with them for five days of "boom boom." It was understood by the men that at the end of the patrol they would have to kill her

and hide her body. Lang used pseudonyms for the five soldiers and
the real name of the victim, Phan Thi Mao, a name that the
soldiers never learned until their court-martial proceedings.

Mao was picked out by the men because for some reason a
gold tooth in her mouth amused them. She was perhaps twenty
years old. As the soldiers knew precisely the intent of their action,
so, too, did the women of the village, who cowered, wept and clung
to one another as Mao's hands were bound efficiently behind her
back before she was marched down the road. In one of the most
pathetic incidents of the entire affair, Mao's mother ran after the
soldiers with her daughter's scarf, the only act of protection she
could think of. One of the men took it and tied it around their
captive's mouth.

Of the five men in the patrol only one, Private First Class
Sven Eriksson, did not participate in Mao's rape and murder. As
Lang described the ordeal, individual acts of superfluous cruelty
practiced on Mao appeared to be a competition for a masculinity
pecking order. Eriksson, for refusing to take his turn in Mao's gang
rape, was derided by the patrol leader, Sergeant Tony Meserve, as a
queer and a chicken. One of the followers, Manuel Diaz, later
haltingly told the military prosecutor that fear of ridicule had made
him decide to go along with the rest: "Okay, let's say you are on a
patrol. These guys right here are going to start laughing you out.
Pretty soon you're going to be an outcast from the platoon."

After her murder, Phan Thi Mao was reported as "one VC,
killed in action." Eriksson's resolve that the crime would not go
unpunished met with a curious wall of resistance from his superiors
back in the base camp, and the men in his platoon who heard the
story began to view him as a whistle-blowing troublemaker. He
became half convinced that he narrowly escaped a fragging.
"Whatever I could do depended on finding someone with both the
rank and the conscience to help me," he told Daniel Lang. "Otherwise I'd stay boxed in by the chain of command."

Summarily transferred to another camp one day after the
alleged fragging, Eriksson finally managed to tell his story to a
sympathetic Mormon chaplain who alerted the Criminal Investigation Division. Mao's decomposing body was found on the hill
where Eriksson said it would be and her sister was located and was
carefully interrogated. A separate court-martial was held for each of
the four men in the winter of the following year. In each of the

trials Eriksson's manhood was brought into question by the defense. "It was just that he was less than average as far as being one of the guys," a sergeant in his old platoon testified, while Sergeant Tony Meserve was depicted by his superior officer as "one of the best combat soldiers I have known." With one exception the defendants went through their courts-martial convinced they were guilty of no wrongdoing. The man who drew the heaviest penalty, life imprisonment, had his sentence cut on review to eight years.

Rape played a role during the most infamous atrocity of the Vietnam war, the My Lai massacre of March 16, 1968. Thanks to Seymour M. Hersh, who broke the story of the Army investigation of My Lai and the subsequent court-martial of Lieutenant William L. Calley, and who later wrote a meticulous account of My Lai's destruction, we are able to glimpse the casual, continuing war against women contained within a larger assault.

According to Hersh and others, including New York Times reporter Joseph Lelyveld, members of Charlie Company, Captain Ernest Medina's unit within the Americal Division, had begun abusing women near their base camp in Quang Ngai Province a month before the destruction of My Lai. Although these rapes were common knowledge in the unit, there were no official reprimands. One gang rape and murder of a peasant woman, set upon while she labored in a field with her baby at her side, had even been photographed step by step by one of the participants with his Instamatic camera.

Charlie Company was a "grunt" unit. "As always," Hersh wrote, "the men assigned to infantry units were those who upon entering service performed poorly on the various Army qualification and aptitude examinations." Most of the men in C Company had volunteered for the draft; most were between the ages of eighteen and twenty-two; nearly half were black.

The systematic shooting of old men, women and children at My Lai began at breakfast time. By 10:30 A.M. most of the wanton destruction of unarmed human beings (accounts vary between 109 and 567 lives; the Army's Criminal Investigation Division settled on 347) had already been accomplished and the soldiers were cooling themselves out—loafing, smoking, methodically setting fire to whatever huts and houses remained standing, and shooting stragglers and wounded survivors with short bursts of fire. It was at this time that enlisted men Jay Roberts and Ron Haeberle, a reporter-photographer team assigned by the Department of Defense to officially record the My Lai "operation," witnessed their first attempted rape of the day. Hersh transcribed their impressions: "A few men now singled out a slender Vietnamese girl of about fifteen. They tore her from the group and started to pull at her blouse. They attempted to fondle her breasts. The women and children were screaming and crying. One G.I. yelled, 'Let's see what she's made of.' Another said, 'V.C. Boom Boom,' meaning she was a Viet Cong whore. . . . An old lady began fighting with fanatical fury, trying to protect the girl. Roberts said, 'She was fighting off two or three guys at once. She was fantastic. Usually they're pretty passive. . . . They hadn't even gotten that chick's blouse off when Haeberle came along.' One of the G.I.s finally smacked the old woman with his rifle butt; another booted her in the rear."

Aware of the presence of an Army photographer, a GI abruptly resolved the incident by shooting both women. Haeberle's photograph, a shot taken seconds before the double murder, was published in Life magazine twenty-one months later when the story of My Lai was made public. Back in Vietnam, Senator Tran Van Don, a leader of the "loyal opposition" to the Thieu-Ky government, was conducting his own investigation into the My Lai affair. He routinely showed the Life photograph to Do Tan Nhon, a hamlet chief who had survived the massacre. Nhon identified the two women in the picture as his wife and daughter.

Senator Don's investigation turned up further accounts of rape, attempted rape and rape-murder during the assault on My Lai. A rice farmer named Le Tong saw a woman raped after the GI's had killed her children. A peasant named Khoa witnessed the rape and murder of a thirteen-year-old girl. The same attackers then turned on Khoa's wife, but before they could rape her, Khoa's small son, riddled with bullets, fell on his mother's body, covering her with blood. The soldiers lost interest in the woman and moved away.

Seymour Hersh questioned each of his soldier-informants about rape at My Lai. He concluded, "Most of the company knew there were rapes that day in March, but remained reluctant to talk about them." A philosophic explanation from John Smail, a squad leader in the 3rd Platoon, struck Hersh as quotable. "That's an everyday affair," Smail said. "You can nail just about everybody on that—at least once. The guys are human, man."

Informant John Paul told Hersh that later in the evening some of the GI's brought two women from one of the My Lai hamlets down to the beach, but Paul wasn't certain what happened to them. Gregory Olsen and Roy Wood recalled a vivid incident during the following morning's mopping-up operation. Three Vietnamese men and a woman were sighted running from a burning hut in one of the hamlets and members of the 2nd Platoon gave chase. The men got away but the woman was caught. Olsen saw the woman stripped naked and flung over a GI's shoulder. "He said he was going to put it to her, but she was too dirty," Olsen reported. Roy Wood had a more specific recollection. The whole 2nd Platoon "caught her ass," he remembered. "They all raped her . . . tore her up." Bleeding badly, the woman later managed to make an escape. Most of Charlie Company eventually learned of the 2nd Platoon's group rape and the grapevine had it that the woman was a North Vietnamese Army nurse. "She sure must have been tough," Wood mused with some wonderment. "She took on all of them."

Helicopter door gunner Ronald L. Ridenhour was the conscience-striken GI whose persistent letters to Washington did much to keep alive the My Lai investigation. Ridenhour's first view was from the air a few days after Charlie Company's assault. The hamlet was deserted. Flying over a rice paddy, Ridenhour and his pilot sighted a body on the field below. The pilot propelled their craft downward for a closer look. "It was a woman," Ridenhour later said with emotion. "She was spread-eagled, as if on display. She had an 11th Brigade patch between her legs—as if it were some type of display, some badge of honor."

At least three members of Charlie Company were formally charged with rape in connection with the My Lai massacre. Although the Army eventually confirmed in its official findings that systematic rapes had indeed taken place, the charges against the accused men were quietly dropped.

Three months after My Lai, another gang rape by members of the 11th Infantry Brigade, Americal Division, occurred near division headquarters at Chu Lai. Adjudged "a serious incident" by the military, this case involved two officers and at least four enlisted men. According to undisputed testimony presented at the various court-martial proceedings—the men, as usual, were tried separately—members of the 1st Platoon of Company B captured some male and two female "Oriental human beings" during the afternoon of June 2, 1968, while on operations in the Dragon Valley. The two females, teen-age girls, were suspected of being Vietcong or NVA nurses The younger one, Yen, was fourteen years old.

Captain Leonard Goldman, commanding officer of Company B, heard from battalion headquarters via radio that no helicopters were available to transport his prisoners to an interrogation unit, so he ordered a sergeant to secure the prisoners for the night. "The events which transpired during the night are not in dispute," reads the stilted language of Goldman's several appeals:

> . . . suffice it to say that the two female detainees were subject to multiple rapes, sodomy, and other mistreatments at the hands of various members of the First Platoon of Company B. On the morning of 3 June 1968, these detainees, including the two females, were escorted to the landing zone where one female nurse [Yen] was murdered by a member of the appellant's unit. Lieutenant D, who had been Acting Company Commander while the appellant was on R & R [rest and recuperation], had ordered a V.C. male detainee to shoot the nurse and provided him with a loaded M-16 rifle to accomplish that purpose. The V.C. shot the nurse in the neck and Lieutenant D thereafter fired two more shots into the nurse's head. The appellant was not present when the killing occurred, and when he was informed of the incident he was advised that "some gink grabbed a rifle and shot one of the nurses."

Yen's body was found on an inspection visit two days later. The older nurse, who had been locked in a shed for three days, was freed. At Goldman's trial there was testimony that he had told his sergeant, "If she's taken back to the MI interrogation and she tells what happened in the field we'll all swing for it."

But nobody swung for it. Captain Goldman, charged with failing to report Yen's rape and murder, was fined $1,200 for "failing to enforce adequate safeguards to protect female Orientals" and was allowed to resign from the Army. Lieutenant William H. DeWitt, referred to as "Lieutenant D" in the briefs, was declared mentally incompetent to stand trial, was released from service and shipped back to the States. Enlisted men Marlyn

D. Guthmiller and William C. Ficke, Jr., one charged with rape, the other with sodomy, each received a year at hard labor, knocked down on review to six months. A fifth man was acquitted, and a sixth, who served as primary witness against the accused, was granted immunity.

A court-martial, a conviction and a knocked-down sentence was not the way it usually went. Rape was, in the words of one Vietnam veteran, "pretty SOP"—standard operating procedure, and it was a rare GI who possessed the individual courage or morality to go against his buddies and report, let alone stop, the offense.

"They only do it when there are a lot of guys around," veteran George Phillips told writer Lucy Komisar. "You know, it makes them feel good. They show each other what they can do—'I can do it,' you know. They won't do it by themselves."

"Did you rape too?"

"Nope."

"Why not?"

"I don't know, I just got a thing. I don't— Of course it got around the company, you know, well, hah, 'the medic didn't do it.'"

"Did anybody report these incidents?"

"No. No one did. You don't dare. Next time you're out in the field you won't come back—you'll come back in a body bag. What the hell, she's only a dink, a gook, this is what they think."

"Me and one of the buck sergeants and two other guys took these four chicks in the elephant grass," a Vietnam deserter who uses the name "Jerry Samuels" told writer Roger Williams in Toronto. "We balled these chicks. They were forcibly willing— they'd rather do that than get shot. Then one of the girls yelled some derogatory thing at the guy who'd balled her. . . . He just reached down for his weapon and blew her away. Well, right away the three other guys, including myself, picked up our weapons and blew away the other three chicks. Just like that. . . . Me and this other guy, we got high together in the bunker a lot, and we talked a lot about why we did it. The thing we couldn't understand was that when this other guy shot the first chick, we picked up our weapons without giving it a second thought and fired up the rest."

In February, 1971, more than one hundred veterans convened in Detroit to give testimony in a public forum concerning atrocities they had witnessed and committed during their period of service in Vietnam. They were now Vietnam Veterans Against the War and they named their convocation "The Winter Soldier Investigation: An Inquiry into American War Crimes." Using the vernacular of young men whose wartime aggressor experience had left them cynical, guilt-ridden and wised-up fast, they spoke to one another and to their audience with a mixture of anguish and toughness. From vet to vet, the stories they told were amazingly similar: cans of C rations thrown from trucks and deliberately aimed at the heads of Vietnamese beggar children who lined the road; "Mad Minutes"—indiscriminate firing along the perimeter of the base camp; "the Bell Telephone Hour"—wiring the genital areas of male and female prisoners to field phones during interrogation procedures; the burning of villages; the destruction of crops; and always, the special systematic abuse of women.

Sergeant Scott Camil, a forward observer with the 1st Battalion, 11th Marine Regiment, 1st Marine Division from March, 1966, to November, 1967, and later a leader of the VVAW, had this exchange with a panel moderator:

> CAMIL: When we went through the villages and searched people the women would have all their clothes taken off and the men would use their penises to probe them to make sure they didn't have anything hidden anywhere. And this was raping but it was done as searching.
>
> MODERATOR: As searching. Were there any officers present there?
>
> CAMIL: Yes there were.
>
> MODERATOR: Was this done on a company level?
>
> CAMIL: Company level.
>
> MODERATOR: The company commander was around when this happened?
>
> CAMIL: Right.
>
> MODERATOR: Did he approve of it or did he look the other way or—
>
> CAMIL: He never said not to or never said anything about it. The main thing was that if an operation was covered by the press there were certain things we weren't supposed to do, but if there was no press there, it was okay. I saw one case where a woman was shot by a sniper, one of our snipers. When we got up to her she was asking for water. And the lieutenant said to kill her. So he

ripped off her clothes, they stabbed her in both breasts, they spread her eagle and shoved an E tool up her vagina, an entrenching tool, and she was still asking for water. And then they took that out and they used a tree limb and then she was shot.

MODERATOR: Did the men in your outfit, or when you witnessed these things, did they seem to think it was all right to do anything to the Vietnamese?

CAMIL: It wasn't like they were humans. . . . They were a gook or a Commie and it was okay.*

Lance Corporal Thomas Heidtman, 3rd Battalion, 5th Marine Regiment, 1st Marine Division, 1966–1967, described a sideline of the "Burning 5th Marines":

One thing that was more or less like a joke . . . and it would get a laugh every time from somebody, was if we were moving through a village and there was a woman present. Her clothes, at least the top half of her clothes, were just ripped. I've seen that happen, and done it several times, probably thirty, forty times I've seen civilians with their clothes just—just because they were female and they were old enough for somebody to get a laugh at—their clothes, the top of their clothes, at least, would be ripped. Just torn right down. It only takes one hand to rip those kind of clothing. They're real thin silk or whatever, and they would be shoved out into the ditch and we'd just keep going.

Sergeant Michael McClusker was with the Public Information Office, I Corps, 1st Marine Division in 1966–1967, "which meant that I was a reporter-photographer and spent all of my time out in the field. It was almost like watching the same film strip continually, time after time after time."

The next instance happened also in the same month of September when a squad of nine men, that was a Chu Lai rifle squad, went into this village. They were supposed to go after what they called a Viet Cong whore. They went into the village and instead of capturing her, they raped her—every man raped her.

---

* From the testimony of Camil and others it becomes evident that the grotesqueries and mutilations practiced by America's famous Boston Strangler (see pages 200 to 206) were no different in concept and execution from those performed by American GI's in Vietnam.

As a matter of fact, one man said to me later that it was the first time he had ever made love to a woman with his boots on. The man who led the squad was actually a private. The squad leader was a sergeant but he was a useless person and he let the private take over his squad. Later he said he took no part in the raid, it was against his morals. So instead of telling his squad not to do it, because they wouldn't listen to him anyway, the sergeant went into another side of the village and just sat and stared bleakly at the ground, feeling sorry for himself. But at any rate, they raped the girl, and then, the last man to make love to her shot her in the head.

Sergeant Jamie Henry was nineteen years old in 1967–1968 when he served with the 4th Infantry Division. He told the conference that he had reported his information to the Army's Criminal Investigation Division. "I gave them names, dates, grid coordinates, etc., but they'll probably say it's a lie."

We moved into a small hamlet, 19 women and children were rounded up as VCS—Viet Cong Suspects—and the lieutenant that rounded them up called the captain on the radio and he asked what should be done with them. The captain simply repeated the order that came down from the colonel that morning, to kill anything that moves, which you can take any way you want to take it. . . . I looked toward where the supposed VCS were, and two men were leading a young girl, approximately 19 years old, very pretty, out of a hootch. She had no clothes on so I assumed she had been raped, which was pretty SOP, and she was thrown onto the pile of the 19 women and children, and five men around the circle opened up on full automatic with their M-16s. And that was the end of that. Now there was a lieutenant who heard this over the radio in our company—he was going nuts. He was going to report it to everybody. After that day he calmed down and the next day he didn't say anything about it.

Specialist/4 Joe Galbally, who served in the 198th Light Infantry Brigade, Americal Division, 1967–1968, said, "I was a Pfc. in an infantry company, which meant that there was about seventy-five of us turned loose on the civilian population in Vietnam."

These people are aware of what American soldiers do to them, so naturally they tried to hide the young girls. We found one hiding in a bomb shelter in sort of the basement of her house. She was taken out, raped by six or seven people in front of her family, in front of us, and the villagers. This wasn't just one incident; this was just the first one I can remember. I know of 10 or 15 of such incidents at least.

Sergeant Michael Hunter served two tours of duty in Vietnam, from 1968 to 1970. His first tour was with the 1st Air Cavalry Division.

Now as far as atrocities, my company, Bravo Company, 5th of the 7th, when we were outside of Hué shortly after the Tet offensive, went into a village—and this happened repeatedly afterwards—and searched for enemy activity. We encountered a large amount of civilian population. The civilian population was brought out to one end of the village, and the women, who were guarded by a squad and a squad leader at that time, were separated. I might say the young women were separated. . . . They were told at gunpoint that if they did not submit to the sexual desires of any GI who was there guarding them, they would be shot for running away. And this was put in the language as best possible for people who cannot speak Vietnamese, and they got the point across because three women submitted to the raping of the GIs.

Specialist/4 Timon Hagelin from Philadelphia was assigned to the Graves Registration Platoon, 243rd Field Service Company, 1st Logistics Command in 1968–1969. He was sent to Dak To.

While I was on the base taking care of KIAs as they came through, I made friends with people in my company that I considered basically nice people. We used to get together at night and talk. I went down to a certain place where they all were and as I approached it, I heard a scream. Someone was obviously very scared. As I got down to the door, I called one of my friends. He punched this chick on the side of the head. The girl was, you know, Vietnamese people are a lot smaller than American people. It doesn't take that much to hurt one of those people, you know? They gave her a couple of good shots and the girl finally started yelling, "Me do, me do, me do," and about seven of them ripped her off. I know the guys, and I know basically they're not really bad people, you know? I just couldn't figure out what was going on to make the people like this do it. It was just part of the everyday routine, you know.

Captain John Mallory, civic action officer for the 1st Squadron, 11th Armored Cavalry Regiment, 1st Air Cavalry Division in 1969–1970, testified with precision.

> On one occasion a North Vietnamese Army nurse was killed by the 11th Armored Cavalry troops; subsequently a grease gun of the type used in automotive work was placed in her vagina and she was packed full of grease.

Specialist/5 Don Dzagulones, an interrogator with the 635th Military Intelligence Detachment, attached to the 11th Infantry Brigade, Americal Division in Quang Ngai Province in 1969, mentioned that "most of the prisoners we had were women. It wasn't uncommon to have a mother and daughter coming in the same group of prisoners."

> Another time they brought in a woman prisoner who also was alleged to be a spy. They continued the interrogation in a bunker and she wouldn't talk. I don't think she even gave them her name. So they stripped off her clothing and they threatened to rape her, which had no effect on her at all. She was very stoic. She just stood there and looked at them defiantly. So they threatened to burn her pubic hairs. And I guess it wasn't done on purpose, I'm sure of that, but they lighted a cigarette lighter and she caught on fire. She went into shock. I guess she was unconscious, so they called the medics. The medics came and they gave the medics instructions to take her to the hospital under the pretext of being in a coma from malaria, which they did. And nothing was ever done about that.

As a matter of historical record, by the time The Winter Soldier Investigation had been convened, the feminist movement and the antiwar movement had gone their separate and distinct ways, each absorbed with its own issues to the exclusion of the other, with no small amount of bitterness among movement troopers whose energies, ideologies and sense of priority pulled them in one direction or the other. As a woman totally committed to the feminist cause I received several requests during this time to march, speak and "bring out my sisters" to antiwar demonstrations "to show women's liberation solidarity with the peace movement," and my response was that if the peace movement cared to raise the issue of rape and prostitution in Vietnam, I would certainly join in. This was met with stony silence on the part of antiwar activists whose catchwords of the day were "anti-imperialism" and "American aggression," and for whom the slogan—it appeared on buttons—"Stop the Rape of Vietnam" meant the defoliation of crops, not the abuse of women. Communications between feminist groups and antiwar groups were tense as they sought to raise our consciousness and we sought to raise our own. I am sorry that the peace movement did not consider the abuse of women in Vietnam an issue important and distinctive enough to stand on its own merits, and I am sorry that we in the women's movement, struggling to find our independent voices, could not call attention to this women's side of the war by ourselves. The time was not right.

4

Riots, Pogroms and Revolutions

Uprisings, riots, revolutions and minor skirmishes with racial and political overtones all have provided an outlet, and sometimes even an ideological excuse, for men to practice rape on women. And sometimes, when it suited propaganda purposes, individual cases of rape were actually preserved in the form of depositions taken from the injured women, eyewitness accounts from unimpeachable observers, newspaper stories and agitational pamphlets—admittedly with partisan motive, and most rarely, long after the fact in official investigations.

The attitude of historians toward this kind of documentation has usually been to ignore it as tangential, inconsequential or as possessing dubious validity. Occasionally an account of rape slips into a history book as a bit of color, a paragraph of vivid, gutsy writing, but it is never treated as more than an isolated incident. And nowhere has this mob rape been equated with the everyday "domestic" occurrence, the kind that until recently was viewed as "aberrant" behavior. Instead, historical rape—rape connected with those apocalyptic events that try men's souls, etc.—has been equated with the nether regions of "atrocity" that after the fact is always suspect because it is so unpleasant, so shocking that we would prefer to consider it exaggeration. And too, as we know, the experience of women is always suspect, and discounted. Another reason for the relegation of rape to the area of suspect is that those who sought to expose it invariably had a political motivation; and those who believed it or didn't believe it based their conclusions on their own political perspective. (I have been guilty of this myself.) Only when all accounts of rape are collected and correlated does the true underside of women's history emerge.

THE AMERICAN REVOLUTION

As early as 1768 American patriots began collecting reports of sexual abuses by British soldiers. In response to colonial unrest because of the unpopular Townshend Acts, British troops landed in Boston that September, creating in effect a garrison city. Continuing friction between the soldiers and the local populace eventually culminated in the famous Boston Massacre, but from the moment the British forces landed, an anonymous group of Americans—Henry Knox, the Greenleafs, John Adams and Josiah Quincy may have been among them—secretly prepared a weekly account of city life under military rule and distributed their reports to sympathetic liberal newspapers in Boston, New York and London. The weekly unsigned column, known as A Journal of the Times or A Journal of Occurrences, appeared in print for more than a year, terminating as suddenly as it began. The Journal, according to one historian, was "the first systematic gathering and retailing of news found in American newspapers," a sort of pre-wire-service syndication.

It was the patriots' stated purpose to show what happens to a city under "the insolence of power." Among the news items they gathered to give evidence of "the great impropriety and grievance of quartering troops in town" was a considerable amount of attempted rape. Continuing sexual harassment of Boston's women by the British forces was viewed by the patriots not as a series of unrelated, irrational acts performed by boisterous soldiers, but as an integral part of colonial oppression. "Perhaps," they wrote, "by treating the most respectable of our inhabitants in this sort, it is intended to impress our minds with formidable ideas of a military government, that we may be induced the sooner to give up such trifling things as rights and privileges." Some relevant items:

> November 9, 1768: A married woman living in Long Lane, returning home in the night, was seized by the neck and almost

strangled, she was then thrown upon the ground and treated with great indecencies. Another woman at New Boston was rudely handled. . . . The mention of such abuses as these is by no means intended to insinuate a want of care in the commanding officers, but to show the great impropriety and grievance of quartering troops in the town. . . . These are times in which no inhabitant knows what ground he stands upon, or can call his own.

December 12, 1768: A married lady of this town was the other evening, when passing from one house to another, taken hold of by a soldier, who otherways behaved to her with great rudeness. A woman near Long Lane was stopped by several soldiers, one of whom cried out seize her and carry her off; she was much surprised, but luckily got shelter in a house nearby. Another woman was pursued by a soldier into a house near the north end, who dared to enter the same, and behave with great insolence. . . . These are further specimens of what we are to expect from our new conservators of the peace.

April 30, 1769: The quartering of troops in the body of a town is as ruinous to the soldiery as it is distressing to the inhabitants; every day furnishes out instances of their debaucheries and consequent violences. As an aged woman at the north end of Boston was setting the other evening in a lower room, having no person in the house with her, a soldier came in and seeing her have a Bible on the table before her, he expressed his approbation of her piety and attempted a kind of exposition upon some parts thereof. But soon dropping this discourse, he acquainted her that he had a bad swelling on his hip and should be glad of her advice. While the good woman was attending to his relation, this abandoned wretch seized her by the shoulders, threw her upon the floor, and not withstanding her years, attempted a rape upon her, which was prevented by the resistance and screams occasioned by his brutal behavior. He thought it proper to hurry off, taking with him a bundle of shirts and other linen, which had just been sent into the house for washing and ironing, a business which the person followed to obtain a livelihood.

May 17, 1769: A woman at the north end enter'd a complaint with Mr. Justice Ruddock against a soldier and some others for a violent attempt upon her, but a rape was prevented by the timely appearance of a number of persons for protection, when the soldier made his escape.

July 3, 1769: On Tuesday morning the 27th of June, a woman going to the south market for a fish stopt at the shop of Mr. Chase, under Liberty Tree, appearing to be faint. They got some water, but on raising her up she died instantly. A jury of inquest was summoned, and upon examination she appeared to be one Sarah Johnson, of Bridgewater, on whom it appeared by evidence and several marks that violence had been perpetrated the 24th inst. by soldiers unknown, which probably was the cause of her death. Several physicians who were called in upon the occasion declared that upon examining the body, they observed sundry livid spots, which evidently demonstrated violence. From the combined appearances, upon opening the body, they were of the opinion that she had been recently ravished, and had resisted to the utmost; and that the over exertion of her strength might probably terminate in a syncope or faintness, which they thought might be the immediate cause of her death.

A cavalier view from the other side was recorded when the American Revolution was in full swing by Captain Francis Rawdon, who wrote to his uncle, the Earl of Huntingdon, in August, 1776, that he appreciated Southern women because they did not publicly take issue after being raped by British soldiers. As for the women of Staten Island, they were "fair nymphs" for the British soldiers, who were "as riotous as satyrs. A girl cannot step into the bushes to pluck a rose without running the most imminent risk of being ravished, and they are so little accustomed to these vigorous methods that they don't bear them with the proper resignation, and of consequence we have most entertaining courts martial every day."

By contrast a terse communiqué from Colonel George Measam to General Anthony Wayne in January, 1777: "The enemy make great devastation in their retreat, burning without distinction Tory's as well as Whig's houses. Great part of Princetown destroyed. Tory's as well as Whig's wives and daughters ravished and carried off with them."

The British and Hessian campaigns in New York and New Jersey were the most notorious for abuses against civilians, and accounts of rape were sometimes written up by correspondents for the *Pennsylvania Evening Post*.

Since I wrote to you this morning I have had an opportunity of hearing a number of the particulars of the horrid depredations committed by that part of the British army which was stationed at and near Pennytown, under the command of Lord Cornwallis.

Besides the sixteen women who had fled to the woods to avoid their brutality and were there seized and carried off, one man had the cruel mortification to have his wife and only daughter (a child of ten years of age) ravished; this he himself, almost choked with grief, uttered in lamentations to his friend, who told me of it, and also informed me that another girl of thirteen years of age was taken from her father's house, carried to a barn about a mile, there ravished, and afterwards made use of by five more of these brutes. Numbers of instances of the same kind of behavior I am assured of have happened. . . . Another instance of their brutality happened near Woodbridge: one of the most respectable gentlemen in that part of the country was alarmed by the cries and shrieks of a most lovely daughter; he found an officer, a British officer, in the act of ravishing her. He instantly put him to death; two other officers rushed in with fusees, and fired two balls into the father, who is now languishing under his wounds.

An unsigned contemporary narrative of the battles of Trenton and Princeton, written in 1777, described specific burnings, robbings and plunderings during "26 days of tyranny" and then remarked:

The Damages Done by these Plunderings and Desolations must amount very high and Occasion much Trouble to the Sufferers. Yet they are Vastly short of Another Horrid Outrage that I have not yet mentioned, I mean the Ravishing of Women, which by a Great Defect in Human Nature that is against both Justice and Reason We Despise these poor Innocent Sufferers in this Brutal Crime Even as long as they live. In time of Peace to avoid so miserable and lasting Reproach I am of the Opinion That many honest virtuous women have suffered in this Manner and kept it Secret for fear of making their lives miserable and so many of those Capital Crimes escape Punishment. In time of War when those Unnatural Miscreants are sure of Getting off with Impunity they commit them the more frequently.

The anonymous narrator took note of the ravishments already mentioned in "the Friendly Post" and added "Another Tretcherous Villany":

There was two of Gen. Howe's light Horsemen Quartered at Pensneck about two miles from Princetown Who Pretended to a

Young Woman that they was Searching for Rebels, and had been Informed that some of them were Secreeted in the Barn and desired her to go with them and Show them the most Secret Places there. And She (Knowing that no body was there) to convince them, Went to the Barn with them to show them that no body was there. And when they had got her there, one of them Laid hold on her Strangled her to Prevent her crying out while the Villain Ravisht her, and when he had done, he Strangled her Again While the Other Brute Repeated the horrid crime upon her again. She is a Farmer's Daughter but her name with her Father's must be kept Secreet to Avoid the Reproach above Mentioned.

Not only was this author mindful that guilt for a rape devolves upon the female victim—a lifetime of observation led also to this conclusion: "This is far Worse in this Respect than an Indian War, for I Never heard nor read of their Ravishing of Women Notwithstanding their cruelty to their captives."

On New Year's Day, 1777, General George Washington issued a special order to his Continental Army forbidding the "plundering of any person": ". . . it is expected that humanity and tenderness to women and children will distinguish brave Americans, contending for liberty, from infamous mercenary ravagers, whether British or Hessians." Washington's army was not rape-free and there were executions for this crime (see page 31), but as might be expected, the pattern of sexual abuse was imposed by the aggressor army fighting on foreign soil. That same January the Continental Congress appointed a committee to look into irregular conduct on the part of King George's army and in April the committee issued its report.

The report was divided into four sections: devastation of country and destruction of property; inhumane treatment of prisoners; savage butchery of those incapable of resistance; and the abuse of women. Part Four, the abuse of women, was written with great delicacy.

The committee had authentic information of many instances of the most indecent treatment and actual ravishment of married and single women; but such is the nature of that most irreparable injury that the persons suffering it, though perfectly innocent, look upon it as a kind of reproach to have the facts related and their names known. Some complaints were made to the commanding

officers on this subject, and one affidavit made before a justice of
the peace, but the committee could not learn that any satisfaction
was ever given, or punishment inflicted, except that one soldier in
Pennington was kept in custody for part of a day.

Attempting a political analysis, the committee concluded that
these abuses reflected the attitude of a soldiery "towards a people
whom they have been taught to look upon, not as freemen defending their rights on principle, but as desperadoes and profligates who
have risen up against law and order in general and wish the subver-
sion of society itself. This is the most charitable and candid manner in which the committee can account for the melancholy truths
which they have been obliged to report."

The Continental Congress ordered the printing of six thousand copies of the committee report (two thousand in German)
for distribution among enemy soldiers, but historians are uncertain
that this proviso was ever carried out. As a matter of fact, the
committee had far more than one affidavit at its disposal. In the
county of Hunterdon, New Jersey, a justice of the peace named
Jared Saxton collected six affidavits in a two-day period. Each
incident of rape had taken place in Hunterdon County "sometime
in December last past," most of the abuses involved three or more
soldiers who came to the house saying they were looking for rebels,
and at least two of the women were dragged off to the British
encampment for further assaults. Each of the victims (Mary
Campbell, five months' pregnant; Abigail Palmer, thirteen years
old; the sisters Elizabeth and Sarah Cain; Mary Phillips, a widow;
and Rebekhah Christopher) was illiterate and signed her deposition with her mark.

Mary Campbell's affidavit was fairly typical:

New Jersey   Mary Campbell wife of Daniel Campbell
Hunterdon County   in the County aforesaid being Sworn
                    on the Holy Evangelists of Almighty God
Deposeth and saith that sometime in December last past, a number of Soldiers belonging to the King of Great Britain's Army
came to the House of her Father, where she the Deponent then
was, when one of the Soldiers asked her to go to the Door & said
he wanted to speak with her, which she Refused & told him he
might speak to her in the House if he had anything to say, when
Two of them Seized hold of her Arms & dragged her out of the

House to an old Shop near the Dwelling House, Broke open the Door & pulled her in against all her cries & Intreaties & Swore if she did not hold her Tongue they would Run her thro with a Bayonet; her mother also plead with them & Intreated of them not to use her Daughter in such a Base & Cruel manner, but to no purpose. But finally three of said Soldiers Successively had Knowledge of the Body of this Deponent, she being five months & upwards Advanced in her Pregnancy at that Time & further this Deponent Saith not.

Sworn Before me March the 22 Day 1777—
Jared Saxton, one of the Justices

Assigned to keep the Peace in & for
the said County of Hunterdon

her

Mary m Campbell

mark

Pogroms

As members of a scapegoat minority, Jewish women were historical victims of rape during the fearful pogroms in Poland and Russia or wherever they happened to live. The Cossack revolt of 1648 under the leadership of the Hetman Bogdan Chmelnitzky was significant to Ukrainian nationalism but it was a memorable disaster for the Ukrainian Jews, who were known to the Cossacks as the people who collected the rent for the hated Polish absentee landlords. (Jews, who were not allowed by law to own land, had been forced into a disagreeable role as agents of commerce.) Chmelnitzky's Cossacks rode through the tiny villages and gave vent to their nationalism by raping Jewish women and maiming and killing others of both sexes, including children, who happened to cross their path.

Chmelnitzky's pogroms were replicated in the Ukraine in 1881–1882, where again the issue for the peasants was the presence of the Jewish rent collectors, and periodically thereafter: 1891–1892, 1903–1906 and 1919–1920. Each wave had its own set of ideological circumstances, each wave raised the slogan "Beat the Jews" as a rallying cry for God and country, and each wave featured the rape of Jewish women. The Czarist government was not without complicity, for with its existence threatened by revolution, "Beat the Jews" became a strategic divertisement from its own repressions.

A writer, Ande Manners, has noted that the early pogroms "had a desultory, amateurish quality: a few hundred feather beds slashed; houses and shops looted; several dozen people killed; here and there, a few skulls fractured, broken limbs, and girls and women raped." The slashing of feather beds had a double significance, she tells us. Besides being symbolic of the good married life—the soft mattresses were the dowries of Jewish brides—"occasionally apprehensive parents rolled up their pretty young daughters in them, to conceal the girls from predatory, lustful Cossacks." Other hiding places were pickle barrels—the opera singer Beverly Sills's mother was hidden in one during a pogrom—and mounds of earth or sand. (Similar hiding places were used by Southern blacks when the KKK was riding.) Later pogroms were characterized by all-out murder, but rape was not abandoned as a tactic. It became a prelude to murder, forgotten in the horror of the larger act.*

The wave of pogroms that began in 1919 took place amid the general confusion (and umbrella) of the Russian Revolution, during the bitter civil war between the Whites and the Reds. Rowdy volunteers from Denikin and Kornilov's White Army, for whom "Beat the Jews" had long been the answer to everything, including, now, the Communist menace, had a field day of wanton destruction. Reports from the Russian Red Cross and from Zionist organizations have furnished the documentation. (The Soviets were concerned about the plight of the Jews, but not overly so; they were waging a revolution. Their advice was "Join the Red Army!") According to a Red Cross report, a typical pogrom on a small Jewish *shtetl* went like this: "The gang breaks into the township, spreads all over the streets, separate groups break into the Jewish houses, killing without distinction of age and sex everybody they meet, with the exception of women, who are bestially violated before they are murdered."

The Red Cross meticulously reported on some Jewish refugees from Ladyshenka, "where an ordinary, simple pogrom took place": "On July 9th, a peasant brought to the Jewish hospital in Uman the last two Jews from Ladyshenka. . . . These were two young

---

* Assaults on Jewish women during the pogroms had their geographic parallel during this period of time in the massive rape of Armenian women by the Turks in 1895 and 1915, as part of a continuing Turkish effort to destroy the Armenian people. See the account by Henry Morgenthau, *Ambassador Morgenthau's Story*, Doubleday, 1918.

Jewish girls, frightfully beaten and bruised, one with her nose cut off and the other with her arms broken. They are both in Kiev now and both suffer from venereal disease."

A Zionist group reported from Kremenchug: "No sooner had the Volunteers entered the town than destruction commenced. . . . All houses, without exception, were plundered. Three hundred and fifty cases of rape have been registered; neither children of 12 nor old women of 60 were spared. After they had been ravished, the little girls were thrown down the water-closets."

A report from Fastov, where six hundred were killed and twelve hundred were wounded: "The soldiers threw themselves upon the girls under age with a perfectly brutal fury and ravished them before the very eyes of their parents, powerless to interfere. Some particularly atrocious scenes took place in the courtyard of the synagogue where the Jews had sought refuge. The courtyard was covered with the bodies of women, children, old men, and young girls who had been ravished. Many people became insane."

Some anti-Bolshevik Jews in Ekaterinoslav sent an urgent, obsequious appeal to General Denikin:

> The tired and oppressed Jews are longing for order and peace. Inasmuch as the large majority of the Jewish population belong to the bourgeoisie, they have been impatiently waiting for the Volunteer Army to redeem them from the proletarian dictatorship. With joy they greeted the oncoming armies and were prepared to help them with money and men. But to our great misfortune, the Jews were disappointed in their hopes. . . . We understand full well that in an occupation there usually occurs unpleasantness, but to our great regret we must say that what is taking place is not an infrequent occurrence in scattered places but occurs systematically wherever the Volunteer Army enters. Especially violent were the outbreaks in Ekaterinoslav, where all the Jewish houses in four streets were plundered and outrages committed upon hundreds of Jewish girls and many Jews killed. The pogrom in Ekaterinoslav is still in progress . . .

Ideology was never absent. A Jewish witness to a pogrom in Kharkov was told by a marauder, "All this is the fault of your Trotsky."

Periodic rape of Jewish women by hostiles sorely taxed the rabbinical concept that a married woman who was raped became an adulteress who was unfit to return to her husband's bed. Pragmatism eventually won out. Since the Jewish people were spread throughout the Diaspora and lived under other nation's laws, rabbinical law could not really be enforced. But defilement of women had and continues to have a deep psychological hold on the minds of men who have traditionally viewed women as "their" women. This attitude is hardly restricted to Jews; it is quite universal. Divorce after rape is not uncommon.

It is reasonable to conjecture that the reputation for unbridled sensuality that has followed Jewish woman throughout history (Rebecca as opposed to Rowena; Henry Miller's frequent reference to "thick Jewish cunt") has its origins in the Jewish woman's historical experience of forcible rape, and is a projection onto them of male sex fantasies. In this respect, Jewish women and black women have a common bond: the reputation for lasciviousness and promiscuity that haunts black women in America today may be attributed to the same high degree of historical forcible rape.

Sartre's famous quote about Jewish women in *Anti-Semite and Jew*, written at the close of World War II, is a poetic insight into this phenomenon: "There is in the words 'a beautiful Jewess' a very special sexual signification, one quite different from that contained in the words 'beautiful Rumanian,' 'beautiful Greek,' or 'beautiful American,' for example. This phrase carries an aura of rape and massacre. The 'beautiful Jewess' is she whom the Cossacks under the czars dragged by her hair through the streets of her burning village. And the special works which are given over to accounts of flagellation reserve a place of honor for the Jewess . . ."

THE MORMON PERSECUTIONS

It is worth noting the similarity of experience, as far as women were concerned, between such disparate events in time and place as the Ukrainian pogroms and, for example, the Mormon persecutions in this country and the periodic outbreaks of white mob violence against blacks. In each historic interlude a mob of men, sometimes an official militia, armed itself with an ideology that offered a moral justification—"for the public good"—to commit acts of degradation upon women. In each interlude a campaign of terror, and a goal that included the annihilation of a people, provided a license to rape. In each interlude the symbol of the mob's hatred and contempt became its exuberant destruction of other men's property, be it furniture, cattle, or women. Further, it mattered little to the rapists acting under the cover of a mob whether or not their victims were "attractive." This, too, is significant, since it argues that sexual appeal, as we understand it, has little to do with the act of rape. A mob turns to rape as an expression of power and dominance. Women are used almost as inanimate objects, to prove a point among men.

Latter-day Saints, or Mormons, began settling in and around Independence, Missouri, in 1831, to the local residents' dismay. Polygamy was not at issue—it had not yet become a church canon. The Missourians could not tolerate the Mormon belief in their living prophet, Joseph Smith, who communicated directly with God, their strange clannish ways and, surprisingly, in view of later history, the Mormon readiness to accept free Negro and mulatto converts, which the locals felt "would corrupt our blacks and instigate them to bloodshed." (Missouri was a slave state.)

A rowdy mass meeting was held in Independence in April, 1833, and two months later a "call" was circulated to rid the state of the undesirables, "peaceably if we can, forcibly if we must," for the sake of "our wives and daughters." (A Mormon version of the mob's call adds the line, "We will whip and kill the men; we will destroy their children, and ravish their women!") The Mormons replied that their settlement was already at the western limits of United States territory and a further move would put them squarely among the Indians, who "might massacre our defenseless women and children with impunity." To show that they meant business, a mob broke into the offices of the Mormon newspaper and destroyed the press. The Mormons signed an agreement to leave the county within the year. Most of them crossed the wide Missouri and moved northward to Clay and Caldwell counties.

That wasn't good enough for the Missourians. In October, 1838, the governor called up the militia and issued his notorious order: "The Mormons must be treated as enemies and must be exterminated or driven from the State if necessary, for the public good." By this time the principal Mormon settlement was located in Far West, Caldwell County. The militiamen marched on Far West, tricked the Mormon leaders, including Joseph Smith, into surrendering, and then, according to official Mormon history:

> The mob was now let loose upon the unarmed citizens of Far West, and under the pretext of searching for arms they ransacked every house, tore up the floors, upset haystacks, wantonly destroyed much property, and shot down a number of cattle, just for the sport it afforded them. The people were robbed of their most valuable property, insulted and whipped; but this was not the worst. The chastity of a number of women was defiled by force; some of them were strapped to benches and repeatedly ravished by brutes in human form until they died from the effects of this treatment. The horrible threat made a few years before . . . had been at last carried out—*We will ravish their women!*

Back in the camp where Joseph Smith and the others were under guard, the militiamen "related to each other their deeds of murder and rapine, and boasted of raping virtuous wives and maidens, until the prisoners were heartsick with the disgusting details of their crimes." The Latter-day Saints were driven from Missouri. They began the trek to Illinois, where prophet Smith was lynched in a jail cell, and eventually to peace and prosperity in Utah.

Mob Violence Against Blacks: The KKK

White mob action against communities of Southern blacks during the Reconstruction period featured the rape of women along with the burning of churches, schools and homes. The Memphis Riot of May, 1866, grew out of white hostility to the presence in town of a black state militia unit. The mob, whom the victims judged to be largely Irish, and in collusion with the local white police force, wreaked its vengeance on the entire black community. Forty-six blacks and five whites were killed. In the Congressional investigation that followed, several black women spoke of rape.

> FRANCES THOMPSON: Between one and two o'clock Tuesday night seven men, two of whom were policemen, came to my house I know they were policemen by their stars. . . . They said they

must have some eggs, and ham, and biscuit. I made them some biscuit and some strong coffee, and they all sat down and ate. A girl lives with me; her name is Lucy Smith; she is about 16 years old. When they had eaten supper, they said they wanted some women to sleep with. I said we were not that sort of women, and they must go. . . . One of them laid hold of me and hit me on the side of my face, and holding my throat, choked me. Lucy tried to get out of the window, when one of them knocked her down and choked her. They drew their pistols and said they would shoot us and fire the house if we did not let them have their way with us. All seven of the men violated us two. Four of them had to do with me, and the rest with Lucy.

Q.—Were you injured?

A.—I was sick for two weeks. I lay for three days with a hot, burning fever.

LUCY SMITH: We had two trunks. They did not unlock them but just jerked them open. They took $100 belonging to Frances, and $200 belonging to a friend of Frances, given to her to take care of. . . . They tried to take advantage of me, and did. I told them I did not do such things, and would not. One of them said he would make me, and choked me by the neck. . . . After the first man had connexion with me, another got hold of me and tried to violate me, but I was so bad he did not. He gave me a lick with his fist and said that I was so damned near dead he would not have anything to do with me.

Q.—Were you injured?

A.—I bled from what the first man had done to me.

LUCY TIBBS: A crowd of men came in that night. . . . They just broke the door open and asked me where was my husband; I replied he was gone . . . I said, "Please do not do anything to me; I am just here with two little children."

Q.—Did they do anything to you?

A.—They done a very bad act.

Q.—Did they ravish you?

A.—Yes, sir. . . . There was but one that did it. Another man said, "Let that woman alone—that she was not in any situation to be doing that." . . . They put me on the bed, and the other men were plundering the house while this man was carrying on. . . .

Q.—What did they mean by saying you were not in a condition to be doing that?

A.—I have been in the family way ever since Christmas. . . .

Q.—How many rooms were there in your house?
A.—Only one.
Q.—And this took place in the presence of all these men?
A.—Yes, sir.

CYNTHIA TOWNSEND:

Q.—Do you know of any violence being committed on the women in your neighborhood?
A.—Yes, sir; I know of some very bad acts. . . . There is a woman who lives near me by the name of Harriet; Merriweather was her name before she married. . . . There were as many as three or four men at a time had connexion with her; she was lying there by herself. They all had connexion with her in turn around, and then one of them tried to use her mouth. . . .

Q.—Did you see these men go into the house?
A.—Yes; I saw them going into the house and saw them coming out, and afterwards she came out and said they made her do what I told you they did; she has sometimes been a little deranged since then, her husband left her for it. When he came out of the fort and found what had been done, he said he would not have anything to do with her any more.

The Memphis Riot of 1866 was an uncoordinated mob action. About the same time, in Tennessee, a secret, organized force of terror haphazardly came into being and rapidly spread from state to state: the Ku Klux Klan, dedicated in the name of chivalry and patriotism to stopping the Radical Reconstruction movement. The ideology of the Klan as regards rape was typically two-faced. Blood oaths, mumbo jumbo and sworn compacts to "protect" Southern womanhood from the black menace, as sympathetically dramatized by D. W. Griffith in *The Birth of a Nation*, were predicated on the false assumption, no doubt spread by the Klan itself, that rape of white women by black men was unheard of before the Civil War, thanks to the law and order maintained by the institution of slavery. The holy mission of the Klan was ostensibly to step into the law-and-order gap created by Reconstruction. Actually, the true political mission of the Klan had little to do with white women, although it was not the first and hardly the last time that "protection" of women has been used to hide a male group's real purpose. The Klan's nightriding was aimed at frightening off newly enfranchised black male voters, who were naturally drawn to the Radical Republicans, the party of Reconstruction. Raping black women was one method of intimidation, along with unsigned threats, spooky costumes, whipping, burning and outright murder.

In 1871 a joint Congressional committee began an investigation into the activities of the Klan, recently outlawed by an Act of Congress. It was a mite late: Reconstruction had already faltered, but the evidence collected as the investigation moved from state to state was most telling. Several black women who were called to testify spoke of rape.

HARRIET SIMRIL of York County, South Carolina: They came back after the first time on Sunday night after my old man again, and this second time the crowd was bigger. . . . They called for him and I told them he wasn't there. . . . They searched about in the house a long time, and staid with me an hour that time. . . . they were spitting in my face and throwing dirt in my eyes . . . they busted open my cupboard, and they ate all my pies up, and they took two pieces of meat . . . and after a while they took me out of doors and told me all they wanted was my old man to join the Democratic ticket; if he joined the Democratic ticket they would have no more to do with him; and after they had got me out of doors, they dragged me out into the big road, and they ravished me out there.
Q.—How many of them?
A.—There were three.
Q.—One right after the other?
A.—Yes, sir.
Q.—Threw you down on the ground?
A.—Yes, sir, they throwed me down.
Q.—Do you know who the men were who ravished you?
A.—Yes, sir, I can tell who the men were; there was Ches Mc-Collum, Tom McCollum, and this big Jim Harper . . .

ELLEN PARTON of Meridian, Mississippi: . . . Wednesday night was the last night they came to my house . . . they came on Monday, Tuesday and Wednesday; on Monday night they said they came to do us no harm; on Tuesday night they said they came for the arms; I told them there was none, and they said they would take my word for it; on Wednesday night they came and broke open the wardrobe and trunks, and committed rape upon me; there was eight

of them in the house; I do not know how many there were outside;
they were white men . . . I called upon Mr. Mike Slamon, who was
one of the crowd, for protection . . . Mr. Slamon had an oil-cloth
and put it before his face, trying to conceal himself, and the man
that had hold of me told me not to call Mr. Slamon's name anymore; he then took me in the dining room, and told me I had to do
just what he said; I told him I could do nothing of the sort; that was
not my way, and he replied, "by God, you have got to," and then
threw me down . . . he had a black velvet cap on; after he got
through with me he came through the house and said he was after
the Union Leagues; I yielded to him because he had a pistol drawn;
when he took me down he hurt me . . . I yielded to him on that
account; he . . hurt me with his pistol . . .

HANNAH TUTSON of Clay County, Florida, was visited by Klansmen who wanted her land: When they came to my house that night
the dog barked twice . . . I got up and went out of doors . . . but
I could see nothing; I went back into the house, and just as I got into
bed five men bulged right against the door, and it fell right in the
middle of the floor, and they fell down. George McRae was the first
to get up. . . . He said, "Come in, True-Klux." I started to scream,
and George McRae catched me right by the throat and choked me.
. . . Then there were so many hold of me that they got me out of
doors. After they got me out, I looked and I saw Jim Phillips, George
McRae, and Henry Baxter. . . . They took and carried me to a
pine, just as large as I could get my arms around, and then they tied
my hands there. They pulled off all my linen, tore it up so that I
did not have a piece of rag on me as big as my hand. They tied me,
and I said, "Men, what are you going to do with me?" They said,
"God damn you, we will show you; you are living on another man's
premises." I said, "No; I am living on my own premises; I gave $150
for it and Captain Buddington and Mr. Mundy told me to stay
here." They . . . whipped me for a while. . . . George McRae
would act scandalously and ridiculously toward me and treat me
shamefully. . . . He would get his knees between my legs and say,
"God damn you, open your legs." I tell you men, he did act ridiculously and shamefully, that same George McRae. He sat down there
and said, "Old lady, if you don't let me have to do with you, I will
kill you." . . . They whipped me . . . and got liquor of some kind
and poured it on my head, and I smelled it for three weeks, so that
it made me sick. . . .

Q.—How many crops had you made?
A.—Two crops. . . .

Q.—You spoke about some of them "wanting to do with you," as you expressed it.

A.—Yes, sir.

Q.—What one was that?

A.—George McRae.

Q.—Did you give way to him?

A.—No, sir; George McRae acted so bad, and I was stark naked. I tell you men, he pulled my womb down so that sometimes now I can hardly walk.

Gerda Lerner, who unearthed and published much of the testimony quoted above in her documentary history, *Black Women in White America*, makes the point that "there are no records of the rape and violation of white women whose husbands or male relatives were associated with the Republican cause. Such practices were confined to black women." Since she called attention to an omission for the purpose of making a case for the *special* political abuse of black women through sexual means, and since this line of reasoning comes perilously close to the old leftist position that "when a black woman is raped the crime is political, but when a white woman is raped the charge is hysterical" (see Chapter 7, "A Question of Race"), I feel I must try to set the record straight.

Under the guise of punishing immorality, Klansmen often whipped white women they accused of adultery, ". . . and sometimes faithful wives who wouldn't come across to a Kluxer," according to one historian of Klan activity. The celebrated trial in 1925 of D. C. Stephenson, Grand Dragon of the Klan in Indiana, for the rape and murder of a white woman—Stephenson was actually convicted—is another example of the use of Klan power to create sexual terror irrespective of race. Further, William M. Kunstler speculated at length on the role played by the New Jersey Klan in *The Minister and the Choir Singer*, his account of the Hall-Mills adultery and murder case.

No one would want to deny that blacks were the special target of the Klan, and that black women suffered special abuse because they were women, but rather than try to separate out white women and claim they got off scot-free, a higher political understanding is gained by recognizing that sexual intimidation knows no racial distinctions, and that the sexual oppression of white women and black women is commonly shared.

MOB VIOLENCE AGAINST WHITES: THE CONGO

When Congolese forces began celebrating independence in July, 1960, by raping Belgian women, including nuns, and a few scattered accounts appeared in the papers, my attitude was one of disbelief. I chalked up the stories to fraudulent rumors, basically racist, designed to embarrass the cause of Patrice Lumumba, hero and martyr of Congo self-determination. I was not alone in my skepticism. The entire world press tended to divide along political lines. Pro-Lumumba papers in England, such as the well-bred *Manchester Guardian*, ignored the rape stories altogether, while papers that took a jaundiced view of African nationalism, such as the sensationalist *Daily Mail* and *Daily Express*, reported the rapes with gusto. In this country the small, vociferous left-wing press considered the rapes to be vicious, deliberate lies; while to William Buckley's conservative *National Review*, which supported secessionist Katanga, the rapes were proof of "what the black savages are doing." The battle lines of truth were drawn, as they frequently are, on the bodies of women.

Fifteen years have passed since those tragic early days of the Congo's struggle for independence, and my views remain unchanged as far as Lumumba is concerned. I still believe he was the hope of the Congo. But a woman's *politik* operates independent of traditional male forces of left and right, as everything in this book should make clear. There was rape in the Congo, a lot of it, Lumumba's denials notwithstanding. And it was not a plot of the CIA or Belgian mining interests, nor was it an hysterical fantasy of sex-starved nuns.

To understand the politics of rape in the Congo, one needs to know a little history. The Force Publique was created by King Leopold II at the close of the nineteenth century and used by the Belgian colonialists to enforce their rule—a rule unmatched in brutality by other colonial powers. The Force was a native army, illiterate and poorly paid, black myrmidons who did the bidding of an elite corps of European officers. To supplement their wages, the black troops were allowed to live off the land. One penetrating observer, the British anticolonialist E. D. Morel, wrote in 1909, "Wherever its operations have ranged, native livestock has almost totally disappeared; native preventive measures against the spread of venereal disease have been impossible of application. From far and wide . . . women have been raided in enormous numbers to satisfy its lusts. . . . It has been admitted in one official document that 'a veritable slave trade in women' was carried out by them."

In 1960 the Force Publique became a rogue elephant—loyal neither to Lumumba, Kasavubu, nor to the hated, departing Belgians, who knew they had created an irresponsible monster. A few days after the formal ceremonies of independence, the Force mutinied at the Thysville barracks. The mutiny spread quickly to other cities. Helen Kitchen, editor in chief of *Africa Report*, observed: "The attacks on European women, many in the Congo believe, were a product of heavy drinking and a gesture of revenge for humiliations suffered in the past. But it probably should also be taken into account that some politicians had led the Congolese people to believe that independence would deliver to them not only jobs, the cars, and the government houses heretofore enjoyed by the Belgians but also their personal property. And to many Congolese soldiers, a woman is still regarded as 'property.' "

Young King Baudouin set up a commission in Brussels to document accounts of rape, and a white paper, "Congo July 1960: Evidence," was published that year as a Belgian government propaganda pamphlet. It is a meticulous document in many respects. Dates and hours of the rapes are recorded. Women's names are conspicuously deleted. All told, the Belgian white paper reported 794 instances of rape of European nationals in a ten-day period from July 5 to July 14, with individual women reporting as many as twenty violations in a single night. Some excerpts:

KISANTU, July 5, 1960: Mrs. **** was in her home with her mother and four children. Towards 1600 hours a number of native soldiers sequestered her in a bedroom, and four of them raped her in turn. Between 1900 and 2000 hours, 12 more soldiers and a gendarme arrived. After pushing her husband and children outside, 12 of these men raped her in the same room. Mrs. **** was therefore raped 16 times.

BANZA-BOMA, July 5, 1960: Mrs. **** together with a small child stated that she was two months' pregnant when soldiers took her onto a verandah and four of them raped her in turn.

MATADI: On July 8, towards 1100 hours, 12 native policemen arrived in Matadi and took away the fit men at gunpoint. Mrs. **** sought refuge in a house with four women and some children. The native policemen returned to loot the houses. . . . One of the policemen entered the room where the women and children were. He took away at gunpoint a girl aged 14. From the cries and moans of the child, Mrs. **** realized the policeman was raping her. Then Mrs. **** was herself raped. . . . Mrs. **** [later] perceived traces of blood which convinced her that the little girl had indeed been raped . . .

KIMPESE: On July 13, 1960, around 1800 hours, a dozen soldiers and about a hundred civilians arrived at the home of Mr. ****. With his wife and three children under 16 years of age, he was taken by car in the direction of Leopoldville. His wife was separated from him, and in the car which was carrying her and her youngest children, she was raped three times by native soldiers. They struck the 9-year-old child and undressed the 2-year-old baby "to make sure it was a boy."

KIMPESE: Mrs. **** was raped during the night of July 13–14, 1960, at the same time as Mrs. B***. She was raped a second time, together with five other women. The following day while being taken to Thysville, the line of women were raped a third time, some in the presence of their children.

KIMPESE: Mrs. X*** was raped 10 times during the night of July 13–14, in the presence of her children and her husband, who had been bound and beaten with a club.

KIMPESE: Mrs. A*** was raped four times during the night of July 13–14, in the presence of her 3-year-old child.

CAMP HARDY (Thysville): Mrs. **** with her husband and two children left Malanga Station at July 11, 1960. In the vicinity of Block 110 they were stopped by ABAKO civilians,* searched, imprisoned and beaten all night. They were all sent on to Thysville where they arrived on the 12th towards midnight. Mrs. **** was alone in a cell with her children under 7 years of age when a party of about 10 soldiers arrived. One held her arms, one her legs, a third placed his hand on her mouth to stifle her cries, and a fourth pulled her hair and struck her in the face. She was raped about a dozen times in the presence of her children who were huddled in a corner, one holding the other. These attacks lasted from 0200 to 0430 hours. The family was saved by a white doctor.

CAMP HARDY (Thysville): On July 11, 1960, Mrs. A*** with a small child was at the house of Mrs. B***. Her husband had been imprisoned by native soldiers, who invaded the house and there found also Mrs. C***, seven months' pregnant, and Mrs. D***

---

* Loyal to Kasavubu.

with a small child. Mrs. A*** was taken home. The soldiers fought over her and Mrs. A*** was finally handed over to two soldiers belonging to the transport company at Camp Hardy, both of whom raped her. She was then taken to the house of Mrs. D*** where she found Mrs. E***, Mrs. F*** and Mrs. G*** who told her that they too had been raped.

CAMP HARDY: (Thysville), July 11, 1960: While Mrs. **** was in bed with 2 of her children, a soldier tried 4 times to rape her even though she was still torn from the birth of her baby and the sutures were still in place.

LULUABOURG, July 9, 1960: Two families . . . were molested and beaten. Mrs. Z*** was raped at gunpoint in her home by 2 policemen. Both families were then taken to the military camp. . . . The 2 mothers were stripped of their clothing, molested and beaten. They were then locked into the prison. In the presence of her children, a soldier lifted Mrs. Z***'s skirts and pretended to insert a hand grenade in her vagina.

LULUABOURG: Mrs. Y*** was taken out of her house and raped in the road before the eyes of her 3 children and her husband, who had previously been beaten. Other women, including an old lady, were stripped of their clothing, molested and publicly humiliated.

BOENDE: On the evening of July 11 Mrs. **** and her family left Djolu. Stopped on the road by native soldiers, they were taken to Djolu prison and the women were separated from the men. . . . Mrs. **** was standing up with her two months' old baby in her arms. In this posture, Mrs. **** was held firmly by some natives while other natives raped her and yet another trained a gun on her. During the night Mrs. **** was raped about twenty times. Knocking her down, the natives threw themselves on her, tearing her clothes and pulling her body hair. The women with her were also raped in the presence of their children . . .

BOENDE, July 12, 1960: The nuns were put into a punishment cell with two women and a baby, according to a statement made by two of the nuns. The native soldiers attacked the first nun, and, after a painful struggle, managed to rape her. Then they attacked another and with the help of yet another soldier, tried to rape the Sister. Two of the soldiers stamped on her. The nun fainted, and one of the other sisters asserted that the victim had just expired. The soldiers were frightened and ran away; other soldiers reproached them for having killed her when it was not permitted to do so. The nun remained unconscious for a long time. At 0530 hours the party of white prisoners, both men and women, were taken to another prison. They were all naked, including the religious, and their hands were tied behind their backs. They were incarcerated in a cell block where some twenty women and children were already imprisoned. The soldiers wanted to know why the nuns were not affiliated to Lumumba's political party, and whether they had sexual relations with priests; each was promised a soldier for the night. Subsequently the captives were taken to Mompono by truck accompanied by insults of the native population.

In July, 1960, the American Universities Field Staff sent an energetic observer named Edwin S. Munger to Leopoldville (now Kinshasa, Zaïre) to write a report on the Congo situation. Munger's newsletter for the month of September is an attempt to verify the rape accounts. Interestingly, he spoke to no raped women, but restricted his investigation to interviews with government officials, doctors and missionaries. Written in the typical, somewhat breathless fashion of an Institute Fellow who has just landed at the airport, Munger's reportage contained some remarkable insights.

Relying on the Belgian white paper as his starting point, Munger spoke first to an ambassador from Ghana. "Did you see anyone raped yourself?" the ambassador asked him. Nodding at Munger's negative reply, the ambassador said chummily, "It is typical of a wartime situation. During the last war American troops used to take Ghanaian girls down to the beach all the time and we never made any objections." A member of the Force Publique confided over a cup of coffee, "The Belgian women have hurt their vaginas to make accusations against the Congolese." A black American minister told him quietly, "It is hard on the children and women but the Belgians deserve it. That's hard for a minister to say, isn't it?"

Munger did better when he spoke to some French and Belgian doctors. One told him, "I saw very much the same thing in the last war when soldiers lost their discipline in Europe. My own gyne-cological examinations were limited to 13 women here. . . . Believe me they were raped." A husband and wife medical team at the Leopoldville airport emergency center had processed scores of rape victims. The wife, Dr. Deniese Malderez, spoke freely: "I do not know how many rapes there were. We announced we had penicillin available as protection against venereal disease. Over 350 women were injected at this station. Approximately 50 women said they feared conception and asked for hormonal treatment. This we did not give because they were flying direct to Brussels. I believe many who were raped did not come to our station. As I went through the waiting hall downstairs to treat bruised women, several told me they had been raped but would not come for an injection. I couldn't go around calling, 'Those who have been raped report here.' In our ward I heard again and again the women whispering to each other, 'How many times for you?' Two girls of eight and eleven were brought to me. Their father said they were in the last car from Thysville and had been cut off. He said many Congolese had raped his daughters for 24 hours. One girl sat here for ten hours without saying a word. One girl had her legs drawn up and could not move them. . . . Over 150 women from Thysville asked for injections. I do not believe they were hysterical and asked for treatment if they were not raped. Many were ashamed to admit it. I went to four nuns who had been beaten and admitted they had been raped but would not come for treatment. The priests were shocked. You know Belgium is a Catholic country and abortion is illegal, but several priests said curettage must be performed . . ."

Munger also spoke with a Belgian evacuee, an old-time colonialist who had owned a coffee plantation. "Why, I've known these people like the back of my hand," the old-timer told him. "I've been working with them and sleeping with their women for 35 years and I never expected to see this."

It was not just Belgian women who were raped by Congolese soldiers and civilians, but Portuguese, Greeks and Americans—no foreign national was exempt. And the Congolese during those brief, unhappy days in July, 1960, were doing no more, in violent, compacted fashion, than the colonialists had been doing to black women for a century, and that they themselves had been doing throughout history to the women of their own race.

Philippa Schuyler, daughter of George Schuyler, conservative black editor of the Pittsburgh Courier, found herself in Leopoldville that July. She had gone there to give a piano recital and stayed on to do some reporting for the National Review, and then to write a book. As a black conservative and a feminist, Philippa Schuyler hewed to an original course. She was one of the few reporters in the Congo to make the connection between the European women and the native women, and was able to later write with equal indignation, "Thousands of black women have been raped in intertribal fighting."

Schuyler also managed to interview some Belgian victims. One woman who had been attacked by three soldiers showed the pianist her body bruises and torn underwear, thickly smeared with dried, clotted blood. The woman gave her this personal account: "I was a social worker, there to teach the Congolese women sewing, cooking, social adjustment, and so on. I lived alone, and it was easy for the soldiers to break in. I tried to hide in the wardrobe, but they pulled me out, spitting on me, and beat me all over. I grabbed a sewing basket and hit one soldier on the head with it, but he wrenched it out of my grasp. I jabbed him with a pair of scissors but it didn't do any good. My legs were bleeding. I fell on the floor and they kicked me. I tried to get up but the floor was slippery with blood, and I fell in it. I crawled away and tried to run into the WC and bolt the door, but I wasn't fast enough, and they came in after me. . . . The women were helpless. . . . [They] stayed in their houses. Where else? They thought they would be safer there. These houses were a little distant from each other and there were no phones, so one woman could not warn another . . ."

The authenticity of Philippa Schuyler's interview with her social worker and the calm account offered to Edwin Munger by Dr. Deniese Malderez cannot be questioned, but Munger and Schuyler were hardly writing for major outlets. Rape in the Congo during the turbulent days of 1960 was never treated by the establishment press as anything more than peripheral exotica to the "big story" of colonialism and civil war. "One woman could not warn another," Schuyler reported. Who but a woman would find this perception relevant?

"It would be interesting to know whether the correspondents of those papers which made no mention of [rape] knew of these allegations," wrote an editorialist for the British New Statesman that July. "And if so, whether they did not regard them as sufficiently substantiated to include in their cables. Or did they just miss the story?"

Munger tried to find out. He tracked down a battle-hardened reporter with a reputation as "one of the ablest and most experienced men covering the African continent," and put the question to him, recording his answer without comment: "He . . . believed other stories more important for his paper and did not, in his view, waste time investigating charges of rape."

There are several aspects of the Congo story to give one pause. The attitude of tough male reporters that an investigation of mass rape was a waste of time on an unimportant side issue was the same attitude that twelve years later retarded exposure of the mass rapes of Bangladesh, or the systematic rapes of Vietnam. The temporizing by government officials and Congo sympathizers that rape was a typical, and therefore *acceptable*, by-product of colonial uprising, or any clash between men, was part of the standard "war is hell" stance affected by diplomats, generals, soldiers and battle-loving correspondents in every war. At the same time, the documentation of rape by the aggrieved side, in this case the Belgians, was collected to prove a propaganda point: that the departing colonialists were injured innocents of a beloved country "not yet ready" for independence. And finally, the very nature of the rapes themselves: they were acts of undifferentiated hostility of men toward women, perpetrated on nonbelligerents in the course of a celebration, in this case a celebration of independence—part of the general hoopla of flexing muscle, taking over, and tying on a manly drunk—with the raped women cast as symbol of the hated oppressor, a ready, easy target without the means of self-defense. Rape in the Congo was shrouded in the cloak of vengeance and made plausible by an historic view of woman as the property of man, but we should not forget that beyond the shiny patina of ideological excuse, it was also rape amid the levity and frivolity of men having a good time.

5

Two Studies in American History

INDIANS

The rape of Indian women by white men and the rape of white women by Indians was a casual by-product of the move westward and The Great Frontier. Although white men talked freely at the time of the rape of white women—and often used these stories as an inflammatory excuse for their own behavior—the women were reticent. Firsthand narratives of captivity by abducted females that were published and widely circulated in the seventeenth, eighteenth and nineteenth centuries were carefully edited for modesty. Nevertheless, explicit, personal accounts of rape have found their way into history. But in this white man's country, insults to Indian women are largely lost. The rape of a "squaw" by white men was not deemed important. The Indian woman gave her testimony to no one; it was never solicited, except perhaps orally within her tribe. Testaments comparable to those that white abolitionists took from black slaves do not exist for the Indian. Any documentation of the rape of white and Indian women at the hands of their enemy must be lopsided for this reason.

The first full-length narrative of captivity to become a popular success in its time was that of Mary Rowlandson, the "goodwife" of the first ordained minister of Lancaster, Massachusetts. She was taken captive in 1676, the sole adult survivor of a massacre of more than forty persons. Mrs. Rowlandson, as befitting her station, sprinkled her story with quotes from the Scriptures and plentiful thanks to the power of God for her divine deliverance, and her writing style became a model for many of the narratives that followed. Toward the end of her story, Mrs. Rowlandson made the following declaration:

> I have been in the midst of those roaring lions and savage bears that feared neither God nor man nor the devil by night and day, alone and in company, sleeping all sorts together, and yet no one of them ever offered the least abuse of unchastity to me in word or action. Though some are ready to say I speak it for my own credit, I speak it in the presence of God, and to his glory.

Mrs. Rowlandson's case was not atypical. Isabella McCoy, captured by the St. Francis Indians in 1747, also averred that she had not been raped. The anonymous narrator of the battles of Trenton and Princeton, quoted in the previous chapter, claimed that British abuse of women had been "far Worse in this Respect than an Indian War, for I Never heard nor read of their Ravishing of Women . . ." Another anonymous author, who penned A Narrative of the Capture of Certain Americans at Westmoreland (1780), saw fit to comment, "I don't remember to have heard an instance of these savages offering to violate the chastity of any of the fair sex who have fallen into their hands." He offered as reason, "This is principally owing to a natural inappetency in their constitution."

Frederick Drimmer, who edited a collection of captivity narratives, wrote, "Anyone reading early accounts of captivity among the Indians is struck by the fact that female prisoners do not appear to have been abused by the Indians in the eastern section of the country." He presents a blanket summation from General James Clinton, who participated in a punitive expedition against the Iroquois in New York in 1799: "Bad as the savages are, they never violate the chastity of any women their prisoners."

Clinton and the anonymous Westmoreland author were writing of the Iroquois, a most remarkable nation whose structure was based on a matrilineal foundation in which women played an important political role, unlike most other Indian tribes and unlike existing white civilization. This factor may help explain the "natural inappetency." Also, as Drimmer points out, "It was a custom for the braves to make elaborate preparations before going on the warpath, and these included the practice of continence and rites of purification. To abuse a female captive would have weakened the Indians' 'medicine.' "

To this analysis we must add another factor: the natural reluctance on the part of women to admit that sexual abuse has occurred. The common experience of most female captives was to live as an Indian wife for the duration of their captivity. Such was the experience of Mary Jemison, the White Woman of the Gene-see, who was assigned a husband when she came of age. The equation of "to live as Indian wife" with rape is a matter of delicate interpretation, dependent in part on the length of captiv-ity. In any event, the woman had no say in the matter, and "the fate worse than death" could remain a secret if the woman denied it. An admission of sexual use after rescue would bring ridicule and sniggerings from the white society to which she was returned, in addition to rejection as a fitting, chaste partner by husband or future spouse. Female captives were closely scrutinized after rescue for signs of moral degradation.

Love relationships, such as Mary Jemison's, or at least rela-tionships of tolerable accommodation, certainly did occur between captor and captive, and early stories of Indian captivity are dotted with cases of whites, both male and female (and especially chil-dren), who preferred to remain with their new relations after a rescue. In the case of the adult white woman, to replace a relatively secure status as Indian wife with a questionable future in white society as a "defiled" woman could be reason enough to choose to remain with the Indians. "Some women who had been delivered up afterwards found means to escape and run back to the Indian towns," wrote Colonel Henry Bouquet at the close of Pontiac's War in Ohio in 1764. "Some who could not make their escape clung to their savage acquaintance at parting, and continued many days in bitter lamentation, even refusing sustenance."

But these touching cases occurred less and less as the white man pushed westward with increasing violence, and the Indian, in retreat, responded in kind. "From all history and tradition, it would appear that neither seduction, prostitution, nor rape was known in the calendar of crimes of this rude savage race, until the females were contaminated by the embrace of civilized men," wrote historian Ebenezer Mix in 1842. Rape shrouded in the polite language of "insult," "outrage," and "submission," or the euphemism, "he treated me as his wife," began to make an appearance in the later narratives of white female captives, and male captives who lived to tell the tale offered succinct commentary on the treatment of the female captives that they saw.

The enterprising Abbie Gardner-Sharp twenty-eight years after the fact wrote and published a lengthy narrative of her three months' captivity among the Sioux in Iowa when she was thirteen years old. Young Abbie and three adult white women, Mrs. Thatcher, Mrs. Marble and Mrs. Noble, were the sole survivors of the Spirit Lake Massacre, a bloody ambush on a settlement of pioneer families in March of 1857. Abbie and Mrs. Noble were sold by their captors to a band of Yanktons. Abbie writes nothing of her own sexual abuse, or lack of it, during captivity, except by implication in her story of the death of Mrs. Noble.

One evening as she and Mrs. Noble were preparing to go to sleep, a son of Chief Inkpaduta by the name of Roaring Cloud came into their tepee and "ordered Mrs. Noble out." This was highly irregular behavior. By Indian custom, the two women belonged to the master of the tepee, an old Yankton warrior with only one leg, but the son of the chief apparently felt he had privileges. Abbie records:

> I told her she had better, as I feared he would kill her if she did not. But still she refused. Mrs. Noble was the only one of us who ever dared to refuse obedience to our masters. Naturally of an independent nature, and conscious of her superiority to her masters in everything except brute force, it was hard for her to submit to their arbitrary and inhuman mandates. Frequently before, she had refused obedience, but in the end was always compelled to submit . . . No sooner did she positively refuse to comply with Roaring Cloud's demand, than, seizing her by the arm with one hand, and a great stick of wood . . . in the other, he dragged her from the tent.

Roaring Cloud dealt Mrs. Noble three blows that killed her while Abbie trembled in the tent, "expecting he would return to serve me in the same manner." But the son of Inkpaduta came back to the tent, "washed his bloody hands, had a few high words with the Yankton, and lay down to sleep."

The narrative of spirited Fanny Kelly, captured by the Oglala Sioux in South Dakota in 1864 and later traded to the Blackfoot Sioux who traded her back to the whites, is blithely free of any hint of sexual use by her captors, although she describes with apparent innocence the several braves who went out of their way to do her favors. An altogether different version of Mrs. Kelly's captivity— from a male Indian point of view—is told in Stanley Vestal's *Sitting Bull*, a history of the Sioux leader gathered from the big chief's descendants. In the Indian version the white woman was plainly "used as a wife." Fanny Kelly may be forgiven for her sins of omission. Vestal's book was published seventy years after Mrs. Kelly's captivity and still he could not resist some between-us-boys jokes surrounding her predicament and her given name of Fanny.

In *Massacres of the Mountains*, an early history of the Indian wars of the Far West by J. P. Dunn, published in 1886, the author took pains to distinguish the mores of the Plains Indians, on the run and highly victimized by whites, from the mores of the eastern Indians in less desperate times. He quoted a Captain Johnson regarding the treatment of women (white, Mexican, or Indian) by the Apaches: "Women when captured are taken as wives by those who capture them. . . . The most unfortunate thing which can befall a captive woman is to be claimed by two persons. In this case she is either shot or delivered up for indiscriminate violence." This system of adjudication, Dunn said, was the standard Apache method of preventing quarrels. "Other property was similarly treated. If a horse was claimed as booty by two warriors, they must adjust their differences speedily or the animal was shot."

Discussing the causes that led to the Sand Creek Massacre, in which the Colorado cavalry slaughtered a village of Cheyenne and sexually mutilated the bodies of men, women and children, Dunn wrote:

> There is a certain amount of justice in the theory of *meting to a man in his own measure* [italics mine], and the people of Colorado had old scores to pay in the accounts of murder, robbery and rape. The treatment of women by any Indians is usually bad, but by the Plains Indians especially so. When a woman is captured by a war party she is the common property of all of them, each night, till they reach their village, when she becomes the special property of her individual captor, who may sell or gamble her away when he likes. If

she resists she is "staked out,"* that is to say, four pegs are driven into the ground and a hand or foot tied to each, to prevent struggling. She is also beaten, mutilated, or even killed for resistance.

To support his argument Dunn quoted from the sworn statement of Lucinda Ewbanks, twenty-four, as taken down by two cavalry officers. Mrs. Ewbanks' story and those of Laura Roper, seventeen, Mrs. Martin, and Mrs. Snyder, who hanged herself before the cavalry arrived to rescue her, were well known to the people of Colorado and their misfortunes were used to inflame the troops to commit similar atrocities against Indian women at Sand Creek in the name of vengeance.

Lucinda Ewbanks was captured in August, 1864, when a Cheyenne war party attacked a frontier settlement on the Little Blue River in Kansas. She was taken to the lodge of an old chief whose name she could not remember. According to her sworn statement, "He forced me, by the most terrible threats and menaces, to yield my person to him. He treated me as his wife. He then traded me to Two Face, a Sioux, who did not treat me as a wife, but forced me to do all menial labor done by squaws, and he beat me terribly. Two Face traded me to Black Foot, a Sioux, who treated me as his wife, and because I resisted him, his squaws abused and ill-used me. . . . I was better treated among the Sioux than the Cheyennes; that is, the Sioux gave me more to eat. With the Cheyennes I was often hungry."

Lucinda Ewbanks' short statement, notarized by the two cavalry officers, was appended to an apologia by Governor Evans of Colorado for the Sand Creek Massacre.

The most famous captivity rape of the West, the story of Josie Meeker, Arvilla Meeker and Flora Ellen Price, was printed as a government report by the U.S. House of Representatives. Their reluctant testimony, given under emotional duress, formed the explosive core of the White River Ute Commission Investigation, an investigation that sealed the fate of the Utes in Colorado.

---

* In 1971 one of the Vietnam veterans interviewed by Lucy Komisar told her, "We were recons and we went into a village in Quang Tri Province and they had ARVN's working there. They captured a medic, as they called her, and her boyfriend, who was with her. Automatically they killed him. They just kind of staked her out on the stakes, you know, on pungi stakes, and just everybody repeatedly raped her, even some of the GI's from my platoon."

Nathan Meeker, a newspaperman, poet and agrarian reformer, took a job as Indian Agent in Colorado with the messianic aim of turning the Utes into farmers. When the Utes resisted Meeker's attempts to "civilize" them, the thwarted agent grew increasingly sympathetic to the Colorado mining interests that desired the removal of all Indians from the gold-rich territory. Distrust and minor skirmishes multiplied on both sides, and Meeker finally sent a telegram to Washington calling for the cavalry as a show of force. The cavalry marched to the edge of the Ute reservation at Milk River and met with several bands of armed Utes who demanded to know why they had come. Tensions rose, a shot was fired and general fighting broke out. News of the battle quickly spread to White River, where Meeker had his Agency compound. The White River Utes descended on the unarmed compound on September 29, 1879. They murdered Meeker and his workmen and carried off the three women. The Utes surrendered their female captives twenty-three days later.

Government Agent Charles Adams, who arranged the rescue, conducted the interrogation of the three women. He drew forth the story of their outrage on his second try. The women had compelling reasons for their initial unwillingness to testify. Flora Ellen Price's husband had been murdered in the massacre. Left a widow with two small children at the age of sixteen, she maintained that if the story of her rape became public knowledge it would kill her chance for remarriage. Arvilla Meeker, sixty-four, the murdered Indian Agent's wife, was a devoutly religious pioneer woman who was used to keeping her own counsel. As an example of the sexual mores of the time, her own husband had never been able to mention the subject of obstetrics to her, although she had birthed five children. Yet it was she, and not her solemn daughter, Josie, who eventually demanded that the women's full story be told. Josie Meeker, twenty-two, was perhaps in the greatest conflict. She felt a strong allegiance to many of the local Utes who had studied at her Agency school. Possessed of unquenchable social conscience, she, more than the others, understood the political implications of a public admission of rape, and to what ends the admission would be used.

The three women gave their testimony to Adams in secret, and for a full year afterward they continued to deny it in public to any reporter who questioned them. Their denials did them little good. The press had a field day with innuendos and Josie was a special target. The Denver *Tribune* hinted that Josie's captor had been a lovelorn admirer and a story circulated that she had contracted syphilis during her captivity. In fact this may well have been the case for she died three years later in Washington, where the government had given her a secretarial job as indemnification. During the last three years of her life Josie Meeker managed to maintain her social values. On her own time she taught a Sunday School class for black children. Her students went to her funeral.

Recorded in the newly developed Pitman shorthand and set in type by the Government Printing Office, the women's testimony comes through in all of its ambivalence, fear and modesty.

JOSIE MEEKER: When our room filled with smoke we ran out. The Indians were so busy carrying off blankets and goods that they did not see us at first. We ran across the street and through the gate into the field.

Q.—Were the Indians on foot or horseback?

A.—On foot. They left the blankets and called to us to stop. One called to me and said, "Come to me. No shoot you." I said, "Going to shoot?" he said, "No." I said, "Better not," and then he took me down to the camp.

Q.—Who was that?

A.—Pah-sone. I looked back. One had hold of Mrs. Price and one hold of Mother.

Q.—How long did Pah-sone keep you?

A.—All the time.

Q.—Did Pah-sone treat you well while you were with him?

A.—Well? I do not know. No better than what I expected.

Q.—This of course is an official investigation and I must get at all the facts. It is not to be published in the newspapers or anything of that kind. I wish to hear the full truth in regard to the matter.

A.—Of course we were insulted a good many times; we expected to be.

Q.—What do you mean by insult, and what did it consist of?

A.—Of outrageous treatment at night.

Q.—Am I to understand that they outraged you several times at night?

A.—Yes, sir.

Q.—Did they threaten to kill you if you did not comply?

A.—He did not threaten to kill—Pah-sone did not—only on one occasion. I asked him if he wanted to kill me. He said, "Yes." I said,

"Get up and shoot me and let me alone." He turned over and did not say anything more that night.

Q.—Was it a constant thing?

A.—No, not all the time. He was away twice, making all together a week.

Q.—He was the one who did it first?

A.—Yes, sir.

Q.—How long after the capture?

A.—The same night—Monday. Of course they were drunk and we dared not refuse them to any great extent. A good many times I pushed him off and made a fuss and raised a difficulty.

Q.—Was it done while his own squaws were in the tent?

A.—Yes, sir.

Q.—And they knew about it?

A.—Yes, sir.

Q.—Did any others do the same thing?

A.—No, sir. Not to me. He took me as his squaw, and of course the rest dared not come around.

Q.—Have you told this to anybody besides your mother?

A.—Yes, sir. Inspector Pollock interviewed us. And I believe, also, Dr. Avery of Denver. She is a lady physician in Denver. Of course we don't want the newspapers to get hold of it.

Q.—Did you tell Mrs. Avery that she must not make it known?

A.—She will not. The Indians delight in telling such things. It is generally talked around at the camp, and a good many white settlers who live around the borders call in now and then, and of course they will spread it if they can.

Q.—Did not they [the Indians] seem to think it was very wrong?

A.—No; they thought it was a pretty good thing to have a white squaw. His squaw told me I must not make a fuss about it. I think she felt sorry for me but she did not dare do anything for me. Jane said, "If he wants to protect you I cannot help it." I told her I did not think much of the protection.

Arvilla Delight Meeker was wounded in the shoulder during the massacre. She described how the ambush occurred just as the settlers were finishing dinner.

ARVILLA MEEKER: I guess I had not wiped more than two plates before firing commenced. . . . We were running away and got into the sage brush and when the ball struck me I dropped on the ground so that I would not be so much of a mark, and as I lay there

I saw them capture Josie and Mrs. Price. I thought they would not see me, but as soon as they had captured the others they came to me.

Q.—As to the outrages, what of them?

A.—It was made known to me that if I did not submit I would be killed or subjected to something of that kind, and after I gave up nothing was said about it. Douglas I had connection with once and no more. I was afraid he had disease.

Q.—He forced you to submit?

A.—Yes, sir. His squaw was gone that night. The Indians talked about matters and things until twelve o'clock. After they went away he came to my bed.

Q.—Was he drunk then?

A.—No, sir.

Q.—Had you been notified that you would have to submit?

A.—He himself had not but all the rest had. His children said I had to be Ute squaw that night, and used indecent language. One great advantage in it was that he was protection for me from the other Indians. Douglas was chief and the rest dared not approach me, and so that was better than the rest. The children were cross and all of them were cross. I do not know as his wife ever spoke to me.

Q.—Did she know of what had happened?

A.—I guess she knew it.

After her husband was murdered, Flora Ellen Price and her two children were captured by some Uncompahgre Utes and later were transferred to the camp of Johnson, a White River medicine man.

Q.—Did any of the Utes treat you badly or strike you?

FLORA ELLEN PRICE: No, none of them struck me.

Q.—What did they do?

A.—I do not like to say. You know, of course, and can judge.

Q.—This is an official investigation on the part of the government and I cannot guess at these things. It is your place to state, in order that we may know the extent of the crime and who the guilty parties are.

A.—It will not be made public in the papers, will it?

Q.—Certainly not through this Commission.

A.—Well, this Uncompahgre Ute and Johnson outraged me.

Q.—Johnson, the old man himself?

A.—Yes, sir; the old man himself.

Q.—Did any others besides Johnson outrage your person?

A.—And the Uncompahgre Ute, these two were all.

Q.—Was it by force?

A.—Yes, sir. By force.

Q.—None of the others attempted it?

A.—No, sir; none of the others attempted it.

Q.—Did any of them treat you kindly?

A.—Yes, sir. Mrs. Johnson treated me very kindly—that is, Susan. She wept over my troubles and said she was sorry for what happened at the agency. She said she did not want them to kill at the agency.

Q.—Did she know what Johnson had done to you?

A.—No, sir; she did not.

Q.—Is there anything further you wish to state?

A.—No; only that I want to have those Utes taken and killed, and I want to have the privilege of killing Johnson and that Uncompahgre Ute myself.

The "Susan" mentioned in Flora Price's testimony was the younger sister of Chief Ouray, leader of all the Utes in Colorado. Once she herself had been captured by some Arapahoe. Arvilla Meeker's captivity account also mentioned the friendliness and intercession of Susan, who, when the Ute men held council to decide whether or not to give up the three women, stormed the assembly to demand that the women be freed.

Chief Ouray was the token Indian representative on the government commission that investigated the White River Massacre. When the white women's testimony regarding their outrage was read to him, he replied, "The oath of a woman is almost worthless among the Indians."

Every Indian who came forward to testify at Ouray's urging, including Chiefs Douglas and Johnson, denied any firsthand knowledge of the events at White River. Ouray patiently told the commission, "Show me any act of law by which a man is compelled to 'criminate himself." Nevertheless, Douglas was sent off to Fort Leavenworth and soon after that the Utes were driven from their home to a small, unprofitable corner of Colorado.

It was land the government was after, and the government got it.

And what of the rape of Indian women by white men? Dee

Brown wrote of the American West, "Only occasionally was the voice of an Indian heard, and then more often than not it was recorded by the pen of a white man. The Indian was the dark menace of the myths, and even if he had known how to write in English, where would he have found a printer or a publisher?"

Where would she have found . . . ?

Commission reports, massacre investigations and records of treaty meetings between white men and Indian men offer a rich source of material on American Indian history, but as Chief Ouray said, the oath of an Indian woman was "almost worthless" to all concerned. If the white woman suffered rape at the hands of the Indian, the treatment of a "squaw" at the hands of a white man was far worse—but if she lived to tell the story it was not recorded.

In April, 1871, a vigilante group of Americans, Mexicans and Papago Indians assaulted an enclave of Aripava Apaches near Camp Grant, Arizona. The Apaches had been on friendly terms with the neighboring ranchmen and were even flying the American flag. Dispatched to the scene, Dr. C. B. Briesly, Camp Grant's surgeon, reported, "The dead bodies of some twenty-one women and children were lying scattered over the ground; those who had been wounded in the first instance had their brains beaten out with stones. Two of the best-looking squaws were lying in such a position, and from the appearance of the genital organs and of their wounds, there can be no doubt that they were first ravished and then shot. Nearly all of the dead were mutilated. . . . While going over the ground we came upon a squaw who was unhurt, but were unable to get her to come in and talk, she not feeling very sure of our good intentions."

Lieutenant Royal Whitman, commander of the post at Camp Grant, reported that the vigilantes had taken several Apache children as captives. The survivors pleaded with him, "Get them back for us. Our little boys will grow up slaves and our girls, as soon as they are large enough, will be diseased prostitutes to get money for whoever owns them."

What occurred at Camp Grant was not very different from the Sand Creek Massacre of November 29, 1864, except that Sand Creek was an official U.S. Cavalry operation. Members of the 1st and 3rd Colorado Volunteers, under the direction of Colonel John M. Chivington, whose rallying cry was "Boys, remember our slaughtered women and children," descended on a village of Cheyenne. The boys remembered by practicing sexual mutilation.

In the investigation that followed the Sand Creek disgrace, Corporal Amos C. Miksch of Company E, 1st Colorado Cavalry, testified, "Next morning, after they were dead and stiff, these men pulled out the bodies of the squaws and pulled them open in an indecent manner. I heard men say they had cut out the privates, but did not see it myself. It was the Third Colorado men who did these things."

Lieutenant James Connor added, "In going over the battle-ground the next day I did not see a body of man, woman or child but was scalped, and in many instances their bodies were mutilated in the most horrible manner—men, women and children's privates cut out, etc. I heard one man say that he had cut out a woman's private parts and had them for exhibition on a stick. . . . I also heard of numerous instances in which men had cut out the private parts of females and stretched them over the saddle-bows and wore them over their hats while riding in the ranks."

In the tragic history of the Nez Percé, hounded into oblivion, we can glimpse through indirect reference the special fate of Nez Percé women. L. V. McWhorter, who was adopted into the tribe, wrote down the oral history of the Nez Percé as he heard it. He concluded that the Nez Percé story was full of "ghastly, unprintable disclosures" regarding "the stalking spectre of rape."

So distasteful to him were these stories of rape by white men that McWhorter could not bring himself to deal with them in his book. From the blind centenarian and tribal historian Wottolen, he recorded one edited fragment: "A Nez Percé woman known as Mrs. Jim was found dead one morning somewhere around White Bird [the Nez Percé winter camp]. Three known white men had done this, murdering her in a very brutal manner not printable. Nobody was punished for this crime."

Thus does "unprintability" erase the record.

A short statement regarding the rape of Indian women by United States soldiers is contained in the testament of Young Chief Joseph of the Nez Percé. In a narrative recorded after he and his dwindling band were in captive exile, Joseph described from his own perspective the ambush of some tourist campers in Yellowstone National Park as the faltering Nez Percé were running from General O. O. Howard's cavalry units.

On the way we captured one white man and two white women. We released them at the end of three days. They were treated kindly. The women were not insulted. Can the white soldiers tell me of one time when Indian women were taken prisoners and held three days and then released without being insulted? Were the Nez Percé women who fell into the hands of General Howard's soldiers treated with as much respect? I deny that a Nez Percé was ever guilty of such a crime.

But the Indian woman herself never spoke.

SLAVERY

The American experience of the slave South, which spanned two centuries, is a perfect study of rape in all its complexities, for the black woman's sexual integrity was deliberately crushed in order that slavery might profitably endure.

In contrast to rape during the Indian wars, which was largely casual and retaliatory—men getting even with men through the convenient vehicle of a woman's body—rape under the Patriarchal Institution, as it was named by the patriarchs, was built into the system. The white man wanted the Indian's land, but the coin he extracted from blacks was forced labor. This difference in purpose affected the white man's relations with, and use of, the black woman. Rape in slavery was more than a chance tool of violence. It was an *institutional* crime, part and parcel of the white man's subjugation of a people for economic and psychological gain.

The Patriarchal Institution took the form of white over black but it also took the form of male over female, or more specifically, of white male over black female. Unlike the Indian woman who was peripheral to the conquest of land, the black woman was critical to slavery. She was forced into dual exploitation as both laborer and reproducer. Her body, in all of its parts, belonged outright to her white master. She had no legal right of refusal, and if the mere recognition of her physical bondage was not enough, the knife, the whip and the gun were always there to be used against her. Forced sexual exploitation of the black woman under slavery was no offhand enterprise. Total control over her reproductive system meant a steady supply of slave babies, and slave children, when they reached the age of six or eight, were put to work; it did not matter whether they were full-blooded or mulatto.

An important psychologic advantage, which should not be underestimated, went hand in glove with the economic. Easy access to numerous, submissive female bodies—and individual resistance was doomed—afforded swaggering proof of masculinity to slaveholding males, while it conversely reduced and twisted the black man's concept of *his* role.

"Sexually as well as in every other way, Negroes were utterly subordinated," writes historian Winthrop D. Jordan of the slave South. "White men extended their dominion over the Negroes to the bed, where the sex act itself served as a ritualistic re-enactment of the daily pattern of social dominance." Jordan's words are too temperate. "Bed" is as much a euphemism as not, and "ritualistic re-enactment" implies a stately minuet of manners—a vastly inadequate description of the brutal white takeover and occupation of the black woman's body.

"Lawdy, lawdy, them was tribbolashuns!" an eighty-seven-year-old ex-slave by the name of Martha Jackson told a recorder for the Federal Works Project in Alabama (who wrote down her words in an approximation of her dialect). "Wunner dese here womans was my Antie en she say dad she skacely call to min' he e'r whoppin' her, 'case she was er breeder woman en' brought in chillum ev'y twelve mont's jes lak a cow bringin' in a calf."

Martha Jackson's choice of imagery was grounded in the realities of slavery. Female slaves were expected to "breed"; some were retained expressly for that purpose. In the lexicon of slavery, "breeder woman," "childbearing woman," "too old to breed" and "not a breeding woman" were common descriptive terms. In-country breeding was crucial to the planter economy after the African slave trade was banned in 1807, and the slave woman's value increased in accordance with her ability to produce healthy offspring. Domestic production of slave babies for sale to other slave states became a small industry in the fertile upper South. In fact, it was observed to be the only *reliably* profitable slave-related enterprise. Quite an opposite state of affairs had existed in the North before abolition, where slavery had never been profitable. In colonial Massachusetts, one observer has written, slave babies when weaned "were given away like puppies." But the state of Virginia annually exported between six thousand and twenty thousand homegrown slaves to the deeper South, where the land, the climate and a harsher work load took precedence over fecundity. The Virginia-reared slave, like Virginia leaf tobacco, was always in great demand.

A member of the Virginia legislature used revealing language when he addressed that patrician body in 1831:

> It has always (perhaps erroneously) been considered by steady and old-fashioned people, that the owner of land had a reasonable right to its annual profits; the owner of orchards, to their annual fruits; the owner of brood-mares, to their product; and the owner of female slaves to their increase . . . and I do not hesitate to say, that in its increase consists much of our wealth.

The fellow from Virginia, Mr. Gholson, was attempting to make the point that a slaveholder would not mistreat a female slave *as he would not mistreat his broodmare*, since the "increase" of each needed a period of nurture in order to show a profit. In return for the production of slave babies, the female knowingly bartered for more food and a reduced work load in the weeks before and after birth. But despite Mr. Gholson's protestations, a lightened work load was not an automatic *quid pro quo*.

Nehemiah Caulkins, a white carpenter who worked for a time on a North Carolina rice plantation, presented this picture of breeder women in an antislavery pamphlet of 1839:

> One day the owner ordered the women into the barn, he then went in among them, whip in hand, and told them he meant to flog them all to death; they immediately began to cry out, "What have I done Massa? What have I done Massa?" He replied, "D—n you, I will let you know what you have done, you don't breed, I haven't had a young one from one of you for several months." They told him they could not breed while they had to work in the rice ditches. (The rice grounds are low and marshy, and have to be drained, and while digging or clearing the ditches, the women had to work in mud and water from one to two feet in depth; they were obliged to draw up and secure their frocks about their waist, to keep them out of water, in this manner they frequently had to work from daylight in the morning till it was so dark they could see no longer.) After swearing and threatening for some time, he told them to tell the overseer's wife, when they got in that way, and he would put them upon the land to work.

The Georgia journal of Fanny Kemble, whose husband owned a pair of cotton and rice plantations, records this entry:

> The women who visited me yesterday evening were all in the family way, and came to entreat of me to have the sentence (what else can I call it?) modified which condemns them to assume their labor of hoeing in the field three weeks after their confinement. They knew, of course, that I cannot interfere with their appointed labor, and therefore their sole entreaty was that I would use my influence with Mr. —— [Butler, her husband] to obtain for them a month's respite from labor in the field after childbearing.

Fanny Kemble was unsuccessful in her intercessionary mission.

Breeder women were sometimes blatantly advertised as such, for if they were "proven," they could command a higher price. The following advertisement from the Charleston, South Carolina, *Mercury* became an abolitionist classic:

> NEGROES FOR SALE—A Girl about twenty years of age (raised in Virginia) and her two female children, one four and the other two years old—is remarkably strong and healthy—never having had a day's sickness, with the exception of the small pox, in her life. The children are fine and healthy. She is very prolific in her generating qualities, and affords a rare opportunity to any person who wishes to raise a family of strong and healthy servants for their own use. Any person wishing to purchase will please leave their address at the Mercury office.

It mattered little to the slaveholder who did the actual impregnating, since the "increase" belonged to him by law. Paternity was seldom entered in the slaveholder's record book, and when it did appear, it was strictly for purposes of identification. The female was often *arbitrarily assigned* a sexual partner or "husband" and ordered to mate. Her own preferences in this most intimate of matters may or may not have been taken into account, depending on the paternalistic inclinations of her master. "I wish the three girls you purchest had been all grown," an overseer wrote to an absent master. "They wold then bin a wife a pese for Harise & King & Nathan. Harris has Jane for a wife and Nathan has Edy. But King & Nathan had sum difuculty hoo wold have Edy. I promist

King that I wold in dever to git you to bey a nother woman sow he might have a wife at home."

Sexual activity for the male slave after the day's work was done was considered by the slave and master to be in the nature of a reward, but it is difficult to make such a generalization for the female. The accepted modern authority on slavery, Kenneth M. Stampp, writes, "Having to submit to the superior power of their masters, many slaves were extremely aggressive toward each other." It is consistent with the nature of oppression that within an oppressed group, men abuse women. "We don't care what they do when their tasks are over—we lose sight of them till next day," one planter wrote. "Their morals and manners are in their own keeping. The men may have, for instance, as many wives as they please, so long as they do not quarrel about such matters."

Another slave owner kept marital law and order in the following fashion, as recorded in his diary: "Flogged Joe Goodwyn and ordered him to go back to his wife. Dito Gabriel and Molly and ordered them to come together again. Separate Moses and Anny finally. And flogged Tom Kollock [for] interfering with Maggy Cambell, Sullivan's wife." The narrative of Charles Ball, *Fifty Years in Chains*, tells of a slave woman who was forced to live with a fellow slave whom she thoroughly detested and feared—and who never stopped reminding her that in Africa he had ten wives! That warm, sustained relationships *did* develop between male and female slaves in bondage is a most profound testament to what can only be called humanity, which everything in slave life conspired to destroy.

Field laborer, house servant and breeder woman were the principal economic roles of the female slave, but she was also used by her white owner for his own sexual-recreational pleasure, a hierarchical privilege that spilled over to his neighbors ("I believe it is the custom among the Patriarchs to make an interchange of civilities of this kind," wrote a correspondent in Missouri to a New York newspaper in 1859), and to his young sons eager for initiation into the mysteries of sex. The privilege, apparently, was also expected by visitors. "Will you believe it, I have not humped a single mulatto since I am here," an aide of Steuben's wrote to a friend in condemnation of the lack of hospitality at George Washington's Mount Vernon.

The sexual privilege also filtered down to lower-class white males in the planter's employ (overseers with the power of the whip and craft workers with access to the plantation) and to certain black male slaves ("drivers") who were also handed the whip and directed to play an enforcer role within the system. At the top of the hierarchy, setting the style, was the white master.

Nehemiah Caulkins testified:

> This same planter had a female slave who was a member of the Methodist Church; for a slave she was intelligent and conscientious. He proposed a criminal intercourse with her. She would not comply. He left her and sent for the overseer, and told him to have her flogged. It was done. Not long after, he renewed his proposal. She again refused. She was again whipped. He then told her why she had been twice flogged, and told her he intended to whip her till she should yield. The girl, seeing that her case was hopeless, her back smarting with the scourging she had received and dreading a repetition, gave herself up to be the victim of his brutal lusts.

Solomon Northup, a shanghaied New York freedman who was forced to spend twelve years on a Louisiana plantation and later published his narrative of bondage, wrote a sympathetic description of a field slave, Patsey, who had to endure her master's "attentions."

> Patsey was slim and straight. She stood erect as the human form is capable of standing. There was an air of loftiness in her movement that neither labor, nor weariness, nor punishment could destroy. Truly, Patsey was a splendid animal, and were it not that bondage had enshrouded her intellect in utter and everlasting darkness, would have been chief among ten thousand of her people. She could leap the highest fences, and a fleet hound it was indeed that could outstrip her in a race. No horse could fling her from his back. She was a skillful teamster. She turned as true a furrow as the best, and at splitting rails there was none who could excel her. . . . Such lightning-like motion was in her fingers as no other fingers ever possessed, and therefore it was that in cotton picking time, Patsey was queen of the field.
> Yet Patsey wept oftener, and suffered more, than any of her companions. She had literally been excoriated. Her back bore the scars of a thousand stripes; not because she was of an unmindful and

rebellious spirit, but because it had fallen to her lot to be the slave of a licentious master and a jealous mistress. She shrank before the lustful eye of one, and was in danger even of her life at the hands of the other, and between the two, she was indeed accursed. . . . but not like Joseph, dared she escape from Master Epps, leaving her garment in his hand. Patsey walked under a cloud. If she uttered a word in opposition to her master's will, the lash was resorted to at once, to bring her to subjection; if she was not watchful when about her cabin, or when walking in the yard, a billet of wood, or a broken bottle perhaps, hurled from her mistress's hand, would smite her unexpectedly in the face. The enslaved victim of lust and hate, Patsey had no comfort of her life.

Northup described one incident in the field when he and Patsey were hoeing side by side. Patsey suddenly exclaimed in a low voice, "D'ye see old Hog Jaw beckoning me to come to him?"

Glancing sideways, I discovered him in the edge of the field, motioning and grimacing, as was his habit when half-intoxicated. Aware of his lewd intentions, Patsey began to cry. I whispered her not to look up, and to continue her work as if she had not observed him. Suspecting the truth of the matter, however, he soon staggered up to me in a great rage.

"What did you say to Pats?" he demanded with an oath. I made him some evasive answer which only had the effect of increasing his violence.

"How long have you owned this plantation, say, you d—d nigger?"

Master Epps chased Northup across the field and then returned to Patsey. "He remained about the field an hour or more. . . . Finally Epps came toward the house, by this time nearly sober, walking demurely with his hands behind his back, and attempting to look as innocent as a child."

Patsey's story had a terrible ending. The jealous Epps became convinced that his slave had had relations with a white neighbor. He ordered her stripped, staked and beaten into listlessness. "Indeed, from that time forward she was not what she had been. . . . She no longer moved with that buoyant and elastic step—there was not that mirthful sparkle in her eyes that formerly distinguished her. The bounding vigor—the sprightly, laughter-loving spirit of her youth, was gone."

Narratives such as Northup's, published by the Northern abolitionist press in the nineteenth century, and oral histories of former slaves that the Federal Works Projects Administration collected in the nineteen thirties cast cold light on the life-style of slavery. When the female ex-slave was asked to tell of her experiences, not surprisingly she did not dwell on sex. "Them was tribbolashuns," and a combination of propriety, modesty and acute shame on the part of narrator and recorder must have conspired to close the door on any specific revelations. (Male ex-slaves, because of a freer convention among men, were permitted to discuss the sexual abuse of females.)

But horror at the sexual abuse of enslaved black women was a recurring theme among white female abolitionists. The Grimké sisters of South Carolina and Margaret Douglass and Lydia Maria Child, among others, did not let it rest. They spoke and pamphleteered relentlessly (but alas, delicately—so dictated the times) out of a strong sense of identification with their black sisters in bondage. Margaret Douglass, a Southern white woman who was convicted and jailed in Virginia for teaching black children to read, wrote from prison in 1853:

> The female slave, however fair she may have become by various comminglings of her progenitors, or whatever her mental and moral acquirements may be, knows that she is a slave, and, as such, powerless beneath the whims and fancies of her master. If he casts upon her a desiring eye, she knows that she must submit; and her only thought is, that the more gracefully she yields, the stronger and longer hold she may perchance retain upon the brutal appetite of her master. Still, she feels her degradation, and so do others with whom she is connected. She has parents, brothers, sisters, a lover, perhaps, who all suffer through her and with her.

The politically keen Mrs. Douglass, writing to a white audience, then added these lines:

> White mothers and daughters of the South have suffered under this custom for years; they have seen their dearest affections

trampled upon, their hopes of domestic happiness destroyed. I cannot use too strong language on this subject, for I know it will meet a heartfelt response from every Southern woman. They know the facts, and their hearts bleed under its knowledge, however they may have attempted to conceal their discoveries.*

Mrs. Douglass' analysis went further:

Will not the natural impulses rebel against what becomes with them a matter of force? For the female slave knows that she must submit to the caprices of her master; that there is no way of escape. And when a man, black though he may be, knows that he may be compelled, at any moment, to hand over his wife, his sister, or his daughter, to the loathed embraces of the man whose chains he wears, how can it be expected he will submit without feelings of hatred and revenge taking possession of his heart?

The slave's revenge took many forms—although white retribution was swift and certain. A traveler through the South wrote in 1856:

A Negress was hung this year in Alabama, for the murder of her child. At her trial, she confessed her guilt. She said her owner was the father of the child, and that her mistress knew it, and treated her so cruelly in consequence, that she had killed it to save it from further suffering, and also to remove a provocation to her own ill-treatment.

A visitor to Mississippi in 1836 sent a letter to a Northern friend:

The day I arrived at this place there was a man by the name of G—— murdered by a Negro man that belonged to him. [The black man was publicly lynched.] G—— owned the Negro's wife and was in the habit of sleeping with her! The Negro said he had killed him and he believed he should be rewarded in heaven for it.

---

* Kenneth Stampp unfairly uses this portion of Mrs. Douglass' letter to buttress his contention that "Southern white women apparently believed that they suffered most from the effects of miscegenation."

The narrative of Charles Ball tells of a mulatto slave woman, Lucy, who rebelled against her forced sexual servitude to her white owner and successfully plotted with her slave lover, Frank, to kill him. Charles Ball himself played a role in their apprehension and confession. Lucy and Frank "were tried before some gentlemen of the neighborhood, who held a court for that purpose," and were hanged at a public gallows. "It was estimated by my master," Ball records, "that there were at least fifteen thousand people present at this scene, more than half of whom were blacks; all the masters, for a great distance round the country, having permitted, or compelled their people to come to this hanging."

The case of Peggy and Patrick received considerable notoriety in New Kent County, Virginia, in 1830. This pair of slaves, who were lovers, were condemned to be hanged for murdering their master. Extenuating circumstances caused the local white citizens of New Kent to submit a petition to the governor asking that punishment for the pair be reduced to "transportation."

One black witness whose testimony was solicited declared that

> the deceased to whom Peggy belonged had had a disagreement with Peggy, and generally kept her confined by keeping her chained to a block and locked up in his meat house; that he [the witness] believed the reason why the deceased had treated Peggy in this way was because Peggy would not consent to intercourse with him, and that he had heard the deceased say that if Peggy did not agree to his request in that way, he would beat her almost to death, that he would barely leave the life in her, and would send her to New Orleans. The witness said that Peggy said the reason she would not yield to his request was because the deceased was her father, and she could not do a thing of that sort with her father. The witness heard the deceased say to Peggy that if she did not consent, he would make him, the witness, and Patrick hold her, to enable him to effect his object.

Since it was the slaveholding class that created the language and wrote the laws pertaining to slavery, it is not surprising that legally the concept of raping a slave simply did not exist. One cannot rape one's own property. The rape of one man's slave by another white man was considered a mere "trespass" in the eyes of plantation law. The rape of one man's slave *by another slave* had no official recognition in law at all.*

Moral objections to the "liberties" that the slaveholder and his overseer took as a matter of course were voiced within the oddly angled framework of miscegenation, amalgamation, mixture of the races, licentiousness, degradation and lust. Typically for the power class, the slave's coerced participation in the act was turned on *her*. Her passive submission—the rule of survival in slavery—was styled as concubinage, prostitution or promiscuity when it was alluded to at all. Even the Northern abolitionists shied away from defining coercive sexual abuse under slavery as criminal rape, preferring to speak emotionally, but guardedly, of illicit passion and lust. Modern historians tend to operate under the same set of blinders.

The patriarchal institution of marriage dovetailed with the patriarchal institution of slavery to prevent perception, by even the most enlightened observers, of a concept of sexual rights and bodily integrity for the female slave. In the nineteenth century, a married woman was considered by law to be the property of her husband, and any abuse to her person was considered, by law, to be an abuse to his property. If the woman was not married, the abuse was to *her father's* property. But slaves were not permitted to marry legally, and criminal sexual abuse of a female slave (a rape) could not be considered by law an affront to her slave "husband" or slave father, *who had no rights of their own.* The examples we find in abolitionist literature that express concern over the sexual abuse of female slaves are frequently couched in terms of sympathy for the abused women's *husbands!* As a Maryland lawyer observed at the time, "Slaves are bound by our criminal laws generally, yet we do not consider them as the objects of such laws as relate to the commerce between the sexes. A slave has never maintained an action against the violator of his bed." Of *his* bed.

Statutory prohibitions against interracial sex, or more accurately, against the act of sex between slaveholder and slave, were on

---

* Some evidence exists that masters attempted to police, in their own fashion, the more blatant abuses that male slaves committed against females. An 1828 advertisement in the Elkton, Maryland, *Press* for runaway "Negro George Anderson, about 21 or 22 years of age," declared informatively, "A few days before he absconded he attempted to commit a rape upon a young female of his own color, the punishment for which has caused his running off."

the books of all the slave states from the time they were colonies of the king. Even in South Carolina, where the slave-trading city of Charleston earned a dubious reputation as the libertine capital of North America (a reputation later claimed by New Orleans), and where "interracial liaisons were less carefully concealed than elsewhere on the continent," a grand jury in 1743 took notice of "the too common practice of criminal conversation with Negro and other slave wenches in this province," and scored this conversation—or intercourse—as "an Enormity and Evil of general Ill-Consequence."

But it was "pollution of the white race" and not concern for the rights of slaves that lay behind such pronunciamentos. The laws against "admixture" that white men wrote were not applied to white men. They were applied by white men against white women —as several divorce suits and bastardy charges of the time showed—and they were applied with a special vengeance against those black men who entered into liaisons with white women. (The implications and consequences of this sex-race quadruple standard are still with us. See Chapter 7, "A Question of Race.")

A Louisiana Supreme Court decision of 1851 after some backing and filling proceeded to define concubinage as a "mutual" liaison, although one participant was a slaveholder and the other a female slave bound to him by law and force.

> The slave is undoubtedly subject to the power of his master; but that means a lawful power, such as is consistent with good morals. The laws do not subject the female slave to an involuntary and illicit connexion with her master, but would protect her against that misfortune. It is true, that the female slave is peculiarly exposed . . . to the seductions of an unprincipled master. That is a misfortune; but it is so rare in the case of concubinage that the seduction and temptation are not mutual, that exceptions to the general rule cannot be founded upon it.

It is difficult to gain a clear understanding of concubinage as it was practiced in the slave South. I do not mean to argue the point that all sexual liaisons between white masters and black slaves fall within my extended definition of rape, although such an argument is tempting. For many black women, concubinage was the best bargain that could be struck, a more or less graceful accommodation given the hopeless condition of bondage; certainly for some it was as close to emancipation as possible, short of a run for freedom with Harriet Tubman. But first, last and always, concubinage was a male-imposed condition: a bargain struck on male values exclusively, resting on a foundation of total ownership and control. Accommodation in lieu of forcible seizure could bring a variety of amenities into one's life: relative status, pretty dresses, gold earrings, and the hope—always the hope—of manumission for one's self and children. This last must have been held out to the black concubine like a carrot on a stick. Several slaveholder wills survive in which freedom for a favored slave and her children is provided, along with bequests of money and real property. Sadly, but not surprisingly, the terms of these wills were often successfully challenged in the courts by the slaveholder's lawful heirs.

Sexual exploitation of black women by white men was understood as one of the evils of slavery by the abolitionist movement, even though abolitionists were unable to bring themselves to call it rape. Specific cases of concubinage and "amalgamation" reported by travelers through the South were incorporated, with appropriate moral outrage, into *American Slavery As It Is: Testimony of a Thousand Witnesses*, compiled and collated by the Grimké sisters and Theodore Weld, Angelina Grimké's husband, in 1839. The Grimké testimony, and that of Margaret Douglass, formed the backbone of an 1860 antislavery pamphlet edited by Lydia Maria Child. The abolitionist women, in dealing with the sexual behavior of men, were treading on dangerous ground, bound by conventions that decreed that a man's private life was beyond the pale of political scrutiny. "We forbear to lift the veil of private life any higher," wrote Angelina Grimké, whose brother had sired mulatto slave children. "Let these few hints suffice to give you some idea of what is daily passing behind that curtain which has been so carefully drawn before the scenes of domestic life in slaveholding America."

The "few hints" of which Angelina Grimké wrote and spoke were scandalous enough for the times. "The character of the white ladies of the South, as well as the ladies of color, seems to have been discussed, and the editor of the Courier was of the opinion that the reputation of his paper, and the morals of its readers, might be injuriously affected by publishing the debate," a Northern newspaper reported after a Grimké speech—neatly turning the crime of men into a matter of the "character" of women, in the age-old tradition.

In the winter of 1838–1839, while Weld and the Grimkés were compiling their documentary record of slavery in New York, the English actress Fanny Kemble was in residence on a Georgia island plantation, recording her shocked observations in a journal that remained suppressed for twenty-five years. The celebrated and strong-minded Miss Kemble had inadvisedly married a young Philadelphian, Pierce Butler, who inherited a pair of cotton and rice plantations employing more than one thousand slaves. The marriage went badly, but it proved invaluable to history, for Fanny Kemble traveled with her husband to Georgia and wrote down what she saw in the form of letters to a friend.

As Fanny Kemble made the acquaintance of slaves on her husband's plantation, it dawned on her that the complexion of some of them was decidedly light, and for a very specific reason—the plantation's overseer, John King. She described the slave woman Betty:

> Of this woman's life on the plantation I subsequently learned the following circumstances. She was the wife of head man Frank . . . the head driver—second in command to the overseer. His wife [Betty]—a tidy, trim intelligent woman with a pretty figure . . . was taken from him by the overseer . . . and she had a son by him whose straight features and diluted color . . . bear witness to his Yankee descent. I do not know how long Mr. King's occupation of Frank's wife continued, or *how the latter endured the wrong done to him* [italics mine]. This outrage *upon this man's rights* [italics mine] was perfectly notorious among all the slaves; and his hopeful offspring, Renty, allud[ed] to his superior birth on one occasion.

Betty was not the only slave on the Butler plantation whom the white overseer, King, forced into sexual service, Fanny Kemble discovered.

> Before reaching the house I was stopped by one of our multitudinous Jennies with a request for some meat, and that I would help her with some clothes for Ben and Daphne, of whom she had the sole charge; these are two extremely pretty and interesting looking mulatto children, whose resemblance to Mr. King had induced me to ask Mr. Butler, when I first saw them, if he did not think they

must be his children. He said they were certainly like him, but Mr. King did not acknowledge the relationship. I asked Jenny who their mother was. "Minda." "Who their father?" "Mr. King." . . . "Who told you so?" "Minda, who ought to know." "Mr. King denies it." "That's because he never has looked upon them, nor done a thing for them." "Well, but he acknowledged Renty as his son, why should he deny these?" "Because old master was here then when Renty was born, and he made Betty tell all about it, and Mr. King had to own it; but nobody knows anything about this, and so he denies it."

The Butler plantation operated under absentee ownership for most of the year and the white overseer, King, was left in charge as a virtual dictator. The power of his station, and its sexual privileges, extended to those directly below him in the chain of command, the black drivers, who themselves were slaves. Owners, overseers, drivers, neighboring white men—all could force the black woman against her will, and she was held morally responsible for the injury done to her. Fanny Kemble herself started from this premise, but rejected it in time.

Quizzing more of her husband's slaves about the paternity of their offspring and hearing the names King and Walker (a white mill hand) and Morris (a black driver) repeated by many of them, she recorded:

Almost beyond my patience with this string of detestable details, I exclaimed—foolishly enough, heaven knows— "Ah! but don't you know—did nobody ever tell or teach any of you that it is a sin to live with men who are not your husbands?" Alas, Elizabeth, what could the poor creature answer but what she did, seizing me at the same time vehemently by the wrist: "Oh yes, missis, we know—we know all about dat well enough; but we do anything to get our poor flesh some rest from de whip; when he made me follow him into de bush, what use me tell him no? He have strength to make me." I have written down the woman's words; I wish I could write down the voice and look of abject misery with which they were spoken. Now you will observe that the story was not told to me as a complaint; it was a thing long past and over, of which she only spoke in the natural course of accounting for her children to me. I make no comment; what need, or can I add, to such stories? But how is such a state of things to endure? and again, how is it to end?

Kemble privately circulated a handwritten copy of her journal among her friends and it quickly gained an underground reputation as the most explosive insider's antislavery testament. Lydia Maria Child urged her to publish portions of it, at least, as ammunition for the abolitionist cause but Pierce Butler flatly refused permission. As a slaveholder he thought the journal was unseemly, which it was. As a husband he could withhold consent, by law, to any publication of his wife's, which he did. The journal, Kemble's antislavery views, and her equally daring belief in equality in marriage, figured prominently in Butler's eventual suit for divorce. Butler won custody of their two children and the visitation-rights agreement stipulated that Kemble must do nothing to embarrass him. In 1863, earning her own living again on the English stage, Fanny Kemble finally published her Georgia journal. By that time the War Between the States was well under way and Harriet Beecher Stowe's novel, based in part on the Weld-Grimké pamphlet, had stolen much of her thunder.

The appointed roles of concubine and breeder woman forcibly progressed to outright prostitution in the last decades of slavery. Traders dispensed with pretense and openly sold their prettiest and "near-white" female chattel for sexual use on the New Orleans market. The cavalier term was "fancy girl." The place was the French Exchange in the grand rotunda of the St. Louis Hotel, and the favored hour was noon. This gaudy fillip to the slave trade was no more than a logical extension of institutional rape, the final indignity.

"Every slaveholder is the legalized keeper of a house of ill-fame," the ex-slave and orator Frederick Douglass thundered to an abolitionist meeting in Rochester, New York, in 1850. Douglass' understanding of the dynamics of slavery far surpassed that of any other single person. That night in Rochester he instructed his audience in the dynamics of sexual oppression.

> I hold myself ready to prove that more than a million of women, in the Southern States of this Union, are, by laws of the land, and through no fault of their own, consigned to a life of revolting prostitution; that, by those laws, in many of the States, if a woman, in defence of her own innocence, shall lift her hand against the brutal aggressor, she may be lawfully put to death. I hold myself ready to prove, by the laws of slave states, that three million of the people of

those States are utterly incapacitated to form marriage contracts. I am also prepared to prove that slave breeding is relied upon by Virginia as one of her chief sources of wealth. It has long been known that the best blood of Virginia may now be found in the slave markets of New Orleans. It is also known that slave women, who are nearly white, are sold in those markets, at prices which proclaim, trumpet-tongued, the accursed purposes to which they are to be devoted. Youth and elegance, beauty and innocence, are exposed for sale upon the auction block; while villainous monsters stand around, with pockets lined with gold, gazing with lustful eyes upon their prospective victims.

New Orleans was "fully tenfold the largest market for 'fancy girls,' " Frederic Bancroft wrote in his unmatched study, *Slave Trading in the Old South.* "The prospect of great profit induced their conspicuous display." Beautiful New Orleans! Ambitious slavers chained their prettiest catches to the coffle and headed for the balmy Gulf port. Racing season and Mardi Gras were especially remunerative times. The Hotel St. Louis on Chartres Street was a beehive of activity. Bilingual auctioneers tickled the libido of the sporting men in simultaneous French and English, for a 2 percent commission. The slave women stood near the auctioneer's hammer and smiled, bedecked in bonnets and ribbons. Sales of two thousand dollars and up were not unusual. Private rooms off the main rotunda of the Exchange were always available for the gentleman who wished to inspect his prospective purchase. Inspection at the French Exchange was a serious matter. "To gamblers, traders, saloonkeepers, turfmen and debauchees, owning a 'fancy girl' was a luxurious ideal."

The master-slave relationship is the most popular fantasy perversion in the literature of pornography. The image of a scantily clothed slave girl, always nubile, always beautiful, always docile, who sinks to her knees gracefully and dutifully before her master, who stands with or without boots, with or without whip, is commonly accepted as a scene of titillating sexuality. From the slave harems of the Oriental potentate, celebrated in poetry and dance, to the breathless descriptions of light-skinned fancy women, *de rigueur* in a particular genre of pulp historical fiction, the glorification of forced sex under slavery, institutional rape, has been a part of our cultural heritage, feeding the egos of men while subverting the egos of women—and doing irreparable damage to healthy sexuality in the process. The very words "slave girl" impart to many a vision of voluptuous sensuality redolent of perfumed gardens and soft music strummed on a lyre. Such is the legacy of male-controlled sexuality, under which we struggle.

ADDENDUM: THE CLIOMETRICIANS

By running two sets of statistics into a computer and by making a few unsupported, outlandish statements, "cliometricians" Robert Fogel and Stanley Engerman argue in *Time on the Cross*, their statistical view of slave history, that the sexual abuse of black women by white men was not a common occurrence. Dismissing all known reports collected by the abolitionists, they write:

> Even if all these reports were true, they constituted at most a few hundred cases. By themselves, such a small number of observations out of a population of millions could just as easily be used as proof of the infrequency of the sexual exploitation of black women as of its frequency. The real question is whether such cases were common events that were rarely reported, or whether they were rare events that were frequently reported.

This is a "real question" only for someone who does not want to accept how infrequently cases of sexual assault are reported even in this day and age, let alone in the time when Angelina Grimké wrote, "We forbear to lift the veil of private life any higher."

Fogel and Engerman heap scorn on Fanny Kemble for having a distorted vision of slavery based on her "upper-class English" bias. In fact, Kemble's origins were not upper class. She was the daughter of a family of celebrated but impecunious actors who relied on her income—hence her gamble on a marriage to Pierce Butler. Ignoring the reasons why her *Journal* remained suppressed for twenty-five years, they try to slough it off as "a polemic aimed at rallying British support to the northern cause." It is not a polemic, as the dictionary defines the word, nor was it aimed at the British at the time of its inception. These errors of fact and interpretation could have been cleared up if Fogel and Engerman had read the *Journal* in its entirety, had read the Butler divorce papers, or had read one of the several biographies of Kemble.

Claiming they deal in facts, not conjecture, the authors, by presenting the results of two tangential computer runs, argue that white men did not as a rule molest black women, coyly adding that in their opinion interracial exploitation "would undermine the air of mystery and distinction on which so much of the authority of large planters rested." The first standard they employ is an analysis of the number of mulattoes reported in the 1860 census. Thirty-nine percent of the freedmen in Southern cities were reported as mulatto that year. Among urban slaves the proportion was 20 percent and among rural slaves, who constituted 95 percent of the slave population, the percentage of reported mulattoes was 9.9. Since the overwhelming majority of slaves lived in rural areas, the authors required no sleight of hand to arrive at a figure of 10.4 percent for the census proportion of mulattoes in the entire Southern slave population. From this they conclude, "Far from proving that the exploitation of black women was ubiquitous, the available data on mulattoes strongly militates against that contention."

Several things are wrong here. The progeny of an interracial union can "come up dark" or "come up light," so in itself the color of the offspring is no sure-fire test. Secondly, how were these 1860 census reports obtained? In their supplemental methodology volume Fogel and Engerman tell us that the census was taken by "thousands of enumerators" who were "drawn from the category of literate middle- and upper-class whites," and who used the criterion of skin color. We may assume that the freedmen reported their heritage to the enumerators in person, but do the authors suggest that the slaves did the same, or that the industrious enumerators entered the grounds of each and every plantation and counted heads and judged color from shack to shack?

It is reasonable to assume that the owners did all the reporting for their slaves, particularly in the rural areas, and it is reasonable to assume that plantation owners would be most reluctant to admit to the government that they were siring mulatto children, especially since miscegenation was technically against the law. Plantation owners, I am certain, saw what they wanted to see, and reported what they wanted to report to their class allies, those middle- and upper-class white enumerators. Any census statistic on the proportion of mulattoes on a plantation would be a most unreliable figure. In addition, why do Fogel and Engerman assume that a rape, even in a "non-contraceptive society," as they put it, is necessarily going to result in pregnancy and birth? Periods of fertility being what they are, a rapist plays Russian roulette with more than twenty chambers, yet the authors would have us believe he impregnates every time.

This fallacy in thinking also affects the import of their second set of computed facts. From a limited number of plantation records, the authors of *Time on the Cross* draw up a distribution chart indicating the age of slave mothers at the time they gave birth to their first child. (Unfortunately the cliometricians do not tell us how large a sample was available to them.) Thirty-six percent of all first births took place between the ages of fifteen and nineteen, and an additional 4 percent took place among girls below the age of fifteen. "Some readers might be inclined to stress that 40 percent of all first births took place before the mothers were 20," the authors generously admit—in the fine print of their methodology volume. In their major volume they write only that "the average age at first birth was 22.5, the median age was 20.8."

The *median* age is the more significant of these two figures, since it shows that there were as many first births below the age of 20.8 as there were above. The average age in the Fogel-Engerman computation is beefed up by each first birth that planter records claim occurred at age thirty-five and over; it does not mean that "most" slave women gave birth to their first child at twenty-two.

From this limited presentation Fogel and Engerman extrapolate, "Only abstinence would explain the relative shortage of births in the late-teen ages," and "the high fertility rate of slave women was not the consequence of the wanton impregnation of very young unmarried women by either white or black men." They hopefully conclude, "The high average age of mothers at first birth also suggests that slave parents closely guarded their daughters from sexual contact with men."

Leaving aside the entire question of the accuracy of slave ages, which does not seem to bother the authors, or the incidence of spontaneous miscarriage and folk-remedy abortions for the very young (information certainly not available), what is most troubling about these first-birth statistics is that nowhere are they matched up against the average age of menarche, the time of the first menstrual period. As it happens, the age at which menstruation begins has been perceptibly declining. In 1960 it fell between twelve and thirteen; however, in 1860 first menstruation usually occurred between the ages of sixteen and seventeen. Not only that, there is evidence in modern medicine and anthropology that fertility in the first few years after the onset of menstruation is comparatively low.

Fogel and Engerman's statistics tell us nothing about the sexual exploitation of black women in slavery. Statistical analysis is a valuable tool when it deals with reported crime. Unreported crime, however, remains beyond the magic of computers.

6

The Police-Blotter Rapist

The typical American rapist might be the boy next door. Especially if the boy next door happens to be about 19 years of age and the neighborhood you live in happens to fit the socioeconomic description of lower class or bears the appellation of "ghetto." That is what the statistics show.

One must approach all statistics with caution if one is going to make generalizations, particularly statistics regarding violent crime. Statisticians of crime are routine fact gatherers, and the raw material they work with is usually mined from police-precinct arrest records or from records of convictions. Since there are many acts of rape, few arrests and still fewer convictions, a huge gulf of unavailable information unfortunately exists.

Police in every town and city compile their figures based on those offenders they manage to catch: height, weight, age, race, *modus operandi*, previous arrest record, etc. These figures are forwarded yearly to Washington, fed into computers and ground out again as the most comprehensive national statistics on forcible rape that we have: the *Uniform Crime Reports* put out by the Federal Bureau of Investigation. The *Uniform Crime Reports* and a few intensive studies done by a handful of criminologists allow us to draw up a profile of the All-American rapist.

Before we go any further let us remember that we are traveling on a road marked with cautionary blinking lights. A feminist definition of rape goes beyond the legal, criminal definition with which the nation's system of jurisprudence concerns itself, and later on in this book we will deal with an extended definition of rape and rapists. Then, according to the FBI itself, forcible rape is "one of the most under-reported crimes due primarily to fear and/or embarrassment on the part of the victim," and one in five rapes, or possibly one in twenty, may actually be reported, which skews all recordable statistics. Further, a provable bias by police and juries against the word of the female victim—and particularly the word of a black female victim—drastically cuts down on the number of cases available for study. On a national average, police say that 15 percent of all rape cases reported to them turn out on cursory investigation to be "unfounded"—in other words, they didn't believe the complainant. In reported rape cases where the police do believe the victim, only 51 percent of the offenders are actually apprehended, and of these, 76 percent are prosecuted, and of these, 47 percent are acquitted or have their case dismissed. (In some locales the conviction rate based on arrests is a shocking 3 percent.)

In 1973 the FBI reported 51,000 "founded" cases of forcible rape and attempted rape across the United States, a rise, it noted, of 10 percent over the previous year and a rise of 62 percent over a five-year period. Its figures did not include statutory rape offenses. Seventy-three percent of the FBI's reported cases were completed rapes and the remaining ones were assaults or attempts to commit rape that fell short of completion. If we say conservatively that only one in five rape incidents was actually reported, we arrive at a figure of 255,000 rapes and attempted rapes in these United States in 1973, a figure that I consider to be an unemotional, rock-bottom minimum. For purposes of comparison we should note that during the same year the FBI reported 19,510 murders, 416,270 aggravated assaults and 382,680 robberies.

Murder, assault, rape and robbery are the Big Four of violent crimes, and rape is the fastest-rising. The volume of rapes has increased 62 percent over a five-year period as compared with a 45 percent rise for the other criminal acts. Not given to speculation, the FBI does not venture as to why. It might mean that there has been a rise in the reporting of rapes by victims who have gained courage to speak out from the women's movement—this is most likely—or it could mean a significant rise in hostility and violence directed at women. We simply cannot say for certain.

Of the 51,000 rape cases that the police believed and reported on to the FBI in 1973, they managed a "clearance"—in other words, they made an arrest—in 51 percent of the crimes. Comparatively, the police clearance rate was 79 percent for murder, 63 percent for aggravated assault and 27 percent for robbery offenses. In the field of violent crime, only robbery has a lower clearance rate than rape.

Who, then, are the police-blotter rapists who form the raw material for the *Uniform Crime Reports* analysis? Sixty-one percent are under the age of 25; the largest concentration of offenders is in the 16-to-24-year age range. According to the FBI, 47 percent are black and 51 percent are white, and "all other races comprised the remainder."

Evan Connell, a novelist of some repute, wrote a *tour de force* some years ago entitled *The Diary of a Rapist.* Connell's protagonist, Earl Summerfield, was a timid, white, middle-class civil-service clerk, age 27, who had an inferiority complex, delusions of intellectual brilliance, a wretched, deprived sex life, and an older, nagging, ambitious, "castrating" wife. Connell's book made gripping reading, but the portrait of Earl Summerfield was far from an accurate picture of an average real-life rapist. In fact, Connell's *Diary* contains almost every myth and misconception about rape and rapists that is held in the popular mind. From the no-nonsense FBI statistics and some intensive sociological studies that are beginning to appear, we can see that the typical American rapist is no weirdo, psycho schizophrenic beset by timidity, sexual deprivation, and a domineering wife or mother. Although the psycho rapist, whatever his family background, certainly does exist, just as the psycho murderer certainly does exist, he is the exception and not the rule. The typical American perpetrator of forcible rape is little more than an aggressive, hostile youth who chooses to do violence to women.

We may thank the legacy of Freudian psychology for fostering a totally inaccurate popular conception of rape. Freud himself, remarkable as this may seem, said nothing about rapists. His confederates were slightly more loquacious, but not by much. Jung mentioned rape only in a few of his mythological interpretations. Alfred Adler, a man who understood the power thrust of the male and who was a firm believer in equal rights for women, never mentioned rape in any of his writings. Deutsch and Horney, two brilliant women, looked at rape only from the psychology of the victim.

In the nineteen fifties a school of criminology arose that was decidedly pro-Freudian in its orientation and it quickly dominated a neglected field. But even among the Freudian criminologists there was a curious reluctance to tackle rape head on. The finest library of Freudian and Freudian-related literature, the A. A. Brill Collection, housed at the New York Psychoanalytic Institute, contains an impressive number of weighty tomes devoted to the study of exhibitionism (public exposure of the penis) yet no Freudian or psychoanalytic authority has ever written a major volume on rape. Articles on rape in psychology journals have been sparse to the point of nonexistence.

Why the Freudians could never come to terms with rape is a puzzling question. It would not be too glib to suggest that the male bias of the discipline, with its insistence on the primacy of the penis, rendered it incapable of seeing the forest for the trees. And then, the use of an intuitive approach based largely on analysis of idiosyncratic case studies allowed for no objective sampling. But perhaps most critically, the serious failure of the Freudians stemmed from their rigid unwillingness to make a moral judgment. The major psychoanalytic thrust was always to "understand" what they preferred to call "deviant sexual behavior," but never to condemn.

"Philosophically," wrote Dr. Manfred Guttmacher in 1951, "a sex offense is an act which offends the sex mores of the society in which the individual lives. And it offends chiefly because it generates anxiety among the members of that society. Moreover, prohibited acts generate the greatest anxiety in those individuals who themselves have strong unconscious desires to commit similar or related acts and who have suppressed or repressed them. These actions of others threaten our ego defenses."

This classic paragraph, I believe, explains most clearly the Freudian dilemma.

When the Freudian-oriented criminologists did attempt to grapple with rape they lumped the crime together with exhibitionism (their hands-down favorite!), homosexuality, prostitution, pyromania and even oral intercourse in huge, undigestible volumes that sometimes bore a warning notice on the flyleaf that the material contained herein might advisably be restricted to adults

Guttmacher's *Sex Offenses* and Benjamin Karpman's *The Sexual Offender and His Offenses* were two such products of the fifties. Reading through these and other volumes it is possible to stumble on a nugget of fact or a valuable insight, and we ought to keep in mind, I guess, how brave they must have seemed at the time. After all, they were dealing not only with s-e-x, but with aberrant s-e-x, and in their misguided way they were attempting to forge a new understanding. "Moral opprobrium has no place in medical work," wrote Karpman. A fine sentiment, indeed, yet one hundred pages earlier this same Karpman in this same book defined perversity as "a sexual act that defies the biological goal of procreation."

By and large the Freudian criminologists, who loved to quibble with one another, defined the rapist as a victim of an "uncontrollable urge" that was "infantile" in nature, the result of a thwarted "natural" impulse to have intercourse with his mother. His act of rape was "a neurotic overreaction" that stemmed from his "feelings of inadequacy." To sum up in the Freudian's favorite phrase, he was "a sexual psychopath." Rapists, wrote Karpman, were "victims of a disease from which many of them suffer more than their victims."

This, I should amend, was a picture of the Freudians' favorite rapist, the one they felt they might be able to treat. Dr. Guttmacher, for one, was aware that other types of rapists existed but they frankly bored him. Some, he said, were "sadistic," imbued with an exaggerated concept of masculine sexual activity, and some seemed "like the soldier of a conquering army." "Apparently," he wrote, "sexually well-adjusted youths have in one night committed a series of burglaries and, in the course of one of them, committed rape—apparently just as another act of plunder."

Guttmacher was chief medical officer for the Baltimore criminal courts. His chilling passing observation that rapists might be sexually well-adjusted youths was a reflection of his Freudian belief in the supreme rightness of male dominance and aggression, a common theme that runs through Freudian-oriented criminological literature. But quickly putting the "sexually well-adjusted youths" aside, Guttmacher dove into clinical studies of two rapists put at his disposal who were more to his liking. Both were nail-biters and both had "nagging mothers." One had an undescended testicle. In his dreary record of how frequently they masturbated and wet their beds, he never bothered to write down what they thought of women.

Perhaps the quintessential Freudian approach to rape was a 1954 Rorschach study conducted on the wives of eight, count 'em, eight, convicted rapists, which brought forth this sweeping indictment from one of the authors, the eminent psychoanalyst and criminologist Dr. David Abrahamsen:

> The conclusions reached were that the wives of the sex offenders on the surface behaved toward men in a submissive and masochistic way but latently denied their femininity and showed an aggressive masculine orientation; they unconsciously invited sexual aggression, only to respond to it with coolness and rejection. They stimulated their husbands into attempts to prove themselves, attempts which necessarily ended in frustration and increased their husbands' own doubts about their masculinity. In doing so, the wives unknowingly continued the type of relationship the offender had had with his mother. There can be no doubt that the sexual frustration which the wives caused is one of the factors motivating rape, which might be tentatively described as a displaced attempt to force a seductive but rejecting mother into submission.

In the nineteen sixties, leadership in the field of criminology passed to the sociologists, and a good thing it was.* Concerned

---

* Transitions are never clean. In 1965 a 900-page volume called *Sex Offenders* by Paul Gebhard and other members of the Institute for Sex Research founded by the late Alfred C. Kinsey put in an appearance. The Gebhard volume forms a sort of missing link between the idiosyncratic Freudians and the sociological approach. Suffering from the racial bias that marred the work of Dr. Kinsey, Gebhard's group tried to find meaningful differences—or similarities—among convicted rapists, child molesters and homosexuals but arbitrarily excluded blacks from their study because "their sexual behavior and attitudes differ to some degree." The spirit of Kinsey floats over this work. Gebhard tells us, "As Dr. Kinsey often said, the difference between a 'good time' and a 'rape' may hinge on whether the girl's parents were awake when she finally arrived home." Elsewhere Gebhard divines that the reason there are so few female sex offenders is because "the average woman has a weaker 'sex drive' than the average male." Perhaps the most usable observation to come out of this comparison study (of nocturnal emissions, masturbatory behavior, animal contact, and incidence of premarital, extramarital and postmarital coitus) is a remark that "the heterosexual adjustment" of rapists "is quantitatively well above average" when compared to a control group of

with measuring the behavior of groups and their social values, instead of relying on extrapolation from individual case studies, the sociologists gave us charts, tables, diagrams, theories of social relevance, and, above all, hard, cold statistical facts about crime. (Let us give credit where credit is due. The rise of computer technology greatly facilitated this kind of research.)

In 1971 Menachem Amir, an Israeli sociologist and a student of Marvin E. Wolfgang, America's leading criminologist, published a study of rape in the city of Philadelphia, begun ten years before. *Patterns in Forcible Rape*, a difficult book for those who choke on methodological jargon, was annoyingly obtuse about the culturally conditioned behavior of women in situations involving the threat of force, but despite its shortcomings the Philadelphia study was an eye-opener. It was the first pragmatic, in-depth statistical study of the nature of rape and rapists. Going far beyond the limited vision of the police and the *Uniform Crime Reports*, or the idiosyncratic concerns of the Freudians, Amir fed his computer such variables as *modus operandi*, gang rape versus individual rape, economic class, prior relationships between victim and offender, and both racial and interracial factors. For the first time in history the sharp-edged profile of the typical rapist was allowed to emerge. It turned out that he was, for the most part, an unextraordinary, violence-prone fellow.

Marvin Wolfgang, Amir's mentor at the University of Pennsylvania's school of criminology, deserves credit for the theory of "the subculture of violence," which he developed at length in his own work. An understanding of the subculture of violence is critical to an understanding of the forcible rapist. "Social class," wrote Wolfgang, "looms large in all studies of violent crime." Wolfgang's theory, and I must oversimplify, is that within the dominant value system of our culture there exists a subculture formed of those from the lower classes, the poor, the disenfranchised, the

church members and union men, which says as much about Gebhard's standards of heterosexual adjustment as it does about rapists. Another usable observation, but one that the reader must make, is that the incidence of nocturnal emission, masturbation, animal contact, and premarital, extramarital and postmarital coitus has no relevance whatsoever to the study of why men rape. And perhaps a 900-page volume was necessary to prove it.

black, whose values often run counter to those of the dominant culture, the people in charge. The dominant culture can operate within the laws of civility because it has little need to resort to violence to get what it wants. The subculture, thwarted, inarticulate and angry, is quick to resort to violence; indeed, violence and physical aggression become a common way of life. Particularly for young males.

Wolfgang's theory of crime, and unlike other theories his is soundly based on statistical analysis, may not appear to contain all the answers, particularly the kind of answers desired by liberals who want to excuse crimes of violence strictly on the basis of social inequities in the system, but Wolfgang would be the first to say that social injustice is one of the root causes of the subculture of violence. His theory also would not satisfy radical thinkers who prefer to interpret all violence as the product of the governmental hierarchy and its superstructure of repression.

But there is no getting around the fact that most of those who engage in antisocial, criminal violence (murder, assault, rape and robbery) come from the lower socioeconomic classes; and that because of their historic oppression the majority of black people are contained within the lower socioeconomic classes and contribute to crimes of violence in numbers disproportionate to their population ratio in the census figures *but not disproportionate* to their position on the economic ladder.

We are not talking about Jean Valjean, who stole a loaf of bread in *Les Misérables*, but about physical aggression as "a demonstration of masculinity and toughness"—this phrase is Wolfgang's—the prime tenet of the subculture of violence. Or, to use a current phrase, the *machismo* factor. Allegiance or conformity to *machismo*, particularly in a group or gang, is the *sine qua non* of status, reputation and identity for lower-class male youth. Sexual aggression, of course, is a major part of *machismo*.

The single most important contribution of Amir's Philadelphia study was to place the rapist squarely within the subculture of violence. The rapist, it was revealed, had no separate identifiable pathology aside from the individual quirks and personality disturbances that might characterize any single offender who commits any sort of crime.

The patterns of rape that Amir was able to trace were drawn

from the central files of the Philadelphia police department for 1958 and 1960, a total of 646 cases and 1,292 offenders.* One important fact that Amir's study revealed right off the bat was that in 43 percent of the Philadelphia cases, the rapists operated in pairs or groups, giving the lie to one of the more commonly held myths that the rapist is a secretive, solitary offender.

The median age of the Philadelphia rapist was 23, but the age group most likely to commit rape was the 15-to-19 bracket. A preponderant number of the Philadelphia rapists were not married, a status attributable to their youthful age. Ninety percent of the Philadelphia rapists "belonged to the lower part of the occupational scale," in descending order "from skilled workers to the unemployed." Half of the Philadelphia rapists had a prior arrest record, and most of these had the usual run of offenses such as burglary, robbery, disorderly conduct and assault. Only 9 percent of those with prior records had been previously arrested for rape. In other words, rapists were in the mold of the typical youthful offender.†

Not surprisingly, the Philadelphia rapist generally lived in one of those inner-city neighborhoods that according to the census tracts are known for a high degree of crime, and most particularly for "crime against the person." His victim *also* tended to live in the same neighborhood. Since Amir was studying a large Northern city with an extensive black ghetto population, the sociologist's proportion of black offenders was higher than the national average. The FBI, as I have mentioned, records that 47 percent of all arrested rapists are black. Amir in Philadelphia found that 82 percent of his reported rapists were black, as were 80 percent of the rapists'

---

* Amir's raw material differed from the FBI's. The FBI releases data based on those men actually arrested for rape and attempted rape. Amir's data was based on statistical information about all reported rapes that the police felt were "founded." Amir did not include cases of attempted rape, but he did include profiles of "known" offenders who were never apprehended. The sociologist used "known" to mean "undeniably existing," not necessarily "known to the police." Of the 1,292 offenders that form the basis of Amir's study, only 845 men were actually arrested.

† The FBI's "Careers in Crime" file, using more current statistics, shows that nationally more than 70 percent of all arrested rapists have prior records. In addition, more than 85 percent go on to be repeaters in crime and show up on later police blotters, in descending order of frequency, for burglary, assault, robbery, rape and homicide.

victims. He concluded, "Rape was found to be an intraracial event, especially between Negro men and women." In other words, forcible rape in Philadelphia was overwhelmingly black on black. Black men raped black women. In lesser numbers, white men raped white women. Most rapists, conveniently for them, raped women who lived in their neighborhood or close by. The percentage of interracial rape in the city of Philadelphia for the years 1958 and 1960, Amir discovered, was small. (More recent studies differ with Amir on this point. A full discussion of interracial rape will be found in my chapter "A Question of Race.")

"Contrary to past impression," Amir wrote, "analysis revealed that 71 percent of the rapes were planned." This observation was another of Amir's most significant contributions to the study of rape. Far from being a spontaneous explosion by an individual with pent-up emotions and uncontrollable lusts, he discovered the act was usually planned in advance and elaborately arranged by a single rapist or a group of buddies. In some cases the lone rapist or the gang had a particular victim in mind and coolly took the necessary steps to lure her into an advantageous position. In other cases the decision to rape was made in advance by a gang, a pair of cohorts or a lone-wolf rapist, but selection of the female was left to chance. Whoever happened by and could be seized, coerced or enticed to a favorable place became the victim. As might be expected, almost all group rapes in Philadelphia police files were found to have been planned. As a matter of fact, advance planning and coordination proved absolutely essential to the commission of gang rape. A "secure" place had to be located; precautions had to be taken to guarantee that the rape-in-progress would remain undetected by passers-by, police or neighbors; and selection of the victim had to be agreed upon by the group.

One-quarter of the single-offender rapes in Amir's study were not planned. In his words, the spontaneous offender had "no previous idea of committing the crime . . . but opportunities (place of meeting, victim's behavior, etc.) created the impulse, or the offender's judgment was impaired, usually by the consumption of alcohol before the event."

Further observations that Amir drew from his computer were these: Forcible rape in Philadelphia increased slightly during the hot summer months, but not by much. Rape was an all-year-round event, although group rape did show a noticeable summer increase.

Friday night, Saturday and Sunday appeared to be the favored time for commission of the crime, giving rape—for the rapists—an interesting aspect of weekend conviviality and paycheck (or lack of paycheck) celebration. Nights in general were favored over days: the top-risk hours for women were between 8 P.M. and 2 A.M. In 85 percent of the 646 cases Amir examined, some form of physical force or the display of a weapon was required by the rapist or rapists to achieve their goal. In the remaining 15 percent, verbal intimidation or the sheer physical presence of the offenders sufficed to overcome a victim's resistance.

When other crimes of violence are compared statistically with rape, the profile of the forcible rapist falls at a point midway between the profile of the man who commits aggravated assault and the man who commits robbery.* Variables that go into a profile include age, race, occupation, spatial patterns of the crime, modus operandi, the role played by alcohol, prior arrest record, etc. When offender profiles for rape, robbery and assault are viewed side by side, the rapist emerges as the man in the middle. His is the least sharp image. His profile "borrows" characteristics from the others, so to speak. The rapist is slightly younger than the assaultive offender and slightly older than the robber or mugger. He uses less physical force than the average man arrested for aggravated assault, but he employs more force than the average robber. He drinks less alcohol before committing his crime than the man who is arrested for assault, but he drinks more alcohol prior to his crime than the man who goes out to rob. He commits his crime less in his own neighborhood than the average man picked up for assault, but he does not range so far afield as the man who commits armed robbery.

Two further comparisons are somewhat related: Rape is more frequently committed against a total stranger than assault, but less

---

* I owe this valuable insight to the sociologist Lynn Curtis, another protégé and student of Marvin Wolfgang's. The rapist as "man in the middle" is apparent from the FBI's *Uniform Crime Reports*; from Volumes 11 and 12 of *Crimes of Violence* (1969), the staff report submitted to the National Commission on the Causes and Prevention of Violence on which Curtis worked as assistant director; and from Curtis' own work on the Big Four of violent crimes, which I read in manuscript. The profile of the murderer, by the way, is distinctively set off from the three other types of violent offenders.

frequently committed against a total stranger than robbery. Finally, a case of rape stands a greater chance of being interracial than a case of assault, but the interracial element is more frequent in robbery.

It seems likely that this "man in the middle" profile of the forcible rapist reflects the nature of his act, which "borrows" characteristics from the other two offenses. Like assault, rape is an act of physical damage to another person, and like robbery it is also an act of acquiring property: the intent is to "have" the female body in the acquisitory meaning of the term. A woman is perceived by the rapist both as hated person and desired property. Hostility against her and possession of her may be simultaneous motivations, and the hatred for her is expressed in the same act that is the attempt to "take" her against her will. In one violent crime, rape is an act against person and property.

Contrary to popular opinion, New York and Washington are not the rape capitals of the nation. That honor, bestowed yearly by the FBI as a sort of negative Oscar, usually goes to Los Angeles, but Denver, Little Rock, Memphis, San Francisco-Oakland, Las Vegas, Tallahassee and Albuquerque are right up there in the running, and a good student of rape must always keep in mind that police reporting procedures vary dramatically from city to city. The FBI does note emphatically that cities with populations in excess of a quarter of a million show higher rape rates per capita than suburban areas while rural areas lag far behind, so in this sense, rape can be said to be a big-city crime, although the rape rate in suburbia is noticeably rising. When rapes per capita are viewed geographically, the Southwestern states emerge as the champions. Southwestern states also lead the nation in rates for homicide and assault, so Southern and Western traditions of violence would appear to be an operative factor.

One statistical consideration that has received too much attention to the detriment of other aspects is the actual site of the crime. Brenda Brown's 1973 Memphis police department study reported that 34 percent of all rapes occurred in the victim's residence, usually by forced, illegal entry; 22 percent took place in automobiles; 26 percent occurred in "open spaces" (alleys, parks, roads, on the street, in the bushes, behind a building, etc.); 9 percent took place in the offender's residence; and the remaining 9 percent occurred indoors in a variety of places ranging from a church to an abandoned building.

The 17-city survey conducted by the task force of the National Commission on the Causes and Prevention of Violence reported that 52 percent of all rapes occurred in the home (most frequently in the bedroom); 23 percent occurred outside; 14 percent occurred in commercial establishments and other inside locations; and 11 percent occurred in automobiles.

Menachem Amir's Philadelphia study reported that 56 percent of all rapes occurred in the home; 18 percent occurred in open spaces; 11 percent occurred in other indoor locations; and 15 percent occurred in automobiles. Taking into account that an offender often escorts a victim, either by duress or through a ploy, to a propitious rape location, Amir was also concerned with what he called "the initial meeting place in a rape event." He found that in 48 percent of the cases, offenders first spotted their victims on the street.

According to these three sets of statistics, the street, the home and the automobile emerge as dangerous, high-risk places, so what is left? Good locks on doors and windows and admonitions against hitchhiking and walking alone at night in deserted places are the usual palliatives, but they do nothing to affect the rape ideology, or to increase our understanding of the crime.

Rape begins in the rapist's mind, and place may be irrelevant. A small comparison study of rape patterns in Boston and Los Angeles is interesting in this respect. Densely packed Boston has a relatively low reported rape rate while vast, sprawling Los Angeles, where people need cars to get about, is a leader. Two sociologists who scrutinized police reports in these two cities discovered that the Boston rapist was more likely to break into an apartment and confront his victim while the Los Angeles rapist was more likely to pick up his victim while cruising about in an automobile. They also found that gang rape was more common in Los Angeles than it was in Boston, which seems directly related to a transportation and mobility problem that encourages the practice of hitchhiking. Weapons were more frequently employed by the Boston rapist, a phenomenon that seems reasonable since solitary offenders have more need for a show of force than gang rapists whose very number provides the display of power.

Pairs, Groups and Gangs

Although it is not unusual to hear of one rapist who manages to keep a second victim at bay and immobilized while he methodically attends to the first, the numerical odds in rape situations are more typically in the rapist's favor. This in itself tells us much about the nature of the act.

Group rape may be defined as two or more men assaulting one woman. As I have mentioned, Amir found that in 43 percent of his Philadelphia cases the female victim had two or more assailants. A Toronto survey came up with a figure of 50 percent. A Washington, D.C., study reported 30 percent. In Toronto and Philadelphia, rapists who operated in groups accounted for 71 percent of the total number of offenders.

"Whatever may be the causal explanation, these results are amazing," wrote Amir, a man not given to hyperbole. The sociologist expressed this astonishment because psychiatric literature on rape had treated the phenomenon of group rape "with silence." Police departments, as a rule, do not tally group-rape statistics for public consumption and the FBI's *Uniform Crime Reports* do not analyze such information.

When men rape in pairs or in gangs, the sheer physical advantage of their position is clear-cut and unquestionable. No simple conquest of man over woman, group rape is the conquest of men over Woman. It is within the phenomenon of group rape, stripped of the possibility of equal combat, that the male ideology of rape is most strikingly evident. Numerical odds are proof of brutal intention. They are proof, too, of male bonding, to borrow a phrase made popular by Lionel Tiger, and proof of a desire to humiliate the victim *beyond* the act of rape through the process of anonymous mass assault.

As we have seen in Bangladesh and Vietnam, men in war tend to rape in groups in which they are anonymous and secure, and against the backdrop of an all-male army to which they have a strong male allegiance. In domestic group rape, male bonding is similarly operative, whether the young men have loosely gotten together of an evening or whether their relationship had been previously formalized into a *bona fide* gang. The act of group rape forges an alliance among men against the female victim who becomes, for their purposes, Anonymous Woman.

Rape in war, because it is so routine and casual and twinned with the opportunity to loot and kill, has rarely been considered an indication of mental disorder. Domestic group rape, with its reliance on the buddy system for planning, security and coordination, its overtones of competitive *machismo*, its sometime link with robbery or theft, and its aspect of sport and rousing conviviality, has also provided meager grist for the psychiatric mill. Recall the remark of Dr. Guttmacher, "just . . . another act of plunder."

Out of the total number of police-blotter rapists that Menachem Amir looked into, 55 percent raped in gangs and another 16 percent chose to rape in pairs. Pair rape has never been studied as an isolated phenomenon. Studies of gang rape have been sparse but interesting.

A California group psychologist, W. H. Blanchard, published a fascinating paper on two sets of youthful gang rapists he studied, one white and one black. He did not divulge their ages but he called them "boys" and mentioned their placement in a juvenile custodial institution. The psychologist put each set of youths through what he called a Group Process Rorschach. A series of Rorschach cards, that pack of random blobs and splashes that offer an infinite variety of personal interpretations, was shown to each boy after a personal interview. The test was then repeated with the entire group present and the boys were told to agree upon one response to each card. In Blanchard's words, "This affords an excellent opportunity to discover how the boys modify their original responses . . . in order to conform to the dynamics of the group." Blanchard quickly discovered that the group response to the cards was richer and more elaborate because of "the pressure of competition for dominance in the group and under the stimulus of group activity."

The white group, Blanchard wrote, had "participated in a particularly vicious assault on a pair of lovers at a secluded spot in the Hollywood Hills of Los Angeles." (Actually, as gang rapes go, the Hollywood Hills rape was not especially vicious.) Five boys had taken part in the assault but only their acknowledged leader, Keith, and Harry and Don were in custody. The rape had gone like this: Boozing it up among themselves the boys decided it might be fun to "scare" some lovers in a parked car. When they approached the car the situation escalated. Keith grabbed the ignition keys, the boy in the car got out and protested, and Keith took a sock at him. The others then jumped on the boy and Harry grabbed his wallet. According to Blanchard, "The girl agreed to do whatever Keith wanted if he would leave her boyfriend alone." Keith raped her first in the car while the other boys were grabbing at her breasts and helping to pull off her clothes. Don was next. By this time the girl was in pain and she pleaded to be allowed to "masturbate" him instead. Don agreed. "During this incident," Blanchard reported, "the other boys were running around the car yelling and knocking on windows." When Don was finished, a third boy made his try, but by this time Keith was getting anxious that they would be discovered. He pulled the third boy out of the car and gave the order to run.

In Blanchard's interviews, Harry, whose major act of violence had been directed against the boyfriend—he never got his "chance" at the girl—gave this description of Keith, the leader:

> Some girl would be taking a sun bath [at the beach] and have her sun glasses on and he would pour sand all over her, and she would get all mad and everything, you know. You can't be relaxed when you are around him, you know, he'll grab you or pinch you or something. . . . You can't lay down on the beach with him without the feeling that he will haul off and slug you in the stomach or something. When you're around Keith, you always have to be watching for him to pull one of his little stunts. . . . It built up my courage, my being with him.

About himself and the rape event, Harry said:

> I was scared when it began to happen. I wanted to leave but I didn't want to say it to the other guys—you know—that I was scared. Then when this guy got out of his car and wanted his keys back, he pushed me and I hit him. . . . When somebody pushes me I hit him. . . . Almost everything I do is kind of—like on a dare.

After their arrest Harry and Don attempted to repudiate Keith and drew closer to each other. When Blanchard brought them together for the group Rorschach, Keith was quick to reassert his leadership. His interpretations prevailed in readings of three out of four cards. Keith saw sexual images, such as a brassiere, on cards he hadn't read that way on his individual test. If Harry would disagree, Keith would snap, "That's what it looks like, doesn't it, Don?" and Don, his "lieutenant," who had been allowed "seconds" on the girl, went along. "It was almost," wrote Blanchard, "as though there was an attempt on Keith's part to re-create the entire rape experience in a symbolic manner. . . . This would tend to substantiate the fact that the sexual relationship and the sexual feeling in the previous rape experience was largely a relationship between the boys rather than between any of the boys and the girl involved."

In an interesting sidelight, Blanchard reported that the mothers of Keith and Don both told him that the entire incident had been "the girl's fault." After all, the girl had told Keith to "do what he wanted," and the girl had "masturbated" Don—a practice, his mother insisted, her son hadn't known about. Wrote Blanchard in irony, "They [the mothers] are so exquisitely sensitive to the unconscious motivation of the girl in this case while being so blind to the dynamics of their own children."

Blanchard's interviews were conducted in 1957, and since that time women's collective consciousness regarding rape has been rising. Yet in 1972 while I was sitting in on a New York City pair-rape trial, and was identified in the courtroom corridor as an active feminist—the victim in this case was eleven years old and the offenders were thirteen and fifteen—the fifteen-year-old's mother lunged and tried to take a sock at me. (Her son had just been given ninety days after a lackluster defense by a male lawyer who tried to argue that the boy had taken his directions from the thirteen-year-old offender.)

When Blanchard conducted his interviews with the black youths, he found that they "did not communicate verbally to the same extent as the white boys." He wrote, "The social distance from the white examiner may have been one of the reasons for this." Spontaneity ran high, however, on the group Rorschach.

In this case Blanchard had four youths to examine. A fifth was processed as an adult offender and was not sequestered with his buddies in the juvenile detention center. The group rape had taken place after the five youths had picked up three black girls in their car. There was a bit of drinking and the boys suggested a drive into the hills for sex. The girls refused, but the boys drove on anyway.

When they stopped the car, two of the young girls managed to escape. The third was caught and gang-raped by all five males.

The four at Blanchard's disposal were Pete, "the leader," Joe, his "lieutenant," Bill and Kenny. What leadership role, if any, was played by the fifth, the "adult," offender was not recorded. Pete and Joe had previously been involved in a string of street robberies and muggings. Like the white boy, Keith, Pete appeared to his examiner as "a very sadistic youngster with a strong need to prove his masculinity." Pete went first in the gang rape, but he had to push Bill out of the way to do it.

In the "guarded" interviews the youths gave to Blanchard, the psychologist felt that the boys were trying to "protect" their leader, and "would not admit that there was a definite leader." It seems to me from what Blanchard presented that in this particular group the leadership lines were not very clear, as often happens—psychologists and sociologists notwithstanding. On the individual Rorschachs only Kenny "showed considerable creative ability [and] a willingness to give more than one response to a card." Coincidentally, Kenny was the only youth who did not strike the victim and he was also the last to have intercourse with her. His background, incidentally, was decidedly more middle class than the rest.

When Blanchard got the boys together for the group Rorschach, the "rather sterile" individual responses evaporated and a lively exchange took place, marked by a pull in one direction by Pete and a pull in another direction by Kenny. None of the individual Rorschachs had stimulated any sexual imagery, but in the group process Pete, "who had shown perhaps the least imaginative ability," suddenly began to see sex symbols, and homosexual symbols at that. He was overruled by Kenny who had to win the support of Joe. Blanchard quotes the following response to Card III. We must make careful note, however, that the role of the examiner is far from neutral.

> KENNY: It look like two men picking up something.
> BILL: It look like two ladies to me.
> KENNY: Yeah, you can see the high heels down there.
> PETE: It look like two homosexuals. (*Laughter.*)
> KENNY: Ah, man, what you thinkin'?

JOE: It do, man, it do!

BILL: It got high heels on, huh?

PETE (*laughter*): See, it got this up here and this down here. (*Pointing to the breast area and phallic area.*)

KENNY: Man, that's a knee.

PETE (*more laughter*): Man, that ain't no knee.

JOE: That ain't no knee.

BILL: Man, what you talkin' about?

THE EXAMINER: Yes, show us what makes it look like a homosexual.

PETE (*giggling*): This sticking out up here and this stickin' out down here.

THE EXAMINER: You mean the person has a breast and a penis both?

PETE: Yeah, that's it.

KENNY: It don't look like that to me.

JOE: It sure look like it to me.

BILL: It don't look like it to me either, man.

PETE: The way it's drawn, like that— and like that.

BILL: It look like two ladies washing clothes or beating on something.

JOE: To me, in my estimation, it look like opossums hanging on a tree or something.

KENNY: Well, what is it?

BILL: I don't know.

KENNY: Could be two ladies beating on something, on a drum

JOE: Two ladies. I say it's two ladies.

BILL: Two ladies beating on a drum.

THE EXAMINER: Have you decided?

JOE: Two ladies beating on a drum.

THE EXAMINER: Do you all agree?

ALL: Yes, yeah, that's it.

Of Freudian persuasion, Blanchard introduced his paper with the comment, "The idea of 'sharing the girl among us fellows,' congregating around a common sexual object, and being sexually stimulated together as a group certainly have their homosexual implications." After presenting his evidence, he concluded that Harry's admiration of Keith's toughness was "almost masochistic" and an "erotized attachment . . . so strong that it is just short of being overtly homosexual in its content." Pete and Keith as leaders, he felt, were sexually stimulated by the group's presence and were able to stimulate the group in turn, but Keith's feeling was "not as obviously homosexual" as Pete's. Presented with one Rorschach card, Pete tried to get his group "to accept the concept of an anus," the psychologist reported. (Whatever the concept, the word was clearly Blanchard's, not Pete's.)

Blanchard wrote in his summation, "It is felt that the most interesting and unique aspect of the group examination is the degree to which the sexual feeling in the leader is stimulated by the presence of the group, his feeling that he must perform for them, and, in a sense, 'exhibit himself.'* The degree to which the leader channels, crystallizes, and directs the attention of the group to sexual matters seems to be of primary importance in the development of a group rape."

I don't think we need go as far afield as Blanchard to gain some understanding of the group-rape phenomenon. Homosexuality, overt or latent, may be present in a variety of innocuous situations, such as Friday-night bowling "with the boys," and so what? (It may also be present in a Tuesday-night consciousness-raising session with the women, and so what?) The Freudian approach to latent homosexuality, or ambivalence about homosexuality, has always been to sniff it out as a dangerous, causative factor, and *this* I believe is dangerous.

Harry may indeed have had a crush on Keith, and Pete, if he continued his life of crime, may today be happily raping other men in Soledad prison, but the reinforced sadistic impulses of both gangs, stemming from a need to find or prove their masculinity—a far cry from the need to either hide or "act out" their homosexuality—is much more central to the rape of women. I have seen boys like Harry on New York City subway trains being jabbed and pummeled by "leaders" like Keith or Pete, and I have seen the mixture of fear and respect in their eyes and watched them in turn jab and pummel younger boys or Wrigley gum machines. This has nothing to do with masochism or homosexuality. I read it as directly related to Wolfgang's theory of the subculture of violence. These youths on the subway platform, or hanging around a rural gas station, are schooling themselves in the ways of violence; they

---

* The phrase "exhibit himself" harks back to the Freudian preoccupation with exhibitionism and the penis.

are following the leader and studying *machismo*. They are desperately trying to learn the way to be successful men.* When I have stood, almost mesmerized, on my Fourteenth Street subway platform and watched a gang of youths methodically assault a gum machine for its pennies—in escalation of a dare—I could only think *That could be my body.*

Male bonding stems from a contempt for women, bolstered by distrust, and it is not, *per se*, homosexual. It is also, in this culture with its forced and exaggerated male/female polarities, an easier way to get along with other human beings than a male-female group bonding, such as in, say, a Vermont commune. Activists in the women's movement have found that female bonding—eating together, socializing together, *thinking* together—works nicely too. But male bonding set the model (a theory of matriarchy notwithstanding) and, as usual, exaggerated the model in the form of group violence and rape. "Sharing the girl among us fellows" strengthens the notion of group masculinity and power, a distorted notion to be sure, in much the same way that an executive dining room "open to males only" strengthens the notion of group masculinity and power, or the way an all-male climb up Mount Everest to conquer the mountain or an all-male canoe trip to shoot the rapids (listen to the language) strengthens the notion of group masculinity and power. Corporate executive dining rooms and climbs up Mount Everest are not usually accessible to those who form the subculture of violence. Access to a female body—through force—is within their ken.

"Gratuitous Acts, Extravagant Defilements"

Hubert Selby did a brilliant fictional treatment of gang rape in *Last Exit to Brooklyn*. Tralala, a young bar hooker down on her luck, returns to her old familiar stamping grounds in Brooklyn where she tries to hustle a customer away from two regulars. She is very drunk and more out of a spirit of competition than anything

---

* I have also watched gangs of tough girls on the New York City subways take jabs or pokes at one another in what I can only call imitation *machismo*. The tragedy of these young girls is that they are imitating a role model that ends in disaster.

else, she offers to take on the entire bar. Set up in the back of a wrecked car on a vacant lot, Tralala is at first a willing participant in a gang bang as she swills her beer and the guys in the line fight over who is going to be first. Soon the Greeks from the luncheonette come over, and then someone puts in a call to the Navy base and the seamen join the swelling ranks. Someone complains that the car is beginning to smell and Tralala, car seat and all, is placed on the ground. Beer is passed down the line and somebody shoves a can against Tralala's mouth. It splits her lip and Tralala spits out a piece of tooth. Everybody laughs. Guys who have had their turn join the end of the line for seconds. Tralala passes out.

> they slapped her a few times and she mumbled and turned her head but they couldn't revive her so they continued to fuck her as she lay unconscious on the seat in the lot and soon they tired of the dead piece and the daisychain brokeup and they went back to Willies the Greeks and the base and the kids who were watching and waiting to take a turn took out their disappointment on Tralala and tore her clothes to small scraps put out a few cigarettes on her nipples pissed on her jerkedoff on her jammed a broomstick up her snatch then bored they left her lying amongst the broken bottles rusty cans and rubble of the lot and Jack and Freddy and Ruthy and Annie stumbled into a cab still laughing and they leaned toward the window as they passed the lot and got a good look at Tralala lying naked covered with blood urine and semen and a small blot forming on the seat between her legs as blood seeped from her crotch . . .

As I discovered during my research into wartime rape, the ramming of a stick, a bottle or some other object into a woman's vagina is a not uncommon *coup de grâce.* Just how frequently this occurs statistically remains a mystery, for it has never been studied. Police department m.o. sheets in Los Angeles and Denver provide blanks to be checked off next to "inserts object in vagina." The Denver form lists "inserts foreign object into rectum" as well.

A law professor with a sociological bent once tried to analyze the phenomenon of gang rape in Sydney, Australia. Gang rape in Sydney, or "pack rape," was found to be mainly a lower-class and lower-middle-class product, like the American experience.

> The grouping is usually just a gang of youths who behave, for the most part, in an aimless, non-goal directed manner [the profes-

sor wrote]. The leader tends to become the repository and epitome of the qualities highly valued in the group. All members must behave in such a way as to positively affirm these highly valued qualities, but the leader must do so even more. . . . This might explain why in certain of the pack rape cases, in addition to the actual physical penetration of the victim, there take place certain gratuitous acts and extravagant defilements which are only darkly hinted at by judges giving sentence but are often excretory in nature. Such behavior as this seems clearly aimed towards gaining or maintaining prestige within the group by overemphasizing the values of toughness and disregard for femininity other than as a sexual tool.

Besides the well-gossiped Fatty Arbuckle Coke-bottle case, the most famous foreign-object rape in our American heritage is in William Faulkner's *Sanctuary*, where Popeye brutally jams a corncob into the well-bred college girl, Temple Drake. Faulkner was making the point that Popeye was impotent, a novelist's rendition of the traditional Freudian view of sexual violence. Amir deals with what he politely calls "sexual humiliation" in his Philadelphia study. Ignoring such acts as urination, ejaculation into the victim's face and hair, and other defilements—perhaps they did not appear in the Philadelphia police reports—he does deal with the incidence of forced cunnilingus, fellatio and "pederasty" or "sodomy." By these last two imprecise terms I think he was referring to anal penetration. He concludes that "these are not the acts of an 'impotent,' which the psychiatric school so emphatically suggests."

Including repeated intercourse in his definition of "sexual humiliation" Amir found that in more than one-quarter of his cases the victim was subjected to some form of extra insult beyond the simple rape. Sexual humiliation ran higher in group rapes than in individual rapes, and the most common form of extra insult in group rape was repeated intercourse. Amir remarked, "Taking repeated turns is part of what group rape can 'offer' to the participants."

As the act of intercourse itself is deliberately perverted in rape by forcing it on an unwilling participant, so, too, the purpose of any sidebar activity is to further humiliate and degrade, and not to engage in sophisticated erotics. (The purpose is never to satisfy the victim.) At best, fringe defilements can be in the nature of clinical experiments performed by initiates who are convinced that all sex is dirty and demeaning. Not surprisingly in Amir's study, when it came to oral sex few rapists showed interest in cunnilingus. What they demanded was fellatio done on them. What these rapists were looking for was another avenue or orifice by which to invade and thus humiliate their victim's physical integrity, her private inner space.

RAPE-MURDER

A former deputy police commissioner with a flair for words divulged in print, "In New York City last year we had 1,466 murders and many attempted murders. We in the police hierarchy took a personal interest in a few of these: the murder of cops, the Joe Colombo hit, and one or two rape-murders distinguished by the youth and beauty of the victim."

Leaving aside the obvious sexism of this remark (for the rape-murder of an elderly and homely woman is just as horrible a crime), what the fellow said was significant. When the police take a personal interest, the newspapers take a personal interest, and vice versa, and so one could almost get the idea from reading the tabloids that a rape can easily wind up as a murder.

Unfortunately for those who take comfort in statistics, there are no available national figures on the yearly number of rape-murders because the act is treated as a homicide by most police departments and the courts. The New York City Police Department's sex crimes analysis squad reported 28 rape-murders in 1973; the sex crime squad in Memphis reported six. In Washington, D.C., rape-murders are not classified separately; the homicide bureau estimated five out of a total of 286 murders (one was an 86-year-old woman).

Homicide statistics as they relate to the sexes are revealing. While 63 percent of all murders are male on male and a scant 4 percent are female on female, 18 percent are male on female and 16 percent are female on male. I know this adds up to 101 percent, but that's how the National Commission on the Causes and Prevention of Violence rounded off its numbers. One out of every four homicides is a killing within a family unit. Sixteen percent of all homicides involve legal or common-law husbands and wives—who kill each other off in fairly equal numbers. From these few facts one can gather that when it comes to murder *between* the sexes, women give almost as much as they get, with a slight edge to the men. Not that everything evens out so nicely, for females invariably kill people they know and males *do* kill strangers—the figure runs higher than 15 percent. (When race is added to the picture, it develops that *white* females as a class commit the least amount of murder.) Our elusive rape-murder statistic must be contained within the 2 percent differential between male/female and female/male homicides, in a catchall that would also include female victims of random shootings and female children murdered by their fathers.

Playing around with numbers, purely speculatively, if rape-murder accounts for 2 percent of all murders (the outside possibility), there are perhaps 400 rape-murders committed per year. This would amount to .8 percent of all reported rapes and .2 percent of all actual rapes and rape attempts. An understanding that rapists seldom murder their victims is critical, and I will return to this theme in my "Victims" section, but here we are defining the beast, not his prey.

Aggravated assault, as defined by the law, is also a predominantly male-on-male phenomenon, displaying many of the statistical characteristics found in patterns of homicide, with some critical exceptions. More assaults—a total of 20 percent—are committed against strangers. Physical violence between husbands and wives (7 percent of all *reported* assaults, and I stress *reported* because police are notoriously reluctant to step into a family "squabble" in the age-old belief, once law, that a man's home is his castle) is 75 percent male against female. When assault statistics are viewed as a whole, only 9 percent of all offenders are females aggressing against males, but 27 percent (more than one in four) are males aggressing against females. These percentages *do not include* forcible rape and assault with intent to commit rape, in which the offenders are exclusively male.

So, while murder between the sexes appears to be almost equally divided, violent physical aggression by males against females, short of murder but committed with brutal, punishing intent, is a serious problem. The occasional rape-murder, with all its attendant publicity, is the ultimate manifestation and the perfect symbol of this unequal aggression.

Although 85 percent of all police-blotter rapists go on to commit additional criminal acts that range over the entire spectrum of antisocial behavior, few advance to become rape-murderers. But the few who do cannot be ignored—because it seems probable that the "support" they received during their raping careers, I mean either their success at eluding capture or the minimal and nontherapeutic prison sentences they served, allowed their escalating violence to proceed unchecked.

It comes as a surprise to most people that the murder of Kitty Genovese, stalked and stabbed to death shortly after 3 A.M. on a bleak commercial-residential street in Queens on March 13, 1964—a much-discussed case in the nineteen sixties because thirty-eight people heard the victim's cries or witnessed some part of her ordeal without calling the police—ended in her rape as she lay dying. Winston Moseley, Genovese's 29-year-old killer, later made an extraordinary confession. "I just set out to find any girl that was unattended and I was going to kill her," he calmly announced in court.

Moseley, a business-machine operator, had cruised about the quiet neighborhood in his white sports car until he spotted his prey. He recalled, "I could run much faster than she could—I jumped on her back and stabbed her several times." This was his first assault on his victim, when Kitty Genovese screamed, "Oh, my God, I've been stabbed! Please help me." Lights flashed on in a middle-class apartment building across the street and a man stuck his head out his bedroom window and bellowed, "Let that girl alone." Moseley backed off and returned to his car. Kitty Genovese, stabbed four times and bleeding, staggered around the corner toward her tenement flat that faced the railroad tracks.

But the killer was just biding his time. He told the court, "I had a feeling that this man would close his window and go back to sleep." He found Genovese lying in the downstairs vestibule of her building. "She was twisting and turning, and I don't know how many times or where I stabbed her until she was fairly quiet." Then Moseley tore at her clothes and attacked her sexually. "I heard the upstairs door open at least twice, maybe three times," he testified, "but when I looked up there was nobody."

Among other salient facts revealed by Winston Moseley in the courtroom and in confessions to the police was the information that he had murdered three other women, setting fire to the genital area of one, raped "four or five others," and robbed and attempted to rape even more, all without getting caught. In the course of his unchecked career he discovered he preferred to rape when his victims were, in his chilling words, "fairly quiet" and dying. Moseley was sentenced to life imprisonment for the murder of Kitty Genovese, but there is an addendum to his story. In 1968 he escaped from a prison hospital and captured a couple at gunpoint. He beat up the husband and raped the wife before he was reapprehended. The New York State Court of Appeals agreed that the state had shown negligence in Moseley's escape and awarded the injured couple $60,000 in damages.

Albert DeSalvo, known far and wide as the Boston Strangler, was another escalator in violence who gained courage from success as he went along. From June, 1962, to January, 1964, the city of Boston was beset by a killer who strangled and stabbed eleven women, many of them elderly, and left their sexually mutilated bodies in garish postures with a nylon stocking knotted about the neck. Dumbfounded police conducted a nationwide manhunt for the elusive phantom, employing the services of seers and psychiatrists, but to no avail. Then the killings stopped as suddenly as they began. Had ego not gotten the better of DeSalvo, confined to Bridgewater State Hospital in 1964 for observation in relation to a tying-up and abusing crime that happened to be his true specialty, we might never have learned the identity of the notorious Strangler and the full extent of his crimes.

As reconstructed by Gerold Frank in his excellent book, the burly, five-foot-eight DeSalvo had begun his assaultive career years before. Hardly the mild-mannered, unprepossessing fellow of his press clippings, DeSalvo had spent nine years in the United States Army, much of it in boxing competitions, and had won the Army's title of European middleweight champion, which helps explain the phenomenal strength the Strangler had in his hands. But Frank dug up something else from DeSalvo's Army days. He had once been indicted for child molestation while stationed at Fort Dix. The child's mother later withdrew the complaint because she feared unwelcome publicity and the charge was dropped.

A full two years before the Boston murders, DeSalvo, then 29, came to police attention in Cambridge, Massachusetts, as The Measuring Man, a nutty fellow who gained entrance to young women's apartments in and around Harvard Square by claiming he was a representative of a model agency. Once inside an apartment

DeSalvo would proceed to impertinently "measure" his "prospective client's" breasts and hips. While Cambridge police were puzzling (or laughing?) over their Measuring Man, police in New Haven, Hartford and other nearby Connecticut towns were collecting information on an elusive Green Man. The Green Man, so named because he usually wore green work pants, was a quick-strike rapist who gained admission to apartments by posing as a building maintenance employee. As the phantom Green Man, DeSalvo's modus operandi was an advance over his Measuring Man activities. Now he tied his victims to the bed and raped or sodomized them. Or tried to. In one of his misspelled, confessional letters to the police from Bridgewater, DeSalvo claimed that half the time, "I just put my hand on them and was finished . . . you see I was so build up by the time I found a woman I just got near her and I was releaved." (This matched the account of several of his victims.)

DeSalvo was eventually picked up and identified as the Cambridge Measuring Man, but the charge that sent him to prison was "breaking and entering." A jury found him not guilty of two counts of lewdness, and the police impression, too, was that they had cornered a petty thief with a curious m.o. This erroneous assumption proved costly in terms of lives, for when DeSalvo was released eleven months later and the Boston stranglings began, his name did not turn up on any computerized list of known sex offenders.

As the proverbial bluebird was found in the proverbial backyard, so DeSalvo, chafing in anonymity and eager to let the world in on his secret, was finally found at Bridgewater. Through the summer and fall of 1965 he volunteered to his interrogators a step-by-step confession, adding new information as he won their growing interest. Some of his details were not letter-perfect. "I've been in so many apartments," he'd sigh, and offer his confessor an animated, man-to-man description of a victim's breast size. In addition to the Boston murders DeSalvo confessed to hundreds of sexual assaults without murder in Massachusetts and Connecticut, in which he usually tied up a victim and ejaculated on her body or in her mouth. His lifetime total of abuses, he volunteered, might run as high as 2,000 if the women he assaulted in Germany while a member of the armed forces were added to his record. (DeSalvo rarely committed a legally defined rape, in the strict definition of genital intercourse. When he did, he preferred to cover up his victim's face.)

Employing techniques he perfected as the Green Man for the Boston stranglings, DeSalvo confessed that he always committed his crimes during the day, sometimes on his lunch hour. He worked on and off as a mechanic and would "shoot over" by car to Lawrence or Cambridge or Salem whenever the mood overtook him. Finding a likely building, he'd check for the names of single women, ring a doorbell and fast-talk his way inside an apartment by claiming the landlord had sent him to do some repairs. If a prospect seemed overly reluctant to open her door he'd retreat and try another doorbell. If a prospect did allow him to enter, he'd wait until her back was turned and grab her in a hammer lock about the neck. Rarely in the Boston killings did he commit a sex abuse first and then murder. His preferred style, like Winston Moseley's, was to murder first and then commit his atrocities.*

DeSalvo's confession was at odds with police reports on a couple of points. In one case he claimed rape but the medical men had found no trace of semen. (This in itself is not particularly significant, since semen is not traceable after a period of time; however, it seems probable that DeSalvo preferred to take credit for a "normal" sex act rather than the wild ejaculation that was his usual style.) Yet he was eerily precise on the stylized grotesqueries that marked the Strangler killings, which he could vividly recall but not explain: the nylon stocking used as garrote, the stab wounds or bite marks tattooed on the breast, the wine bottle or broomstick rammed up the vagina as the final coup de grâce. As an extra touch of authenticity he even added two more killings to his list that the

---

* The ease with which the Strangler got his victims to open their doors was a continuing source of wonderment to police detectives and reporters. Before DeSalvo's confession a popular theory held that the mysterious killer must have posed as a priest. After DeSalvo owned up to the maintenance-man ploy, his success was attributed to his "charm" and to his victims' gullibility. More than likely his success was a tribute to the state of disrepair in many of Boston's older apartment buildings, and to female dependence on men for repair work. All of DeSalvo's murders were committed in shabby, run-down neighborhoods where a landlord's handyman is akin to a messenger from heaven, particularly to women who live alone and usually have something that "needs fixing."

police had not attributed to the Strangler. One was a bludgeon murder and the other was an 85-year-old woman whose death had been officially recorded as heart failure. Abashed, DeSalvo confessed that she had suffered a heart attack in his arms. "I didn't touch her," he whispered. "I picked her up and put her on the couch and I left."

In all, it was a convincing performance and the mystery of the Boston Strangler should have ended then and there. It didn't. One reason for the nagging doubts was that DeSalvo's case history did not match a psychiatric profile of the Strangler drummed up by a team of doctors working close to the investigation.

A Medical-Psychiatric Committee, upon invitation of the stymied police, had put together an imaginative, detailed profile of the phantom Strangler. Or, to be more precise, they put together an imaginative profile of the Strangler's mother. Struck by the advanced age of the first victims, one of whom was 75, the committee postulated with the kind of certainty that seems endemic to their profession that the elusive killer was a neat, punctual, conservatively dressed, possibly middle-aged, probably impotent, probably homosexual fellow who was consumed by raging hatred for his "sweet, orderly, neat, compulsive, seductive, punitive, overwhelming" mother. The Strangler's mother was probably dead, they agreed, but during his childhood she had walked about "half-exposed in their apartment, but punished him severely for any sexual curiosity." Consumed by mother hatred, the psychiatrists divined, the Strangler had chosen to murder and mutilate old women in a manner "both sadistic and loving."

When the next six of the Strangler's victims turned out with one exception to be young women, the Medical-Psychiatric Committee broke ranks. Some were of the opinion that the second batch of murders was the work of another, "more heterosexually adjusted" killer, while others maintained that the more recent killings showed that the Strangler had been "cured" of his mother fetish and had found his potency, at last, with young girls. On one point the psychiatric group voiced unanimity: The older women had been Pure Victims but the younger women Might Have Brought Their Fate on Themselves.*

---

* Gerold Frank records that the only two women allowed in the inner sanctum of the Strangler investigation, a research assistant in charge of the files

Armed with this learned psychiatric analysis, the police pro-grammed themselves to look for "an impotent male bearing an unendurable rage toward his mother and all women like her."

Albert DeSalvo, as he revealed himself and as his juvenile records bore out, was genuinely attached to his mother. Moreover, she was still alive and not particularly sweet, neat or overwhelming. The consuming rage DeSalvo bore was uncompromisingly directed against his drunken, brutalizing father, who had regularly beaten him, his mother and the other children during a wretched youth. DeSalvo's father had engaged in sex acts with prostitutes in front of his children, had taught his sons to shoplift, had broken every finger on his wife's hand and knocked out her teeth, and had gone on periodic rampages where he smashed up all the furniture in the house. As a final act of rejection he abandoned the family when Albert was eight.

At one point during his meandering confessions DeSalvo bristled at the suggestion that a 75-year-old woman like Ida Irga might be an unusual choice of sex object. "Attractiveness has nothing to do with it," he patiently explained. "She was a woman. When this certain time comes on me, it's a very immediate thing." He did not consider himself an impotent, and neither did the police. The idea of homosexuality made him embarrassed. As far as DeSalvo understood DeSalvo, he was unhappily blessed with a powerful sex drive and he petulantly whined that if his German-born wife and the mother of his two children had not "denied me my rights as a husband" things might have worked out a little better. On the other hand, he knew he had gone from a "nothing"

---

and a secretary to the assistant attorney general, fought spiritedly against the police detectives who, in Frank's words, "were inclined to agree with the psychiatrists that the younger victims might have brought their fate on themselves." On a related point, Frank notes that a woman reporter on Boston's *Record-American* proposed to do an investigative series after the fourth murder of an older woman took place, at a time when the police still publicly maintained that the killings were unrelated. Her city editor vetoed the assignment, arguing, "They're nobodies. Who'd be interested in them?" Victims Number One through Four were Anna Slesers, 55; Nina Nichols, 68; Helen Blake, 65; and Ida Irga, 75. Victim Number Five was Jane Sullivan, 67. Victim Number Six was the first of the young women, Sophie Clark, age 20 and black. The *Record-American's* Strangler series, in 29 parts, did not begin until after the murder of Patricia Bissette, 23, DeSalvo's first young, white victim.

to a "something" and "Boy, it made me feel powerful." Once he hopefully ventured, "I was like any other normal guy, trying to make out."

Cleared of Oedipal interpretations, DeSalvo's graduation from older victims to young ones loses much of its mystery. He told his police interrogators that he was a terrible coward as a boy because he ran away from fights. When he started boxing in the Army he astounded himself by his ability to "drop" bigger men. It seems highly logical that he deliberately began his murdering career by "dropping" older women, who would certainly present less physical resistance, and then, as he gained in confidence, began testing his strength against younger women. Sophie Clark, his first young victim, who happened to be black, was 5 foot 10, a fact that impressed him more than her color. "Tall, very tall, taller than me," he exclaimed over and over. "She was the one I had to tie really tight."

DeSalvo always chose to murder under the safest conditions, where the odds were clearly in his favor. Twice he backed off after selecting a victim. On one occasion a strongly built waitress kept up a loud, sustained scream while she bit his finger down to the bone. He fled in anger and confusion. Another time during his "check" for leaks and falling plaster he discovered a six-year-old boy in an adjoining room. He turned on his heels, walked up a flight of stairs and rang another doorbell.

Albert Desalvo single-handedly smashed every cherished psychiatric concept of a sex murderer. To add a final irony, the flamboyant Dutch psychic Peter Hurkos, whose secret entry into the case caused an uproar early in the investigation, had conjured up a description of the Strangler that matched the real DeSalvo more closely than the Medical-Psychiatric Committee's "profile." With equal certainty Hurkos had instructed the police to search for a religious shoe fetishist (false) about 5 foot 8 (true) with a big nose (true) who worked with diesel engines (true) and who bore a scar on his left arm (true).

DeSalvo was never put on trial as the Boston Strangler. Instead, with F. Lee Bailey as his lawyer, he went to court in Massachusetts for Green Man-style offenses against four women and pleaded not guilty by reason of insanity. Bailey, who did not have any doubt that DeSalvo and the Strangler were one and the same, shrewdly hoped that an insanity verdict on these lesser crimes (the specific charges were breaking and entering, assault and battery, unnatural and lascivious acts, and burglary) would guarantee that his client would not face the electric chair for the Boston murders. He was partially correct. DeSalvo never did face the chair, but an all-male jury,* fully aware of the notorious celebrity they had in the dock, voted life imprisonment.

"Life" proved somewhat shorter than expected. Late in 1973 DeSalvo was murdered by some fellow inmates at Walpole State Prison. In the news stories surrounding his death it was reported that he had become rather skilled at making costume jewelry and had been an active leader of an inmates' union seeking reforms. "The only problem we had with Albert," an official said, "was his trafficking in drugs." Nowhere was there a mention of how his "powerful sex drive" adjusted to a society without women, and how it got "releaved."

Winston Moseley and Albert DeSalvo represent fairly typical, if unusually dramatic, examples of the men who commit rape-murder. Far from the stereotypic, psychiatric construct of mild-mannered, repressed, impotent homosexuals with an Oedipus complex, they are better understood as brutalized, violence-prone men who act out their raging hatred against the world through an object offering the least amount of physical resistance, a woman's body. They do not provide a complete composite of the crime of rape-murder, for no individual case studies can.

Some rape-murders are frivolously accidental and occur in the course of what was intended to be a routine break and entry. A victim dies because the gag stuffed in her mouth suffocated her and her inexperienced assailant didn't know any better. Or a victim dies because her attacker got carried away by the awful power of his violence, which became more important to him than the act of rape or robbery that was his initial intent.

It is a rare rapist who intends to kill, except in war, where killing is cheap, just as it is a rare robber who expects his act to end in a fatal stabbing. And yet accidental, totally inexplicable murder does occur, and although as yet it cannot be proved by statistical

---

* DeSalvo's jury was all male not entirely by accident. Under Massachusetts law a judge may bar all women from juries hearing cases of child rape, statutory rape, obscenity and various sex-related crimes because women might be "embarrassed" by the testimony. (This law was still on the books in 1974.)

incidence, it appears to be committed with increasing frequency in our violence-oriented culture by youths whose overriding impulse seems to be to stab or bludgeon, rather than to rob or rape. Increasingly, it seems, we hear of cases where something snaps and a compliant victim is fatally wounded. Who can explain the lifetime of built-up rage that led inevitably to this senseless explosion?

I think it is important to mention here that despite the popular myths of male violence and the alleged safety in submission, it has never been demonstrated that resistance on the part of a rape victim in an attempt to escape "provokes" an assailant to commit an act of murder.

At this point we will skip the critical processes that bring a rapist to his confinement or let him go scot-free to wreak more damage on further victims, and proceed to a brief look at the rapist in prison, where he serves an average of less than four years, and where he is indistinguishable from the rest of the prison population except in one interesting aspect. *He is more than twice as likely to continue to insist on his innocence than the nonsexual offender.*

A study completed at Sing Sing (now the Ossining Correctional Facility) in 1955 reported that 80 percent of the prison's rapists were partially or markedly evasive about their crimes while only 26 percent of the control group of general offenders displayed this attitude. An earlier New York City report emphasized the convicted rapist's tendency to project his blame on others, most notably on his victim, "even in the face of conclusive evidence."

A 1967 Canadian study of thirty rapists confined at Kingston Penitentiary, Ontario, bore out the American results. R. J. McCaldon, a prison psychiatrist, noted that the Canadian rapists, like their American counterparts, were "generally young men" from the lower socioeconomic classes, who had a total number of forty-six previous offenses among them, "mainly acquisitive." McCaldon broke down the Canadian offenders' attitudes toward their rape convictions in this manner:

Admits	33%
Denies	27%
Rationalizes	33%
Amnesic	7%

He summed up, "In two-thirds of the cases one hears, 'I'm here on a phoney beef,' or 'So I might have been a little rough with her but she was asking for it,' or 'I might have done it but I was too drunk to remember.' "

Ten years ago Clinton Duffy, the famous warden of San Quentin, put his thoughts on sex and crime together in a breezy, opinionated book. In command of one of America's toughest penal institutions for almost thirty-five years, Duffy didn't require any sociological studies to tell him what he knew from practical experience in the yard. He had learned first hand that the typical felon's cry was "I'm no rapo," and it amused him. He had seen men return to his care again and again with "a three-page rap sheet of burglary convictions without one mention of rape," but they didn't fool him. The yard-wise warden knew they were rapists. As he patiently explained to the general reader, each time up the man had copped a plea in court. By arrangement he had pleaded guilty to burglary and in return the rape charge had been quietly dropped. For good reason. Burglary could mean a one-to-five-year sentence while rape could mean twenty years to life. "Rape is often so difficult to prove," he airily explained, "that prosecutors will settle for a burglary conviction."

Duffy spoke from strength when he wrote, "Rapists are usually all-round offenders with a long list of convictions. The opportunity for rape often crops up while they're in the course of committing another felony, and they take advantage of it. Actually, practically every offender who is not an overt homosexual is a potential rapist. And most habitual criminals have rape, or the burglary conviction that really means rape, somewhere on their rap sheets. I have never known of a 'second-story' burglar who climbed into the window of a man's apartment."

When Duffy fished out one of these pseudo burglars, he rarely let the fellow off his hook. What happened next was usually a fierce battle of wills. He reported with no small degree of satisfaction, " 'I'm no rapo!' may cut some ice in the yard but it adds years to the time [a man] spends in prison. If he's on an indeterminate sentence he won't get out until he responds to treatment, and if he refuses therapy there's nothing for him to respond to." Few prison wardens took their jobs as seriously as Clinton Duffy.

As described by Warden Duffy or as defined by the statistical profiles of the sociologists and the FBI, America's police-blotter rapists are dreary and banal. To those who know them, no magic, no mystery, no Robin Hood bravura, infuses their style. Rape is a dull, blunt, ugly act committed by punk kids, their cousins and older brothers, not by charming, witty, unscrupulous, heroic, sensual rakes, or by timid souls deprived of a "normal" sexual outlet, or by *super-menschen* possessed of uncontrollable lust. And yet, on the shoulders of these unthinking, predictable, insensitive, violence-prone young men there rests an age-old burden that amounts to an historic mission: the perpetuation of male domination over women by force.

The Greek warrior Achilles used a swarm of men descended from ants, the Myrmidons, to do his bidding as hired henchmen in battle. Loyal and unquestioning, the Myrmidons served their master well, functioning in anonymity as effective agents of terror. Police-blotter rapists in a very real sense perform a myrmidon function for all men in our society. Cloaked in myths that obscure their identity, they, too, function as anonymous agents of terror. Although they are the ones who do the dirty work, the actual *attentat*, to other men, their superiors in class and station, the lasting benefits of their simple-minded evil have always accrued.

A world without rapists would be a world in which women moved freely without fear of men. That *some* men rape provides a sufficient threat to keep all women in a constant state of intimidation, forever conscious of the knowledge that the biological tool must be held in awe for it may turn to weapon with sudden swiftness borne of harmful intent. Myrmidons to the cause of male dominance, police-blotter rapists have performed their duty well, so well in fact that the true meaning of their act has largely gone unnoticed. Rather than society's aberrants or "spoilers of purity," men who commit rape have served in effect as front-line masculine shock troops, terrorist guerrillas in the longest sustained battle the world has ever known.

7

A Question of Race

No single event ticks off America's political schizophrenia with greater certainty than the case of a black man accused of raping a white woman. Facts are irrelevant to the public imagination. Objectivity is thrown out the window. A maze of angled mirrors buried deep within the individual psyche rises to confront the perceiver and distort the vision. What is the truth? Upon hearing the bare outlines of such a case—no, upon merely learning the race of defendant and victim—a convulsive reaction sets in. Part of the public screams guilty while another part, equally vociferous, equally certain, screams innocent, a frame-up. Racism and sexism and the fight against both converge at the point of interracial rape, the baffling crossroads of an authentic, peculiarly American dilemma.

There is no unemotional way to approach the subject of interracial rape, and no way for me to pretend to an objectivity of my own. I speak as a white woman whose first stirrings of social conscience occurred when I read of certain famous cases, now legend, in which black men had been put to death for coming too close to white women. Tales of Scottsboro, Emmett Till and Willie McGee were part of my formative experience. As a rebellious young woman during the height of McCarthyism, when most people could not say the word "Communist" without trembling, I took myself down to the old Jefferson School and enrolled in a night course taught by Dr. Herbert Aptheker, the American Communist historian. There, while the outside world screeched and red-baited, I sat as a respectful student and listened to Aptheker's analysis of black slavery. Thunderous and dogmatic, Aptheker was an impressive teacher. In his classroom I heard for the first time in my life that rape was a political act, for it was Aptheker's thesis that the white man imposed a special burden of humiliation and oppression on the black woman by forcing her to submit to his sexual will.

My political and intellectual debt to Herbert Aptheker is great and this is as good a place as any to acknowledge it, for as the child grows up and finds the parent wanting, so too, from my present vantage point, I find the Aptheker thesis severely limited. Aptheker and the Communist Party understood rape as a political act of subjugation only when the victim was black and the offender was white. White-on-white rape was merely "criminal" and had no part in their Marxist canon. Black-on-black rape was ignored. And black-on-white rape, about which the rest of the country was phobic, was discussed in the oddly reversed world of the Jefferson School as if it never existed except as a spurious charge that "the state" employed to persecute black men.

But as I said, I owe a debt to Aptheker, who was the first to tell me that rape was a political crime, who taught me the tools of dialectic logic, and who shouldn't be surprised that I have carried his argument further than he intended.

In 1968 I wrote a long piece for *Esquire* which appeared under the title "Rashomon in Maryland." It was the story of three black youths who had received a death sentence for raping a sixteen-year-old white girl near a lovers' lane. At the time I asked for the assignment, the young men had spent six years on Death Row, their case had been to the Supreme Court twice and an active citizens' defense committee, formed to protest the severity of the sentence, had become convinced of their innocence. To the defense committee, the original crime appeared to be nothing more than a little escapade of consensual sex that upon discovery a promiscuous, unstable white girl decided to call rape. It didn't take them long to convince me. As it happened, while I was preparing my final copy, a new trial was ordered, the case was dismissed, and the three defendants were set free, which wrapped things up neatly in terms of the piece.

But while I was pursuing my single-minded researches, a friend who lived in Washington and was following the case asked me one day, "How can you be so sure they're innocent?"

"What do you mean?" I testily replied. "There's a long line of these cases. It's a little Scottsboro, there's a defense committee."

"Yes, I know," she answered. "But what makes you so positive? You weren't there. How do you *really know* what went on? How does anyone know?"

How did I "know"? I didn't. At the time it was enough for me to know that the defendants were poor and black, that the girl's "reputation for chastity" was not good, and that an unpaid defense committee was working itself to a frazzle to get the conviction overturned. That was all the proof I needed. My knee-jerk reactions were as fast as anybody's, left or right.

One other thing I had learned at the Jefferson School was the value of the Schomburg Center for Research in Black Culture housed on 135th Street in Harlem. And so when I began my researches for this book and knew I wanted to have a chapter on rape in slavery, I went to the Schomburg to see what it had in the way of documentation.

"I'm writing a book on rape," I told a librarian. "You wouldn't by any chance have any special files."

He looked acutely unhappy. I was soon to learn that no library in the world has efficiently catalogued rape material, but that wasn't the cause of this librarian's discomfort. "Why did you come here?" he asked with caution.

"Because I thought this would be the best place to find historical stuff on the rape of black women. I'm writing a serious book."

"Then you mean to ask about the lynching of black men."

"Sir, I know about that," I answered, "and I know where to find the material when I'm ready for it. At this point I really need to know about the rape of black women."

"I'm sorry, young lady. If you're serious about your subject you need to start with the historic injustice to black men. That must be your approach."

"That has been your approach, sir. I'm interested in the historic injustice to women."

"To black people, rape has meant the lynching of the black man," he said with his voice rising.

It was an awful facedown, this confrontation between an aging black man with old left values and an irascible white feminist with beginning-a-book anxieties. He directed me to a seat and for the next two hours he patiently filled the long wood table in front of me with bound volumes of trial records, comparative studies of conviction rates and sentences, NAACP anti-lynch pamphlets and the like. True to his word, all the material focused on the black man as victim. Finally I screwed up my courage to try again. "There's nothing here about women," I said in what I hoped were even tones.

He disappeared into a back room and re-emerged with two manilla folders. "Perhaps this is what you're looking for."

One folder was marked "Rape." It was a collection of newspaper clippings dating back to the nineteen forties and culled from New York tabloids and the *Daily Worker*. The tabloid clips were garish features on black rapists and rape-murderers, complete with pictures of wild-eyed men in handcuffs and high-school graduation photos of their white victims, articles clearly designed to exploit racial fears. In contrast, the *Worker* articles were short, pamphleteering accounts of Southern interracial rape trials, lynchings, near-lynchings, and the work of defense and/or justice committees. The second folder was marked "Women." It contained a pile of invitations and souvenir programs from some national Negro sororities.

Why should I have found the male bias of the Schomburg Center any more distressing than the male bias of the A. A. Brill Collection at the New York Psychoanalytic Institute where I did my research on Freudian theories of rape? I don't know. But I did.

According to the FBI's *Uniform Crime Reports*, 47 percent of all Americans arrested for rape in 1973 were black, as opposed to 58 percent of all those arrested for murder and 63 percent of those arrested for armed robbery. These statistics are interesting from several angles. For one thing, the black crime rate in this country appears to be wildly out of proportion to the 1970 census figures, which show a black population of 11 percent, although blacks claim they are chronically undercounted in the census, and I would agree. But what is really interesting about these figures, once we stipulate that poverty and ghetto conditions are breeding grounds for violent crime, is that the black rapist lags behind other black criminals by eleven to sixteen percentage points. This may be due to underreporting and undercounting of black-on-black rape (see pages 366–67).

The FBI holds to a firm policy of not reporting arrest figures for interracial rape. This is unfortunate because these figures would be a valuable national statistic. Four other studies that I know of have been more revealing. The staff of the National Commission on the Causes and Prevention of Violence did a 17-city survey based on 1967 police statistics and came up with a figure of 10 percent for black-on-white rape and a "negligible" percent (.3) for white-on-black rape, which the staff report qualified with the statement, "Because white males have long had nearly institutionalized access to Negro women with relatively little fear of being reported, it is likely that the true proportion of Negroes raped by whites is larger."*

A Memphis police department study by Brenda A. Brown of reported rapes and attempted rapes, using 1973 statistics, discovered that 16 percent of all rapes in Memphis were black on white, but only .56 percent were white on black.

Menachem Amir, studying the files of the Philadelphia police department for 1958 and 1960, found that in those years only 7 percent of the Philadelphia rapes were interracial. Breaking it down, Amir found that in 4 percent of the cases white men raped black women and in 3 percent of the cases black men raped white women.

Dr. Charles Hayman did a yearly analysis of rape victims admitted to D.C. General Hospital in Washington from 1965 to 1971, during a period of time in which 95 percent of all Washington's reported rape victims were taken to D.C. General for their medical examinations. Hayman found that in this city with a black population of 70 percent, black-on-black rape accounted for 76 percent of all his cases, white-on-white rape accounted for 3 percent, white-on-black rape amounted to less than half of a percent-

---

* The staff report of the National Commission on the Causes and Prevention of Violence also discussed interracial aspects of other crimes that the FBI's *Uniform Crime Reports* avoid. In the same 17-city survey it was estimated that 47 percent of all reported robberies were cases of "younger black males robbing older white males." Robbery, generally characterized by "have-nots" forcibly taking from those they perceive as "haves," contains the highest interracial component of any violent crime. Rape has the second-highest interracial component.

age point, but black-on-white rape accounted for a significant 21 percent of all reported Washington rapes.

Hayman's Washington data and Brown's Memphis data were compiled more than a decade after Amir's Philadelphia study, and that decade, the sixties, was marked by an explosion of racial tension throughout the United States. As a matter of fact Hayman discovered that the percentage of black-on-white rapes rose each year. Amir did not publish his findings until 1971 and Hayman, a public health administrator for the city of Washington, felt compelled to write, "In contrast to Amir's finding very few cases of white females raped by blacks, these constituted a significant proportion of our series, especially when physical injury was sustained and in victims 25 years and older. Although we agree that reported rape is mostly a black-black phenomenon, the increasing number and proportion of black-white rapes indicates to us an increase in aggression and violence, in hostility to females, and to white females."

The difference between an incidence of 3 percent for black-on-white rapes (Philadelphia, c. 1960) and 21 percent (Washington, c. 1970) is startling. It is also unsettling, inflammatory and somehow illiberal even to talk about. Why? For the answer we need to look at another series of statistics.

Professor Marvin Wolfgang of the University of Pennsylvania's school of criminology and Professor Anthony Amsterdam of the university's law school did a comparison study of three thousand rape convictions in eleven Southern states between 1945 and 1965. Thirteen percent of all convicted blacks were executed. By comparing the rate of black executions to white executions, Wolfgang and Amsterdam found that blacks were seven times as likely as whites to receive this maximum penalty. If, however, a black was convicted of raping a white woman, he was 18 times as likely to be executed as a black who raped a black, a white who raped a white, or a white who raped a black woman. (Wolfgang's extensive research into comparative patterns of punishment made him conclude that blacks usually receive longer prison terms than whites for most—but not, as we shall see, *all*—criminal offenses.)

Statistics from the U.S. Department of Justice show that of all men executed in these United States for rape since 1930 (the last execution for rape was in 1964; the last execution for any crime was in 1967), 89 percent have been black. (The Justice Department does not reveal how many of these executions were for interracial rape.)

A study of rape convictions in the city of Baltimore conducted by a black bar association in 1967 also shows a pattern of discriminatory sentencing. Seventy-five percent of the 629 men brought to trial for rape in Baltimore between 1962 and 1966 were black. Black-on-black cases accounted for 449 of these trials. Conviction rates for black-on-black rape and white-on-white rape matched each other at 57 percent. Conviction rates for interracial rape were considerably higher: 78 percent for black-on-white rape and 83 percent for white-on-black rape, but in one-fifth as many trials.

Of the four categories of rapist and victim in a racial mix, blacks received the stiffest sentences for raping white women *and the mildest sentences for raping black women*. Of the 26 blacks convicted in Baltimore of raping white women, 13 received sentences of from 20 years to life, three received a life sentence, and one was sentenced to death. Only one got less than five-to-ten years. Of the five white men convicted in Baltimore of raping black women, one received a sentence of from 15 to 20 years, three received less than five years, and one received a suspended sentence.

Excluding the death penalty and the life sentence, punishment for Baltimore rapists in each of the four categories looked like this:

RACIAL MIX OF CRIME	NO. OF MEN BROUGHT TO TRIAL	CONVICTION RATE	NO. OF CONVICTIONS	SENTENCE IN YEARS, EXCL. LIFE OR DEATH
b/w	33	78%	26	15.4
w/b	6	83%	5	4.6
w/w	141	57%	81	3.67
b/b	449	57%	258	3.18

Other studies in my files, some extending back to 1890, show the same discriminatory pattern. Heavier sentences imposed on blacks for raping white women is an incontestable historic fact.

This chapter is going to concern itself with interracial rape as a national obsession, and by that I mean the phenomenon of black men raping white women, both fear of and fact, how the meaning of the act is understood by white men and black men, and how the white woman and the black woman have been used by both as a pawn in the cause of politics, ideology and power.

In the slaveholding South, revolt and rape by dehumanized black hordes was the classic white male nightmare. The purity of white womanhood, enforced by social mores as compelling as the whip, was as critical a touchstone of white masculinity as the system of slaveholding itself. Aware of his wholesale transgression against the black female slave, which he refused to conceptualize as criminal rape, the slaveholder was eternally vigilant against a reverse of the syndrome. Rumors and scare stories of slave conspiracies usually featured the rape of white women as the ultimate purpose of the slaves' revenge.

"The entire Negro population, at least the greater part, had conspired to assault their masters on a certain night, massacre all the population [and] make the women either their slaves or use them to gratify their desires," a soldier in Charleston wrote in his diary in 1736 after listening to the local gossip—but historians have been unable to verify this alleged Charleston conspiracy. "After confessing the conspiracy, each of them declar[ed] whose wife, daughter or sister he had fixed on for his future bedfellow," a magazine reported in 1757, but no documentation exists for this conspiracy either.

In fact, organized slave revolts in the South were few and there is no evidence that rape played a part in any of them, perhaps because those that did get beyond the planning stage were quickly snuffed out.

William Styron was roundly criticized by several black writers a few years ago for injecting a "thwarted rape" motif into his fictional account of the Nat Turner rebellion. "Infuriating sexual slander of the Negro male," Mike Thelwell called it, continuing, "this kind of neurotic frustration finds expression in solitary, suicidal acts of violence, not in planned, public, political acts of rebellion." A noble revolutionary sentiment from Thelwell, and accurate enough in Nat Turner's case, but as the quixotic Marxist historian Eugene Genovese suggested in his own countercriticism of the anti-Styron broadside, Styron's literary license is not without some basis in fact if one wants to extend one's horizon to Haiti, where the slave rebellion led by Toussaint L'Ouverture was partially successful. Toussaint's black biographer, C. L. R. James, wrote of the Haitian revolt, "The slaves destroyed tirelessly. . .

They, whose women had undergone countless violations, violated all the women who fell into their hands, often on the bodies of their still bleeding husbands, fathers and brothers."

But this wasn't the pattern in the American South, except in the morbid imagination of the slaveholder. Individual acts of rape by black slaves upon white women, "solitary, suicidal acts of violence," did occur, and taking the broadest possible perspective on the nature of rebellion, they were probably as "political" as any individual act of slave arson, for a slave might have a firm understanding of what constituted hit-and-run damage to the white man's property, being property himself.

Sifting through the state of Virginia's records of slaves sentenced to death during the eighty-year period prior to emancipation, Ulrich B. Phillips, the grand old man of American slavery historians, found 105 convictions for sexual assault: 73 for rape and 32 for attempted rape. Two of the rape victims had been free mulatto women; all the rest were white. "That no slave women were mentioned among the victims is of course far from proving that these were never violated," Phillips carefully noted, "for such offenses appear to have been largely left to the private cognizance of the masters."*

Harking back to concepts of retribution found in early English law, the Southern slaveholders wrote their codes to include the penalty of castration. Once legal punishment for a variety of slave crimes, including running away, when the colony of Virginia decided to phase out dismemberment in 1769, it kept the penalty on the books for slaves convicted of raping white women. Among those troubled by the castration statute was Thomas Jefferson, who wrote to James Madison from Paris in 1786 advising him of French opinion: "The principle of retaliation is much criticized here, particularly in the case of Rape. They think the punishment indecent and unjustifiable. I should be for altering it, but for a different reason: that is on account of the temptation women would be under to make it the instrument of vengeance against an inconstant lover, and of disappointment to a rival."

---

* During the same time span Phillips found 346 convictions for murder (85 of the victims were fellow slaves; 39 of the murderers were women), 257 convictions for burglary, 90 for arson (29 of the arsonists were women), and 111 convictions for miscellaneous assault.

But castration was not the usual punishment. Throughout most of the South's slaveholding history a simple, mandatory sentence of death awaited the slave found guilty of interracial rape. Black freedmen found guilty of raping white women fared little better than slaves. The 1860 Code of Virginia provided a maximum penalty of 20 years in jail for any white rapist but a freedman could be punished by death, even for attempted rape. (During Reconstruction, Virginia's statutes were amended to remove the blatant race distinction.)

And beyond the legal apparatus stood the lynch mob, the unveiled expression of violent retaliation reminiscent of the blood-vengeance codes of prehistory. The role that lynching was later to play in American history as the chief extralegal weapon for intimidating Southern blacks was modeled after the pattern set during the slaveholding years when rape or suspicion of rape was one sure way to call the citizenry to arms. A Mississippi newspaper editorialized in 1843 after a band of whites pursued and hanged two slaves who had raped a farmer's wife, "We have ever been and now are opposed to any kind of punishment being administered under the statutes of Judge Lynch; but . . . a due regard for . . . all that is most dear to man in the domestic circles of life impels us to acknowledge the fact that if the perpetrators of this excessively revolting crime had been burned alive . . . their fate would have been too good for such diabolical and inhuman wretches."

What precisely was it that was dear to man in the domestic circles of his life? A slaveholder's wife once blurted out to Harriet Martineau that she was nothing more than the "chief slave of the harem" on her husband's plantation. Legal bearer of his children, prized decorative ornament, sometime companion, bestowed with the external trappings of privilege but denied real power, the white woman was her husband's choicest piece of property. Valued for her chastity, access to her sexuality was wholly owned by the same white master who could daily violate the sexual integrity of his black female slave. Chastity of the white woman was a serious matter that the rule of marriage required to ensure legal heirs, just as a corresponding denial of chastity and legal marriage to the black woman gave the slaveholder clear title to ownership of all children born of slaves.

White men, whether they were slaveholders or not, viewed white women as a private fief of less than equal beings. A white woman could not vote, hold office, or sit on a jury; she could not attain a higher education, and she could not own land, slaves or money in her own right after marriage. The highly vaunted pedestal on which she was placed had a hard-rock base of economic dependence, and the fastest way to get knocked off that pedestal was to show an inclination for sexual freedom. Evidence of a white woman's sexual independence was considered a direct challenge to the white man's inviolable holdings, and when a white woman was discovered to have "had connection" with a black man in voluntary association, the collective white male mind felt it had sustained a property loss.

Vindictiveness toward white women who took black lovers or married them was written into the white man's law. Colonial legislation in North Carolina, South Carolina, Maryland and Virginia directed a white woman who bore a mulatto child to pay a fine to the court; in addition, her child might be placed in indentured servitude until the age of 31 and the woman herself was bound out as a servant for five years or more. This one-way discouragement of interracial relations was not restricted to the South. A colonial Pennsylvania court ordered a white woman who bore a mulatto "bastard childe" to receive 21 lashes "on her beare backe." Enforcement like this was designed to serve as a fierce deterrent, for the white man saw sexual activity between a black man and a white woman as a horrible threat to his hegemony. Rape, then, was merely a matter of degree.

But when a white woman's reputation for chastity was open to question, the collective rage regarding her rape by a black man was considerably abated. During a forty-four year period in slaveholding Virginia (1789–1833), out of sixty cases in which the courts imposed a death sentence on blacks convicted of interracial rape, the white woman's sullied past was raised as an issue after the trial in 27 instances, either in a jury's recommendation to the governor for mercy or in a citizens' petition demanding full pardon. Mitigating circumstances incorporated into these mercy pleas included the presence of mulatto children, no visible means of support, socializing on an equal basis with families of free blacks, a mother who socialized freely with blacks, and in the case of a slave named Peter convicted of raping one Patsy Hooker, a petition signed by 62 white men of Hanover County who swore, "The said Patsy Hooker . . . is a common strumpet."

When a freedman named Tasco Thompson was sentenced to death in 1833 for an attempted rape of a young girl named Mary Jane Stevens in her mother's house, the foreman of the jury that voted to convict him filed a plea for mercy that contained a revealing discourse on the nature and purpose of the white man's rape law.

> It was notorious [he wrote] that the mother had long entertained Negroes, and that all her associations, with one or two exceptions, were with blacks. . . . In a word she was below the level of the ordinary grade of free Negroes. . . . There is no doubt that [Tasco Thompson] repaired to the house of Mrs. Stevens in the belief that she would cheerfully submit to his embraces, as she doubtless had often done before, but finding her absent he probably supposed his embraces would be equally agreeable to her daughter . . .

Having thus disposed of the facts in the case to his satisfaction, the foreman went on to say that he and his fellow jurors

> considered that the law was made to preserve the distinction which should exist between our two kinds of population, and to protect the whites in the possession of their superiority; but here the whites had yielded their claims to the protection of the law by their voluntary associations with those whom the law distinguishes as their inferiors. As a prosecution would not have a claim in the case if the female concerned had been a colored girl, so the jury thought it hard to convict the prisoner for an offence not greater in enormity than had the prosecutrix been colored; but her maker had given her a white skin, and they had no discretion.

What was the argument in this and other pleas? Not that the crime of rape did not take place—the petitions do not address themselves to this point—but that the poor reputations of a certain class of white women render their rape a lesser crime *even if* their rapists are black. In the eyes of white men these women were damaged property before the crime and not worth the loss of a good slave or laborer.

Thus from slavery onward, the black man's fortune was inextricably and historically linked to the white woman's reputation for chastity, a terrifying imbroglio that the black man and the white woman neither created nor controlled.

A memorable scene in D. W. Griffith's epic *The Birth of a Nation* shows a glorious gallop by white-hooded knights of the Ku Klux Klan in pursuit of a rolling-eyed black intent on rape who drove a beautiful and virginal blonde to suicide. It was Griffith's view, pictorially expressed, that the rise of the Klan was an heroic effort to save white womanhood from wholesale black assault during the crisis of Reconstruction. This particular scene and others caused near-riots in front of some Northern movie houses when *The Birth of a Nation* was first released in 1915. As I have detailed in another chapter, some of the Klan's nightriding, in fact, had ended in the rape of black women, or in the murder of black men whose crime had been not the desire for white women but the ownership of valuable land or the desire to vote. But as unpopular as *The Birth of a Nation* was among radicals in the North, it accurately reflected popular opinion in the white South, which did regard the Klan as heroic in its "defense" of white womanhood.

W. J. Cash, a thoughtful white Southerner, was at pains to define what he called a pervasive Southern "rape complex" during the Reconstruction in *The Mind of the South.* "What the Southerners felt," he wrote, "was that any assertion of any kind on the part of the Negro constituted in a perfectly real manner an attack on the Southern woman. What they saw, more or less consciously, in the conditions of Reconstruction was a passage toward a condition for her as degrading, in their view, as rape itself."

Cash articulated the deepest fears of Southern white men in his book. Was not the logical result of emancipation, he wrote, that the black man would "one day advance the whole way and lay claim to complete equality, including, specifically, the crucial right of marriage?" And if this happened, the proudest privilege of white men would be destroyed—"the right of their sons in the legitimate line, through all the generations to come, to be born to the great heritage of white men." Adding to the white man's fears in Cash's analysis was the role played by Yankee scalawags and carpetbaggers who "provocatively" told their black friends "about the coming of a day when Negroes would take the daughters of their late masters for concubines."

As for the daughters, the object of all this attention and speculation, Cash wrote, "There was real fear, and in some districts even terror, on the part of the white women themselves. And there were neurotic old maids and wives, hysterical young girls, to react to all this in a fashion well understood now, but understood by almost nobody then."

Cash published *The Mind of the South* in 1941, and by that time the view that Southern white women were given to neurotic, hysterical overreactions was being loudly trumpeted. Curiously, no such hysterical apprehension appears in Mary Boykin Chestnut's authentic *Diary from Dixie:* a little nervousness regarding attitudes toward women on the part of Sherman's advancing army, but no morbid fear of being raped by blacks. Nor had the prescient Fanny Kemble sensed any threat to her bodily safety during her stay on her husband's Georgia plantation, although she had been acutely sensitive to the rape of black women by both whites and blacks. And Margaret Mitchell, who achieved total empathy with the mind of a nineteenth-century white Southern woman in *Gone with the Wind*, imparted no such fears and terrors to Scarlett O'Hara. Scarlett's closest scrape with a criminal black during Reconstruction was over her money and not her body.

Whether or not one cares to accept an analysis of Southern white women as prone to neurosis and hysteria, and I do not accept it, the Southern rape complex that Cash described was all too real. Identification of the lynching of a black man with the rape of a white woman was so complete that a whispered euphemism, "the one crime," sufficed as explanation in both black and white circles.

When the newly formed National Association for the Advancement of Colored People took on the job of tabulating lynch statistics in 1912, one of its priorities was an attempt to verify just how many lynchings had been motivated by rape or the faintest suspicion of it. The tabulation was published in *Thirty Years of Lynching in the United States*, a painfully documented booklet of more than 100 pages. From 1889 to 1918, the NAACP reported, 3,224 persons had been killed by lynch mobs, 2,838 of them (seven-eighths of the total) in the South. Seventy-eight percent of the victims were black. Sixty-one women were also among those lynched, 50 of them black.*

Of the white men lynched, 8.4 percent had been accused of

---

* A terse NAACP report on a black female lynch victim: "May 26, 1911, Okemah, Oklahoma.—A colored woman accused of having shot a sheriff was taken by a mob and, together with her fourteen-year-old son, was hanged from a bridge. The woman was raped before she was hanged."

"rape and attacks upon women." Among the blacks the percentage was 28.4. The NAACP cautiously summed up,

> It may be fairly pointed out that in a number of cases where Negroes have been lynched for rape and "attacks upon white women," the alleged attacks rest upon no stronger evidence than "entering the room of a woman" or brushing against her. . . . In many cases, of course, the evidence points to *bona fide* attacks upon women. . . . It is apparent that lynchings of Negroes for other causes than the so-called "one crime" have for the whole period been a large majority of all lynchings and that for the past five years [1914–1918], less than one in five of the colored victims have been accused of rape or "attacks on women."

Yet "the one crime" myth persisted in the popular imagination and those who joined the fight against lynching in the next two decades were forced to deal with it head on. Not surprisingly, political groups of differing persuasions in the nineteen thirties and forties developed divergent methods of exposing the rape excuse, which often set them at each other's throats.

In 1931, eleven years after the enfranchisement of women, which the South had bitterly resisted to the end, a white church-woman from Atlanta named Jessie Daniel Ames organized the Association of Southern Women for the Prevention of Lynching in direct response to lynch-law propaganda that summary mob action was needed to protect white female chastity. Working through church groups in fifteen states and one thousand counties, the Association women (white, middle- and upper-class) began their political education work with a massive campaign for signatures to a strongly worded declaration.

"We declare lynching is an indefensible crime," their statement began.

> We believe that . . . public opinion has accepted too easily the claim of lynchers and mobsters that they were acting solely in the defense of womanhood. In the light of facts, women dare not longer permit the claim to pass unchallenged nor allow themselves to be the cloak behind which those bent upon personal revenge and savagery commit acts of violence and lawlessness in the name of women. We repudiate this disgraceful claim for all time.

Jessie Ames later credited female suffrage with helping to change the public climate in regard to lynching since the vote freed Southern women from "the oft-repeated and generally accepted statement that no real lady would degrade herself by participating in politics." Despite hooting opposition from many white male community leaders who felt the ladies were stepping into a dangerous area in which they had no business, the Association collected more than forty thousand signatures from their white Southern sisters in the next few years. Their activism did not end with the signature drive, or with pamphlets, conferences, questionnaires to politicians and plays performed at church suppers. With a bravery that equaled that of the Southern blacks who worked with the NAACP, they undertook their own investigations of lynchings to determine the real root cause and published their information in special bulletins.

> *Lowndes County, Miss. 1933,—1.* Accused of insulting white woman—Hanged. Rumored that charge of insult to white woman furnished excuse to landlord to "put away" Negro tenant whose crop the landlord wanted. Visiting preacher conducting revival services for local church was told that meeting might be disturbed because "there was to be a lynching that night." He made no effort to prevent the lynching. Lynching was not known outside the community until body, thrown in creek, came to surface some days later. (Mob of about 10 men.)

"Taken from the sheriff," "taken from the courthouse," "taken from the jail," was the common way a lynching began. Outside the South the collusion of Southern sheriffs was a glaring fact that did not require any mincing of words. Inside the South, in the very communities in which lynchings took place, these sheriffs had a vivid personal reality and identity to members of the Association. A sheriff might be a relative or neighbor; in any event, he was the known local figure entrusted with the maintenance of law and order, someone to greet by name, someone who might drop in on that church supper, someone with whom one was used to exchanging civilities. To white Southern women, a white Southern sheriff was one of *their own men.*

"Whatever else may be said about Southern women, it cannot

be said that they lack the moral courage to act according to their convictions," Jessie Ames was to write. "When from their own investigations of lynchings allegedly committed to protect Southern womanhood, they found that they were used as a shield behind which their own men committed cowardly acts of violence against a helpless people, they took the only action they could." By 1937 the Southern women began naming names.

Abbeville, Henry County, Alabama, February 2—Negro accused of criminal assault on a white woman; taken from custody of Sheriff J. L. Corbitt. . . . Impeachment proceedings brought against sheriff, who was exonerated by a 4 to 2 vote. . . . Testimony disclosed that the sheriff waited about four hours before he began to search for the mob. . . . The sheriff and his deputy never overtook the mob.

Milton, Santa Rosa County, Florida, October 3—Negro accused of "unnatural crime" against a white boy and robbery of a filling station was taken from Sheriff Joe Allen on highway and shot. Prisoner had been held at Panama City for safekeeping until time for his trial; he was being brought back to Milton for trial when the mob got him.

"WHERE WERE THE PEACE OFFICERS?" the Association's bulletin asked. "All eight victims of lynching in 1937 were in the hands of Peace Officers. In seven of the lynchings, investigations indicate that officers of the law were either in the mob or were in collusion with the mob. In the eighth lynching no conclusive evidence has yet been obtained. . . . It is difficult to believe, however, that any officer who has custody of a prisoner is entirely ignorant of an intention to lynch on the part of his constituents or is unable to identify any of the mob."

Someday I hope someone will write the full story of the fight to eradicate lynching in the South with special attention to the interorganizational squabbles, typical of radical politics, that usurped the energies and debilitated the efforts of all of the groups. Whose statistics were the most reliable, whether or not to support federal anti-lynching legislation, who was being namby-pamby, who was being inflammatory, who had the right to speak and who was an outside agitator, was lynching a product of "lawless elements" or was it "carefully organized . . . with the cooperation of every ruling class agency," was it better to work quietly within the community or was it better to put forward a political overview—the battles never ceased to rage.

The role of the Communist Party deserves careful study, for this was the grouping that put forward an all-encompassing political overview couched in ferocious rhetoric. Sometimes the rhetoric contained brilliant insights that few had seen before and sometimes it was nothing more than a frenetic jumble of misstated facts. In 1932, during a time when the Communists were at loggerheads with the NAACP, International Publishers put out its own pamphlet on lynching that laid down the party line. Reserving a good part of their venom for NAACP leaders W. E. B. Du Bois, Walter White and Clarence Darrow—for their "dastardly evasion of the real cause of lynching"—the authors of "International Pamphlet No. 25" denounced the NAACP for promoting the theory that lynching might be understood as an isolated phenomenon, the terrible sport of lawless, uneducated poor whites. "No," they thundered. "Lynchings defend profits! Lynchings are a warning to the Negro toilers. Lynching is one of the weapons with which the white ruling class enforces its national oppression of the Negro people and tries to maintain division between the white workers and the Negro toilers."

The rhetoric was terrible, the attack on Du Bois and the others was patently unfair, but the germ of the idea was sound. In 1947 The President's Committee on Civil Rights issued a famous report, *To Secure These Rights*, which showed that Communist Party theory, in part, had been absorbed into mainstream thinking. *To Secure These Rights* concluded, "Lynching is the ultimate threat by which his inferior status is driven home to the Negro. As a terrorist device, it reinforces all the other disabilities placed upon him."

"International Pamphlet No. 25" also had thunderous words to say about rape. In a style that C.P. literature favored, rape was never written as rape but always in quotation marks as "rape" and sometimes contained within the phrase "the capitalist rape lie":

The "Rape" Lie

To incite the white workers against the Negroes and to further build the myth of "white superiority," the white ruling class has

coined the poisonous and insane lie that Negroes are "rapists." . . .
The cry of "rape" is raised whenever any Negro worker begins to
rise from his knees. We may be certain that of the Negro workers
lynched for "rape," practically none, if any, were guilty of a crime
committed innumerable times by whites against Negro women, and
punished, if ever at all, by a few months in jail. . . . The first time
we hear this lie is about the year 1830, two hundred years after the
Negroes were first unloaded from the slave ships in Virginia. Why
did it appear at this time? *Because this year marks the beginning of
the abolition movement in the North, and the sharpening struggle
of the slaves themselves for freedom.* For 200 years the Negro
workers were not "rapists." But as soon as their position as valuable
slaves was endangered, then they suddenly became "rapists." . . .
Many whites take advantage of the capitalist "rape" lie to protect
themselves . . .

If rape was a lie, with whom did the lie originate? "International Pamphlet No. 25" hedged the question, but it allowed the
reader to draw a fairly obvious conclusion. After all, phrases like
"the cry of 'rape' " and "the 'rape' lie" had a history to them.
Potiphar's wife had been a liar who maliciously cried rape. Thomas
Jefferson had warned of those women who might cry rape as an
instrument of vengeance. That Bible of American jurisprudence,
Wigmore on *Evidence*, required reading for students in law school,
cautioned against the female's tendency to lie.

Disbelief of a woman who said she had been raped had been
built into male logic since the days when men first allowed a
limited concept of criminal rape into their law, and the male
leaders of the Communist Party did not question this logic although they had forthrightly exposed and challenged other aspects
of property law. To Communists, feminism was always a dirty
word, a right-wing deviation, a bourgeois "error"—Lenin had said
as much to Clara Zetkin; Mother Bloor had made it plain. The
Communist Party, for all its talk about equality, maintained (and
still maintains, although it hardly matters today) that male supremacy was nothing more than an unfortunate "attitude" among
workers that would be eliminated after socialism had been
achieved. So it was historically inevitable that the American Communist Party of the nineteen thirties, controlled and directed by
white men, like all other political parties, would slight the veracity

of women and charge them with the sins of Potiphar's wife in its effort to clear the reputation of blacks.

Still, it took a woman, a Viennese disciple of Freud who had probably ventured no farther south than Boston, to provide the clincher. In the turbulent thirties two strains of thinking, Marxism and Freudianism, the one concerned with social forces and the other concerned with the individual psyche, collided and crashed against each other in the public arena. Yet these two currents of thinking, arising from such vastly different ideological wellsprings, managed to dovetail with startling precision on the role of the white woman in interracial rape. Once Dr. Helene Deutsch laid down her dictum of the hysterical, masochistic female, it was adopted with astonishing speed by those who wanted, or needed for their own peace of mind, to dilute white male responsibility for the Southern rape complex.

Describing the rape complex of the Reconstruction period from the vantage point of 1941, W. J. Cash had written of "neurotic old maids and wives, hysterical young girls," borrowing from a latter-day Freudian perspective. From where had the idea sprung? Four years earlier John Dollard, a Yale professor of psychology, had published a well-received appraisal of modern life in the South, *Caste and Class in a Southern Town*. In it Dollard quoted verbatim the views of Helene Deutsch, which he claimed to find "illuminating." Deutsch, he reported, had analyzed several white Southern women in whom she had found "marked sexual attraction to Negro men and masochistic fantasies connected with this attraction." Her blanket indictment followed: "The fact that the white men believe so readily the hysterical and masochistic fantasies and lies of the white women, who claim they have been assaulted and raped by Negroes, is related to the fact that they (the men) sense the unconscious wishes of the women, the psychic reality of these declarations, and react emotionally to them as if they were *real*. The social situation permits them to discharge this emotion upon the Negroes."

When Deutsch produced her two-volume *Psychology of Women* in 1944–1945 she reiterated her thesis. "Rape fantasies," she wrote, "often have such irresistible verisimilitude that even the most experienced judges are misled in trials of innocent men accused of rape by hysterical women. My own experience of ac-

counts by white women of rape by Negroes (who are often subjected to terrible penalties as a result of these accusations) has
convinced me that many fantastic stories are produced by the
masochistic yearnings of these women."

If one case convinced the American public—and international
opinion—that lying, scheming white women who cried rape were
directly responsible for the terrible penalties inflicted on black
men, the name of that case was Scottsboro. Most famous of all the
Southern rape cases for its miscarriage of justice, for the awesome
fact that it almost claimed nine lives, for its incredible longevity—
it dragged through the courts and the penal system for two decades
before the last defendant was finally set free—Scottsboro remains
an ugly blot on American history and Southern jurisprudence, and
damning proof to liberals everywhere that Eve Incarnate and the
concept of Original Sin was a no-good, promiscuous woman who
rode a freight train through Alabama.

It began routinely enough for the Depression year of 1931.
Two young women, "po' white trash," millworkers from Huntsville
recently laid off and used to supplementing their earnings with a
little catch-as-catch-can hustling, hopped a freight to Chattanooga
for a bit of adventure. Ruby Bates was seventeen and Victoria Price
was in her mid-twenties. They spent the night in an open field
known as a hobo jungle with some male companions and the next
morning, outfitted in denim overalls on top of their dresses, they
climbed aboard a Southern Railway gondola for the trip back to
Huntsville. Victoria Price had already known trouble with the law,
an arrest for violating the Volstead (Prohibition) Act and a short
stretch in the workhouse on an adultery conviction. Ruby Bates
was clean, but a minor.

They were not the only rootless young people riding the rails
that morning. Scattered the length of the train in open gondolas
and boxcars were black youths and white. Somewhere past Steven-
son a fistfight broke out between the blacks and the whites and the
white youths were forced off the train. News of the race fight was
telegraphed ahead to Paint Rock along with the information, volunteered by the vanquished white boys, that two white women
were still aboard the train and were in serious trouble. When the
train pulled into the Paint Rock station, rape was already in the air
and an armed posse of seventy-five men, augmented by an angry

crowd, was waiting. Nine blacks, ranging in age from thirteen to twenty, were rounded up. Victoria and Ruby tried to duck away and vanish in the confusion but they were cornered by the station-master. Ruby was the one who first answered his question with a faltering Yes.

Two years later Ruby Bates wrote a letter to her boyfriend. "Dearest Earl," she began,

> I want too make a statement too you Mary Sanders is a goddam lie about those Negroes jazzing me those policemen made me tell a lie that is my statement because I want too clear myself that is all too if you want too believe me Ok. If not that is ok. You will be sorry some day if you had too stay in jail with eight Negroes you would tell a lie two those Negroes did not touch me or those white boys I hope you will believe me the law dont. i love you better than Mary does ore any body else in the world that is why i am telling you of this thing i was drunk at the time and did not know what i was doing. i know it was wrong too let those Negroes die on account of me i hope you will believe my statement because it is the gods truth i hope you will believe me i was jazzed but those white boys jazzed me i wish those Negroes are not Burnt on account of me it is those white Boys fault that is my statement and that is all i know i hope you tell the law hope you will answer
>
> Ruby Bates

The first set of trials held at Scottsboro were quick affairs that might be termed farcical were it not for the fact that eight of the nine defendants were sentenced to death. A court-appointed lawyer reluctantly provided a defense and Ruby Bates and Victoria Price, who were kept in jail with possible vagrancy and/or prostitution charges held over their heads, testified for the prosecution. The singular opportunity afforded Price and Bates should be appreciated by every woman. From languishing in a jail cell as the lowest of the low, vagrant women who stole rides on freight cars, it was a short step to the witness stand where dignity of a sort could be reclaimed by charging that they had been pathetic, innocent victims of rape. (Victoria Price could never get herself to admit in court that she had spent a night in a Chattanooga hobo jungle. No, she stubbornly insisted in trial after trial, she had stayed in the home of a respectable lady.) Operating from precisely the same

motivation—to save their own skins—some of the black defendants tried to exculpate themselves in court by swearing they had
seen the others do the raping.

After the plight of the Scottsboro Boys had received international attention through world-wide publicity from the Communist movement—the Communists must be credited with keeping
the youths alive—and a million dollars had been raised in their
behalf, a new series of trials began. Samuel Leibowitz, hired by the
International Labor Defense to represent the defendants, made
legal history by getting the Supreme Court to acknowledge that
black men had been systematically excluded from serving on Alabama juries. Leibowitz later said that this was the proudest accomplishment of his life, and yet a feminist looking at the Scottsboro
case today must note that while every person who ever served on a
Scottsboro jury and voted to convict was white, he was also male,
and no one, no political grouping, no appellate lawyer, no Scottsboro pamphlet ever raised the question of the exclusion of women
from the jury rolls of Alabama, although many a pamphlet charged
that Victoria Price was a prostitute. (Women did not win the
right to sit on Alabama juries until 1966.)

Would a fair number of women, white and black, have made a
difference on a Scottsboro jury? Maybe so. Particularly when the
prosecuting attorney went into his standard "protection of Southern womanhood" speech. The Association of Southern Women for
the Prevention of Lynching had been formed to fight this approach. Would women sitting on those juries have been able to
understand the predicament faced by Victoria Price and Ruby
Bates? Perhaps. Might they have been able to distinguish a fake
rape story from a true one? Would they have been quicker to
understand the import of dead, nonmotile sperm in Victoria
Price's vagina to the exclusion of living sperm, which the defense
vainly argued was proof that whatever recent intercourse Virginia
Price had experienced had occurred in Huntsville or in the hobo
jungle but not on the train?

But why carry on with these speculations? The unalterable
fact remains that no woman ever served on a jury of the Scottsboro
nine, and each and every vote to convict was cast by a white man.
As the black defendants sat in an alien courtroom in which all the
forces of the law—judge, prosecution, defense and jury—were
white, so too the forces arrayed before them were all male. It was a

white man's game that was played out in the Scottsboro trials, with black men and white women as movable pawns, and white men judged interracial rape according to their own particular property code.

Sam Leibowitz, later Judge Leibowitz, once remarked that if Victoria Price and Ruby Bates had walked into a New York City police station and charged nine blacks with rape, after five minutes of questioning they would have been "tossed out of the precinct and that would have been the end of the whole affair. Even the dumbest cop on the force would have spotted those two as tramps and liars." While this may have been a fair assessment of the stereotypic Northern cop mentality, it seems to me that Leibowitz deliberately missed an essential point. Victoria and Ruby didn't quite walk into an Alabama police station either. They were corralled by a posse of white men who already believed a rape had taken place. Confused and fearful, they fell into line.

This is not an *ex post facto* deduction on my part, nor a fanciful rearrangement of sequences. It is a critical truth about Scottsboro. Early observers on the scene had also considered the time element a matter of some significance. Hollace Ransdell, a white woman sent south by the American Civil Liberties Union to conduct a private investigation of the Scottsboro case, filed her report to the ACLU in May, 1931, one month after the initial verdict. In it she stated that George Chamlee, the ILD attorney from Chattanooga who followed the case from the very beginning, was certain "that when the two girls were taken from the train at Paint Rock they made no charges against the Negroes until they were taken into custody; that their charges were made after they had found out the spirit of the armed men that came to meet the train and catch the Negroes, and that they were swept into making wholesale accusation against the Negroes merely by assenting to the charges as presented by the men who seized the nine Negroes."* Mary Heaton Vorse, writing in *The New Republic* in

---

* Hollace Ransdell obtained personal interviews with both young women, their mothers, neighbors and local social workers (the fathers had long vanished from the home). She pointed out with prescience that the quick-witted Victoria Price prided herself on being able to give the prosecution what it needed, thus becoming the star witness and courtroom pet, while the less articulate Ruby Bates had been shoved into the background and was seething with resentment. Two years later Ruby Bates exploded her bombshell.

1933, said tersely, "The girls in overalls, fearing a vagrancy charge, then accused the Negro boys of assault." This lucid explanation of the origin of the rape complaint later got lost in the avalanche of Scottsboro publicity.

After Ruby Bates made her spectacular recantation in the second trial of "ringleader" Haywood Patterson—Victoria Price desperately stuck to her original story and even embellished upon it—a new jury of twelve white men still voted a sentence of death. It was then that Judge James E. Horton, the "good" judge of the Scottsboro trials, set aside Patterson's conviction and ordered a third trial. He hadn't believed Victoria Price, and it cost him his judicial career in the next election. But Judge Horton's legal opinion did not explore the reasons why a jury of his white brothers might feel emotionally driven to convict a black man for rape and sentence him to death on insubstantial evidence. Nor did he stick to unraveling "the uncorroborated, improbable testimony of the prosecutrix." Horton had a grander theme, one that reached back to man's oldest suspicions.

"History, sacred and profane," he wrote, "and the common experience of mankind teaches that women of the character shown in this case are prone for selfish reasons to make false accusations both of rape and of insult upon the slightest provocation, or even without provocation for ulterior purposes. . . . The tendency on the part of the women shows they are predisposed to make false accusations upon any occasion whereby their selfish ends may be gained."

Blaming Scottsboro on the predisposition of a certain class of woman to make false accusations was an easy handle for the liberal mentality to grasp. Trouble was a white woman of murky virtue—the root of all evil—how neatly everything fell into place, how cleanly white men were absolved of guilt.

A study of penalties for rape in Louisiana from 1900 to 1950 showed that thirty-seven blacks had been duly executed by the state yet only two whites had met that extreme fate during the same fifty-year period. A study of executions for rape or attempted rape in Virginia during the years 1908 to 1963 showed that fifty-six blacks and no whites had been given the maximum penalty. As Southern white men continued to round up black men, lynch them or try them in a courtroom and give them the maximum sentence for the holy purpose of "protecting their women," Northern liberals looking at the ghastly pattern through an inverted prism saw the picture of a lying white woman crying rape-rape-rape.

In 1951 the last Scottsboro "Boy," by then a man of thirty-eight, had finally won his freedom, his name superseded in the pantheon of obscure Southern black men suddenly elevated to the position of international martyr by a succession of new cases, new trials, new convictions and death sentences pronounced in Southern courts for interracial rape, and corresponding new picket lines, petitions and protest rallies staged by leftists in the North and in Europe. The early fifties were a bad time for the American left. Its own house was under sharp attack from McCarthyism, the McCarran Act, the House Un-American Activities Committee, the Rosenberg case and the patriotic, anti-Red fervor whipped up by the Korean War. To Communists and those within their orbit who believed in the political strategy of mass action built around an emotional symbol, the Southern interracial rape case came to epitomize everything that was rotten or unjust about the American way of life. It was also a dramatic focal point for civil-rights efforts, the one last area in which the beleaguered Communist Party could —and did—have an effect that rippled beyond its diminishing ranks.

As a natural outgrowth of its *politik*, the Communist Party deliberately propagandized a series of interracial rape cases as symbolic of the perfidy of the American system. The injustice of Southern justice when it came to blacks was pronounced in many areas above and beyond the issue of rape and a sentence of death. When an authentic, black-originated Southern civil-rights movement got off the ground in the nineteen sixties, the new movement started not with symbolic cases but with pragmatic efforts at lunch-counter desegregation and voter registration. But rape had the historic violence of Southern lynch law behind it, a rape case had inherent drama, and a rape story could be told in such a fashion as to convince a listener of guilt or innocence or reasonable doubt. Moreover, many people outside the left were opposed to capital punishment (the Communist Party wasn't), particularly for a crime that did not take a life. Even more people cherished male-biased doubts that a woman could be raped against her will. All things considered, the left had done well, comparatively, on Scottsboro—as well as or better than it had done on the Haymarket case, Joe Hill, Tom Mooney, or Sacco and Vanzetti. Lives had been saved and thousands of new people had been politicized during the struggle. Liberals who were unwilling to buy the left's political and economic reasons for the historic oppression of blacks could mourn the tragedy of the South's mucked-up sexual racial relations, preferring to see sex, rather than politics or economics, as the root cause of a host of evils from segregation to genocide. And sex, of course, meant women.

Just once, as far as I have been able to determine, did the left go all out to publicize a rape case from the victim's perspective. In September, 1944, Recy Taylor, a twenty-four-year-old wife and mother, and a black woman, was abducted and raped by a gang of whites as she left a nighttime service of the Rock Hill Holiness Church in Abbeville, Alabama. Despite a confession from one member of the gang who named his accomplices, a grand jury repeatedly refused to indict the young men. A national Committee for Equal Justice for Mrs. Recy Taylor ("Send contributions to treasurer, Hon. Hulan Jack") tried to keep the case alive by distributing a pamphlet written by Earl Conrad, the biographer of Harriet Tubman, and Eugene Gordon, a black newspaperman. Gordon's contribution to the effort came as close as the left ever came to a feminist analysis of rape, a flash forward into the rhetoric of the seventies:

> The attack on Mrs. Taylor was an attack on all women. Mrs. Taylor is Negro. But the only reason a black woman was singled out was that owing to economic, social and political inequality established during and held over from slavery, she was unprotected, and, therefore, easy prey. A part of her helplessness came from the fact that the criminals believed they wouldn't be punished. The black woman, and not the white, is generally the object of debasement, but only because the black woman is less well protected economically and socially. The white woman is safe only to a degree above the safety of the black woman. No woman is safe or free until all women are free.

Recy Taylor never secured her equal justice and the Conrad-Gordon pamphlet remains an anomaly in left-wing literature. The left was more at ease politicizing rape as "rape," a fantasy charge designed to kill black men.

We Charge Genocide, the famous petition to the United Nations that was widely circulated by the Civil Rights Congress in

1951 (the Congress replaced the disbanded International Labor Defense as the left's mass-protest organization for civil-rights activities), devoted several paragraphs of hard-line rhetoric to a definition of "rape" as "one of the methods of the conspiracy whereby finance joins with the state and terrorist organizations to disfranchise Americans for political power and private profit":

> The conspiracy has made potent use of the spurious charge of "rape" as a political weapon. The charge of "rape" was consciously forged as a matter of state policy. It emerged in the Southern states at the same historic moment as the poll tax. It has since consistently been used to terrorize militant Negroes with the ever-present menace of death by lynching or by "legal murder" through police, incited mobs, and venal courts. Examples of how the cry of "rape" is used, invariably on the basis of race, abound in numerous cases. . . . The genocidal, murderous quality of the charge of "rape" is apparent . . .

It was not the *charge* of rape that was murderous and genocidal to Southern blacks, it was the overkill retaliation at the hands of white men, but this important distinction perpetually eluded the left's ideologues.

I need to tread gently here. The left fought hard for its symbols of racial injustice, making bewildered heroes out of a handful of pathetic, semiliterate fellows caught in the jaws of Southern jurisprudence who only wanted to beat the rap. Whatever else one cares to believe about the Communist Party and the progressive movement, one should be forever mindful of its individual members' selfless, pioneering devotion to the question of black equality long before it became fashionable or politically urgent within liberal circles. Yet because of the national hysteria of the McCarthyite years, any case the Communists took on and publicized became for all practical purposes a Communist cause from which others ran as if from a plague. Few people did not line up according to their political perspective on any given issue the Communists chose to publicize, and many a case was decided in the timid court of public opinion on the basis of whether or not a modest compromise—a commutation of the death sentence— would give aid and succor to the Communist cause.

For its part, the left, in *its* increasing paranoia and raging impotence, vilified and excoriated the hapless white woman whose original charge had wreaked such total destruction upon the hapless black. The standard defense strategy for puncturing holes in a rape case was (and is) an attempt to destroy the credibility of the complaining witness by smearing her as mentally unbalanced, or as sexually frustrated, or as an oversexed, promiscuous whore. In its mass-protest campaigns to save the lives of convicted black rapists, the left employed all these tactics, and more, against white women with a virulence that bordered on hate.

Most of the cases have since passed into oblivion, except in the minds of readers of the old *Daily Worker* who are blessed with total recall. Some, like the Martinsville Seven, executed by the state of Virginia in February, 1951, for gang-raping a thirty-two-year-old white woman, a Jehovah's Witness who sold the *Watchtower* in the black part of town, barely broke through the sound barrier of the left, perhaps because their case had no complexity to it, little room for speculation, and the nation had yet to be sensitized to the issue of capital punishment even when a state felled seven with one blow. And perhaps because the left had been able to make so little headway on the Martinsville case, vilification of the white woman reached an all-time high. In a signed article printed in the *Worker* for two days running while the Martinsville Seven met their death, a writer put forward a series of feverish questions:

> Why did she change her story between the time of the alleged "attack" and the preliminary hearing a month later?
>
> Why did she say at first that she was "attacked" by 13 or 14 men and then later changed it to "12 or 13 times"?
>
> Was it not a fact that she had been promised $5?
>
> Was it not a fact that she accepted the offer?
>
> Was it not a fact that she had dates in the past with one of the men?
>
> Why did she insist on leaving the hospital on the night of the alleged "attack" after speaking with her husband?
>
> Who came to visit her that night at her home?
>
> What instructions did those visitors give her?
>
> What promises of financial support were made, and by whom?
>
> What organizations and individuals gave her money, and how much?
>
> What promises did she make in return for this money?

Questions like these were being asked all over town. The answers to these questions would have exposed the frameup in this case. That's why they weren't asked. That's why they were carefully avoided . . .

"Questions like these" were a hodgepodge of innuendo, but they fueled the *Worker* reader who thrived on conspiracy.

And then there was Willie McGee, the filling station attendant and truck driver whose death in a portable electric chair trundled for the occasion to the Laurel, Mississippi, courtroom where he was first convicted made page one of *The New York Times* for May 8, 1951, and the front page of newspapers throughout the world.

McGee had three trials in all, and three convictions—two by all-white, all-male juries and the third by an all-male jury of nine whites and three blacks (as in Alabama, women were not permitted to serve on Mississippi juries). According to the prosecution, in the early morning of November 2, 1945, while Willametta Hawkins, the wife of a postal worker, lay asleep with her sick child—her husband and two other children were sleeping in an adjoining room—a black intruder stole into her bed, warning that if she screamed or cried out he would cut her throat. Mrs. Hawkins could not identify her rapist in the darkness except to say that he had been drinking, but police investigation led to McGee within a day. A grocery firm had reported that one of its trucks was missing overnight along with driver Willie McGee and $15.85 of the company's money; and a neighbor had noticed a grocery truck parked near the Hawkins' home at 4:30 A.M. McGee was picked up the following afternoon. He turned in the company's money, saying he had not meant to keep it, and the larceny charge was dropped. Instead he was charged with rape. A deputy sheriff extracted a confession from him, a confession that McGee later repudiated by saying he had been beaten and kept in a sweatbox until he cried guilty.

In all three trials McGee never took the stand in his own defense. His lawyers vainly claimed that he had been drinking in Hattiesburg, thirty miles away, when the rape took place. The first trial was a one-day affair in which the jury deliberated for two and a half minutes while guardsmen kept an angry mob in the streets at bay. The second trial, granted on a change-of-venue appeal that a fair trial for McGee had been impossible in Laurel, was conducted in Hattiesburg with similar results. The third trial, granted on the appeal that black men had been kept off the jury, was held back in Laurel. Circuit Judge Burkitt Collins, who presided at all three trials, three times sentenced Willie McGee to death.

No white man had ever been executed for rape in Mississippi, while McGee was the latest in a long row of condemned blacks. On this basis—unequal treatment under the law—a national Save Willie McGee campaign began to mount. McGee's new lawyers, hired by the Civil Rights Congress, had hinted at the third trial that there was more to the McGee case than had been divulged in court, and in March of 1951 Mrs. Rosalee McGee, McGee's wife and the mother of his four children, held an emotional press conference in New York. Her husband was no drunken intruder whom Mrs. Hawkins couldn't identify in the dark, she told reporters; he was the victim of a frame-up. According to Rosalee McGee, Willametta Hawkins knew Willie quite well—they'd been having an on-and-off affair for years, an affair that Mrs. Hawkins had instigated and McGee had tried to break off.

As Mrs. McGee told it, the affair started back in 1942 before her husband had gone into the Army when Mrs. Hawkins propositioned McGee by leaving a note for him in the nozzle of a gas hose in the filling station where he worked. "Down South you tell a woman like that 'no' and she'll cry rape anyway," Rosalee McGee explained. When McGee came out of the Army the following year and returned to Laurel, the notes and the affair resumed, with McGee as a most reluctant participant, according to his wife. Once he had even gone out to California with the idea of settling there, just to escape Mrs. Hawkins, she said, but he couldn't find work and had to come back. Rosalee McGee informed the press that she had not spoken up and told this story in court "because the lynch mob would've got me." She concluded, "I don't know what happened between Mrs. Hawkins and her husband. But after Willie was picked up by the police that night, everybody in the block said that they had a big argument and that he was chasing her right out into the street at five o'clock in the morning. So she could save herself from her husband, she figured she'll say she was raped."

One of the few newspapers to report Mrs. McGee's press conference in full was the Daily Worker, which stoked the fire and kept the McGee case on its front page for the next two months. The Worker called Willametta Hawkins a Potiphar's wife and McGee became a modern-day Joseph, "a slave in the kingdom of jimcrow," who had tried to run from Mrs. Hawkins' clutches. Worker reporters sent out to interview "the ordinary people" came back with quotes like "I've always been skeptical about this rape business" and "I'm convinced it is almost impossible to rape a woman if she doesn't really want it." Inevitably, the rhetoric grew bolder as the days grew shorter for Willie McGee. At the end of March the Worker editorialized, "The woman who said McGee 'raped' her was known to the entire community as having had a prolonged relationship with him . . . that she initiated and insisted on continuing against the will of her victim." The following month Mrs. McGee told a rally, "If there was any raping done, it was Mrs. Hawkins who raped my husband."

The U.S. Supreme Court refused to consider Rosalee McGee's story as new evidence warranting another trial and shortly after midnight on May 8, as one writer put it, the string ran out after five and one-half years. Mrs. Hawkins' husband, brother and two brothers-in-law were among those who watched McGee's execution. The following day the Worker let loose with one last blast: "Willie McGee was murdered," the paper editorialized on page one, "because the white woman who had forced an illicit affair upon him for more than four years suddenly shouted 'rape' after the whole town discovered the story."

To turn from the Worker's coverage of the McGee case to Time and Life is an object lesson in political schizophrenia. The one and only story Life ran was printed after McGee's execution and was headlined, appropriately enough, "The End of Willie McGee." Its subtitle: "A Mississippi rapist with a slender chance to escape death is 'aided' by the Reds and gets the chair." Life breathed not a word of Rosalee McGee's version of the case, except to remark obliquely that Mrs. McGee had been "taken over by the Communists." The burden of Life's story was that "something very unfortunate happened to Willie. His case fitted too well into the strategy of the Communist International . . . which sought to convince Chinese and Indians and Indonesians that capitalism hates and tortures anyone who is not white." Life seemed particularly incensed that left-wing rhetoric had constantly called McGee a World War II veteran. "He was never in the Armed Services," the magazine said flatly. Time magazine, which subtitled its story "Justice & the Communists," did refer to what it called the "new and ugly accusation," answering, "In the small (pop. 20,000) town of Laurel, there was utterly no evidence of such a relationship."

So to *Time* and *Life*, waging their cold war on the home front, it was the Communists who killed McGee, and to the *Daily Worker* it was a lustful white woman who suddenly cried rape. There was little middle ground to hang on to in 1951.*

That year Carl Rowan, the distinguished black journalist, former ambassador to Finland and one-time director of the United States Information Agency, was a cub reporter on the Minneapolis *Tribune*. He had asked for and received a very special assignment— to return to his birthplace and write a series of articles on the Southern way of life. One of the stops on Rowan's itinerary, an unplanned stop, he later recalled, was Laurel, Mississippi. The McGee case had drawn him, for he was more than mildly curious about the so-called "new evidence" hinted at during the third trial. "Some of the things filtering out of Mississippi," he later wrote, "read like an episode from my youth in Tennessee." (As a teen-ager in McMinnville, Rowan had once sneaked up on a buddy of his and a local white girl who were making out in a secluded spot down by the riverbank. When the girl heard his footsteps she screamed, "Get up! Stop, you black sonofabitch! Jesus, he's raping me!" Later the girl explained in tears, "I was afraid they'd kill me. I thought they had come to kill me.") To Rowan, "The overtones of sex in its role as the dominant factor in Dixie Negro-white relations were spelled out clearly in the case of Willie McGee," and further, "the whole ugly issue of Communism as it affects the Negro's fight for full equality was on review."

Rowan got off the bus and played sleuth in the black section of town. He interviewed some middle-class professionals and then, disguised as a jobless loafer, he spoke with some folks in "a junky café." He found no shortage of black people willing to fill him in on The Case. To Laurel's black citizens Willie McGee was "a fool." "It was pretty much whispered around among Negroes that McGee was going to get in trouble with that woman," a teacher

---

* One exception was a short article written for *The Nation* by Mary Mostert, a Southern social worker. She wrote: "Many questions are left unanswered by both sides, but certainly there seems pitifully little evidence to warrant taking a man's life. Probably no one except those directly involved will ever know the true story. . . . Of course in the minds of professional Southerners there is no such thing as a voluntary sex relation between a Negro man and a white woman—any relation at all, to them, is rape."

told him. From someone else he heard about the note that was left for McGee when he worked at the filling station. In the little café someone who claimed he knew McGee "pretty well" said, "Yeah, I knowed what was going on. I knowed that McGee told his wife he been doing 'er wrong. He said the only way for him to straighten up was to leave. So he went out west, supposedly to get away from this woman."

But Rowan had a journalist's problem. No one he spoke with was willing to be quoted and the men in the café, he learned, had even given him false names. When it came to an interracial rape case and the fearsome charge of "playing ball with the Commies," one informant told him, "nobody wanted to get his fingers burned." Rowan didn't file his story. He later wrote, "Even I took the cowardly way out by sheltering my own fingers and proceeding to forget that I ever visited Laurel." A few weeks later Rosalee McGee held her press conference in New York City and the young black reporter learned that her story was substantially the same one that he had dug up.

Rowan eventually did write about the McGee case, and with great sensitivity to its lasting ambiguities. He included a chapter on McGee in *South of Freedom*, a report on his year of travel. "Only the craziest Negro," Rowan wrote, "would walk into a white man's house and rape his wife while the white man slept in the next room—unless he knew his way around in the pitch-black house, and unless he had reason to believe that the white woman wouldn't cry out. And the one thing nobody had accused Willie McGee of was insanity." Yet on the other side of the "tiring, weird befuddlement" was this:

> The defense was wishy-washy. The story of long-standing illicit relations between McGee and the alleged victim appeared to be an admission that the defendant might have been in bed with the woman, but at her invitation. How did this square with Communist contention that McGee was driving his truck in Hattiesburg, thirty miles away, at the time of the attack? And how did either of these stories jibe with testimony of a woman defense witness that McGee was with her at the time of the alleged attack? And why was McGee silent all this time; why didn't he tell his own story?

Almost twenty-five years have passed and Rowan's questions remain unanswered, but to Congresswoman Bella Abzug, who as a young labor lawyer directed McGee's defense for the third and last trial and presented his high-court appeals, the Willie McGee case is a closed chapter in a life that has since been filled with more successful battles.

Bella Abzug agrees today that the McGee case was filled with ambiguities but the ambiguities are too far in the past for her to want to sort out. "I placed my own investigators in town," she told me one afternoon in her office. "The affair between the two was common knowledge among blacks and whites." Then why hadn't she put McGee or his wife on the stand? "No jury was going to believe it. Challenging the word of a white woman just wasn't done. The strategy was to depend on a lack of concrete evidence. Nobody believed you could win an interracial rape case in a Southern court. You could only win on appeal."

"Do you think McGee was in the Hawkins' house that night?"

"I don't think he was there that night. I think she had to entrap him to get out of the situation. We had lots of debates and discussions over that."

"Look, Bella," I ventured, "even from your point of view McGee was a philanderer and Rosalee McGee knew it. It must have been difficult for her to come to terms with her husband's long-standing affair with a white woman. Is that why, when she finally did talk, she pictured her husband as an unwilling participant? Four years is a long time to be an unwilling participant in any affair. If McGee wasn't unwilling, he probably was in her bedroom that night. Do you believe Willametta Hawkins simply woke up in the middle of the night and started shouting that she'd just been raped by an unknown black man, and that an accidental chain of circumstances led the police to the very man with whom she'd been having a clandestine affair?"

Abzug agreed that these were debatable questions, but insignificant compared to the horror of McGee's execution in what she still terms "the Southern slavocracy."

"Bella, do you believe today that Southern white women have a history of crying rape?"

"I believe," Abzug said heavily, "that the white woman was always the pivot, the excuse. The black man was played off against the white woman and the white woman was played off against the black man, to keep both oppressed groups down."

"You successfully raised the issue of the exclusion of blacks from McGee's jury, why didn't you raise the issue of the exclusion of women?"

"I don't think it ever came up. In those days we were never consciously raising that issue."

I understand Bella Abzug's desire to leave forgotten, painful history undisturbed, but the questions of journalists are seldom compatible with the concerns of defense lawyers, who seek to leave judge, jury and public with reasonable doubt. I would like to believe that the defense of Willie McGee was based on truth, that McGee and Mrs. Hawkins had been carrying on a secret liaison and that perhaps Troy Hawkins had awakened that night to discover the presence of a black man in the bed of his wife. I would also like to believe that McGee fled in haste and that Willametta Hawkins had no alternative but to say she had been raped.

Willametta Hawkins never wavered. She had been raped, she said, but she could not identify her assailant. For this she was vilified and harassed by leftists who smeared her in print as an oversexed and vengeful white witch. Willie McGee, too, did not waver. He kept his silence to the end. Perhaps he had come to a philosophic acceptance of his fate for crossing the forbidden barrier and encroaching on the white man's property. Perhaps to him also this encroachment bore the same gravity as rape.

It took the "wolf whistle" murder of Emmett Till to shock the entire nation into seeing the Southern white man's property code for what it was. Amid a traceable pattern of retaliatory strikes, death sentences and lynchings that went unpunished, the murder of Till stands out in stark relief. Nothing in recent times can match it for sheer outrageousness, for indefensible overkill with community support. Old patterns die and new ones arise to take their place. In the following decade a new movement for civil rights forced the South to reorder its priorities and placed the battle to preserve the old way of life on grounds apart from the white woman's body. The murder of Till, we can see now in retrospect, came toward the end of a definable era. It was the landmark case of white male retaliation for black male transgression. In a sense, it broke the mold.

In August, 1955, a fisherman pulled the decomposed body of a dead black boy out of the Tallahatchie River. The corpse bore signs of a terrible beating and the face was mutilated beyond recognition. A ring on one finger led to a positive identification: Emmett

Louis Till, fourteen years old, who had come to the rural hamlet of Money, Mississippi, from Chicago to spend a summer vacation with his uncle. There was little mystery in town as to who killed Emmett Till and why. Two white men, J. W. Millam and his half brother, Roy Bryant, were promptly arrested.

Since the facts in the Till case were never in serious dispute, even by Millam and Bryant after a jury found them not guilty, a straightforward story can be told. Till, nicknamed Bobo, had been regaling the black youth of Money with tales of his exploits with white girls up North, proudly displaying the picture of one girl he carried in his wallet. His skeptical buddies dared the Chicago braggart to walk into Bryant's general store at the crossroads and ask the lady who was alone behind the counter, Bryant's young wife, for a date. According to a telescoped version provided by William Bradford Huie, who wrote several articles and a book about the Till case, "While the Delta Negroes peered, in delicious awe, through the front windows, Bobo took the dare; Carolyn Bryant chased him with a pistol and, in a gesture of adolescent bravado, Bobo 'wolf-whistled' at her."

At two o'clock the next morning, Millam and Bryant strode into his uncle's shack on a tenant farm and ordered Till to go with them. As Huie got the story from the unrepentant half brothers, the white men intended only to rough up the boy and send him packing to Chicago but Till did not display the proper cowering attitude. Instead he repeated his brag about having "had" white women. Enraged, Millam shot him in the head with his Army .45. The two men tied a weight around Till's neck and dumped him in the Tallahatchie.

An all-male, all-white jury (women were excluded by law from Mississippi juries until 1968) acquitted Millam and Bryant after an hour's deliberation, accepting the defense contention that there was no real proof that the body from the river was actually Till's. In a courtroom tableau preserved for posterity by a news photographer, Millam chomped on a big cigar as the two half brothers embraced their wives.

Never again was the Southern white man's property code so blatantly expressed. Four years after the murder of Till, Mack Charles Parker would be dragged from a jail cell in Poplarville, Mississippi, two days before his scheduled trial for rape, but

Parker's murder was an anticlimactic echo to the whistle heard round the world.

Rarely has one single case exposed so clearly as Till's the underlying group-male antagonisms over access to women, for what began in Bryant's store should not be misconstrued as an innocent flirtation. Till's action was more than a kid's brash prank and his murder was more than a husband's revenge. The scene that was acted out in Money, Mississippi, had all the elements of a classical Greek drama. Emmett Till was going to show his black buddies that he, and by inference *they*, could get a white woman and Carolyn Bryant was the nearest convenient object. In concrete terms, the accessibility of *all* white women was on review. This is how it must have been perceived by Till's companions, who set him up with some degree of cruelty and then, sensing that things had gone too far, called him off. And we know this is how it was perceived by Millam and Bryant. "Hell," Millam told William Bradford Huie when he recalled the night of the murder. "He showed me the white gal's picture! Bragged o' what he'd done to her! What else could I do? No use letting him get no bigger!"

And what of the wolf whistle, Till's "gesture of adolescent bravado"? We are rightly aghast that a whistle could be cause for murder but we must also accept that Emmett Till and J. W. Millam shared something in common. *They both understood* that the whistle was no small tweet of hubba-hubba or melodious approval for a well-turned ankle. Given the deteriorated situation—she with a pistol in her hand, he scampering back to safety with his buddies—it was a deliberate insult just short of physical assault, a last reminder to Carolyn Bryant that this black boy, Till, had in mind to possess her.

A murder for a wolf whistle and a jury that refused to convict. The Till case became a lesson of instruction to an entire generation of appalled Americans. I know how I reacted. At age twenty and for a period of fifteen years after the murder of Emmett Till whenever a black teen-ager whistled at me on a New York City street or uttered in passing one of several variations on an invitation to congress, I smiled my nicest smile of comradely equality— no supersensitive flower of white womanhood, I—a largess I extended with equal sincerity to white construction workers, truck drivers, street-corner cowboys, indeed, to any and all who let me know from a safe distance their theoretical intent. After all, were not women for flirting? Wasn't a whistle or a murmured "May I fuck you?" an innocent compliment? And did not white women in particular have to bear the white man's burden of making amends for Southern racism? It took fifteen years for me to resolve these questions in my own mind, and to understand the insult implicit in Emmett Till's whistle, the depersonalized challenge of "I can have you" with or without the racial aspect. Today a sexual remark on the street causes within me a fleeting but murderous rage.

And we know from the record how another person, Eldridge Cleaver, reacted to the murder of Till. In *Soul on Ice* Cleaver writes that he was nineteen years old when he "saw in a magazine a picture of the white woman with whom Emmett Till was said to have flirted." Cleaver spelled out his reactions in full, for the Till case was a critical event in his life, one that turned him "inside out."

> While looking at the picture, I felt that little tension in the center of my chest I experience when a woman appeals to me. I was disgusted and angry with myself. Here was a woman who had caused the death of a black, possibly because, when he looked at her, he also felt the same tensions of lust and desire in his chest— and probably for the same general reasons that I felt them. . . . I looked at the picture again and again, and in spite of everything and against my will and the hate I felt for the woman and all that she represented, she appealed to me. I flew into a rage at myself, at America, at white women, at the history that had placed those tensions of lust and desire in my chest.

Cleaver had a small breakdown two days later during which he says he "ranted and raved . . . against white women in particular," and then, "Somehow I arrived at the conclusion that, as a matter of principle, it was of paramount importance for me to have an antagonistic, ruthless attitude toward white women. The term *outlaw* appealed to me . . ." His solution: "I became a rapist."

Cleaver's thought pattern and the ideological construct he used to justify his career as a rapist, a career cut short by imprisonment, is interesting on several levels. Besides being a rare glimpse into the mind of an actual rapist, it reflects a strain of thinking among black male intellectuals and writers that became quite fashionable in the late nineteen sixties and was taken up with astonishing enthusiasm by white male radicals and parts of the white intellectual extablishment as a *perfectly acceptable* excuse for rape committed by black men. The key to the ready acceptability of Cleaver's thesis is obvious. The blame, as he saw it, belonged on white women.

Before I quote further from Cleaver the practitioner it might be instructive to hear from some of his contemporaneous brothers who struck a similar chord when attempting to explain or exhort the black man. Cleaver himself makes passing reference to the poetry of LeRoi Jones (Imamu Amiri Baraka): "Come up, black dada nihilismus. Rape the white girls. Rape their fathers. Cut the mothers' throats," and comments coolly, "LeRoi is expressing the funky facts of life."

Funky or extreme as the poetry and plays of Jones-Baraka might be, no such criticism could be leveled at the black sociologist Calvin C. Hernton, who made a serious stab at defining the black male perspective in *Sex and Racism in America.* "I am well aware," writes Hernton, "that, like murder, rape has many motives. But when the motive for rape, however psychotic, is basically racial, that is a different matter. I think now that, at one time or another, in every Negro who grows up in the South, there is a rapist, no matter how hidden. And that rapist has been conceived in the Negro by a system of morals based on guilt, hatred, and human denial."

Hernton's concept of *human denial* implies that free access to white women, or indeed, to any woman, is some sort of inalienable male right that has been *inhumanely denied* to blacks. He states as doctrine without questioning the implications, "Any oppressed group, when obtaining power, tends to acquire the females of the group that has been the oppressor." To Hernton and to many black intellectuals (shades of the white Helene Deutsch) the role of the white woman is eagerly complicitous: "A Negro is more prone than anyone else to comply with the white woman's fantasies of rape and martyrdom." With a twist, this too was the theme of Jones-Baraka's *Dutchman.*

But Hernton's analysis was tame compared to the pronunciamentos of Frantz Fanon, the darling of the New Left. Rape runs as a curious subtheme in all of Fanon's writings. As a doctor of psychiatry and a student of colonialism, Fanon was in an excellent position to make a substantial, original contribution to the world's understanding of rape as a means of oppressing native women in Algeria and the Antilles, but Fanon's concern, to which he returns again and again (it is something of an obsession), is with the native man and the *white* woman. "Whoever says rape says Negro," he announces in *Black Skin, White Masks* in preface to his morbid rehash of the super-Freudian "A Negro Is Raping Me" theory of white female masochism propounded by Marie Bonaparte and Helene Deutsch.

Here is Fanon's rendition of the familiar theme: "When a woman lives the fantasy of rape by a Negro, it is in some way the fulfillment of a private dream, of an inner wish . . . it is the woman who rapes herself. . . . The fantasy of rape by a Negro is a variation of this emotion: 'I wish the Negro would rip me open as I would have ripped a woman open.' " One cannot but be affected by the private anguish and personal confusion of Frantz Fanon when one reads these lines: "Basically does this *fear* of rape not itself cry out for rape? Just as there are faces that ask to be slapped, can one not speak of women who ask to be raped?"

Purely and simply, this radical theorist of third-world liberation was a hater of women. With an arrogance rarely matched by other radical male writers, Fanon goes on, "Those who grant our conclusions on the psychosexuality of the white woman may ask what we have to say about the woman of color. I know nothing about her."*

---

* Nor did he ever take the trouble to find out. In Fanon's *politik*, rape of third-world women was a devious colonial trick to emasculate third-world men. *The Wretched of the Earth* reports several cases of "mental disorders" that Fanon attributes to the French colonization of Algeria. Case One, Series A: "Impotence in an Algerian following the rape of his wife." A twenty-six-year-old fighter for the National Liberation Front discovered he had become impotent when he tried to conduct an affair in a foreign country where he was sent on a mission. During interviews with Dr. Fanon, the patient explained that his wife had been raped by French soldiers while he was fighting for liberation. The Algerian's problem, in addition to his impotence, was that he didn't want to see his violated wife. He confessed, "Often, while I was looking at the photo of my daughter, I used to think that she too was dishonored, as if everything that had to do with my wife was rotten. If they'd tortured her or knocked out all her teeth or broken an arm I wouldn't have minded. But that thing—how can you forget a thing like that? And why did she have to tell me about it all?" The FLN fighter then asked Fanon, "Would you take back your wife?" The best Fanon could answer was "I think I would . . ." and a concession that he was not quite sure.

Fanon's haughty dismissal of "the woman of color" was more than matched by Eldridge Cleaver in his early raping career. "To refine my technique and *modus operandi*," wrote the man who was to become a Black Panther theorist, "I started out by practicing on black girls in the ghetto . . ."

No comment I might interject at this point seems adequate. Cleaver sheds no further light on his unusual form of target practice, although he implies in a sudden spurt of fancy language that he never got caught for raping black women because he was operating within a milieu of high crime, continuing in the same sentence, ". . . and when I considered myself smooth enough, I crossed the tracks and sought out white prey." Thereafter follows his extraordinary rationale:

> Rape was an insurrectionary act. It delighted me that I was defying and trampling upon the white man's law, upon his system of values, and that I was defiling his women—and this point, I believe, was the most satisfying to me because I was very resentful over the historical fact of how the white man has used the black woman. I felt I was getting revenge.

Cleaver also reports in *Soul on Ice* that later on in the solitude of prison he found he could no longer "approve the act of rape": "I lost my self-respect. My pride as a man dissolved . . ." This was as close as he ever got to an apology to women, white or black, but it was not a very meaningful apology. Years later he blithely told an interviewer for *Playboy*, "I was in a wild frame of mind and rape was simply one of the weird forms my rebellion took at that stage. So it was probably a combination of business and pleasure."

As Fanon had his Jean-Paul Sartre and Calvin Hernton his Nat Hentoff, Cleaver, too, had his champions and interpreters among the white male literati. "It takes a certain boldness on Cleaver's part," the critic Maxwell Geismar raved in his introduction to *Soul on Ice*, "to open this collection of essays not merely on rape but on the whole profound relationship of black men and white women. There is a secret kind of sexual mysticism in this writer which adds depth and tone to his social commentary; this is a highly literary and imaginative mind surveying the salient aspects of our common life."

The spectacle of white radicals and intellectuals falling all over each other in their rush to accept the Cleaver rationale for rape was a sorry sight in the late nineteen sixties and early seventies when the Neanderthal slogan, "All black prisoners are political prisoners," was raised as a rallying cry of the New Left. As an indication of how far this ideology traveled, I clipped and saved a printed exchange that New York Times reporter Tad Szulc conducted with Soledad Brother George Jackson shortly before Jackson's death during the San Quentin riot. Szulc appeared to have bought Cleaver's "insurrectionary" excuse for raping white women, for he carefully asked George Jackson, "Aren't any black people guilty of crimes in American society? Aren't any of them criminals—for example, a black man who rapes and murders a black woman?" Jackson, for his part, did not appear unduly concerned with what he sloughed off as "the relatively small percentage . . . of thrill crimes" committed against black women. He countered in political jargon, "Every revolutionary theoretician and psychiatrist accepts as elementary the tendency of violence to turn inward when the oppressed can find no externalization . . ."

The recurrent nightmare in the eighteenth-century slaveholding South had been the white male dream of black men rising up to rape "their" women, and in the second half of the twentieth century the black man in his fiercest rhetoric seems intent on fulfilling that prophecy. This cannot be chalked off to the chickens coming home to roost, payback for injustice past, or the pressure cooker of "human denial" that finally explodes. Nor does the postulation that males of an oppressed class tend to "acquire" the females of the oppressor class when the opportunity arises suffice as full explanation. In the past the acquiring of women, largely through marriage, has been a useful gauge of progress, and it is true that on this level women have been consciously complicitous, giving their bodies to the oppressed male as their small contribution to eliminating inequalities and "making things all right," a logical extension of woman's traditional service role. But we are talking about rape, the one-sided acquisition, and male power politics. It is also historically observable that oppressed males take on the values of those who have oppressed them. When Eldridge Cleaver quotes a prison buddy who says that the white woman has been dangled before him "like a carrot on a stick," this is what he is talking about. We white women did not dangle ourselves, yet everything the black man has been exposed to would lead him to this conclusion, and then to action, in imitation of the white man who raped "his" woman.

So well is this political lesson understood that today's white radical male, imbued with Marcuse's theory of rising expectations, feels it would be reactionary on his part to question a black man who felt it was his insurrectionary right to rape. (It is unfashionable in extreme white radical circles to question any misguided aspiration articulated by blacks.) When the women's movement first began to discuss rape as a feminist issue, those women who still identified themselves with the male left reacted like their brothers with noncomprehension or hostility. (They have since shown signs of change.) And again, it was the interracial aspect, the fear of playing into the hands of racists, or an undifferentiated sympathy for the criminal as society's victim that dictated their emotional response.

A fascinating psychiatric study of thirteen young white victims of rape in Boston and Washington, each of whom "had moved into a low-income (not necessarily black) community to implement her conviction about 'doing something real' in contemporary society," revealed a reluctance on the part of the victim to prosecute her rapist, or even to report the crime, stemming partially from her political belief that her rape was "an extension of the social struggle of black against white or poor against rich," Sandra Sutherland, co-director of the Metropolitan Mental Health Skills Center in Washington and the senior author of the study, concluded that this self-sacrificial, altruistic response "was no doubt a product in part of the same internal factors which led the women to live in low-income areas in the first place." (Several of the women, despite their rationalizations and repressed angers, were traumatized by what had happened to them. They left the neighborhood centers and poverty programs in which they had been working and retreated back to their middle-class environments.)

A young white woman with radical politics who had been raped by a black youth on Manhattan's lower East Side told New York *Post* reporter Roberta Brandes Gratz, "I just can't throw off history. I feel like I'm being used to pay off the old debts to men falsely accused in the South of raping white women. Even my friends were reluctant to see me press charges."

"Locking up individual rapists may satisfy our urge to retaliate," a member of a Los Angeles anti-rape group agonized in *Sister*, a women's newspaper, "but will this lead to the further oppression of all people, and Third World people in particular?"

Interracial rape remains a huge political embarrassment to liberals. A recognition of the long history of the white man's overkill for "the one crime" has left many whites with deep feelings of guilt. The fight against capital punishment waged by the NAACP Legal Defense Fund was based in large measure on the discriminatory application of the death sentence to blacks convicted of raping white women. A civil-libertarian movement to protect the rights of defendants has led many people, Jessica Mitford among them, to question the very idea of imprisonment, and most particularly, it seems, for rape.

The shock to liberals in 1971 when the women's movement first began to discuss rape was profound. I remember the looks of incredulity and the charge, "Why you're on the side of the prosecution," as if that per se was evidence of racism and reaction. But liberals are nothing if not elastic in their ability to absorb new ideas. Two years later the director of the New York Civil Liberties Union expressed his confusion over whom to root for now that the right of a woman not to be raped had been perceived by him as a political issue. "It's a little bit like cowboy-and-Indian movies," he admitted.

By pitting white women against black men in their effort to alert the nation to the extra punishment wreaked on blacks for a case of interracial rape, leftists and liberals with a defense-lawyer mentality drove a wedge between two movements for human rights and today we are still struggling to overcome this historic legacy. Yet the similarities between the types of oppression suffered by blacks and women, and heaped upon black women, are more impressive than the antagonisms between us. As I have stated elsewhere, the rapist performs a myrmidon function for all men by keeping all women in a thrall of anxiety and fear. Rape is to women as lynching was to blacks: the ultimate physical threat by which all men keep all women in a state of psychological intimidation.

Women have been raped by men, most often by gangs of men, for many of the same reasons that blacks were lynched by gangs of whites: as group punishment for being uppity, for getting out of line, for failing to recognize "one's place," for assuming sexual freedoms, or for behavior no more provocative than walking down the wrong road at night in the wrong part of town and presenting a convenient, isolated target for group hatred and rage. Castration, the traditional coup de grâce of a lynching, has its counterpart in the gratuitous acts of defilement that often accompany a rape, the stick rammed up the vagina, the attempt to annihilate the sexual core.

History is never "behind" us, and we must not forget how the white man has used the rape of "his" women as an excuse to act against black men. But today the incidence of actual rape combined with the looming spectre of the rapist in the mind's eye, and in particular the mythified spectre of the black man as rapist to which the black man in the name of his manhood now contributes, must be understood as a control mechanism against the freedom, mobility and aspirations of all women, white and black. The crossroads of racism and sexism had to be a violent meeting place. There is no use pretending it doesn't exist.

8

Power:
Institution and Authority

All rape is an exercise in power, but some rapists have an edge that is more than physical. They operate within an institution-alized setting that works to their advantage and in which a victim has little chance to redress her grievance. Rape in slavery and rape in wartime are two such examples. But rapists may also operate within an emotional setting or within a dependent relationship that provides a hierarchical, authoritarian structure of its own that weakens a victim's resistance, distorts her perspective and confounds her will. A therapist who suggests to his patient that the solution to her problem of frigidity lies in having sex with him is practicing rape upon a vulnerable victim, although the patient may be slow to discover that she has been "had," and a court of law would not recognize such emotional coercion as a forcible act.

Similarly the glamour attached to cultural heroes, such as a movie star, sports figure, rock singer or respected-man-in-the-community, provides a psychologic edge that lessens the need for physical coercion until it is too late for the victim to recognize her predicament. Cases of celebrity rape pop up in the news from time to time and usually vanish again with immoderate speed. These cases are "tainted" from several angles: the glamour that emotion-ally disarmed the unwitting or foolish victim (and the fact that a victim has been foolish should not diminish the import of the offender's crime; many robbery and con-game victims are also fool-ish and unwitting) also acts as a shield in the rapist's defense—

police and prosecutors have little enthusiasm for ruining reputations over a charge of rape.

Date rapes and rapes by men who have had prior relationships with their victims also contain elements of coercive authority that militates against decisive resistance. Here the "authority" takes the form of *expected behavior*. In a dating situation an aggressor may press his advantage to the point where pleasantness quickly turns to unpleasantness and more than the woman bargained for, yet social propriety and the strictures of conventional female behavior that dictate politeness and femininity demand that the female gracefully endure, or wriggle away if she can, but a direct confrontation falls outside of the behavioral norms. These are the cases about which the police are wont to say, "She changed her mind afterward," with no recognition that it was only *afterward* that she dared pull herself together and face up to the fact that she had truly been raped.

Date rapes look especially bad for the victim in court, if they ever get to court, nor do they look good on paper. The intangibles of victim behavior (which I deal with in my "Victims" section) present a poor case. Upon hearing such cases, even with my feminist perspective, I often feel like shouting "Idiot, why didn't you see the warning signs earlier?" But that, of course, is precisely the point. As debatable as the case may appear when one tries to apply objective standards, it is the *subjective* behavioral factors that may determine a rape.

In this chapter I will deal only with certain objective conditions that are institutionalized or so overwhelmingly authority-ridden as to be incontestable. These are prison rapes and rapes within juvenile correctional facilities, which provide the statistical bulk of all homosexual rapes, and rape or molestation of children by adults, often within the family. Because of its Kafkaesque quality—the ultimate nightmare of rape by the ultimate authority charged with the duty of protection—the small incidence of rape by policemen that has come to public light also deserves mention.

Prison Rape: The Homosexual Experience

The prison movie *Fortune and Men's Eyes* portrays the ideological evolution of Smitty, an attractive heterosexual youth. Because of his tensile good looks Smitty has been forcibly raped by King Rocco-Rocky, who turns the unhappy victim into his prison "girl." There are certain advantages to being the girl of a punk like Rocky, small favors of food, cigarettes, dope and protection from other predatory males, but Smitty wants desperately to break out of his sexual bondage. One day in the showers, after Rocky has told him to go get the Vaseline, the prelude to anal penetration, Smitty turns on his tormentor. Summoning all his courage, he manages to beat down Rocky in a wet and steaming brawl. When the other inmates learn what has happened, Rocky is dethroned and Smitty becomes the acknowledged king of the cellblock. Smitty's first act as victor is to command his gentle friend and cellmate, Jan-Mona, to smear himself with the Vaseline. Bewildered, Jan-Mona pleads, "You have power now, Smitty—do you need sex, too?" But Smitty does "need sex." How else within the confines of prison can he exercise his hard-won power?

It is finally being acknowledged that one of the main problems of prison life is the assault and rape of other inmates by their fellow men. Shrouded in secrecy and misinformation, so-called homosexual "abuse" in prison was formerly thought to be symptomatic of the deranged brutality of a few prison guards or an "infection" spread throughout a cellblock by a certain number of avowed homosexuals within the prison population. More information and a relatively enlightened modern perspective has drastically altered this old-fashioned view. Prison rape is generally seen today for what it is: an acting out of power roles within an all-male, authoritarian environment in which the younger, weaker inmate, usually a first offender, is forced to play the role that in the outside world is assigned to women. In a wicked twist of irony, it is often the avowedly homosexual youths, because of their "feminine" mannerisms and pariah status, who fall victim to the most brutal of prison gang rapes—and when prison authorities segregate homosexuals these days, as they do in the New York City Tombs, it is for their own protection. The other favored category of inmate who is earmarked for prison rape—perhaps the favored victim—is the slight, sensitive young man, whatever his sexual persuasion, who cannot or does not wish to fight.

In the summer of 1973 a 28-year-old Quaker pacifist named Robert A. Martin, a former seaman with a background in journalism, held a stunning press conference in Washington, D.C. Arrested during a peace demonstration in front of the White House, Martin had chosen to go to prison rather than post a $10 bond. His first week in the District of Columbia jail, Martin told reporters, passed uneventfully enough in a quiet cellblock populated by older prisoners including Watergate burglar C. Gordon Liddy, but then he was transferred to Cellblock 2, a tier of "predominantly young black prisoners, many of them in jail for serious crimes of violence." During his first evening recreation period on the new tier, the boyish-looking pacifist was invited into a cell on the pretext that some of the men wanted to talk with him. Once inside, he said, "My exit was blocked and my pants were forcibly taken off me, and I was raped. Then I was dragged from cell to cell all evening." Martin was promised protection from further assaults by two of his violators. The next night his "protectors" initiated a second general round of oral and rectal rape. The pair stood outside his cell and collected packs of cigarettes from other prisoners wanting a turn. When his attackers gave him a brief rest period to overcome his gagging and nausea, Martin made his escape and alerted a guard. He was taken to D.C. General Hospital where he underwent VD tests and a rectal examination. The following morning a Quaker friend posted his bond.

When a skeptical reporter asked where the prison guards had been during his two nights of multiple assault, in which Martin estimated he had been ganged by 45 to 50 men, he replied in all honesty, "That's a good question." Trying to make some sense out of a terrorizing experience, the nonviolent Quaker strongly suggested that he had been deliberately transferred to the violent cellblock as a sure-fire way of getting a political demonstrator and potential troublemaker out of the jail. He told the assembled group that the guard captain who transferred him "put me in Cellblock 2 knowing what Cellblock 2 is like, probably knowing what would happen to me in there and figuring that it would induce me to leave, which it did. But I suspect he was also counting on the silence which rape victims have maintained. In the past most of the victims have been kids with hang-ups about their masculine image. There have been countless rapes in there, but I'm the first óne who has stood up to make it public. If something can be changed, my experience will have been meaningful."

Public recognition of rape in prison is increasing. From a pile of newsclips I can pull the following items:

• Nine inmates at Sumter Correctional Institute in Florida are charged with raping other prisoners during a prison riot.

• Two inmates at Florida's Raiford Prison are charged with raping other inmates at knife point.

• A county judge in upstate New York refuses to send a young offender, who is homosexual, to Attica. His stated reason: "I just couldn't see throwing him into that situation. He'd become an object of barter there, completely dehumanized if he wasn't killed. This is a heck of a thing, and the public ought to know about it."

• Two bright young Nixon aides who plead guilty to Watergate offenses and know they face a jail sentence admit they are apprehensive about the possibility of a sexual assault.

(The concern of the Nixon men, as a matter of fact, was exaggerated, since federal prisons hold the least violent criminals, those convicted largely of white-collar crimes. Prison rape is more typically a product of state and city penal institutions, where those convicted of crimes of violence predominate.)

A straightforward account of the hierarchic sex code as it operated in prison almost forty years ago appears in the autobiography of Haywood Patterson, chief defendant in America's most famous rape case, the Scottsboro affair. (See pages 230 to 235.) By his own admission the most ornery and unbowed of the Scottsboro "Boys," when Patterson landed in Alabama's tough Atmore State Prison Farm in 1937 he was confronted with a cut-and-dried option: either submit to the older men and become a "gal-boy" or defend his bodily integrity by becoming a "wolf." The issue, as the 25-year-old Patterson saw it, was manhood. He reasoned, "If any of that stuff goes on with me in on it I'll do all the fucking myself. I been a man all my life."

There was little neutral ground at Atmore in Patterson's estimation. Some inmates escaped becoming predator or prey but "that was a minority." Rape was tolerated, even encouraged, by the prison authorities, Patterson believed, because "it helped them control the men. Especially the tough ones they called devils. They believed that if a devil had a gal-boy he would be quiet. He would be a good worker and he wouldn't kill guards and prisoners and try to escape. He would be like a settled married man."

The most sought-after raw material for a gal-boy was a tender young teen-ager. "A fifteen-year-old stood no chance at Atmore," Patterson reported. "Prisoner and warden were against him and he was quickly made into a woman." The womanizing process was methodical and brutal. "I've seen young boys stand up and fight for hours for their rights," he related. "Some wouldn't give up." Prisoners and guards would watch the assaults on young boys with impassive interest. "They knew a young woman was being born. Some just looked forward to using her a little later themselves."

After a gal-boy was broken he might accept his new nature with abject, promiscuous surrender. "Some carried on like real prostitutes," Patterson told in wonder. "They sold themselves around on the weekends just like whore women of the streets. . . . Usually you could hunk up with a gal-boy for two or three dollars. Gal-boys got sold off to different men. If a guy had a gal-boy but didn't get along with him any more, he could put him up for sale. He could sell him for twenty-five dollars. News of a sale went through the prison pretty fast and bids came in every time." Patterson mentioned with satisfaction, "I once heard Deputy Warden Lige Lambert tell some state patrolmen that fifty percent of the Negro prisoners in Atmore were gal-boys—and seventy percent of the white."

Patterson's own acid test came early in his stay at Atmore. He had already determined, "If I had to be a part of this life I would be a man," and the first step toward manhood was to patronize the weekend gal-boys. "I called them fuk-boys. I called them all sorts of sorry names. . . . I would say to one of them, 'You come here taking your mommy's and your sister's places. You rotten.'" Patterson gradually began to relish his wolf role, but his status had to be periodically defended. In the prison hierarchy there were wolves and bigger wolves. "Even after I had my regular gal-boy it didn't end my troubles with wolves who wanted to use me that way." A wolf named John Peaseley let him know he thought the Scottsboro Boy was too young to be a man—"He wanted to use both me and my gal-boy." Patterson went after the older wolf with a switchblade knife, and this event became the turning point of his stay at Atmore. He reported succinctly, "Peaseley didn't try to make a girl out of me no more. Nobody did. I had taken a gal-boy, whupped a wolf, and set myself up as a devil."

A reversed set of values permeates the prison writing of Jean Genet. Sartre, his interpreter, has called Genet "a raped child" whose early violations determined his "passive" homosexuality, but Sartre sees both rape and homosexuality as metaphor:

An actual rape can become, in our conscience, an iniquitous and yet ineluctable condemnation and, vice versa, a condemnation can be felt as a rape. Both acts transform the guilty person into an object, and if, in his heart, he feels his objectification as a shameful thing, he feels it in his sex as an act of coitus to which he has been subjected. Genet has now been deflowered; an iron embrace has made him a woman.

There is no doubt from a reading of *Miracle of the Rose* that Genet was subjected to repeated assaults by the older boys at Mettray Reformatory, and that he accepted his gal-boy status with gratitude and humility. At Mettray and other prisons inhabited by Genet, wolves and gal-boys are "big shots" and "chickens" and chickenhood to Genet becomes the ultimate in saintliness. No abject humiliation is too degrading for him and he carries his tube of Vaseline with pride, his own inverse stiff prick. In Genet's prison experience, too, chickens are bought and sold, and guards are complicitous in beating youths into girls.

Beauty and tenderness form the fatal attraction, as in the case of Winter: "His pretty mug and his nonchalance excited the big shots. . . . The toughs took a fancy to him, and he had to suffer being reamed by twelve cocks and the shame of its happening almost publicly." Winter cuts off his eyelashes "to be less hand-some." Bulkaen, a chicken's chicken, a "jerk," falls victim to a gang spitting. Nine toughs line up and expectorate into his mouth. Bulkaen speaks through Genet: "I was no longer the adulterous woman being stoned. I was the object of an amorous rite. I wanted them to spit more and thicker slime. Deloffre was the first to realize what was happening. He pointed to a particular part of my tight-fitting pants and cried out: 'Hey! Look at his pussy! It's making him come, the bitch!' "

To read Genet is to read a male *Story of O*. Male homosexual masochism is in its finest flower, and flower not incidentally is Genet's chief metaphor for the love he finds in brutal assault. What is a feminist to make of a man who professes to see a compliment in the threat, "I'd like to give you a shot in the pants," and who considers a furtive tap on the anus the equivalent of a stolen kiss? Genet poses a real problem. His equation of his own male masochism with the female principle is dangerously false. His adoration of the muscular thighs on crooks, cops, Nazis and revolutionary blacks, his personal icons, is no different from the routine stuff, the standard fare, of hard-core heterosexual pornography. Genet would like to see his chickenhood accepted as the true femininity and he toys with the concept in Our Lady of the Flowers that "a male that fucks another male is a double-male." Sartre explains for us that in one masturbatory gesture Genet is "the criminal who rapes and the Saint who lets herself be raped," a religious postulation that is tenable only if God is indeed a phallus.*

Within the current Gay Liberation Movement there is a boisterous minority contained within the outposts of leather bars that would like to see consensual sadomasochism, including the paraphernalia of whips and handcuffs, accepted as a civil-libertarian right, as drag queens are demanding the right to dress in traditionally female attire. Again, what is a feminist to make of this? Does homosexual sadomasochism have its own, peculiarly male, dynamic, or is it an aberration masquerading as the newest issue? The international language of sadomasochism, from the prison argot to the intellectual's musing, and its immutable rites and practices are too revealing to ignore. Sartre explains for Genet that "the rump is the secret femininity of males, their passivity," and both men agree that passivity is defined as being on the receiving end of a penis. In the man-on-man definition, fellatio, too, is a passive act and cock-sucker is the equivalent of chicken. Hardly by accident, sadomasochism has always been defined by male and female terms. It has been codified by those who see in sadism a twisted understanding of their manhood, and it has been accepted by those who see in masochism the abuse and pain that is synonymous with Woman. For this reason alone sadomasochism shall always remain a reactionary antithesis to women's liberation.

Although I believe that masochism is often a dynamic in homosexuality, I am not suggesting that it is in some way integral to noncoercive, one-sex relationships or predilections. More signifi-

---

* Genet was not the only brilliant homosexual to have suggested the deliciousness of rape. The half-humorous double-entendre of Lytton Strachey before the Hampstead Tribunal in 1916, when he argued his case as a conscientious objector, has been widely retold. "Mr. Strachey, what would you do if you saw a German soldier attempting to rape your sister?" the examiner asked. Strachey responded with "ambiguous gravity" according to his biographer, "I should try and come between them."

cant, perhaps, than the masochistic factor has been the blanket assumption of masochism—in the belief that all male homosexuals wish to be forcibly violated—that has been used with telling effect by heterosexual men who wish to avoid the implications and reality of a man's rape by other men. Here again, the parallels to the woman's experience are obvious. I have listened more than once to the story of a homosexual youth who tried without success to convince his local precinct that he was beaten and raped by some strangers he met in a gay bar and thoughtlessly decided to entertain at home. To the cops in the precinct the raped youth was nothing more than a faggot who was "asking for it." Along the same lines, T. E. Lawrence's account of his gang rape by the soldiers of the Nuri Bey in Deraa, laundered in many editions of *Seven Pillars of Wisdom*, has been quartered and dissected by a host of Lawrence scholars who feel that the "truth" of the brutal sodomizing hangs on Lawrence's alleged or suppressed homosexuality. Indeed, I have heard the argument that Lawrence's sphincter muscles should have been sufficient to ward off unwelcome penetration. Correspondingly, some modern sociologists have tried to downplay homosexual rape in American prisons by making use of the biased belief that—this is a direct quote from an accepted source—"there is some question, as in heterosexual situations, as to whether the situation is really in fact rape or whether it is a seduction which has simply gone wrong."

A comprehensive study of rape within the Philadelphia prison system was jointly conducted in 1968 by the district attorney's office and the Phildelphia police department after two embarrassing incidents came to light. One was a gang rape by detainees in a sheriff's van upon a youth who was being transported to court for his trial; the second incident concerned a youth who was sexually assaulted "within minutes of his admission" to the Philadelphia Detention Center for a presentencing evaluation. (In both cases the youth's lawyer reported his rape to the court.)

Alan J. Davis, the chief assistant district attorney who was put in charge of the resulting investigation, was forced to conclude that sexual assault in Philadelphia prisons was "epidemic." Meticulously documenting 156 cases of rape during a two-year period through task-force interviews with more than 3,000 reluctant inmates and guards, the use of lie-detector tests and examination of prison records, Davis believed he had merely touched "the top of the iceberg," and that the true number of rapes during this period was probably closer to 2,000 in a shifting inmate population of 60,000 men. However, a total of only 96 rapes had actually been reported by victimized inmates to prison authorities, and of this number only 64 had been written up in prison records. Prison officials had imposed some form of internal discipline on 40 of the offenders and 26 of the cases had been passed on to the police for legal prosecution.

Davis disclosed that "virtually every slightly built young man committed by the courts is sexually approached within a day or two after his admission to prison. Many of these young men are repeatedly raped by gangs of inmates. Others, because of the threat of gang rape, seek protection by entering into a homosexual relationship with an individual tormentor." Homosexual assault, this district attorney learned, had become an extra form of punishment that was part and parcel of imprisonment, a punishment never intended by the sentence of the court. "Only the tougher and more hardened young men," he wrote, "and those few so obviously frail that they are immediately locked up for their own protection, escape homosexual rape."

Homosexual rape in the Philadelphia prisons turned out to be a microcosm of the female experience with heterosexual rape. Davis discovered that prison guards put pressure on inmates not to report their rapes by using the argument that the victim wouldn't want his parents and friends to find out about his humiliation. But not telling did not cause the humiliation to "go away": "After a young man has been raped," Davis learned, "he is marked as a victim for the duration of his confinement. This mark follows him from institution to institution. Many of these young men return to their communities ashamed and full of hatred."

Matching the woman's experience with rape in the outside world, Davis found that in a closed society without women, men who raped other men in prison as a group were on the average three years older, one inch taller and fifteen pounds heavier than their prison victims. Also in parallel to the outside world, prison rape appeared to be a function of youthful aggression. Although the average age of an inmate within the Philadelphia prison system was 29, the average prison rapist was found to be 23 years old and the average age of his victim was slightly under 21. Men who raped in prison had usually been put there for crimes of violence: robbery, assault and heterosexual rape. Men who were raped in prison looked young for their years, appeared unathletic and were noticeably better looking than their predators. Their crimes, as might be expected, were usually on the nonassaultive end of the spectrum: auto theft, going AWOL, or violating parole. The one criminal category in which there were as many prison victims as prison rapists was homicide, proving once again that the profile of the murderer is unto himself. (See page 184.)

Davis' report was unflinching when it came to interracial rape in prison. Eighty percent of the inmate population in Philadelphia was black but the pattern of sexual assault revealed "a disproportionate number [of] Negro aggressors and white victims." White-on-white rape accounted for 15 percent of the documented assaults, and black-on-black rape accounted for 29 percent. Davis found no incidence of white-on-black rape in the Philadelphia prisons, but black-on-white rape registered 56 percent of the grand total. The district attorney reasoned, correctly I think, that it is "safer" for a member of a powerful majority group, in this case the prison blacks, to aggress against a weak minority group, in this case the prison whites, and he also took note that "Negro victims seemed more reluctant than white victims to disclose assaults by Negro aggressors," but he could not escape the inevitable conclusion: "It also seems true that current racial tensions and hostilities in the outside community are aggravated in a criminal population."

Haywood Patterson had stated forthrightly that by taking a gal-boy he preserved his stature as a man. Davis reported that he and his team of investigators were struck by the fact that the man who rapes another man in prison "does not consider himself to be a homosexual, or even to have engaged in homosexual acts. This seems to be based upon his startlingly primitive view of sexual relationships, one that defines as male whichever partner is aggressive and as homosexual whichever partner is passive."

Homosexual rape in prison could not be primarily motivated by the need for sexual release, Davis observed, since autoerotic masturbation to orgasm is "much easier and more normal." But conquest and degradation did appear to be a primary goal: "We repeatedly found that aggressors used such language as 'Fight or fuck,' 'We're going to take your manhood,' 'You'll have to give up some face,' and 'We're gonna make a girl out of you.'" Significantly, in the penal institution, economic clout proved as persuasive as physical force: "Typically, an experienced inmate will give cigarettes, candy, sedatives, stainless-steel blades, or extra food pilfered from the kitchen to an inexperienced inmate, and after a few days the veteran will demand sexual repayment." In the fear-charged atmosphere of prison society, the "threat of rape, expressed or implied, would prompt an already fearful young man to submit" for a guarantee of future protection from gang assault or for an easier time of it. "Prison officials," Davis concluded, were "too quick to label such activities 'consensual.' "

In sum, Davis found that prison rape was a product of the violent subculture's definition of masculinity through physical triumph, and those who emerged as "women" were those who were subjugated by real or threatened force.

Here I shall add my own coda to the Davis report. Well-meaning people from time to time put forward the suggestion that the way to curb homosexual activity in prison lies in supplying real women—wives, girlfriends and volunteer prostitutes—for the inmate population, a highly touted feature of some Mexican jails. At their most sincere those who advocate this solution hold to the mistaken belief that prison homosexuality is the fallout of an unfortunate situation in which men have no heterosexual outlet for their emotions and physical needs, and that so-called "deviant" behavior can be curtailed by a stock of willing women. Besides being an embarrassingly simplistic view of the nature of true homosexuality, which is not dependent in the slightest on the availability of women, this "solution" misreads the ideology of rape in the prison experience: that is, the need of some men to prove their mastery through physical and sexual assault, and to establish, most strikingly within the special crucible of the male-violent, a coercive hierarchy of the strong on top of the weak.

Incidents of rape by guards, trusties or other inmates also surface from time to time in periodic exposés of mental hospitals, women's prisons and juvenile detention centers. An imitative rape ideology among females is not unknown in the women's institutions, although it nowhere matches the male experience. The inmate hierarchy in a women's prison, according to those who have made a study of it, expresses itself in an intricate emotional super-structure imitative of an extended family life rather than in raw domination by physical power. Women who remain in prison for any length of time tend to form families consisting of a butch husband, femme wife, and assorted aunts, uncles, brothers, sisters and children. The female acculturation process, so different from the male's, leads to a preference for nest-building over the simpler tyranny of the strong over the weak.

Yet there is evidence enough that outright sexual assault among women does occur. In her autobiography, the actress Frances Farmer described in frightening detail the lesbian rape of an inmate by a trusty on the women's ward of a state mental hospital in the nineteen forties. Recently in New York City a newspaper exposé of conditions at the temporary Children's Center reported that an adolescent girl, shortly after her admission, was taken by a group of girls into a room where she was raped by a gang of youths that included some young men who had come into the building from the street.

This was not an isolated incident. Workers at this shelter for truant and retarded teen-agers described a deteriorated situation in which gangs of girls, in cahoots with outside gangs of boys from whom they took orders, terrorized staff members and newer inmates. On one occasion a woman counselor was stripped by a gang of girls intent on abusing her sexually. Complaints of sexual assault at the Children's Center, including abuse of girls by girls, were common according to a deputy police inspector from the nearby precinct who remarked, "There is no way of knowing if this is lesbian or sadistic. All we do know is that we don't hear of most of the crimes because the victims—and this includes counselors—are afraid to complain."

POLICE RAPE

Consider the case of James J. Farley, a New York City police detective assigned to the robbery squad and the holder of four special citations in six outstanding years of service. In October, 1972, officer Farley was quietly suspended from the force when he was arrested and charged with raping a fifteen-year-old girl in Suffolk County near his home the previous June. A small item about his arrest and suspension appeared in the newspapers and I filed it away as a curio in a manilla folder marked POLICE. In February, 1974, another small news item caught my eye. James

Farley had been sentenced to fifteen years in prison for the admitted rape at gunpoint of two women on the West Side of Manhattan. Not only that, Farley had received a twelve-year sentence in another jurisdiction for three other rapes in the borough of Queens and his Suffolk County case was still pending. Farley's entire raping career, as it came to light, had occurred while he was a member in good standing of the New York police department.

In the course of monitoring New York newspapers over a four-year period, I collected reports on one new police rapist per year—that is, one new case per year in which the evidence against a policeman was sufficient to warrant his arrest and departmental suspension *that subsequently came to public attention.* Less systematic monitoring of some other big-city newspapers leads me to suspect that the pattern holds true for Washington, Cleveland, Houston and Detroit. Detroit might win a mention in the *Guinness Book of World Records.* On Thanksgiving Day, 1973, three Detroit policemen were suspended from the force and charged with rape and sodomy after a departmental investigation. One of the Detroit officers had done his work solo, while the other two, one white and one black, had utilized the buddy system. On routine patrol one evening they picked up a young woman on a drunk-and-disorderly charge in front of a bar and took her to the precinct house for booking. There the commander on duty determined that the young detainee, age 19, was not drunk and ordered the patrolmen to drive her home. Instead, according to the official charges, the officers drove her to a deserted street and proceeded to rape her.

The two policemen were dismissed from the force (as was the third and solo operator) after a departmental trial affirmed the charges. Interestingly, in an outside criminal court procedure they were found not guilty on a technicality, but this did not affect the departmental ruling.

I want to say that this Detroit case represents a distinctive *modus operandi* of police rape—on-the-job abuse of power within the protective cover of "duty" by men invested with the sanctioned authority of a badge and a gun and the power to make an arrest—that has been far more prevalent than any of us realize. But to support such a serious indictment I would have to rely on unprovable folklore as it has been told and retold by ranks of bitter women, especially black women, who never won the satisfaction of having their police rapists charged with the crime, let alone convicted.

One item out of several from We Charge Genocide:

> Memphis, Tennessee, August 3, 1945: Two young Negro women were raped by uniformed police officers. They were waiting for a street car to take them home from work when the officers took them into custody. They were then driven to an isolated spot where the officers raped them. The officers warned them that they would be killed if they reported the incident. A complaint to the Chief of Police from the mother of one of the young women brought the advice that she keep her mouth shut. The two officers were acquitted by an all-white jury.

Those who bear the awesome responsibility for maintaining law and order are demonstrably reluctant to face up to evidence of criminality within their own house, as periodic exposés of police brutality, graft and corruption plainly show. That this much documentary evidence of police rape has surfaced is in itself remarkable in view of the solidarity of the police brotherhood and the reluctance of policemen in general to believe a rape complainant. Equivocators might argue that the phenomenon of police rape, whatever its statistical incidence—it has never been formally studied—proves that officers of the law are no different from anyone else and that occasional acts of miscreance are an all-too-human failing. This will not do. The horror of police rape is special, for it is an abuse of power committed by those whose job is to control such abuses of power. A police department, like a prison or an army, is by nature and structure a traditionally male, authoritarian institution, but one empowered by law to employ force where necessary to protect us from crime. Operating through sanctioned force, the local police precinct has always been a bastion of male attitudes and responses that are inimical to women. (See Chapter 11.) The policeman who rapes is at the extreme end of a value system that also tolerates the policeman who does not believe that the crime of rape exists.

Police rape, as I have said, represents the ultimate Kafkaesque nightmare, for when society's chosen figure of lawful authority commits a criminal act upon one of those persons he has been sanctioned to protect, to whom can a woman turn for justice?

The women's folklore of rape—cases that seldom, if ever, reach a court of law—is an oral history of abuses by men in positions of authority. The therapist who applies his personal kind of sexual therapy, the doctor or dentist who suddenly turns a routine examination into a physical overture that the bewildered patient feels helpless to halt, the producer who preys on a starlet's ambition, the professor who twists to his advantage his student's interest in his field of scholarship—these are examples of what men would call seduction since the sexual goal may be accomplished without the use, or even the threat, of physical force, but the imposition of sex by an authority figure is hardly consensual or "equal."

Coercion can take many forms, economic and emotional coercion are among them, and not only is the victim afraid to resist, but after the fact, she is seldom believed. Rape by an authority figure can befuddle a victim who has been trained to respect authority so that she believes herself complicitous. Authority figures emanate an aura of rightness; their actions cannot easily be challenged. What else can the victim be but "wrong"?

No area of sexual abuse is characterized by unchallengeable authority to a greater degree than the sexual abuse of children, for to a child *all* adults are authority figures. When a child is sexually abused by an adult, the entire world of adult authority bears down to confuse and confound the hapless victim.

THE SEXUAL ABUSE OF CHILDREN

"Dear Abby," a mother who signed herself "DAZED" wrote to the syndicated columnist Abigail Van Buren,

> I wrote to you several months ago about a male relative molesting my 3-year-old girl. Your answer was to confront him with it and get him to a doctor, fast. We had already confronted him, and of course, he denied everything. "She makes up stories," he said. Abby, how can a 3-year-old make up stories of this kind? I talked with the police department and was told you cannot accuse someone of molesting without proof. . . . Will they take the word of a 3-year-old against that of a grown man who is admired and respected by all? NO! I was made to look like an hysterical mother having hallu-

cinations. Can you understand why each night I pray for God to take him?

Columnist Van Buren did understand. This was not the first such letter she, or her real-life sister Ann Landers, had printed.

The sexual abuse of children is an outrage to which people universally react in uncontained horror when that rare manifestation, a mutilation murder, occurs. Yet the *routine* occurrence of child molestation remains a subject from which people prefer to avert their eyes. "Never take candy from a stranger" is a lesson all mothers drum into their unsuspecting children, for in the popular imagination the child molester is the dirty old man who lurks outside the schoolyard or the sniveling Peter Lorre character in *M*. In the hierarchic world of the prison inmate, where assaultive criminals rank high, the child molester is considered the lowest of the low, on a par with the squealer as a figure of scorn and derision. In stunning contrast to the prison population's own view, in the all-forgiving liberal's attitude toward crime, the child molester has come to be personified by the nice, timid man with a fear of grown-up relationships (I'm thinking of that curious movie of some years back, *The Mark*) or as a confused, conflicted man with a "morality" problem or bad judgment.

What is the national incidence of child molestation in these United States and who are the molesters? Is the sexual abuse of minors extreme and aberrant behavior committed by a small number of unfortunates who cannot help themselves—and whose crimes have been blown out of proportion by the tabloids to such an extent that they have ticked off hallucinating fantasies in "hysterical" mothers and their "lying" children? Or is it an all-too-real and rather common experience? The FBI's *Uniform Crime Reports* are no help to us here, for incredible as it sounds, although they can tell us all about the theft of automobiles, the government's crime fighters have never produced a national analysis of sex crimes committed against the defenseless young.

Dr. Charles Hayman's Washington study disclosed that the ages of rape victims brought to D.C. General Hospital ranged from 15 months to 82 years. Twelve percent of his intake were children age 12 and younger. Brenda Brown's study of rapes reported to the Memphis police department showed that 6 percent of all victims were age 12 and under. Menachem Amir's study of reported rapes in Philadelphia showed that 8 percent of all victims were age 10 and under; a total of 28 percent were age 14 and below.

Recent literature by and about women has turned up a remarkable number of accounts of childhood molestation and rape. Quentin Bell's intimate biography of his famous aunt, Virginia Woolf, informed the literary world of what had been a well-kept family secret, that young Virginia had been cornered and molested in the nursery at age six by her 19-year-old half brother George Duckworth, who continued his furtive, insistent grapplings until the young writer was into her teens. *Lady Sings the Blues*, the autobiography of Billie Holiday, told of her rape by a 45-year-old neighbor when she was ten. Underground film star Viva has described being regularly molested by the trusted family doctor during her childhood years. The most moving and painful account of childhood rape ever put to paper appears in *I Know Why the Caged Bird Sings*, a personal memoir by Maya Angelou, the extraordinary and multitalented black woman. It begins, "Mother's boyfriend, Mr. Freeman, lived with us, or we lived with him (I never knew quite which)."

Eight-year-old Maya and her brother Bailey, she tells us, had gone to live with their mother and Mr. Freeman in St. Louis. One morning the child awoke to feel a strange sensation of pressure on her leg. "It was too soft to be a hand, and it wasn't the touch of clothes. . . . I knew, as if I had always known, it was his 'thing' on my leg. He said, 'Just stay right there, Ritie, I ain't gonna hurt you.'" And so began an off-and-on-again fondling that the fatherless young girl desperately wanted to believe was a sign of love. "Get up," Mr. Freeman would say irritably after a flurry of motion. "You peed in the bed." The child knew she hadn't, but Mr. Freeman would pour a cup of water over a telling spot. The funny activity continued for some months, with Mr. Freeman pressing "his thing" against the confused young girl when they were alone and then refusing to speak to her for weeks at a time. One morning when Bailey and Mother weren't home, Mr. Freeman called out, "Ritie, come here."

> I didn't think about the holding time until I got close to him. His pants were open and his "thing" was standing out of his britches by itself.
>
> "No, sir, Mr. Freeman." I started to back away. I didn't want

to touch that mush-hard thing again, and I didn't need him to hold me any more. He grabbed my arm and pulled me between his legs. His face was still and looked kind, but he didn't smile or blink his eyes. Nothing. He did nothing, except reach his left hand around to turn on the radio without even looking at it. Over the noise of the music and static he said, "Now, this ain't gonna hurt you much. You liked it before, didn't you?"

. . .

And then there was the pain. A breaking and entering when even the senses are torn apart. The act of rape upon an eight-year-old body is a matter of the needle giving because the camel can't. The child gives, because the body can, and the mind of the violator cannot.

I thought I had died—I woke up in a white-walled world, and it had to be heaven. But Mr. Freeman was there and he was washing me. His hands shook, but he held me upright in the tub and washed my legs. "I didn't mean to hurt you, Ritie. I didn't mean it. But don't you tell . . . Remember, don't you tell a soul."

Young Maya was hospitalized, and eventually she did tell. There was a trial and the courtroom was filled.

"What was the defendant wearing?" That was Mr. Freeman's lawyer.

"I don't know."

"You mean to say this man raped you and you don't know what he was wearing?" He snickered as if I had raped Mr. Freeman. "Do you know if you were raped?"

A sound pushed in the air of the court (I was sure it was laughter). . . .

"Was that the first time the accused touched you?" The question stopped me. Mr. Freeman had surely done something very wrong, but I was convinced that I had helped him to do it. I didn't want to lie, but the lawyer wouldn't let me think . . .

"Did the accused try to touch you before the time he—or rather you say he raped you?"

I couldn't say yes and tell them how he had loved me once for a few minutes and how he had held me close before he thought I had peed in my bed. My uncles would kill me and Grandmother Baxter would stop speaking, as she often did when she was angry. And all those people in the court would stone me as they had stoned the harlot in the Bible. And Mother, who thought I was such a good girl, would be so disappointed. But most important, there was Bailey. I had kept a big secret from him.

"Marguerite, answer the question. Did the accused touch you before the occasion on which you claim he raped you?"

Everyone in the court knew that the answer had to be No. Everyone except Mr. Freeman and me. I looked at his heavy face trying to look as if he would have liked me to say No. I said No.

       •   •   •

Mr. Freeman was given one year and one day, but he never got a chance to do his time. His lawyer (or someone) got him released that very afternoon.

That night a tall white policeman came to the house to report, "Freeman's been found dead on the lot behind the slaughter-house. . . . Seems like he was dropped there. Some say he was kicked to death." To the logic of an eight-year-old child, "a man was dead because I lied. . . . I could feel the evilness flowing through my body and waiting, pent up, to rush off my tongue if I tried to open my mouth. I clamped my teeth shut, I'd hold it in. If it escaped, wouldn't it flood the world and all the innocent people?"

Maya Angelou stopped talking. For a long time.

What would Sigmund Freud have made of Maya Angelou's story, or of Viva, Billie Holiday, Virginia Woolf and the woman who signed herself "DAZED" if, perchance, they had sought an audience with him in Vienna? The father of psychoanalysis had noticed that many of his hysterical female patients reported a childhood experience of rape or molestation, most often at the hands of their own father. At first the good doctor believed the women. Later he developed the theory in his famous essay on femininity that these disturbing reports of childhood assault were fantasies that the child contrived as a defense against her own genital pleasure and her guilty wish to sleep with her father.

Freud's peremptory dismissal of what his female patients told him and his dogmatic construct of the sexually fantasizing child influenced several generations of his devoted followers. Psychoanalytic literature on child molestation points a wagging finger at the victim. In fact, the thrust of the psychoanalytic approach has been to pinpoint the child victim's "seductive" behavior. A frequently quoted study from the nineteen thirties described the "unusually attractive and charming personalities" of victimized children and cheerfully remarked that they showed less evidence of fear, anxiety, guilt or psychic trauma "than might be expected." A follow-up study posited that in many cases "it was highly probable that the child had used his [sic] charm in the role of seducer rather than that he [sic] had been the innocent one who had been seduced." After the experts had ferreted out the hidden complicity of children, they sighed and chastised "submissive," "passive" or "negligent" mothers for failing to protect their young.

So children were to blame and mothers were to blame. What about the offenders? America's own original sex expert, Alfred C. Kinsey, he who said that the difference between a rape and a good time depends on whether the girl's parents were awake when she finally came home (see footnote page 179), paused in the middle of a discourse on impotence in *Sexual Behavior in the Human Male* to remark:

> A problem which deserves noting is that of the old men who are apprehended and sentenced to penal institutions as sex offenders. These men are usually charged with contributing to delinquency by fondling minor girls or boys; often they are charged with attempted rape. . . . Many small girls reflect the public hysteria over "being touched" by a strange person; and many a child, who has no idea at all of the mechanics of intercourse, interprets affection and simple caressing from anyone except her own parents as attempts at rape. In consequence, not a few older men serve time in penal institutions for attempting to engage in a sexual act which at their age would not interest most of them, and of which many of them are undoubtedly incapable.

This represented almost the sum total of Dr. Kinsey's thoughts on rape in his opus on the human male. In *Sexual Behavior in the Human Female*, Kinsey returned to his singular theme. One in four women interviewed (*all white, predominantly middle-class*) had reported an unwanted preadolescent sex experience of some sort with an adult male. Trying to deal with this astonishing incidence—80 percent reported that they had been frightened—Kinsey theorized:

> It is difficult to understand why a child, except for its cultural conditioning, should be disturbed by having its genitalia touched,

or disturbed by seeing the genitalia of another person. . . . Some of the more experienced students of juvenile problems have come to believe that the emotional reactions of the parents, police and other adults . . . may disturb the child more seriously than the contacts themselves. The current hysteria over sex offenders may well have serious effects on the ability of many of these children to work out sexual adjustments some years later in their marriages.

As the social worker and writer Florence Rush has written, "With the usual male arrogance, Kinsey could not imagine that a sexual assault on a child constitutes a gross and devastating shock and insult, and so he blamed everyone *but* the offender. The fact remains that sexual offenses against children are barely noticed except in the most violent and sensational instances. Most offenses are never revealed, and when revealed, most are either ignored or not reported. If reported, a large percentage are dismissed for lack of proof, and even when proof can be established, many cases are dropped because of the pressure and humiliation forced on the victim and family."*

In 1969 the Children's Division of the American Humane Association, under the direction of Vincent DeFrancis, released a detailed analysis of adult sex crimes against children in Brooklyn and the Bronx, using as its core sample 250 cases that had been reported during an eighteen-month period to police and child-protection agencies. No case involving an offender below the age of 16 (or victim above 16) was included. The Association's definition of a sex crime encompassed rape, attempted rape, incest, sodomy and carnal abuse. In other words, some form of abusive physical contact was the determining criterion. Noncontact cases of indecent exposure and "impairing the morals of a minor" were omitted. The core sample represented a fraction, less than one-sixth, of all reported cases at the Association's disposal, for well over one thousand cases were reported in Brooklyn alone during a single year. Those who worked on the study cautiously estimated that the actual incidence was probably twice that. Among their major findings were these:

---

* I am deeply grateful to Florence Rush for putting much of her material on child molestation at my disposal, and I eagerly await the publication of her book.

• The sexually abused child is statistically more prevalent than the physically abused, or battered, child.

• The median age of sexually abused children is 11, but infants have not escaped molestation.

• Ten girls are molested for every one boy.

• Ninety-seven percent of the offenders are male.

In a book-length report of specific findings the Humane Association disclosed that

• In three-quarters of the Brooklyn-Bronx cases the offender was known to the child or her family. Twenty-seven percent lived in the child's home (father, stepfather, mother's lover, brother). Another 11 percent did not live in the home but were related by blood or marriage. A significant number of offenders were local storekeepers, next-door neighbors, landlords, janitors and youths entrusted to baby-sit. Only 25 percent of the offenders were reported to be total strangers.

• In more than 40 percent of the cases the sexual abuse was not a single, isolated event but occurred over a period of time ranging from weeks to, in one case, seven years.

• Force or the threat of force was used against 60 percent of the children. Another 15 percent were enticed by money or gifts. For the remaining one-quarter, "the lure was more subtle and was based on the child's natural loyalty and affection for a relative or near-relative."

Out of the 250 cases in the Brooklyn-Bronx study, police managed to make 173 arrests. In some of the outstanding cases the offender remained unknown; however, in 48 cases a parent of the child withdrew the complaint—usually because the offender was a relative or friend. In order to prosecute the 173 offenders, the victimized children put in an aggregate of more than 1,000 personal appearances in court. Nearly half of the cases were eventually dismissed because of a New York State law requiring corroboration of a victim's testimony.*

The Humane Association, unlike some of its predecessors in

---

* In 1974 the New York State legislature repealed the corroborative requirement for sex offenses committed against adults, but kept the additional evidence requirement for cases of assaults against children. The precept that children lie is more deeply entrenched in the law than the precept that adult women lie.

the field, was acutely sensitive to the emotional damage done to the child victim. It found that two-thirds of all sexually abused children had suffered some form of identifiable emotional disturbance and 14 percent had become severely disturbed. The most common reaction among the children was the taking on of deep feelings of guilt (articulated by the victims as "the trouble" that they "had caused the family"), shame and loss of self-esteem. "To shatter the ego even further," the report noted, "some parents projected blame on the child and used every opportunity to upbraid and remind the child of the consequences of bad behavior." Emotional damage also appeared in the form of disruptive, rebellious behavior at home and at school, truancy and an inability to concentrate in the classroom. A few children began to display behavior imitative of the offense. A four-year-old who had been abused by her father was later observed playing a similar "game" with her three-year-old brother. Some of the older girls careened into promiscuity. In addition to the emotional trauma, 29 of the girls had become pregnant as a result of the offense.*

An interesting profile of the adult offender emerged from the Brooklyn-Bronx study. The age of reported offenders ranged from 17 to 68, with a median age of 31. More than 30 percent were under the age of 24 and almost 60 percent were under the age of 34. Still, on the whole, police-blotter child molesters appeared significantly older than police-blotter rapists, and a full 10 percent were above the age of 50. (Amir's combined Philadelphia statistics on men and boys who raped women and children showed a median age of 23; a negligible 1 percent were above the age of 50.) Half of all offenders had had a previous brush with the law, an observation that closely matched the Philadelphia statistics.

---

* Psychiatric case studies of prostitutes unearth accounts of childhood rape or molestation by relatives with stunning regularity, but although these cases have been reported individually, no serious study of the prostitute, as far as I know, has tried to put together any statistical evidence. A recent magazine interview with a New York pimp who prided himself on his stable of teen-age runaways contained the quote, "The majority of girls I've gotten so far got raped by their fathers or uncles or somebody." Pimps, who are acknowledged experts in the field of female psychology, intuitively, or perhaps empirically, understand that rape is the fastest way to "turn out" a likely teen-age candidate, and they have been known to set up intricate gang-rape situations when they have spotted a prospect, as a sort of good-business practice.

The victimized child's natural father had committed the abuse in 13 percent of the cases, and the child's stepfather or the man with whom the child's mother was living was responsible for another 14 percent of the crimes. Victims and offenders came mainly, though not entirely, from the lower end of the economic ladder. Reflecting the ethnic composition of lower-class neighborhoods in the Bronx and Brooklyn, 22 percent of the offenders were white, 42 percent were black and 37 percent were Puerto Rican. By and large, offenders molested children of their own class and kind, but as members of the newest immigrant group and with a language barrier to boot, Puerto Rican children were found to have been frequently victimized by neighbors and storekeepers of other ethnic backgrounds.

One serious and unanswerable criticism of the Humane Association study would be that middle- and upper-class families do not bare their internal disorders to the police or to child-protection agencies that essentially service the poor. And since so many of the sex crimes committed against children turn out to be what the sociologists call an interfamily event, the study was unavoidably skewed to the disadvantaged end of the social spectrum. Florence Rush believes that the sexual abuse of children crosses all class lines and economic distinctions quite without favoritism, and the report of Dr. Kinsey, despite himself, would tend to confirm this, since his subjects were all white and largely middle-class. Not much force is needed to molest a young child, and for this reason, I think, older men prove quite successful at it, whereas young men use rape as a test of male prowess and male solidarity. This last point is important. Amir found that 43 percent of all adult rape in Philadelphia was committed by pairs or gangs, but the Brooklyn-Bronx study revealed that only 10 percent of the abuses against children involved more than one offender, and few of these were group assaults. They were, for the most part, "situations where more than one member of a household or more than one relative had each separately committed offenses against the same victim. When the child's victimization was discovered all of the offenders were reported."

Are men who rape their daughters a subspecies of brute monster? Gebhard's group from the Institute for Sex Research, for all its studying, found *nothing at all special* about father rapists when compared to ordinary rapists and the rest of the prison population. In fact as a group they appeared "conservative, moralistic, restrained and religiously devout," to name a few of their sterling qualities as defined by Gebhard's researchers. Throwing up his hands in dismay, Gebhard concluded that "propinquity" and alcohol, and a possible "cultural tolerance" of incest within their backgrounds, had led these quite ordinary men to abuse their daughters.

The unholy silence that shrouds the interfamily sexual abuse of children and prevents a realistic appraisal of its true incidence and meaning is rooted in the same patriarchal philosophy of sexual private property that shaped and determined historic male attitudes toward rape. For if woman was man's original corporal property, then children were, and are, a wholly owned subsidiary. A careful reader might recall from my chapter "In the Beginning Was the Law" that in the Code of Hammurabi a man who "knew" his own daughter was merely banished from the city while a man who stole the virginity of another man's daughter might be lawfully killed. Incest, a misnamed term that implies mutuality—I prefer the explicit description of father rape—has hardly been the universal or uncompromising taboo that psychologists and anthropologists would have us believe; or rather, the taboo against father rape is superseded by a stronger, possibly older taboo—there shall be no outside interference in the absolute dictatorship of father rule. Am I expressing this point in an exaggerated fashion? As recently as the beginning of this century the Washington State Supreme Court dismissed a suit for damages brought by a girl named Lulu Roller, who had been raped by her father—on the grounds that "the rule of law prohibiting suits between parent and child is based on the interest that society has in preserving harmony in the domestic relations."*

---

* It has been suggested, I forgot by whom, that the origin of the incest taboo was an agreement wrung from the father by the mother when she consented to accept male authority in return for protection of herself and her children. I like this theory but I'll admit it is only speculation, but no wilder speculation than the theory that the incest taboo sprung from the father's own recognition of his desire to sleep with his daughter, or was a compact a tribe wrung from each male member, either to increase their number through marrying out (exogamy) or to discourage inbreeding and hereditary flaws. At any rate, the incest taboo, when it works, does protect children, and that is important.

All adults, and especially male adults, are authority figures to a child. Fathers, uncles, big brothers, next-door neighbors and store-keepers are invested with an assumed benevolence that may not exist—that certainly did not exist for those unfortunates in the Brooklyn-Bronx study.

9

The Myth
of the Heroic Rapist

People often ask what the classic Greek myths reveal about rape. Actually, they reveal very little. For one thing, myths about any given god or goddess are often contradictory and impossible to date; and for another, it is far too easy to retell a Greek myth to fit any interpretation one chooses. It does seem evident that up there on Olympus and down here on earth and in the sea and below, the male gods, Zeus, Poseidon, Apollo, Hades and Pan, raped with zest, trickery and frequency. Yet on the other hand, the goddesses and mortal women who were victim to these rapes, Hera, Io, Europa, Cassandra, Leda, rarely suffered serious consequences beyond getting pregnant and bearing a child, which served to move the story line forward. Hera, Zeus's sister, wife or consort, had a foolproof method of recovery. She would bathe yearly in a river to restore her virginity and be none the worse for wear. Aphrodite was a champion seducer in her own right.

Philomela was raped by Tereus, King of Thrace, who took the precaution of cutting out her tongue so she could not tell her story. Philomela cleverly embroidered her woes into a piece of needlework that she sent to her sister, Prokne, who happened to be Tereus' wife. In sisterly revenge, Prokne killed Tereus' son. (Later all of them were turned into birds.) The young girl Kainis, raped by Poseidon, chose an unusual and highly personal solution to her problems. She asked Poseidon to change her into a man in order to avoid future violations. Kainis the girl promptly became Kaineus the warrior, who worshiped his spear.

Zeus's rape of Leda by taking the form of a swan, which resulted in the birth of Helen, was considered by Yeats to be a myth of superheroic proportions responsible for the eventual fall of Troy: "A shudder in the loins engenders there / The broken wall, the burning roof and tower / And Agamemnon dead." For Helene Deutsch's interpretation of the same myth, see page 318.

Robert Graves has suggested that Zeus's many rapes refer to the Hellenic conquest of the goddess shrines, or more simply, to the triumph of the patriarchy over the matriarchy. This is an interesting interpretation, and others have elaborated on it to suggest that men began to rape women when they discovered that sexual intercourse was responsible for pregnancy, but I frankly do not believe that men needed to wait that long to discover the benefits that accrued to them from rape. It is more sensible, I think, to consider the Greek myths charming fables whose origins have been hopelessly lost and proceed to more tangible substance.

Some anthropological studies of primitive societies have been revealing. Dr. Margaret Mead, a pioneer in so many respects, seldom failed to inquire about the role rape played among the peoples she studied in New Guinea. Her beloved mountain-dwelling Arapesh, a mild and gentle people whose major battle in life was survival, did not rape, she categorically reported. "Of rape the Arapesh know nothing beyond the fact that it is the unpleasant custom of the Nugum people to the southeast of them," Mead wrote. "To people who conceive sex as dangerous even within a sanctioned relationship where both partners give complete acquiescence, the dangers of rape do not need to be pointed out. Nor do the Arapesh have any conception of male nature that might make rape understandable to them."

The Arapesh had evolved an intricate survival philosophy and if a woman was not to belong to a man permanently it was "much safer never to possess her at all." However, within one hundred miles of the Arapesh lived the cannibalistic, river-dwelling Mundugumor. Among the violent Mundugumor, "a woman of equal violence who continually tries to attach new lovers and is insatiable in her demands may in the end be handed over to another community to be communally raped." Iatmul headhunters, another river-dwelling people of New Guinea, she reported, also used communal rape to force a recalcitrant wife into submission.

When Mead studied the remnants of Plains Indian culture, she found that in the remembered history of these dislocated native Americans, "A bad woman was fair game for any man. No discipline, no set of standards were enjoined upon the young men who, like male members of many puritan societies, regarded rape as a great adventure. . . . A woman would be taken out by a gang of men, and after long and brutal abuse, turned loose naked, to find shelter as best she could." A "bad" woman was defined by the Plains Indians as a divorced woman who did not have male protection, or a woman who was quarrelsome and vituperative.

The use of gang rape as a control mechanism to keep women in line was hardly restricted to the cultures Margaret Mead happened to study, yet anthropologists who preceded or followed her professed surprise when they stumbled on it and they sometimes resolved their confusion as to its implications by treating it with humor or else they dismissed it as an oddment of backward peoples. Other, wiser students in the field paid more attention.

Robert F. Murphy of the anthropology department at Columbia University came across gang rape as a mechanism of social control when he studied the men's secret society of the Mundurucú Indians of central Brazil. Mundurucú culture was strongly male-oriented, Murphy reported, and a Mundurucú woman was "supposed to be docile and submissive, obedient and faithful to her husband." Mundurucú men hunted in groups and engaged in warfare while Mundurucú women stayed home and communally helped one another in manioc processing. In a Mundurucú village men and women lived in separate houses. The chief secret of the men's secret society was a set of sacred musical instruments closeted in the men's house that the women were not allowed to see or hear, and which the men believed contained the magical key to their own sex-role dominance.

"I was unable to obtain an actual case in which a woman spied upon the sacred instruments," Murphy wrote, "but the Mundurucú men were firm in their insistence that any such violation would be immediately punished by dragging the offender into the underbrush and submitting her to gang rape by all the village men."

Murphy did find gang rape enforced on village women who strayed from their sex-ascribed roles. "When a woman is openly promiscuous and actually takes the initiative in sex relations," Murphy wrote of the Mundurucú, "she is then manifesting behavior appropriate only to the male and thereby intrudes upon and threatens the masculine role. Her acts are thus a community concern, a public delict, and her punishment becomes the proper duty of all the village men."

Gang rape by Mundurucú men was not reserved exclusively for sexual transgressions. Murphy reported that village children were sent against their will, and against their parents' will, for that matter, to a missionary school and the children usually made "every effort to escape. Now when a boy flees the school, he has universal sympathy, but when an adolescent girl runs away, she is raped by the men of the first village near which she passes. . . . By running away, she has placed herself beyond masculine protection, and she has also flouted male authority, albeit that of foreign missionaries whose objectives find limited support among the Mundurucú."

"We tame our women with the banana," an informant quipped to Murphy, using a euphemism for his penis, and the anthropologist noted that among Mundurucú men, the subject of gang rape was treated "with some hilarity. Gang rapes are carnival occasions that become the topic of endless anecdotes told in men's houses."

Institutionalized gang rape, Murphy wrote, had been personally observed by Charles Wagley, another prominent anthropologist, among the Tapirapé Indians of Brazil in the case of an independent young woman who refused to join the other females in manioc processing. "The woman in this case was unmarried and she was turned over to the village men for punishment by her brother. The action of the Tapirapé brother suggests that the deviation of a female constitutes a crisis that requires direct and immediate action regardless of bonds of kinship."

Napoleon Chagnon, a University of Michigan anthropologist, spent nineteen months among the fierce Yanomamö of southern Venezuela and northern Brazil who lived in a state of chronic warfare. "The Yanomamö themselves," he wrote in 1968, "regard fights over women as the primary causes of their wars. . . . A captured woman is raped by all the men in the raiding party and, later, by the men in the village who wish to do so but did not participate in the raid. She is then given to one of the men as a wife." The bonds of kinship are apparently more immutable among the Yanomamö than among the Tapirapé, for "if the captured woman is related to her captors, she is not raped."

A specific anthropological study of rape, which may be the only one of its kind, was conducted among the Gusii tribes of southwest Kenya shortly before that country's hard-won independence from Britain. There had been two famous mass outbreaks of rape in Gusiiland, once in 1937 and once in 1950. Robert LeVine, an anthropologist from Northwestern University, investigated and discovered that in both years the price of a bride had soared beyond the reach of Gusii young men. An exchange rate of eight to twelve head of cattle, one to three bulls and eight to twelve goats for one woman "was the highest . . . since before the great cattle plague of the 1890's," LeVine wrote of the 1937 outbreak. "Many young men could find no legitimate way of getting married, and they resorted to cattle theft and all types of rapes." On one eventful market day, "a large group of young men gathered and decided to procure mates for themselves by abduction. They grabbed the girls in the marketplace and carried them off."

Many of the Gusii girls managed to escape and came home crying to their villages. The British colonial administration, in an effort to restore some semblance of law and order, negotiated a settlement with the male Gusii elders whereby the bride price was formally reduced to six cows, one bull and ten goats. But by 1950, prices had soared once again and the second serious outbreak of mass rape occurred, "though without the dramatic or organized qualities of the earlier one."

LeVine discovered that the Bantu-speaking Gusii had no special word for rape, but used a number of revealing euphemisms such as "to fight," "to stamp on" and "to spoil." Before the imposition of British rule in 1907, the patrilocal Gusii had often "imported" wives from related but hostile clans with whom they conducted blood feuds. Virginity was not especially prized. As mentioned earlier, a famous Gusii proverb went, "Those whom we marry are those whom we fight." Interclan rape and abduction was kept in check by the constant threat of retaliation. After the British moved in, traditional clan life and self-regulation broke down: "Whereas previously a prospective rapist could anticipate the possibility of annihilation of himself and his fellows by the clansmen of his victim, nowadays he faces an indecent assault charge with a maximum prison sentence of one year," LeVine wrote in 1959. "Furthermore, two-thirds of indecent assault indictments are dismissed, mostly because the enforcement agencies cannot prevent the escape of rapists to European plantations . . . where they stay and work until the charges are dropped."

The Gusii experience baldly highlights the concept of woman as property, secured by rape. An extreme example, it has its Western counterpart in recurring stories of the rape and abduction of Sicilian women. LeVine called the Gusii a "high-rape culture" and reported that their annual rape rate for 1955–1956 was estimated at 47.2 per 100,000 population. The current rape rate for certain American cities, such as Denver, Little Rock and Los Angeles, it should be noted, actually exceeds the Gusii's.

Ethnological studies of primitive peoples far removed from us suggest the use of rape as an expression of manhood, as an indication of the property concept of women, and as a mechanism of social control to keep women in line. It has been no different in other parts of the world, if not in actual fact then often in the private and public fantasies of the men who dominate and define the culture.

Male bonding employed against women in a collectively violent fashion is not a recent nor an ethnic phenomenon, nor has it been restricted historically to a war situation or a lower-class mob. In Renaissance Italy the dashing corps of noblemen who led the *condottieri*, the mercenary bands who carried out skilled warfare, were feared as ruthless abusers of women in their spare time, and at least one, Sigismondo Malatesta, was convicted in 1450 of raping the Duchess of Bavaria, who was on her way to the Roman Jubilee. A staple of modern Japanese pornography, comic-book variety, depicts the noble samurai of feudal times vanquishing their foes and then stripping the kimonos off women won in battle. In eighteenth-century London, societies of young dandies named the Mohocks and the Bold Bucks terrorized the streets without fear of trial or prison, secure within their class privilege. "The ravages of the Bold Bucks," Christopher Hibbert has written, "were more specifically sexual than those of the Mohocks and consequently, as it was practically impossible to obtain a conviction for rape and as the age of consent was twelve, they were more openly conducted."

My favorite scene in Nathanael West's *Miss Lonelyhearts* occurs when the tired, anguished newspaperman stops off in Delehanty's for a drink and joins a group of his friends at the bar.

> One of them was complaining about the number of female writers.
>
> "And they've all got three names," he said. "Mary Roberts Wilcox, Ella Wheeler Catheter, Ford Mary Rinehart . . ."
>
> Then someone started a train of stories by suggesting that what they all needed was a good rape.
>
> "I knew a gal who was regular until she fell in with a group and went literary. She began writing for the little magazines about how much Beauty hurt her and ditched the boy friend who set up pins in a bowling alley. The guys on the block got sore and took her into the lots one night. About eight of them. They ganged her proper . . ."
>
> "That's like the one they tell about another female writer. When this hard-boiled stuff first came in, she dropped the trick English accent and went in for scram and lam. She got to hanging around with a lot of mugs in a speak, gathering material for a novel. Well, the mugs didn't know they were picturesque and thought she was regular until the barkeep put them wise. They got her into the back room to teach her a new word and put the boots to her. They didn't let her out for three days. On the last day they sold tickets to niggers . . ."
>
> Miss Lonelyhearts stopped listening. His friends would go on telling these stories until they were too drunk to talk. They were aware of their childishness, but did not know how else to revenge themselves.

Throughout history no theme grips the masculine imagination with greater constancy and less honor than the myth of the heroic rapist. As man conquers the world, so too he conquers the female. Down through the ages, imperial conquest, exploits of valor and expressions of love have gone hand in hand with violence to women in thought and in deed. And so it was the poet Ovid, the Roman celebrant of love, who wrote of the rape of the Sabine women, "Grant me such wage and I'll enlist today," setting a flippant attitude toward rape in war that has persisted for two thousand years.

James Bond, the mythic superagent creation of Ian Fleming, fights SMERSH and wins women with equal success. Of a new

sexual interest Bond muses, ". . . however long they were together, there would always be a private room inside her which he
could never invade. . . . And now he knew that she was profoundly, excitingly sensual, but that the conquest of her body,
because of the central privacy in her, would each time have the
tang of rape."

But writers are known to exaggerate, and what, after all, do
they truly know of war or women? A man who did know was
Genghis Khan, who led the great thirteenth-century Mongol conquest. Genghis explained his divine mission with a seriousness that
befitted his successful station. "A man's highest job in life," said
the man who practiced what he preached, "is to break his enemies,
to drive them before him, to take from them all the things that
have been theirs, to hear the weeping of those who cherished them,
to take their horses between his knees, and to press in his arms the
most desirable of their women." This remains, I think, the defini-
tive statement of heroic rape: woman as warrior's booty, taken like
their proud horses. We owe a debt to Genghis for expressing so
eloquently the direct connection between manhood, achievement,
conquest and rape.

Permissible rape as an act of manhood infused the theories of
courtly love propounded by the social arbiters of the Middle Ages.
Andrew the Chaplain, a most secular fellow who served in the
twelfth-century court of Marie of Champagne, wrote a treatise to
guide the behavior of knights in love. His rules were somewhat
rigid when a pair of would-be lovers were of equal station, but with
women of peasant stock no stately minuet was needed. Wrote
Andrew, "When you find a convenient place do not hesitate to
take what you seek and embrace them by force. For you can hardly
soften their outward inflexibility so far that they will grant you
their embraces quietly or permit you to have the solaces you desire
unless first you use a little compulsion as a convenient cure for
their shyness." The Chaplain's approach to women of the peasant
class was grounded in his exquisite understanding of feudal labor.
Peasant women ought not be instructed in the delicate art of
courtship, he warned, "lest while they are devoting themselves to
conduct which is not natural to them the kindly farms which are
usually made fruitful by their efforts may through lack of cultiva-
tion prove useless to us."

Andrew's contemporary, Chrétien de Troyes, poetically restated the rules of chivalry in his romances of the King Arthur legend. As Chrétien defined the Arthurian ethic,

> If a knight found a damsel or wench alone, he would, if he wished to preserve his good name, sooner think of cutting his own throat than of offering her dishonour; if he forced her against her will, he would have been scorned in every court. But, on the other hand, if the damsel were accompanied by another knight, and if it pleased him to give combat to that knight and win the lady by arms, then he might do his will with her just as he pleased, and no shame or blame whatsoever would be held to attach to him.

So much for theory. Sir Gawain the courteous, the "most perfect knight" of King Arthur's Round Table, gallantly ravished the unprotected Gran de Lis "in spite of her tears and screams." According to some commentators on medieval England's social mores, "To judge from contemporary poems and romances, the first thought of every knight on finding a lady unprotected and alone was to do her violence."

The fifteenth-century English narrator of the Arthurian cycle, Sir Thomas Malory, shed some unexpected light on the chivalric code of gallant rape. In Le Morte d'Arthur he tells of a rapacious knight who drags a weeping, screaming lady from the hall of the King during supper. Not only did the other knights not rush to her aid, but the King was glad at her removal, "for she made such a noise."

Malory's concept of heroic rape was no mere fantasy, as it turned out. Morte d'Arthur was written while he languished in Newgate Prison on a variety of charges, the particular nature of which remained a mystery until 1927 when a painstaking scholar sifting through some dusty records in Warwickshire found a parchment of his original indictment. The dashing poet-knight of Newbold Revell apparently had supported his life-style by plundering the local monasteries and on two occasions he "did feloniously seize and have carnal knowledge with Joan, the wife of Hugh Smyth," in addition to stealing the Smyth family's household goods.

Sir Thomas Malory a rapist! The discovery and shock were more than the academic community could bear. Response to the unwelcome news was a closing of ranks and a stirring twentieth-century defense brief that appeared to take its cue from the Legal Aid Society. G. L. Kittredge of Harvard, the dean of Malory scholars, took to himself the role of an F. Lee Bailey and scoffed, "The double charge of rape was manifestly absurd—a mere legal formula." Edward Hicks, the embarrassed scholar who found the indictment, did as much as he could to make amends. He was convinced, he wrote, that Malory had been a faithful husband and the awful rape charge was probably no more than "piling on the agony." Hicks could not resist a parting shot at the reputation of the woman who five centuries earlier had caused his Malory such grief. Seeking to leave the court of public opinion with reasonable doubt, he wrote, "Whether Joan Smyth of Monks Kirby played the part of Potiphar's Wife it is impossible to say."

Another chivalric fifteenth-century figure whose personal life-style was so truly shocking that history gave him a new identity and modified image is Gilles de Rais, the original Bluebeard. A French nobleman and soldier extraordinaire who served as Joan of Arc's lieutenant on the field of battle, in his later life Gilles indulged a fondness for small boys to extravagant proportions. He abducted, raped and murdered between forty and one hundred (estimates vary) peasant youths at his Brittany castle. After a notorious trial he was executed in 1440. In his final confession Gilles admitted to having been influenced by the life of Caligula and other Caesars who "sported with children and took singular pleasure in martyring them." The most amazing part of the Gilles de Rais story is that the legend of Bluebeard's Castle that we know today has metamorphosed from a terrifying account of a sex-murderer of small boys to a glorified fantasy of a devilish rake who killed seven wives for their "curiosity." It is almost as if the *truth* of Bluebeard's atrocities was too frightening to men to survive in the popular imagination—but turned about so that Bluebeard's victims were acceptably female, the horror was sufficiently diminished (but not, of course, to women). Charles Perrault, who included the heterosexual version in his tales of Mother Goose, probably deserves the credit for the turnabout of the Bluebeard legend, which had its most recent incarnation in the form of a Richard Burton movie widely advertised with the pictures of seven pretty, young women, each in the throes of a different, terrible and violent death.

Gilles de Rais, the original model and not the transmogrified Bluebeard, made a brief return to the public consciousness in the summer of 1973 when the grisly story of Dean Allen Corll came to the surface in Houston along with the plastic bags that held his victims' remains. In a three-year spree of undetected evil, Corll and two disciples had lured and made captives of more than a score of teen-age boys, torturing, sodomizing and finally killing them for orgiastic pleasure. Some bright researcher at *Time* had made the appropriate connection, for when I turned to that magazine's account of the Houston boy murders, there, right at the top of the page, was an archive portrait of Gilles himself. It set me to wondering. How will history remember Corll? His cultish rituals, his disregard for law and human life—this is the stuff of which the legends of sexual *Übermenschen* are formed. For less ambitious crimes Charles Manson has already won deification as a Satan of Sex. In one night of evil Richard Speck secured a permanent spot in the history of infamy. The Boston Strangler and Jack the Ripper are icons in an international chamber of horrors. But Dean Allen Corll, I suspect, will be conveniently forgotten as quickly as possible. Not that his acts of violence were too disgusting; canonization of a sex killer depends on a plethora of lurid details. Dean Allen Corll must fall in the dustbin of unremembered villains because of the homosexual nature of his crime. Corll raped and killed his own kind, and what heterosexual man with a rich, imaginative, *socially acceptable* fantasy life could safely identify with Corll without at the height of his fantasy slipping a little and becoming for one dread instant that cringing, whimpering naked lad manacled wrist and foot to the makeshift wooden torture board? What a turnoff that would be! What a short circuit of the power lines!

Within the heterosexual world that most of us inhabit by choice, sexual violence is exalted by men to the level of ideology only when the victims are female and the victimizers are male. Hard-core pornography is the most extreme manifestation of this destructive principle. By long-standing tradition based on sales experience, run-of-the-mill pornography geared to the heterosexual taste has one big no-no: scenes in which men "do it" to men are *verboten*. But we needn't look to the extreme example to prove the point. The popularity of quite ordinary books, movies and songs that depict violence to women and glorify the man who perpetrates the violence is so entrenched in our culture that an entire book could be devoted to the subject. How women perceive these messages from the culture and how men perceive them are obviously worlds apart. In another chapter I attempt to deal with the lasting effect on women; here I shall restrict myself to the male end of the fantasy.

Jack the Ripper's grip on the masculine imagination is so out of proportion to the case of an unknown man who stalked, mutilated and murdered five prostitutes in London's East End in the autumn of 1888 that we must wonder precisely what his attraction holds. I have seen a couple of Ripper movies on the *Late Late Show*, and the only emotion they inspired in me was terror. As a woman I could not help but identify with the female victims who walked the fogbound streets unaware of imminent death, and I imagine this would be almost every woman's reaction. Not so for men. "Hero" is the surprising word that men employ when they speak of Jack the Ripper. No less an impeccable critic than Noel Annan (Provost of University College, London), writing in the *New York Review of Books*, called him "the hero of horror in Victorian times." (Annan's article was an abstruse roundup of some recent books on Victorian crime and his paragraphs on the Ripper were tangential, yet the acute editors of the *Review*, knowing their audience, emblazoned "JACK THE RIPPER" among their cover lines.)

Charles McCabe of the San Francisco *Chronicle* once devoted a full column to the Ripper, calling him among other superlatives "that great hero of my youth, that skilled human butcher who did all his work on alcoholic whores." McCabe's rave—he likened the Ripper to a British "national treasure"—offered some insights into the Ripper cult. "The Ripper's greatest historical importance," he wrote, "is that he probably founded a new school of murder, the motiveless crime, usually tied up with sex." This is hogwash, of course, since mutilation murders of women are never motiveless. Elsewhere in his column McCabe ventured that "the Ripper is . . . the only important murderer in history whose name we do not know." This, too, is ridiculous, but it does contain the germ of an idea. Jack the Ripper became an important murderer and mythic figure precisely because his identity remained unknown. In other words, he got away with it. Every time a new theory is raised as to the Ripper's identity (current speculation identifies him as a wastrel member of the Royal Family; all seem to agree that he was "exceptional" and "a gentleman"), there is fresh opportunity to drag out the gory facts of his mutilations and the terror he inspired. Terror to women, we must remember, and not to men. If the mystery of Jack the Ripper's real name is ever solved to everyone's satisfaction—a highly unlikely occurrence—the Ripper myth will be severely damaged, for his power over the minds of men lies in his remaining unknown, something the Ripper himself played upon in his taunting catch-me-if-you-can letters to newspapers and local vigilance committees.

I cannot leave the Ripper without paying my respects to the always interesting English writer Colin Wilson, author of *The Outsider*, who expressed his attraction to male slayers of women in his provocative *A Casebook of Murder*. Wilson posited that the Ripper clearly belonged to the talented, dominant, top 5 percent of the population, and he was much taken with "the propaganda of the deed." In his sprightly compendium of sex slayings Wilson finds only one that truly disgusts him, a lesbian murder of two small children. Of this particular murder and why if fictionalized it would make poor reading, he writes, "It is hard to see how [it could be] made bearable for the sexually normal reader." But of the rest of his gallery of heterosexual and male homosexual rapists, necrophiliacs, disembowelers, axe murderers, breast eaters, kidney devourers, etc., he displays no queasiness. He honestly believes they are of interest to the "sexually normal"—for, writes Colin Wilson, "The sexual act has a close affinity with murder. . . . Murderer and victim are in the same sort of relation as the male penetrating the female."

Jack the Ripper's preeminence as the mythic hero of sexual violence has been strongly challenged in recent years by America's own Boston Strangler (see pages 200 to 206). Yet after the confession of Albert DeSalvo the public reacted with a keen sense of feeling cheated by the anticlimax of it all. When DeSalvo was murdered in prison, newspaper feature writers took the opportunity to rehash the Strangler story in a way that left doubts that the real killer of thirteen women had truly been caught. The Boston Strangler's mythic reputation as an unknown Superman of sexual terror who still lurks outside the door at night, I predict, will survive the chunky, dullish *persona* of Albert DeSalvo in life and in death. Besides a book (a good one) and a movie, he has already been memorialized by Mick Jagger and the Rolling Stones in one of their most theatrical numbers, "Midnight Rambler," in which

Mick's scarves, his own personal trademark, become the Strangler's garrote.

A magazine reporter described the frantic audience reaction to "Midnight Rambler": "Keith Richard sways through a long, threateningly erotic guitar introduction as Mick slowly removes a bright gold sash. On the first line, 'You've heard about The Boston Strangler,' the lights suddenly dim and Jagger is outlined in a deep red floodlight. He slinks around the stage, a slim-hipped, multisexual reincarnation of Jack the Ripper [sic]. Grasping the sash like a whip he brings it down with a crack. . . . 'Me, me,' they shout. 'Hit me, Mick.' "

"Midnight Rambler" is Mick Jagger's orgasmic, heightened recreation on stage of the rape-murder of twenty-three-year-old Beverly Samans, the most viciously mutilated of the Strangler's victims, taken from the words of Albert DeSalvo's confession as it appears in Gerold Frank's authenticated book. (Musicologists might want to check Mick's lyrics against pages 354–356 of *The Boston Strangler*, paperback edition.) After Keith Richard's musical bridge, punctuated by a faint "Oh, don't you do that, oh, don't do that" (Beverly's cry), Mick chants,

> Well, you heard about The Boston— aghhhh
> It's not one of those.
> Well, talkin' 'bout the midnight— shhhhh
> The one who closed the bedroom door . . .
> Oh God, hit her head . . . rape her . . . hang her . . .
> The knife sharpened . . . tiptoe . . . uhhhh
> Oh just that . . . She was dead—
> Uhhh, the brain bell jangled,
> Hullo, have you ever seen so dead?

"Midnight Rambler" ends with Jagger's crescendo, "I'm gonna smash down on your plate-glass window/Put a fist, put a fist through your steel-plated door/I'll . . . stick . . . my . . . knife right down your throat." The transformation is complete. Mick has become the mythic Strangler, and with more tensile grace and style than the original model ever possessed.

In the summer of 1965 a strangely compelling bit of graffiti appeared on the wall of a subway station in Greenwich Village. With great economy of word and thought it read "MICK IS SEX."

Those were the days of "Satisfaction," the Stones' first great hit ("*I can't get no satisfaction, well I try, well I try . . .*"). By the early seventies, at least according to "Midnight Rambler," "Sympathy for the Devil" and "Let It Bleed," the search for sexual satisfaction had led to the dark enactment of simulated violence for autoerotic pleasure. A Stones tour in 1969 culminated in the tragedy at Altamont, where the playacting on stage touched off an uncontrollable frenzy of real violence among members of the audience to Jagger's genuine bewilderment, or so it appears from the film documentary *Gimme Shelter*. A man was knifed and beaten to death at Altamont by the Stones' myrmidon guard of Hell's Angels, who needed but a small romantic push to release their anti-social behavior; less publicized but reported in a West Coast women's liberation newspaper was an eyewitness account of several rapes during the free-for-all concert.

Jagger and the Stones were not an isolated example of violent sexuality during the heyday of hard rock. Jim Morrison of The Doors and Jimi Hendrix, both dead, had meteoric careers built on simulated on-stage abuse of women for autoerotic kicks. It is interesting to note the emergence during this period of a group that actually named itself The Amboy Dukes, from the title of a late-forties novel of gang life in Brooklyn by Irving Shulman in which the climactic scene is the rape of a neighborhood girl who wouldn't "put out" for the Dukes—as up-front a case of romantic conjuring as we are wont to find. But the Stones were/are the champions and their brief, unhappy association with the Hell's Angels of California illuminated the danger of glorifying violence.

We have the self-styled hero-outlaw of journalism, Hunter Thompson, to thank for foisting upon a susceptible American public in the mid-nineteen sixties the mythologized exploits of a gang of scruffy, two-bit, overaged hoodlums and motorcycle freaks known as the Hell's Angels. Had it not been for Thompson and his souped-up prose covered with a chrome shine of social significance, the bike-riding thugs in their swastika-studded black-leather jackets might have gunned off into yet another California sunset and oblivion. Instead, the Hell's Angels came to symbolize the bandit-outlaw fighting an oppressive system to a generation of young people newly politicized by the Southern civil-rights movement and soon to be galvanized into opposition to the Vietnam war.

Thompson and the Angels jointly shared their first real publicity break when he wrote a spirited defense of their "outlaw tradition" for *The Nation* in 1965, a piece that was intended to give the lie to what Thompson called the "supercharged hokum" in accounts of Angel gang rape that had appeared in *Time* and *Newsweek*. "The Hell's Angels mean only to defy the world's machinery," he explained, comparing their working-class group loyalty to Joe Hill and the IWW. Thompson knew his audience well enough to tailor his piece to his readers' predilections. The heady combination of Joe Hill, the Wobblies, a swipe at *Time* and not one but two "phony" charges of rape was enough to launch the Angels as the new cultural darlings of the liberal left. "They speak to and about each other with an honesty that more civilized people couldn't bear," Thompson wrote with a sob. As for those nasty *Luftwaffe* insignia and Iron Crosses that the Angels used to adorn their jackets—"Purely for decorative and shock effect," he soothed. "The Angels are apolitical and no more racist than other ignorant young thugs."

In his full-length book *Hell's Angels*, Thompson continued his odd mythologizing of the bike gang's habits, endowing their sadistic sexual antics and swaggering confessions with the imprimatur of Everyman's fantasy but stopping just short of actual endorsement. Or does he stop short? Thompson's high-horsepower writing style managed to neatly straddle the question. He professed to see in the Angels a larger-than-life symbol of society's "rape mania, the old bugaboo." Rape mania, according to Thompson, was composed of several related aspects. "Women," he announced, "are terrified of being raped, but somewhere in the back of every womb there is one rebellious nerve end that tingles with curiosity whenever the word is mentioned." The Angels, he believed, were merely taking advantage of this female curiosity. "Sure, we'll take whatever we can get," he quotes an Angel as saying. "But I've never yet heard a girl yell rape until it was all over and she got to thinking about it." Non-Angel men shared a slightly different perspective: "Men speak of rapists with loathing, and talk about their victims as if they carried some tragic brand. They are sympathetic, but always aware. Raped women·have been divorced by their husbands—who couldn't bear to live with the awful knowledge, the visions, the possibility that it *wasn't really rape*. There is the bone of it, the unspeakable mystery."

There was little unspeakable mystery but remarkable correlation with disciplinary procedures practiced by the Mundurucú and Tapirapé Indians when Thompson described gang rape by the Hell's Angels "as a form of punishment" inflicted on "a girl who squeals on one of the outlaws or who deserts him." "Pulling the Angel train," Thompson wrote, was "a definite ceremony, like the purging of a witch," and he recorded the punishment with the neutral eye of a trained anthropological observer. An errant woman would be apprehended by some of the boys, taken to a safe house, "stripped, held down on the floor and mounted by whoever has seniority." Angel wives and girlfriends ("mamas" and "old ladies") were invited to watch the group disciplinary procedure but few took advantage of the opportunity. The author grandly concluded, "So the Hell's Angels, by several working definitions, including their own, are working rapists—and in this downhill half of the twentieth century they are not so different from the rest of us as they sometimes seem."

Not so different from whom? There is no doubt that Hunter Thompson himself had a case of acute identification with his subject matter and that fact and fiction tend to get confused in his own well-developed fantasy life. Years later, when he had quit mythologizing the Angels and had embarked on a more satisfying career of mythologizing himself through semifictional political-campaign reportage, the Prince of Gonzo told a fellow reporter, "You know I was a real juvenile delinquent . . . got picked up on a phony rape charge, all that." Out of this sort of stuff the image of the heroic male is formed.

The appeal of the sexual outlaw has always been profound. I am certain that part of the mystique attached to Caryl Chessman, and why he became an international rallying point for the fight against capital punishment in 1959–1960, had to do with his legend as the Red Light Bandit, who preyed on women in lovers' lanes. Not that guilty or innocent Chessman should have been executed for crimes that did not include murder, but as a figure around whom a cause was formed, the sex attacks he may or may not have committed added to his image and made him the ideal personification of society's favorite victim: the arrogant, unloved desperado who never had a decent break or a faithful woman.

Legends of rape have helped to mythify a score of bandits, from the notorious eighteenth-century highwayman Dick Turpin, celebrated in story and ballad, who "raped an occasional servant

girl" as he plundered his way through the English countryside, to
that *mucho hombre*, the chubby-faced Pancho Villa, who en-
tranced a corps of impressionable American newsmen, John Reed
among them, with his shoot-'em-up, love-'em-up exploits in the
days when it looked like Mexico might be having a revolution. The
Villa legend, carefully embroidered by Villa himself, stands as the
ultimate in *machismo* mongering. No other semidisreputable figure
won for himself a gushier crew of biographers seeking to exploit,
confirm or deny his rapacious conquests of peasant women and
cantina barmaids as the wily *caudillo* and his ragged troops galloped over the Mexican landscape yelling "*Tierra y Libertad!*"
"After the Sack—the Saturnalia," gushed one *simpático* Boswell.
"The bowed peon of yesterday today reels in a vertigo of freedom
and power—freedom to do what he will, seize what he will; power
to plant his seed where he will, slay whom he will." And John Reed
defended his hero with "What's wrong with that? I believe in
rape."

Central to the Villa legend, indeed, the significant formative
experience that supposedly shaped this illiterate bandit's steal-from-
the-rich, give-to-the-poor ethic, is a tale of rape. Young Pancho's
first taste of murder, it is faithfully recorded, was an act of blood
vengeance against the hated landlord who had violated his virgin
sister. Which sister, and whether the rapist was the landlord or the
landlord's son, or perhaps the local sheriff, depends on which biography one reads. Villa embellished the story as he went along. In
any event and whatever the form, it remains a fixture in his Official
Life, the "key," as it were, to his later ruthlessness toward landlords and women.

Similarly, rape supposedly played a catalytic role in the rise to
power of Brooklyn mobster Abe (Kid Twist) Reles. When Reles
was just getting started in the nineteen thirties, Brooklyn's established mob chieftain Meyer Shapiro decided to teach the Kid a
lesson by raping and beating Abe's 18-year-old girlfriend. Shapiro
sent her back to Reles with the message, "Tell the dirty rat what
happened and who did it." In blood vengeance, so the story goes,
Reles made appropriate new alliances, rubbed out the Shapiro
mob, and established his own suzerainty over Brooklyn. This story
was part of Reles' later confessions to the district attorney. Reles,
some readers may recall, was the fellow who "fell" to his death
from a police-guarded room in the Half Moon Hotel in Coney

Island twenty months after he became an informer. Nothing more is known about the raped girlfriend.

The Villa legend was resurrected in 1971 by Reis Lopez Tijerina, charismatic *macho bandido* of *la raza*, the northern New Mexico land-claim movement, to give historical weight to his charge that a state trooper had raped his wife, Patsy, while he, Tijerina, was held in prison. This case is a sad one, saturated through and through with *machismo*. When Tijerina first got out of jail and learned of his wife's alleged independent sexual adventures he filed for a divorce. His second impulse was to make political hay. He called a press conference in Washington and charged that his wife's alleged infidelity had been "a legal rape" aimed at him because Patsy had the mind of a child and was unable to resist the state trooper's advance. Thus *la raza* briefly had a new issue, at the double expense of Patsy Tijerina.

Sexual assault of a wife, daughter, girlfriend, sister or mother is often appropriated by men as a major traumatic injury to themselves, a manifestation all the more significant when we remember that men have generally tended to discount the emotional injury suffered by women who have been raped. Harold Robbins made use of the Villa legend in *The Adventurers*, a tale of violence, rape and political intrigue spread over four continents, eight hundred pages and twelve million copies. His Latin-American hero, Dax, is six years old when he witnesses the rape-murder of his mother, sister and female servants by a band of soldiers. At age nine, befriended by a group of Villa-style bandits, an emotionally scarred Dax is ready to try it himself.

"If I'm old enough to kill I'm old enough to rape a woman," Dax pleads after an older boy has scoffed that his "pecker isn't big enough."

"Easy, my little cock," he is soothed by a grizzly old bandit. "Everything will come to you in time. Soon enough you will be a man."

And soon enough he is. Sexual conquest and outlawry run as a dual theme throughout *The Adventurers*, becoming the novel's decisive expression of manhood.

"A bandit against the world and women" is also the theme of *A Clockwork Orange*, in which among other antisocial escapades young Alex and his buddies give a slobbering writer's wife the old "in-out, in-out" before his eyes. This particular rape scene is indicative of the male approach. Had the rape not been performed before the husband's eyes there would have been no recognizable expropriation of property, no outrageous impudence from man to man, for we must keep in mind that within the myth of the heroic rapist women play a minor role. Just how small a role may be gauged by the ecstatic reviews accorded Stanley Kubrick's movie version of the Burgess novel in which Kubrick glamorized sadistic little Alex to extravagant proportions. Beside himself with enthusiasm, *Newsweek's* usually rational reviewer forgot that there were two sexes who watched this movie, and that one sex had no role in the picture other than as victim of assault. "At its most profound level," Paul D. Zimmerman intoned, "A *Clockwork Orange* is an odyssey of the human personality, a statement of what it is to be truly human. . . . As a fantasy figure Alex appeals to something dark and primal in all of us. He acts out our desire for instant sexual gratification, for the release of our angers and repressed instincts for revenge, our need for adventure and excitement."

I am certain no woman believes that the punk with the Pinocchio nose and pair of scissors acted out *her* desire for instant gratification, revenge or adventure. We could chalk up the *Newsweek* review to the excesses of one effusive writer did we not have it straight from the horse's mouth. Film-maker Kubrick used similar words to define his grand purpose: "Alex symbolizes man in his natural state, the way he would be if society did not impose its 'civilizing' processes upon him. What we respond to subconsciously is Alex's guiltless sense of freedom to kill and rape, and to be our natural savage selves, and it is in this glimpse of the true nature of man that the power of the story derives."*

A *Clockwork Orange* was no aberration among movies during its box-office season. Hitchcock's *Frenzy*, Peckinpah's *Straw Dogs* and a Robert Mitchum vehicle, *Going Home*, were also notable for their glamorization of rape. There is nothing I can say about *Frenzy* that was not perceived with great sensitivity by Victoria

---

* Another highly respected film maker, Luis Buñuel, was a bit more honest when he discussed his reasons for making *Viridiana*. "As a child," he confessed, "I dreamed of making love to the Queen of Spain, who was very blonde, very white, like a sublime nun. I imagined I stole into the palace, drugged Her Majesty, and then raped her. *Viridiana* is the crystallization of this masturbator's dream."

Sullivan writing in *The New York Times* Sunday entertainment section. The underlying message of *Frenzy*, she wrote, is that "psychopathic rapists are basically nice guys screwed up by their mums . . . [and] to graphically remind a woman of her vulnerability." Her furious conclusion with which I heartily agree: "I suddenly want to retaliate: I want to see films about men getting raped by women. . . . I want to see the camera linger on the look of terror in his eyes when he suddenly realizes that the woman is bigger, stronger and far more brutal than he." (Compare Victoria Sullivan's pro-woman commentary to *Newsweek's* senior reviewer, who once again presumed to speak for all of us with these words, "Hitchcock's graphic, brutalizing handling of a rape sequence with a crescendo of groans from the killer mixed with the recited prayers of the victim triggers our own latent excitement . . . [and makes] his audiences accomplices to his acts of criminal genius.")

What was notable about the Mitchum movie, *Going Home*, which featured the rape of a father's woman friend by his son, was that this picture won a GP (all ages admitted) rating from the Hollywood censors—the movie was deemed acceptable to children! (Thus are young boys taught important lessons.) To achieve the box-office-valuable GP, some footage had to be deleted from the boffo rape scene. The director's outburst when he learned of the studio cuts was unwittingly ironic. He screamed, "They unilaterally and arbitrarily raped my picture."

Although movie makers generally take inordinate delight in glorifying rape—the critic Aljean Harmetz counted twenty such rape scenes in two years of Hollywood productions—and often wrap up the package by having the female victim enjoy it (*Straw Dogs, Blume in Love*), one aspect of the crime has received more sensitive cinematic treatment. This is when the plot line views the rape as man's revenge against another man—either in the case of homosexual rape or in situations where the female victim is merely a passive vehicle of retribution within a larger battle between two men. (Most of the movies that fall into this last category did not have their origins in Hollywood.)

The movie *Deliverance*, made from the James Dickey novel, presented one of the ugliest rapes committed by some of the ugliest rapists in cinematic history. There is no doubt in *Deliverance* that the homosexual rape scene is intended to horrify viewers; in no way can it be construed as a sexual turn-on. Far from being glamorized and heroic, the backwoods rapists in *Deliverance* are physically repulsive and appear to be possessed of subnormal intelligence. What is presented as heroic in *Deliverance* is the justifiable murder of one of the rapists by the victim's buddy, a revenge that is never allowed to women friends of women victims in the movies. I doubt if there exists even one viewer of this powerful film who identified his manhood with the rapist-aggressors. And significantly, lest any viewer have too strong a case of jitters by identifying with the chief victim, he, too, was presented in uncomplimentary terms as fat, huffy-puffy and "womanish." Interestingly, critics who saw *Deliverance* did not use lines like "true nature of man" and "our need for adventure and excitement" when referring to the homosexual rape. Instead, they viewed the scene as some sort of metaphor for the rape of the environment.

In *Twenty-seven Wagons Full of Cotton*, a remarkable short play later turned into the movie *Baby Doll*, Tennessee Williams wove a fascinating tale around an unusual battle of property rights. Jake sets fire to his neighbor's cotton gin in order to secure a contract to process the neighbor's cotton. While Jake is ginning the first of the load in boozy celebration of his good fortune to have his competitor "by the balls," to use an apt colloquial expression, the neighbor enters his house and rapes Jake's wife. The play ends on the implicit note that the neighbor intends to take his vengeance out in trade on the body of Jake's slow-witted wife for every one of his twenty-seven wagons of unprocessed cotton.*

A similar theme of man's revenge against man appears with four variations in Kurosawa's *Rashomon*. In this Japanese film classic, a virile bandit rapes a young nobleman's wife in his pres-

---

* Tennessee Williams has always treated the rape theme with sensitivity. Stanley Kowalski's rape of Blanche DuBois in *Streetcar Named Desire* is also no glamorization, for Blanche, however damaged, represents fragility and aspiration while Stanley is symbolic of the darker forces of nihilism. An additional element here is class antagonism. Stanley has already pulled Stella "down off those white columns" that represented her genteel, Southern, upper-class plantation background, and as this beautifully wrought play proceeds it becomes clear that he intends to perform a similar feat on the woman he contemptuously refers to as Her Majesty, the Queen of the Nile and Dame Blanche. This the climactic rape scene accomplishes. Blanche is vulnerable because she has no male protector. Mitch turns from her when he learns of her past promiscuity and the millionaire Shep Huntleigh of Dallas is an illusion.

ence as a brash thumbing of the nose toward a member of the aristocracy. In the bandit's version of the story he articulates his motivation quite directly. "I wanted to take her right before his eyes," he snarls. And this he does, while the powerless young lord thrashes about, tied and trussed like a chicken. The bandit, consciously or unconsciously, has engaged in class warfare, using the dual means of robbery and rape, *des vols et des viols*, and his triumph is complete because he has rendered his highborn antagonist incapable of defending his property *before* he draws his sword to kill him. As further testament to his manhood the bandit crows with pride that the noble wife actually enjoyed his attentions, an arrogance not uncommon among police-blotter rapists.

The wife in *Rashomon* disputes the bandit's story. She is adamant that she did not enjoy being raped. Interestingly enough, her husband does not endorse her version. Conjured up from his grave, the husband cries that he has been cuckolded, partially by his wife's treacherous, seductive behavior. He also disputes the bandit's story that he was murdered and claims instead that he committed hara-kiri to protect his honor. The final version of the events in *Rashomon* is provided by an itinerant woodcutter who claims to have witnessed everything. In his story all the participants are reduced to less than heroic terms. As the woodcutter tells it, the bandit accidentally killed the husband during a ridiculous sword fight instigated by the wife—because *both men* rejected her as damaged property after the rape.*

---

* Mario Puzo dealt nicely with the damaged-property aspect of rape from another perspective in *The Godfather*. In one of the opening scenes of the book an undertaker petitions Don Corleone for justice. His daughter has been the victim of a brutal attempted rape by two young boys—"not Italian." The petitioner has made the mistake of going through the American court system, and the boys have been let off with a suspended sentence. The girl, disfigured for life, keeps asking, "Father, Father, why did they do this to me?" Don Corleone does not attempt to deal with this question; like the judge who heard the case, he does not believe it is a serious affair. "The boys were young, high-spirited," he tells the distraught man, "and one of them is the son of a powerful politician." He advises the father to send his daughter a box of candy and flowers at the hospital. But the undertaker will not be assuaged—his daughter "will never be beautiful again." When it is understood *between the two men* that Don Corleone is a higher authority to his Mafia "family" than the American system of jurisprudence, the Don dispatches a lieutenant to "take care of" the would-be rapists.

But a movie like *Rashomon* or De Sica's *Two Women* (see page 73) has always been the exception. A typical Hollywood product might throw in a rape scene for a bit of sexy pizzazz and nothing more. Screenwriter Eleanor Perry ran afoul of this unwritten code during the making of *The Man Who Loved Cat Dancing* when she fought against the insertion of a rape scene, and lost. She later said, "I thought [the heroine] would defend herself; she would not be raped. But the director and my co-producer thought otherwise. The rape scene is in the film. One of the men told me, 'Well, rape turns some men on.' " Aljean Harmetz in her quest for why the rape scene has become an ugly movie trend found a producer who told her flatly, "We give the people what they want to see."

An answer that movie producers are giving the public what they want to see will not do. Movie producers, who are male, give the public *their own concept* of what the world is all about, and in this function they perpetuate, shape and influence our popular attitudes. I have dwelt in this chapter on mass-culture figures because I believe it is they who truly affect attitudes, and in particular the attitudes of adolescent males, who are our potential rapists. But I do not mean to suggest that Stanley Kubrick, Mick Jagger or Harold Robbins stand alone in their role as glorifiers of rape. Modern-day proponents of heroic rape pop up all over the place and span the intellectual horizon from the prestigious poetry review *New York Quarterly*, which saw fit to print an early-morning-sex poem brazenly titled "Rape" (*"On top of you this morning on yr flat belly . . . yr eyes open in aversion but no longer fighting"*), to the foolish attempt by some black literati to forge a political theory of "insurrectionary" rape (see pages 248 to 253) to the buffoonery of America's current king of letters, Norman Mailer, who has tied his view of male dominance into a cryptomystic, pseudoscientific doctrine of the aggressive sperm swimming heroically toward the stolid, passive egg, and who treats college audiences on his lecture circuit to the pronunciamento that "a little bit of rape is good for a man's soul."

As patriotism was said to be the last refuge of a scoundrel, buffoonery may well be the last refuge of the heroic rapist. The very concept of heroism, as it has been defined by men, appears to be undergoing a serious re-evaluation these days. The medieval knight in shining armor is rusted and clanking; toughies like the

Hell's Angels are generally perceived as the overaged, two-bit punks they really are. In the future I am confident that men will cease to define their manhood in terms of their aggression toward, or protection of, women. At present, however, they continue to display more than a little public confusion as to their proper stance. For this reason I find a novel by Ed Bullins, *The Reluctant Rapist*, to be of considerable interest. Torn between a concept of heroic, insurrectionary rape, à la Eldridge Cleaver, and an intruding reality that makes such an idea laughably ludicrous, Bullins, who is black, resolves the conflict by presenting contradictory statements and refusing to permit his reader the satisfaction of knowing for certain whether he is deadly earnest or just plain kidding.

Throughout the novel Bullins' protagonist reports his rape of black women and white women with impartiality and gusto, appearing, like Cleaver, to have started on blacks and moved on to whites, but the element of buffoonery and self-mockery wins out. "I'm actually a lover," his hero announces. "I am very reluctant to rape any woman I don't relate to." Professing astonishment that a woman he raped might "misunderstand" and think he was motivated by hostility, he protests, "On the contrary, rarely is it the case that I dislike a source of my pleasure. And I would not knowingly take a woman's body that I did not desire, unless I was drunk or terribly horny, or depressed, or it was very dark, or someone offered her to me out of comradeship and I couldn't refuse . . ."

The Reluctant Rapist wants us to know that some of his conquests have treated his predatory acts "as the compliments they are," once they have "recovered their composure after having been taken advantage of against their will, if it really was against their will." Like Hunter Thompson's Angels and husbands, Bullins' hero worries over female complicity, and he also vaguely worries over why he does not feel any guilt. But dismissing these nagging doubts, the Reluctant Rapist calls his victim "the moon to the sun of my manhood" and declares that "it is not for her to decide how her man is to use her." In his most ambitious and foolish exegesis he argues that committing rape is the highest compliment he can pay a woman: "For to commit rape is to commit oneself to one's own death, if the woman so wills it and if one allows her to live with this power to speak of it to the authorities." In the next breath he tells us, "Though frankly, I would rape a snake if the opportunity presented its slinky self. After all, it's all relative . . ."

Yes, it is all relative, and whether life imitates art or art imitates life is immaterial when we consider the heroic rapist. We can move from fact to fiction and back again to fact with alarming ease, for men have created the mythology and men continue to act it out.

A skyjacker is analyzed from a distance by a psychiatrist who concludes that the wish to kidnap an airplane is symbolic of an impotent's wish to rape a woman, and this is put forward as some kind of deep truth, a "logical" explanation for an irrational act. The police records of two other skyjackers are released to the press and, lo, we discover that both men were wanted on rape charges in Detroit and had jumped bail some months before their grandiose escapade in the air.

Four armed men with nylon stockings over their faces rob a fancy mansion in Greenwich, Connecticut, while the master of the house is away on business. They take the color TV and a sewing machine. They look for cash and silver. While they are searching, one of them forces the governess into a downstairs bedroom and rapes her, tying her with ripped-out telephone wire. An updated version of Dick Turpin?

Two Bronx teen-agers follow a 49-year-old woman to her apartment door and force their way inside. The woman's husband is in the house, convalescing after a brain operation. The youths proceed to rape their victim while her disabled husband watches in tears, unable to move. Did the youths see a movie called A Clockwork Orange?

Three convicts escape from Colorado State Penitentiary and go on a rampage across New Mexico and Texas. There is talk of a "death list" and settling old grudges. For four days the nation follows their trail of killings while hundreds of police close in. What begins as revenge turns into a random binge and a shootout in a mesquite forest. What do you do, you desperate, self-styled "soldiers of fortune," when you realize you will not be able to make it to the Mexican border? You kidnap female hostages at gunpoint and you rape them repeatedly. You let the world know that you are men.

10

Victims:
The Setting

Women are trained to be rape victims. To simply learn the word "rape" is to take instruction in the power relationship between males and females. To talk about rape, even with nervous laughter, is to acknowledge a woman's special victim status. We hear the whispers when we are children: *girls get raped*. Not boys. The message becomes clear. Rape has something to do with our sex. Rape is something awful that happens to females: it is the dark at the top of the stairs, the undefinable abyss that is just around the corner, and unless we watch our step it might become our destiny.

Rape seeps into our childhood consciousness by imperceptible degrees. Even before we learn to read we have become indoctrinated into a victim mentality. Fairy tales are full of a vague dread, a catastrophe that seems to befall only little girls. Sweet, feminine Little Red Riding Hood is off to visit her dear old grandmother in the woods. The wolf lurks in the shadows, contemplating a tender morsel. Red Riding Hood and her grandmother, we learn, are equally defenseless before the male wolf's strength and cunning. His big eyes, his big hands, his big teeth—"The better to see you, to catch you, to eat you, my dear." The wolf swallows both females with no sign of a struggle. But enter the huntsman—he will right this egregious wrong. The kindly huntsman's strength and cunning are superior to the wolf's. With the twist of a knife Red Riding Hood and her grandmother are rescued from inside the wolf's stomach. "Oh, it was so dark in there," Red Riding Hood whimpers. "I will never again wander off into the forest as long as I live . . ."

Red Riding Hood is a parable of rape. There are frightening male figures abroad in the woods—we call them wolves, among other names—and females are helpless before them. Better stick close to the path, better not be adventurous. If you are lucky, a good, friendly male may be able to save you from certain disaster. ("Funny, every man I meet wants to protect me," says Mae West "I can't figure out what from.") In the fairy-tale code book, Jack may kill giants but Little Red Riding Hood must look to a kindly huntsman for protection. Those who doubt that the tale of Red Riding Hood contains this subliminal message should consider how well Peter fared when he met his wolf, or even better, the survival tactics of the Three Little (male) Pigs. Who's Afraid of the Big Bad Wolf? Not they.

The utter passivity of Red Riding Hood in the teeth of the wolf is outdone by Sleeping Beauty, who lay immobile for one hundred years before she was awakened by the kiss of the prince. As a lesson in female sexuality, Sleeping Beauty's message is clear. The beauteous princess remains unresponsive until Mr. Right comes along. The prince is the only one who can awaken the princess. She cannot manage this feat by herself. Her role is to be beautiful and passive. Snow White in her glass coffin also remains immobile until her prince appears. Cinderella, too, needs a prince to extricate her from her miserable environment. Thus is female sexuality defined. Beautiful passivity. Wait, just wait, Prince Charming will soon be by; and if it is not Prince Charming but the Big Bad Wolf who stands at the door, then proper feminine behavior still commands you to stay immobile. The wolf is bigger and stronger than you are. Why try to fight back? But don't you worry, little girl. We have strong and kindly huntsmen patrolling these woods.

I was nursed and nurtured on fairy tales, but as a child of World War II, there were other, stronger rape images that came into the home. My parents had a favorite art book that held a place of honor on the coffee table, and on one of its pages there appeared a popular example of a propaganda poster from World War I. This was the Rape of Belgium, also known as the Rape of the Hun. There are several variations of this poster, but in all of them Belgium is pictured as a beautiful young maiden with long, flowing hair lying prostrate at the feet of the towering Hun, complete with pointed helmet. The purpose of the poster in terms of World War I propaganda is simple: Defenseless Belgium is the tragic victim of the German war machine. But the propaganda message I received at age eight in 1943 was slightly different. Belgium was *beautiful*, even if she was lying on the ground.

I was drawn again and again to the Rape of Belgium because she was so pretty—unlike the overblown, embarrassingly naked Venuses and the stiff Madonnas that filled the rest of the book— but it puzzled me that she was lying down. "Why doesn't she hit him and run away?" I once asked my parents. "It's just a picture, dear" was their response. But was it just a picture? For into the house there soon came Belgium's sister from World War II. In the new drawing, a political cartoon, a porcine Nazi was hauling off two gunnysacks of plunder from a tiny cottage. And cowering prostrate near the doorstep, clutching a baby this time, was a beautiful young girl with long, flowing hair.

What jumps does a child's mind make when confronted with such compelling proof that to be beautiful is to lie crumpled on the ground? This was the middle of World War II, the German Army had marched through Belgium a second time, and I was a Jewish girl growing up in Brooklyn. I could not help but conclude that the Hun and the Nazi were one in the same and, therefore, I had to be Belgium. In the next year I fantasized myself to sleep at night with a strange tableau. A tall and handsome Nazi concentration-camp guard stood near a barbed-wire fence. He did not menace me directly—after all, I had no idea what the actual menace involved. For my part, I lay there motionless, at a safe distance. I was terribly beautiful.

My concentration-camp daydream struck me as peculiar and dangerous even as I conjured it up, and I soon rooted it out of my fantasy life. No doubt the end of World War II helped to speed its annihilation: Jews were no longer international victims. I use this painful remembrance to set the stage for an examination of female victim mentality, and how it is conditioned.

> "ALL WOMEN WANT TO BE RAPED"
> "NO WOMAN CAN BE RAPED AGAINST HER WILL"
> "SHE WAS ASKING FOR IT"
> "IF YOU'RE GOING TO BE RAPED, YOU MIGHT AS WELL RELAX AND ENJOY IT"

These are the deadly male myths of rape, the distorted proverbs that govern female sexuality. These myths are at the heart of our discussion, for they are the beliefs that most men hold, and the nature of male power is such that they have managed to convince many women. For to make a woman a willing participant in her own defeat is half the battle.

Cloaked in intricate phraseology, the male myths of rape appear as cornerstones in most pseudoscientific inquiries into female sexuality; they are quoted by many so-called "experts" on the sex offender. They crop up in literature; they charge the cannons of the dirty jokesters. They deliberately obscure the true nature of rape.

There is good reason for men to hold tenaciously to the notion that "All women want to be raped." Because rape is an act that men do in the name of their masculinity, it is in their interest to believe that women also want rape done, in the name of femininity. In the dichotomy that they have established, one does and one "is done to." This belief is more than arrogant insensitivity; it is a belief in the supreme rightness of male power.

Once the proposition that all women secretly wish to be ravished has been established, it is bolstered by the claim that "No woman can be raped against her will." A variation runs "You can't thread a moving needle," used with wicked wit by Balzac in one of his *Droll Stories*, and retold *ad nauseam*, I am informed, by law professors seeking to inject some classroom humor into their introductory lectures on criminal law. The concept seems to imply at first hearing that if the will of a woman is strong, or if she is sufficiently agile, she can escape unscathed. Four hundred rape-murders a year in this country, and the percentage of gang rapes, should offer strong testament to the cruel lie of this statement, but "No woman can be raped against her will" is not intended to encourage women to do battle against an aggressor—rather, it slyly implies that there is no such thing as forcible rape, and that it is the *will* of women to be ravished.

"She was asking for it" is the classic way a rapist shifts the burden of blame from himself to his victim. The popularity of the belief that a woman seduces or "cock-teases" a man into rape, or precipitates a rape by incautious behavior, is part of the smoke screen that men throw up to obscure their actions. The insecurity of women runs so deep that many, possibly most, rape victims agonize afterward in an effort to uncover what it was in their behavior, their manner, their dress that triggered this awful act against them.

The last little maxim that we must consider with a jaundiced eye, "If you're going to be raped, you might as well relax and enjoy it," deliberately makes light of the physical violation of rape, pooh-poohs the insult and discourages resistance. The humorous advice that a violent sexual encounter not of your choosing can be fun if you play along and suspend your own judgments and feelings is predicated on two propositions: (a) the inevitability of male triumph and (b) "All women want to be raped."

Do women want to be raped? Do we crave humiliation, degradation and violation of our bodily integrity? Do we psychologically need to be seized, taken, ravished and ravaged? Must a feminist deal with this preposterous question?

The sad answer is yes, it must be dealt with, because the popular culture that we inhabit, absorb, and even contribute to, has so decreed. Actually, as we examine it, the cultural messages often conflict. Sometimes the idea is floated that all women want to be raped and sometimes we hear that there is no such thing as rape at all, that the cry of rape is merely the cry of female vengeance in postcoital spite. Either way, the woman is at fault.

One popular reflector of the culture, the highly regarded John Updike, has incorporated both these points of view in his novels. First, a line from *Couples:*

> He fought against her as a raped woman might struggle, to intensify the deed.

Now this exchange of dialogue from *Rabbit Redux*, and notice that it is the woman who makes the telling judgment:

> "This is pretty slummy territory," he complains to Janice. "A lot of rapes lately down here."
> "Oh," she says, "the paper prints nothing but rapes. You know what a rape usually is? It's a woman who changed her mind afterward."

Thus is the victim of rape summarily dismissed by Updike, but, oh, how she is romanticized by Ayn Rand in *The Fountainhead*, the story of Dominique Francon and Howard Roark.

I had not looked at *The Fountainhead* for more than twenty years (it has remained in print for three decades), and when I requested it at the library, I was faintly anxious that the search for Dominique's undoing amid the more than seven hundred pages of Rand's opus might take more time than I cared to spend. I seriously underestimated the universality of my interest. The library's copy of *The Fountainhead* opened itself to Dominique's rape. Hundreds of other readers had, in effect, indexed it for me. And I must say, the two-and-a-half-page scene was as torrid as I had remembered it—all the more remarkable in the light of present-day fiction since the genitals of the two antagonists are not even mentioned.

The vivid picture I had carried in my memory for more than twenty years was surprisingly accurate: architect Roark in work clothes, a stranger from the stone quarry, climbing through aristocrat Dominique's window late at night. The two of them locked in silent struggle. His victory, her defeat, and then his silent departure through the French windows. Not a word has been exchanged, but clearly this has been a coupling of heroes, a flashing signal of superior passion, a harbinger of the superior marriage that finally takes place offstage along about page 700.

And now, with the book before me, I can report verbatim Ayn Rand's philosophy of rape, as posited by Dominique, after the nocturnal visit of Roark:

> It was an act that could be performed in tenderness, as a seal of love, or in contempt, as a symbol of humiliation and conquest. It could be the act of a lover or the act of a soldier violating an enemy woman. He did it as an act of scorn. Not as love, but as defilement. And this made her lie still and submit. One gesture of tenderness from him—and she would have remained cold, untouched by the thing done to her body. But the act of a master taking shameful, contemptuous possession of her was the kind of rapture she had wanted.

A week later Dominique is still mooning:

> I've been raped. . . . I've been raped by some redheaded hoodlum from a stone quarry. . . . I, Dominique Francon. . . . Through the fierce sense of humiliation, the words gave her the same kind of pleasure she had felt in his arms.
>
> She wanted to scream it to the hearing of all.

So this was grand passion! A masochistic wish by a superior woman for humiliation at the hands of a superior man! *The Fountainhead* heated my virgin blood more than twenty years ago and may still be performing that service for schoolgirls today.

Ayn Rand is the chief ideologue of a philosophy she calls Objectivism, essentially a cult of rugged individualism, vaguely right wing, and what I would call spiritually male. She is an example of the ways in which a strong, male-directed woman accommodates herself to what she considers to be superior male thought. Roark is Rand's philosophic hero; Dominique is merely an attendant jewel, a prize of prizes. But if rape for Roark is an act of individual heroism, of manhood, of challenge met and coolly dispatched, then rape for Dominique must embody similar values. When superman rapes superwoman, superwoman has got to enjoy it—that is the bind Rand has gotten herself into. Rand becomes, as does Helene Deutsch, whom I shall soon discuss, a traitor to her own sex.

Men have always raped women, but it wasn't until the advent of Sigmund Freud and his followers that the male ideology of rape began to rely on the tenet that rape was something women desired. The dogma that women are masochistic by nature and crave the "lust of pain" was first enunciated by Freud in a 1924 paper entitled "The Economic Problem in Masochism." This curious little essay, as obscure as it is short,* laid down the psychoanalytic rule that masochism in women is the preferred state, an expression of sexual maturity—or, in Freud's terms, "the final genital stage"— obtaining from "the situation characteristic of womanhood, namely, the passive part in coitus and the act of giving birth."

Freud's male disciples embroidered dutifully on the master's theme, but it remained for a woman, the brilliant Viennese psychoanalyst Helene Deutsch, to construct the epic thesis of female masochism—and to become the ultimate authority for sex-crime experts who wished to explain away the victims of rape. Deutsch is a puzzling, contradictory figure in the history of psychology, who cannot be ignored or laughed at or easily dismissed. A prodigious

---

* Part of the problem, to be perfectly fair to Freud, is that our American understanding of the translated words "economic" and "lust" differs significantly from his German intention. A more accurate substitute for "economic" would be "utilitarian"; a more accurate substitute for "lust" would be "thrill." Still and all, the essay is not one of Freud's finest. It is confused and uncertain and lacks the drama of some of his other works.

intellect and a powerful personality (one can make that judgment from the force of her writing), she rigorously probed the depths of her own psyche and that of her patients to create her dramatic theories of female sexuality. Her first papers were written in German, but after she came to this country in 1935 and settled in Boston she switched, almost effortlessly it seems, to a strong and lucid English. *Psychology of Women*, a two-volume work published here in 1944 and 1945, is the culmination of her ideas. It influenced much of the thinking about women in the conservative, back-to-the-kitchen nineteen fifties.

I became aware of Deutsch's theory that masochism is an essential element of femininity, and a condition of erotic pleasure, when I was in my early teens. Her pronouncements were piously quoted in all the popular books and magazine articles of the day that purported to teach women how to "accept" their female role. Since that time Helene Deutsch has been for me a particular symbol of that which is inimical to women. I believe she has caused real—and incalculable—damage to the female sex, as has, it goes without saying, Freud. But I want to say loudly and clearly that *Psychology of Women* is a towering work. It is a brave, pioneer study, a merciless exploration of the shameful underpinnings of female psychosexuality, *as it has been conditioned by men*. Superstrict Freudian to the end, Deutsch mistook *what sometimes is* for *what must be*, and that is her tragedy—and ours.

Deutsch's belief in the fundamental rightness of rape as an archetypal female experience rested primarily on her view of sexual intercourse as an essentially painful encounter for an essentially passive woman. This attitude was in keeping with the Victorian times in which she and Freud lived and may well have reflected the kind of sex these pioneers of psychoanalysis privately experienced. Deutsch maintained in her writings that women put up with the pain of intercourse and even taught themselves to find a bit of pleasure in it, if they were genitally mature, because of the female's historic mission of reproduction, or as she put it, "service to the species." Service to the species was a holy mission fraught with pain from beginning to end, but most particularly at the moments of labor and birth, and it was clearly a mission any right-thinking person would shirk were it not for a conveniently built-in female masochism.

There is just enough reality in Deutsch's somber view of sex and its reproductive consequences for me to consider granting her a point or two, but then I remember the intense social pressure put upon women to perform this "service to the species" and how the end does often justify the means, and I conclude that a woman does not need any special attraction to pain to want to conceive and give birth.

But let us go back to the sex act, or to Helene Deutsch's picture of it. In true Freudian fashion she quickly disposes of the clitoris. It is "inadequate" compared to you-know-what, and when it is seen in combination with the vagina, it is an "overendowment" from which a woman "suffers." The vagina itself, Deutsch believed, had "physiologically determined pleasure sensations" (modern physiologists would disagree), but she has to admit that the erogenous "transfer" from clitoris to vagina is "never completely successful." With this as background, she then goes on to describe the actual act:

> The "undiscovered" vagina is—in normal, favorable instances—eroticized by an act of rape. By "rape" I do not refer here to that puberal fantasy in which the young girl realistically desires and fears the sexual act as a rape. That fantasy is only a psychologic preparation for a real, milder, but dynamically identical process. This process manifests itself in man's aggressive penetration on the one hand and in the "overpowering" of the vagina and its transformation into an erogenous zone on the other.

That is quite a view of the act of sex. Deutsch bases it, she says, on the biology of a "completely passive vagina" that must await the male sex organ so that it may be "awakened." Ergo, women have "a deeply feminine need to be overpowered." But there is also this aspect: "Woman's frequent fear of coitus originates in the fact that it implies an injury to her physical integrity."

And this, from another page in another chapter: "Woman's entire psychologic preparation for the sexual and reproductive functions is connected with masochistic ideas. In these ideas, coitus is closely associated with the act of defloration, and defloration with rape and a painful penetration of the body. . . . The rape fantasy reveals itself as only an exaggeration of reality."

So, rape is her dramatic definition of intercourse. He tries to conquer, she flees his wooing—and must gradually be won or overpowered by him. Deutsch elevates her theory by ascribing it to man's evolutionary triumph over the apes:

> It is no exaggeration to say that among all living creatures only man, because of his prehensile appendages, is capable of rape in the full meaning of the term—that is, sexual possession of the female against her will.

But apes, too, play a part:

> Every time I see one of the humorous pictures in popular movies or magazines showing an anthropomorphous ape or a powerful bear-like masculine creature with a completely helpless female in his arms I am reminded of my old favorite speculation: thus it was that primitive man took possession of woman and subjected her to sexual desire.

Deutsch is thinking of King Kong (a male mythic figure if ever there was one), the hairy ape who is part destroyer and part misunderstood protector. She conjectures that copulation was originally an act of male violence that women, being weaker, could not successfully resist. Through the ages the mighty embrace and violent penetration, "perhaps accompanied by wooing and caresses," gradually came to be accepted by women as sexual enjoyment: "The powerful embrace of the prehensile arms, combined with the defensive counterpressure, induced strong pleasure sensations in the woman's entire body."

From apes it is but a short flight back to swans. Deutsch offers as evidence the Greek myth of Leda, tricked and seduced by Zeus in the form of a swan. She vividly pictures the god-as-swan enveloping Leda in his plumage, which suggests to the analyst "the feminine wish to feel the seducer's might with the whole surface of her body." This is, she admits, "a phylogenetic hypothesis," but titillation over the entire skin surface could be a happy transfer from the unsatisfactory female genitals.

In support of her theory that it is the pleasure-pain principle that gives female sexuality its masochistic character, Deutsch speaks often of "the pain of defloration." The very word "defloration" has a Victorian ring today as virginity assumes its rightful place of unimportance. (There have always been cultures, in areas little exposed to Christianity, where female virginity has never mattered.) The act of defloration has been of greater psychologic importance to men than it has ever been to women, for as codified by the Hebrew patriarchs in Deuteronomy, proof of virginity was a requirement of the marriage contract. When a husband "deflowered" his wife on their wedding night, in terms of his pragmatic ideology he was breaking open a pristine package that now belonged to him—private property—and he wanted tangible proof of the mint condition of his acquisition. The blood on the sheet and the cry of pain were the proof he demanded. If the tokens of virginity—telltale spots of blood—were missing, there were dire consequences for the Hebrew maiden. She was stoned to death and shame befell her father's house. But female pragmatism in the virginity matter must have asserted itself at some point, for the evidence could always be faked. Wonderful tales have passed down through the ages of anxious mothers or loyal servants who sprinkled a bit of chicken blood on those nuptial sheets in advance of the climactic moment.

My own "deflowering" was so unremarkable (no blood, no pain) that the young man, a wag from the campus humor magazine, brightly inquired if this was really my "first go-round." The question irked me for some time—it had more to do with his expectations than mine—but years later when my consciousness-raising group discussed virginity one evening, it turned out that seven of the eight women present had experienced no discomfort on their first go-round. The eighth had a rough time, and perhaps down through the ages it has been women like her who set the mark. Is the highly touted hymen fast retreating as a vestigial membrane (in which case this is important news and I would like some biologist to formally note its passing) or was its guarding function always exaggerated? I favor the second theory. We can say fairly certainly that as the woman-as-property concept fades and virginity lessens in importance, the "pain of defloration" appears to be going out of style, as all of woman's special gynecological pain seems to be going out of style, from menstrual cramps to the agonies of labor. Or to be more precise, the modern effort is to downplay, control or alleviate the pain, rather than to humbly accept it as a woman's due.

Offering further evidence that the basic and correct stance of females is a "passive-masochistic attitude . . . toward men and life as a whole," Deutsch posits that the fantasy life of young girls is filled with conscious and unconscious thoughts of rape. Rape fantasies often remain on the unconscious level, Deutsch writes, but they "evince their content" in dreams:

> In dreams the rape is symbolic: the terrifying male persecutor with knife in hand, the burglar who breaks in at the window, the thief who steals a particularly valuable object, are the most typical and frequently recurring figures in the dreams of young girls. They are connected with fear, not with pleasure, and thus differ from the boy's puberty dreams.

Girls and women, as we know, have objective reasons to fear hostile, violent men—the burglar, the mugger, the wanton, senseless killer, not to mention the rapist—and this may find justifiable expression in dreams. There is no need to ascribe such fears to "rape fantasy." Recently, after a series of mugging stories in the papers and some firsthand reports from unfortunate friends, I had a dream in which I ran with great strides through the streets with my wallet in my hand, pursued by an unidentified youth. (I got away.) Now this dream could have been a rape fantasy with my wallet representing my hidden, intimate sexuality, or it could have been a straightforward anxiety dream about the real danger of mugging on the city streets, with my wallet representing my wallet.

Freudian dream interpretation, in which a host of plausible, real-life situations are assigned sexual symbolism, can certainly add to one's insecurity. Years ago I once had a dream in which I walked up the stairs to my apartment and was about to open the door when a male figure emerged from the shadows and struck out at me with a hammer. Inundated with popular Freudian psychology, I was distressfully convinced that this dream had to represent a hopeless fear of men and sex—until my Adlerian analyst drew from me the information that I hadn't paid my rent that month and had gotten a dispossess notice from the landlord!

Deutsch was not alone in her faith that young girls' dreams are crowded with symbols of rape. The courageous Karen Horney, who did so much to disabuse her associates of the doctrine of inherent female masochism, got stuck on this idea, too. Dr. Horney cared little for Dr. Deutsch, and Dr. Deutsch cared little for Dr. Horney. The brightest females in the Freudian constellation, one settled in

Boston, the other in New York, conducted a wicked battle of the footnotes as they worked to define their opposing views. In a major break with orthodox psychoanalysis, Horney argued that masochism in women was a neurotic manifestation culturally induced and culturally encouraged, rather than a normal, inevitable result of female biology. Nevertheless, there was enough of the Freudian left in her to make her swallow whole the sexual interpretation of dreams.

Horney believed it was "instinctive" for young girls to dream of rape in various "guises"—and her list of guises was longer than Deutsch's: "Criminals who break in through windows or doors; men with guns who threaten to shoot; animals that creep, fly or run inside some place (e.g., snakes, mice, moths); animals or women stabbed with knives; or, trains running into a station or tunnel." Horney's stake in rape dreams was expressed in a 1933 paper, "The Denial of the Vagina," in which she postulated that the dreams "betray quite unmistakably an instinctive knowledge of the actual sexual process."

Rape dreams to Deutsch were proof of inherent female masochism, but rape dreams to Horney were proof of nothing less than the primacy of the vagina. How a sensible woman like Horney got trapped into such an awkward stance deserves an explanation. Horney put her energy and her professional integrity into a long-running refutation of Freud's theory that all women suffer from penis envy. But instead of attacking the master directly for the inflated importance he bestowed upon the penis, Horney sought to elevate the vagina to a position of equal stature. In her campaign for the primacy of the vagina, all clitoral sensations and corresponding masturbatory impulses in prepubertal girls had to be downgraded, for it wouldn't do to have the vagina take second place and lie erotically dormant, unnoticed even, as per Deutsch, through the critical years of childhood. A young girl's dream into which rape might be read could be construed as an early indication, an actual affirmation, of vaginal sexuality:

> In other words we must assume that both the dread of rape characteristic of puberty and the infantile anxieties of little girls are based on vaginal organ sensations (or the instinctual impulses issuing from these), which imply that something ought to penetrate into that part of the body.

Poor Helene! Poor Karen! Poor us! Freud's most clever—and mutually antagonistic—female disciples thus concurred, for quite different reasons, on the unconscious rape symbolism in young girls' dreams. As Bertha Pappenheim, the German feminist more familiar to us as "Anna O," might have said, "What a pity!"

It is important to distinguish between the unconscious rape fantasies that the Freudians tell us are rife in young girls' dreams and the conscious rape fantasies, the deliberate, waking, sexually distorted daydreams that some women indubitably do have, and that I intend to discuss in the next few pages. Belief in the unconscious rape dream implies belief in an inherent wish for rape on the part of all women—a false assumption that today's Freudian analysts and Freudian-styled criminologists continue to perpetuate. Horney and Deutsch understood that the dreams they reported and interpreted were, for the most part, unpleasant dreams, filled with anxiety and dread, and yet they maintained that these fearful nightmares were the natural condition of womanhood—normal and healthy—either in the service of masochism or in the name of vaginal sexuality. I do not mean to lay the burden of Freudian rape-fantasy theory exclusively at the feet of Deutsch and Horney; many of Freud's male disciples (Rado, Abraham, Fenichel) expounded similar views, though with less authority. But the fact that brilliant women chose to compromise their own sex has particular emotional value. Of course they could not think otherwise and remain within the accepted psychoanalytic orbit—men and men alone determined what was heresy—but that does not give them full pardon.

THE CONSCIOUS RAPE FANTASY

I have examined the Freudian theory of inherent female rape dreams to uncover the origins of much of today's thinking in the fields of criminology, psychology and the law, and to lay the groundwork for an exploration of the conscious female fantasy of rape, the opposite, but hardly equal, polarity of the male rape fantasy, its distorted mirror image.

The rape fantasy exists in women as a man-made iceberg. It can be destroyed—by feminism. But first we must seek to learn the extent of its measurements.

Male sexual fantasies are blatantly obvious in the popular culture (the burden of my previous chapter). Female sexual fantasies are quite another matter. Rarely have we been allowed to explore, discover and present what might be some workable sexual daydreams, if only we could give them free rein. Rather, our female sexual fantasies have been handed to us on a brass platter by those very same men who have labored so lovingly to promote their own fantasies. Because of this deliberate cultural imbalance, most women, I think, have an unsatisfactory fantasy life when it comes to sex. Having no real choice, women have either succumbed to the male notion of appropriate female sexual fantasy or we have found ourselves largely unable to fantasize at all. Women who have accepted male-defined fantasies are often quite uncomfortable with them, and for very good reason. Their contents, as Helene Deutsch would be the first to say, are indubitably masochistic.

What percentage of women fantasize about sex? Frankly, I do not know the answer, nor would I care to hazard a guess. I know of no objective studies that deal with the nature and prevalence of women's sexual fantasies. Kinsey did not delve into this area; nor, as yet, have Masters and Johnson. I am vehemently hostile to suggestions that some known, popular sex fantasies attributed to women are indeed the product of a woman's mind, or the product of a healthy woman's mind. I am thinking here of the scurrilous, anonymous pornographic classic The Story of O by "Pauline Reage," a pseudonym that many men delight in believing masks the name of a real woman. The Story of O and its dreary catalogue of whips, thongs, bonds and iron chastity belts represents the pinnacle, or should I say the nadir, of painful masochism. I first became acquainted with O when it made the rounds of my college dormitory. It was during finals week, as I recall, and I was looking for some diversion. I nearly retched before I closed the book and handed it back to the giver. A few years ago, when I was working for one of the TV news networks, a fellow writer earnestly presented this same book to me as "the truest, deepest account of female sexuality" he had ever encountered. I am sorry I behaved with such civility at my second refusal of O and "her" story.

Because men control the definitions of sex, women are allotted a poor assortment of options. Either we attempt to find enjoyment and sexual stimulation in the kind of passive/masochistic fantasies that men have prepared us to have, or we reject these packaged fantasies as unhealthy and either remain fantasyless or cast about for a private, more original, less harmful daydream. Fantasies are important to the enjoyment of sex, I think, but it is a rare woman who can successfully fight the culture and come up with her own non-exploitative, non-sadomasochistic, non-power-driven imaginative thrust. For this reason, I believe, most women who reject the masochistic fantasy role reject the temptation of all sexual fantasies, to our sexual loss.

Given the pervasive male ideology of rape (the mass psychology of the conqueror) a mirror-image female victim psychology (the mass psychology of the conquered) could not help but arise. Near its extreme, this female psychosexuality indulges in the fantasy of rape. Stated another way, when women do fantasize about sex, the fantasies are usually the product of male conditioning and cannot be otherwise.

Two extreme examples of male fantasy that were commercially palmed off as female fantasy in recent years have been the pornographic movies *Deep Throat* and *The Devil in Miss Jones*, and I cannot deny I know a few women who claim they enjoyed seeing them. But I am not talking about such obvious junk, but of the normal run of books and movies with the theme of man as the conquering sexual hero, works that influence the daydreams of women, unfortunately, as well as men.

I do not mean to suggest that a woman's basic erotic fantasy, through cultural conditioning, is a fantasy of being raped. Rape is simply a noticeable marker near the end of a masochistic scale that ranges from passivity to death. And I do not intend to limit this discussion to specific erotic fantasies. At issue here is Everywoman's attitude toward her sexuality, her being, her attractiveness to men.

I owe it to Helene Deutsch to quote from her writings once more, since she was the first to define the female rape fantasy:

> The conscious masochistic rape fantasies [Deutsch writes] are indubitably erotic, since they are connected with masturbation. They are less genital in character than the symbolic dreams, and involve blows and humiliations; in fact, in rare cases the genitals themselves are the target of the act of violence. In other cases, they are less cruel, and the attack as well as the overpowering of the girl's will constitute the erotic element. Often the fantasy is divided into two

acts: the first, the masochistic act, produces the sexual tension, and the second, the amorous act, supplies all the delights of being loved and desired. These fantasies vanish with the giving up of masturbation and yield to erotic infatuations detached from direct sexuality. The masochistic tendency now betrays itself only in the painful longing and wish to suffer for the lover (often unknown). . . . Many women retain these masochistic fantasies until an advanced age.

The combination of perception and dogma contained in the above paragraph continues to amaze me no matter how many times I read it through. The conscious rape fantasy is offered as proof of inherent female masochism; masturbation is seen as an adolescent stage to be "given up." Yet despite these rigidities in her thought, Deutsch perceives that the female rape fantasy is no simple matter: For some, *the rape of the will* constitutes the erotic element; yet for others, the sufferance of a physical attack, or mental abuse, is a necessary prelude to the acceptance of love and affection. These two quite different sets of responses might have given Deutsch a clue that the most significant factor of all lies precisely in the *lack* of a uniform response. I would conclude that both sets of responses, or utilizations of the rape daydream, indicate a pitiful effort on the part of young girls, as well as older women, to find their sexuality within the context of male sexuality—*as we have seen it operate,* as part and parcel of the male power drive. This effort is the crux of woman's sexual dilemma.*

---

* Karen Horney, while abiding by the dogma of the inherent rape dream, parted company with Helene Deutsch on the importance of the conscious rape fantasy. "The possibility of rape . . . may give rise in women to the fantasy of being attacked, subdued, and injured," she ventured at the close of her paper "The Problem of Feminine Masochism." "In our culture it is hard to see how any woman may escape becoming masochistic to some degree from the effects of the culture alone," she proposed. Beyond such "culture-complex" phenomena as the economic dependence of women on men that must produce an emotional dependence, the societal estimation of women as inferior, the restriction of women to "spheres of life that are built chiefly upon emotional bonds, such as family life, religion, or charity work," and the "blocking of outlets for expansiveness and sexuality," Horney adduced that "women presenting the specified [masochistic] traits are more frequently chosen by men. This implies that women's erotic possibilities depend on their conformity to the image of that which constitutes their 'true nature.'" She then went on to list four "anatomical-physiological factors in

I refer here again to my own concentration-camp fantasy at age eight, at the height of Nazi power, in which I lay passive and beautiful, and offer as a companion piece a favorite childhood fantasy described by Viva in her autobiographical novel, *Superstar:*

> I was naked, strapped in an army cot . . . hung up in a stand-ing position in this contraption, on the wall, very near the ceiling. There were a lot of other little girls hanging around me in the same cots, all on the same level and in the same suspended standing posi-tion. Then the room would fill up with men wearing grey pin-stripe suits. They all had grey hair and glasses and white shirts and ties. When the room was absolutely full of them, they would all look up at once.

Viva makes a point of mentioning that this erotic daydream, which her autobiographical *persona* couldn't-wait-to-finish-her-prayers to begin afresh each night, took place a few years after World War II. She also informs us that during this time she and her sisters had been molested vaginally by the family doctor. Exhi-bitionism and passive masochism, as expressed in her fantasy, marked the early stages of Viva's "superstar" career.

Anaïs Nin, companion to famous men, analysand and writer who chose as her life's work to contemplate her "subjective" femaleness—"My self, woman, womb"—confessed to her diary in the summer of 1937:

> Sometimes in the street, or in a café, I am hypnotized by the "pimp" face of a man, by a big workman with knee-high boots, by a brutal criminal head. I feel a sensual tremor of fear, an obscure attraction. The female in me trembles and is fascinated. For one second only I am a prostitute who expects a stab in the back. I feel anxiety, I am trapped. I forget that I am free. A subterranean primitivism? A de-

---

women that may prepare the soil for the growth of masochistic phenomena [and] fertilize an emotional conception of a masochistic female role." In ad-dition to the "possibility of rape," already mentioned, she suggested in brief outline fashion: the greater physical strength of men over women; menstrua-tion, defloration and childbirth; and "the biologic differences in intercourse." These thoughts of Horney's were published in 1935. They are not incom-patible with the thinking of present-day feminists. We would not, however, be inclined to view her list as either incontrovertible or inevitable.

sire to feel the brutality of man, the force which can violate? To be violated is perhaps a need in women, a secret erotic need. I have to shake myself from the invasion of these violent images, awaken.

How much these thoughts reflect Nin and how much they reflect a dutiful parroting of Otto Rank, her former mentor, remains uncertain. Three years earlier the imperious Rank had informed her, and she had faithfully recorded, that many of the women he analyzed wanted to be "mastered, wanted to lose. It was almost as if they continued to re-enact the old primitive forms of love-making, in which woman was overpowered by the strength of man. To feel themselves conquered, in a more abstract situation, they enjoyed losing."

The morbid attraction of Sylvia Plath to a male Nazi figure ("Panzer-man, panzer-man, O You——") in the poems "Daddy" and "Lady Lazarus" is also pertinent to this discussion. Plath, who was three years older than I and Protestant, appears to have identified as a young girl with the same concentration-camp victims that haunted my childhood: *'I think I may well be a Jew . . . I may be a bit of a Jew.'* Plath's victim identification remained with her throughout her life; she could not shake it. According to "Daddy," she even married *"A man in black with a Meinkampf look/And a love of the rack and the screw."* Her painful emotional credo was expressed in these lines:

> Every woman adores a Fascist,
> The boot in the face, the brute
> Brute heart of a brute like you.

Sylvia Plath committed suicide at the age of thirty-one. (*"Dying/Is an art, like everything else./I do it exceptionally well."*) As Helene Deutsch would have it, the "certain amount of masochism" necessary to a woman "if she is to be adjusted to reality" had gotten out of hand.

Through legend and lore, history has mythified not the strong woman who defends herself successfully against bodily assault, but the *beautiful* woman who dies a violent death while trying. A good heroine is a dead heroine, we are taught, for victory through physical triumph is a male prerogative that is incompatible with feminine behavior. The sacrifice of life, we learn, is the most perfect testament to a woman's integrity and honor.

Raising a woman to the stature of heroine because she has suffered a violent death that carries sexual implications is a Christian concept, unknown to Old Testament Judaism. Parables of female martyrdom—or male martyrdom, for that matter—are conspicuously absent from the pragmatic, Hebraic Old Testament, where traces of strong, physically triumphant females, products of an incomplete patriarchal rule, can be found. Consider the Book of Judith. Described as a glamorous Israelite widow, Judith consciously risked the possibility of sexual assault to slay Holofernes in his tent. Not only did she cut off his head and escape unharmed, Judith inspired her people to military victory. Instructive as the story of Judith might be to little girls, this heroine was not the sort of role model that any patriarchy in its right mind would wish to put forward. Judith and her Book appear in the nether regions of the dubious Apocrypha.

Lucretia, an earlier heroine of ancient Rome, was cast in a more acceptable mold. She, too, in a sense, served as a catalyst to free her people. Raped by the dictator's son, Sextus Tarquinius, the chaste Lucretia took her own life rather than shame her husband, and thereby inspired the Romans to drive the dread Tarquins from their city. Thus was the Roman republic established. The rape of Lucretia (or Lucrece, as Shakespeare renamed her) served patriarchal attitudes better than the triumph of Judith, but neither model—suicide or a clever act of beheading—was quite what Christianity required of its female converts.

As a matter of fact, Saint Augustine, writing in the fifth century A.D., heaped witty scorn on Lucretia's act of suicide as the gesture of a woman "excessively eager for honor."

> When a woman has been ravished without her consenting and forced by another's sin, she has no reason to punish herself by a voluntary death [the saint maintained in City of God]. Her killing of herself . . . was due to the weakness of shame, not to the high value she set on chastity. . . . Since she could not display her pure conscience to the world she thought she must exhibit her punishment before men's eyes as a proof of her state of mind. She blushed at the thought of being regarded as an accomplice in the act if she were to bear with patience what another had inflicted on her with violence.

Augustine was killing two birds with one stone in this clever exposition. He was arguing that Christians had no authority to commit suicide in any circumstance, and he was defending against skeptics the behavior of Christian women raped by the Goths—"the violation of wives, of maidens ready for marriage, and even in some cases of women in the religious life"—who did not choose the course of suicide:

> When they were treated like this they did not take vengeance on themselves for another's crime. They would not add crime to crime by committing murder on themselves in shame because the enemy had committed rape on them in lust. They have the glory of chastity within them, the testimony of their conscience. They have this in the sight of God, and they ask for nothing more. In fact there is nothing else for them to do . . .

That other great Catholic philosopher, the orthodox, scholastic Aquinas, devoted a few dry words to rape in "the second part of the second part" of his *Summa Theologiae*. The brevity of his discourse seems to prove how unimportant to Aquinas (and to other fathers of the Church) the "element of violence"—his phrase—really was in the cosmic system. Since all sexual intercourse outside of marriage was a mortal sin in God's eyes—fornication—what was left to the logician was a mere ordering of the sin in terms of spiritual gravity. The Thomistic pyramid went like this:

> Simple fornication without injustice done to a partner is the least among the sins of lechery. Then, to continue, it is a greater injury to misuse a woman subject to the father of her children [i.e. a wife] than one subject to her guardian [i.e. a virgin], and consequently, adultery is worse than seduction. Both are aggravated by violence, and therefore raping a virgin is worse than seducing her, and raping a wife is worse than committing adultery.

It seems from the above extract that Thomistic reasoning holds the rape of a married woman to be a worse sin than the rape of a virgin. Nevertheless, dating roughly from the third century and the Diocletian persecutions, the Church ingeniously began to dramatize a virgin role model that embodied two critical tenets, chastity and defense of the faith, in one lurid act of annihilation.

Elevated to sainthood for the manner of their violent deaths as much as for the purity of their short lives, Agnes, Agatha, Lucia, Philomena, Susanna and many others became celebrated in Catholic tradition as the virgin martyrs.

It is difficult even for devout Catholics to keep the stories of these tragic maidens separate and distinct. Each was beautiful and wellborn, each willingly chose martyrdom over the option of forced sex or marriage with a pagan nonbeliever, and each suffered a cruel death to maintain her Christian faith and virgin status. Saint Agnes, the most famous virgin martyr of them all, was a child of twelve. She was thrown naked into a brothel as part of the routine punishment of "outrage," but through miraculous intervention her honor was preserved. Virginity intact, little Agnes was beheaded.

Agnes remains the patron saint of bodily purity in the religious instruction of Catholic schoolgirls but in 1950 she acquired a modern and controversial sister. With the canonization of Maria Goretti (1890–1902), the Church of Rome put a stunning update on its concept of the virgin martyr. Maria Goretti was no legendary victim of dimly remembered religious persecutions—she was murdered in twentieth-century Italy during an attempted rape.

A peasant girl of eleven, Maria Goretti suffered fourteen stab wounds inflicted by a twenty-year-old farm hand, Alessandro Serenelli, while insisting, "No, no, Alessandro, it is against God's wishes." Proof of her saintliness in the eyes of the Church was that Maria did not raise a hand to resist Serenelli's blows but directed all her effort toward protecting her virtue. Furthermore, she forgave her attacker before she died, as did her grieving mother.

Maria Goretti was raised to sainthood on the basis of her resistance to sin. In canonical terms, she died in defense of Christian precept as opposed to a general defense of the faith. This was an unprecedented development in the history of martyrology, steeped in political mysteries as well as divine. When the apostolic inquiry into Maria's sanctity began, a Bavarian girl murdered in similar circumstances a century earlier was being promoted by some German Catholics, but she was swiftly displaced by Maria. Italian chauvinism was one factor in Maria's favor, but there were other factors, too. Unlike the original virgin martyrs, Maria Goretti was a poverty-stricken child of the soil, a matter of some importance in the Vatican's effort to renew the faith of the laboring classes in postwar, politically turbulent Europe. But the key factor, curiously enough, was the exemplary behavior of her would-be rapist.

Had Alessandro Serenelli gone through with his intentions, Maria's death would have amounted to a futile gesture, canonically speaking. But Serenelli did more than desist. He confessed at his trial and later to the apostolic investigation that he had given his victim every opportunity to submit before he killed her. Six years into his jail sentence the unremorseful murderer saw a vision of Maria in his cell (she came to him dressed in white and carrying flowers) and became a penitent. After his release—he served twenty-seven years—Serenelli went to Maria's mother to give his apologies. He lived out his days as a lay brother and gardener at a Capuchin monastery, humbly devoted to Maria's saintly cause. Newspaper accounts even placed him in St. Peter's on the occasion of her beatification, a fact that later was sternly denied.

Thousands of women had been raped impartially by invading armies throughout the long years of World War II, but if this experience had anything to do with the popularity of Maria Goretti as a candidate for sainthood, it remained unexpressed. When Pope Pius XII declared her Blessed in 1947 he gave other reasons for this unprecedented Church interest in a virgin victim of attempted rape. Calling Maria Goretti a second Saint Agnes, he took the occasion to lament the corruption of female chastity by movies, press, fashion styles and Communist youth organizations. "In our day," he intoned with appropriate vagueness, "women have even been thrown into military service, with grave consequences." Against the dissolution of female morality stood the shining example of little Maria Goretti, who defended her Christian virtue by death and made a penitent of her attacker. Could there be a more perfect expression of woman's role?

Maria Goretti was declared a saint in three years' time. Hers was the speediest canonization in the annals of modern Church history, witnessed in St. Peter's Square by the largest crowd ever to gather for such an event.

No photograph was ever taken during the short life of the sturdy, robust little peasant girl—her widowed mother was too poor for such an extravagance—but the iconographers have not been deterred. Saint Maria Goretti has been idealized in death as a fragile, delicate beauty clutching lilies of the valley to her breast.

Typically, she is inscribed in Coulson's book of saints as "exceptionally beautiful."*

The Catholic Church has not been alone in promoting as role model the chaste female martyr who dies on the cross of male sin. The rape of women in the 1648 Chmelnitzky pogroms (see page 121) comes down to us in the legends of "beautiful Jewish girls" who threw themselves off bridges or courted slaughter to escape the fate worse than death. A popular Greek legend, celebrated in song, tells of an entire village of women who threw themselves off a cliff to escape certain rape by invading Turks.

World War II (see pages 48–78) spawned an entire new pantheon of dramatized virgin martyrs, even in atheistic Russia. A popular piece of Soviet war propaganda, printed in book form, tells the story of Comrade Genia Demianova, a virgin schoolteacher engaged to a young American (!) engineer named Jimmy. Genia was raped and tortured by invading Nazi soldiers but supposedly lived long enough—"in the mental ward of the Third Garrison Hospital in Moscow"—to write down her story. Published in London, the title page of *Comrade Genia* bears the inscription, "This is the documentary of the rape of a young schoolmistress—no, of an entire Russian village—by the Germans, August, 1941." A short introduction exhorts, "Get into your tank, Jimmy, you and all the other Jimmys, Tommys and Ivans—and let those tanks never stop until you have exterminated those Teutonic beasts to the last, so that horrors like this shall never again happen on this earth."

More sorrowful than *Comrade Genia* through the strength of sheer numbers was a suicide poem that appeared in an American Jewish magazine in 1943, supposedly the last testament from ninety-three girls of the Beth Jakob Seminary in Krakow who took their own lives after being informed that the Nazis intended to turn their seminary into a brothel.

Did ninety-three Jewish girls in Krakow take their own lives to avoid prostitution? Was there a Comrade Genia engaged to an American Jimmy? Evidence of rape and forcible prostitution dur-

---

* There has lately been some indication that Maria Goretti will not remain the only saint in her special category. In 1972 Pope Paul VI beatified Agostina Pietrantoni, a thirty-year-old nun who worked as a nurse in a hospital just outside the Vatican. Sister Pietrantoni was stabbed to death in 1894 after an attempted rape by a former patient.

ing World War II as a routine fact of life exists in scattered documents that most historians have chosen to ignore, an imbalance I have tried to correct. Far more compelling than the male atrocity has been the legend of virgin martyr whose inspirational value rests on being beautiful, chaste and dead.

The Beautiful Victim

The psychic burden under which women function is weighted by a deep belief, borne out by ample evidence, that our attractiveness to men, our sexual desirability, is in direct proportion to our ability to play the victim. This is no mere game that women must play in order to catch and keep a man; this is a lifetime practice in living the part of the walking wounded.

Playing the beautiful victim goes further than clichés like "You're adorable when you cry" or a pretended incompetence amid things technical that many men profess to find so feminine and appealing. It goes to the very core of our sexuality. I used the phrase "catch and keep" in the above paragraph quite deliberately because it implies deceit. Men do not *catch* women; they *win* them, and a woman's ultimate appeal lies in her ability to be a *prize that is won*. Her value is as captured trophy.

A lot of preparation goes into playing a *capturable* trophy, and a lot of schooling is provided for us along the way, in case we have missed the many signposts. There was a custom some years ago, but I think it may be going out of fashion, for dog owners to teach their pets to roll over and play dead. No doubt such total mastery over an animal with the ability to bark and bite brought immense ego satisfaction to some humans, and for the dog's part, perhaps it was just a temporary inconvenience in return for the favors of love and food. I have always felt that the Freudian warning, a strong woman is a castrating woman, springs from the same ego need as that of the master of the docile pet. And is it unfair to say that the woman who responds to this warning by playing up her weakness is also "rolling over" for love and food?

I once read an interview with the movie director Alfred Hitchcock, who was asked to describe what qualities he looked for in his leading ladies. He replied that all of them possessed one quality in common, a certain vulnerability. When I first read this interview I was surprised, because vulnerability would not spring to my mind in appraising such diverse stars as Janet Leigh and Grace Kelly, but then, as a woman appraising other women, vulnerability would not be a huge plus mark for me.

The poet Adrienne Rich wrote the line "*This is the oppressor's language.*" I borrow her phrase now for a small digression into male semantics. The dictionary definition of "vulnerable" is "susceptible to being wounded or hurt, or open to attack or assault." The opposite of "vulnerable" would be "impregnable" or "impenetrable." The sex act, which can result in pregnancy, has as its *modus operandi* something men call "penetration." "Penetration," however, describes what the man does. The feminist Barbara Mehrhof has suggested that if women were in charge of sex and the language, the same act could well be called "enclosure"—a revolutionary concept I'm afraid the world is not yet ready for. (To further digress, in the Latin of Augustine's day *pudenda,* meaning "parts of shame," referred to male and female genitalia alike. In modern usage the term refers only to female genitalia.)

So Hitchcock was on to something, I have concluded. His leading ladies did not have a certain "sensitivity" in common: what they had was vulnerability. They managed to project the feeling that they could be wounded or "had." And I think Hitchcock was speaking for most of his profession. The grand masters of the Hollywood dream machine chose their heroines to fit their own sexual fantasies, and their fantasies became important lessons in our female reality. In the nineteen fifties and sixties the celluloid vision of the desirable female increasingly became the child-woman who was beautiful and vulnerable. Strength, heroism, invincibility and mature middle age were qualities reserved for the men as they rode off into the sunset. For the women, vulnerability was inextricably tied in with being sexy, from the moody Ava Gardner to the wispy Mia Farrow.* The few *grandes dames* who did not fit the stereotype, survivors from the spirited forties like Joan Crawford and Bette Davis, got little work besides the unpleasant character part of "superbitch."

---

* *Love Story,* the most popular movie of 1970, was perhaps the epitome of the trend. The drama, and what little plot there was, turned on the untimely death of a beautiful, fresh-spirited girl. It was heralded by *Time* magazine as a "Return to Romance."

Not only were the Hollywood goddesses vulnerable to destruction, they often managed to self-destruct as well. A movie, *The Goddess*, made precisely that point. On the screen and off, where life has imitated art to a frightening degree, the self-destructive sex queen has been a powerful symbol in our culture, offering a glamorous lesson in the art of victimology. Her divorce, her miscarriage, her battle with alcoholism and drugs, her suicide or suicide attempts, have been presented to us by the popular media as tinsel tragedy, glittering items for public consumption.

The most famous and overworked example is Marilyn Monroe, whose pathetic history of use and abuse is already memorialized in several biographies, plays and paintings. In an earlier time there was the role model of Jeanne Eagels and Jean Harlow. The hard-luck stories of Hedy Lamarr and Betty Hutton crop up in the news from time to time, as have the episodic moments of crisis in the lives of Brigitte Bardot, Susan Hayward, Jennifer Jones and Lana Turner. The untimely deaths of a score of stars, some by their own hand, some by accident (often a car or plane crash), and sometimes from a combination of alcohol and pills, when viewed together present a pattern of glamorous destruction: Judy Garland, Jayne Mansfield, Veronica Lake, Françoise Dorleac, Carole Landis, Carole Lombard, Linda Darnell, Gail Russell, Marie McDonald, Margaret Sullavan, Diana Barrymore, Dorothy Dandridge, Pier Angeli, Inger Stevens, etc. So few women reach the success and fame of the ones I've mentioned, yet in some weird way their tragic deaths become more vivid to us than their lifetime accomplishments.

The line between the real-life players and the movie product blurs. The rare motion picture that tells the story of a real woman's life is often a catalogue of destruction: the Helen Morgan story, the Jeanne Eagels story, the Lillian Roth story, the Grace Moore story, the Billie Holiday story, and the worst instance of the industry feeding upon itself, two versions released simultaneously of the Jean Harlow story. Many of these women won fame as singers. For complex reasons having to do with the nature of the blues and vulnerability, girl singers seem the most ill fated of all, from Billie Holiday to Janis Joplin. Even though she led a full, rich life, it is the *death* of Bessie Smith that has passed into legend.

I think back now to my childhood years and the "required" poetry I dutifully memorized in public school. The little boys in class recited the heroic morality lesson of Abou ben Adhem, may his tribe increase, or gloried in the Charge of the Light Brigade, out of which a fair number did manage to survive. But I, searching for female images, pined with Poe for the death of the beautiful Annabel Lee and suffered again for his beautiful Lenore. I would rise to declaim at the slightest show of interest all twenty-eight stanzas of "The Wreck of the Hesperus," a hoary Longfellow ballad in which the captain's blue-eyed daughter is tied to the mast during an awful storm. She is found the next morning floating near shore, still lashed to the mast, beautiful and dead. Later, in my teens, I recall being puzzled and finally rebelling over the sympathy accorded to Mary Queen of Scots in her battle with Elizabeth in the tragic plays of Schiller and Maxwell Anderson. Mary was imprisoned in her tower and beheaded; Elizabeth won and survived. But it was haughty Mary, reduced in physical size and carefully feminized, who became the subject of romantic glorification, against the grain of history.

One might conclude, if one did not know the facts, that women were more prone to death than men. But the opposite is true. Women live longer than men, have fewer fatal accidents, suffer fewer violent deaths, and are outnumbered by men in suicide by a ratio of three to one. Yet the eternal image of the beautiful, desirable woman is Camille coughing her last on her deathbed, Mimi dying of consumption in her garret, Madame Butterfly killing herself over a broken heart, Carmen stabbed to death outside the arena, the damsel in distress locked into her tower, the sad-eyed Venus of Botticelli, the Hollywood starlet with dark glasses and an unhappy love life, the international fashion model dead at twenty-eight—the list is infinite.

"Blonde Ex-Showgirl Slain in Hotel Suite"

The conceptual link between tragic beauty and sexual desirability was forged long ago, but it is perpetuated in our modern culture by books, movies, popular songs and television serials in which women are most often portrayed as victims, seldom as survivors. "Women Is Losers" ran Janis Joplin's most haunting refrain; and Bob Dylan sings a poignant love song to his "Sad-Eyed Lady of the Lowlands." The staples of television, the doctor, lawyer and private-eye shows (with the pioneering exception of Emma Peel in the English-made *The Avengers*), star handsome men as heroes and beautiful women as victims of disease and murder, or sometimes, for variety, as guilty co-conspirators. At its most bizarre, the concept of glamour-in-destruction is reinforced in the pages of our daily tabloid newspapers where rape, and most particularly rape-murder, is reported with the brightest writing the old hands on the rewrite bank can muster.

Crime is valid news, and rape deserves a place in news coverage. It is also obvious that rape sells newspapers, or the stories would not appear on page one, as they sometimes do. But the tabloid treatment of rape is more complex than simple, factual reporting. The rape story that a big-city "picture newspaper" like the New York *Daily News* is apt to feature is a *selected* rape, enhanced by certain elements of glamour and aided by the use of stimulating adjectives judiciously written in. It is rape dressed up to fit the male fantasy, lurid and "sexy." It is often the only news of women that can be found in the important first few pages of the paper on a given day.

I must stress that I am talking here about tabloid journalism. When I first began to monitor newspaper rape coverage in 1971 in an attempt to gain a national overview, I was struck with how differently rape is treated from paper to paper and from city to city. The Washington *Post*, for example, was consistently informative and unsensational in its handling of rape, and made real efforts to treat the crime as a social issue. But in New York City, where I live, I found little of substance reported on the crime of rape in *The New York Times*, stemming, I believe, from that paper's long-unquestioned editorial policy of sexual conservatism. The small, infrequent, back-page squibs I did unearth in the *Times* concerned victims who had some kind of middle-class status, such as "nurse," "dancer" or "teacher," and with a favored setting of Central Park.* By contrast, the New York *Post* and the *Daily News* were, in an ironic sense, something of a bonanza. My pile of clippings from these two tabloids grew at an alarming rate, but as I cut and clipped and filed, I discovered a pattern that was even more alarm-

---

* In fairness to *The New York Times* I must report that its rape coverage had improved dramatically by 1974, thanks to a new interest in rape inspired by the women's movement.

ing. Although I already knew that the rapist chooses his victim with a striking disregard for conventional "sex appeal"—she may be seventy-four and senile or twelve and a half with braces on her teeth—and although New York City police statistics showed that black women were more frequent victims of rape than white women, the favored victim in the tabloid headline, I discovered, was young, white, middle-class and "attractive."

As the months wore on, I decided to make a special study of the New York Daily News, the very model of the modern tabloid newspaper. More people read the News—more than two million of them every day and more than three million on Sunday—than any other paper in the United States. Half of these people may be presumed to be women, and what we read of the lives of other women—or what other women get into the news for—cannot help but affect our own life and expectations.

The limited concept of the role of women that the Daily News sells each morning for fifteen cents was forcibly driven home to me when I spent a full week exploring the microfilmed front pages of its four-star final for the complete year of 1971. At the end of the week my eyes were aching, but I had learned a lot. The moral code of the News is simple. It is "for" law and order and the good, honest working bloke, as exemplified by cops, firemen and other city employees. It is fascinated by crime but eager to see criminals brought to justice. It has a nose-pressed-against-the-window approach to America's first family in the White House and toward a few other families of our American political aristocracy. He-man style, it likes its women mute and interchangeable, with a show of leg and bosom. Family-man style, it grumbles over higher taxes and is capable of outrage when innocent women, children and animals are hurt—but, he-man again, sometimes it thinks that gals get what is coming to them. (Blacks, too, although the News has shown some uncertainty of late in its vision of blacks, a lesson of the moral suasion of political power that women must learn.) There are two sure ways a woman becomes newsworthy in the eyes of the Daily News, I learned: as wife or daughter of a famous politician or astronaut, or as an anonymous, innocent victim of a rape-murder or some other disaster. A third way is when she herself has committed a crime.

The job of a tabloid is to present the news in an entertaining fashion, and news is mostly made by men since it is men who are engaged in the "real world out there" of government, industry, sports, adventure and crime. Newspapers are edited for men by men. Women readers are tagalongs: advertisements and the "women's pages" alone are designed with us in mind. Tabloid editors operate under the assumption that sex is a necessary spice for their daily stew, and since they are men editing for men, sex means *women*. A standard feature of the *Daily News* is the anonymous bathing beauty, regardless of the weather. In summer she may be of the local variety; in winter the caption reads Miami or Australia. Although her name may be duly printed, it is of no consequence. She is a nobody, strictly there for men to admire. For women readers she can only offer an uncomfortable model for emulation: *so, we think, this is what men find attractive*. A rape-murder story is also presented in the *News* for sex: *so, we cannot help but conclude, this is what happens to attractive women*.

The use of the word "attractive" to describe a rape-murder victim in the lead paragraph of a *Daily News* story is a significant part of the story's formula. In a year's study of the *News* I found only two instances where this did not apply. One was a story of an eight-year-old victim; the other was a second day's follow-up story on a publicized rape-murder that occurred on the street in which I live. In this particular case, the first day's story had duly called the girl "attractive." For the follow-up, the *News* sent one of its few female reporters. She got her facts straight. The victim was *not* attractive, and the reporter broke the formula and wrote it that way. Two sideline facts are of interest here. This was the only instance I could find in a year's study of the *News* in which the paper sent a woman to report on a rape-murder; and at the corner newsstand where I buy my papers, the owner had also noticed that the adjective "attractive" was strangely missing from the story. He thought it showed a marked unkindness to the girl in death.

The use of "attractive" or similar glamour adjectives to describe a young woman in death is employed *in place of* other relevant material—the kind of relevant material that a good reporter writes in when he is describing a man. The following lead paragraph from a Sunday *News* story of January 16, 1972, "CAR FUMES STIFLE TEEN PAIR'S DREAM" (front-page headline and page 3 news story), illustrates what I mean: "A Long Island University

sophomore and the tall, good looking brunette whom he hoped to
marry were killed by carbon monoxide early yesterday as they
attended a drive-in movie in Valley Stream, L.I."

We are immediately told that the young boy who died had a
place in the world: he was a college sophomore. The young girl's
news value, however, is as "tall, good looking brunette whom he
hoped to marry." Not until the third paragraph, after we learn that
the boy was a music major and a part-time messenger, do we
discover that the girl, too, had an identity. She was also a student, a
senior in high school. But this fact could be sacrificed to her
physical description: that way the story had more "sex appeal."

Women who die violently are memorialized in the *Daily
News* in bold headlines that attest to their physical appeal to men.
In life they would not rate a story. The violence of their death has
made them newsworthy, but it does not lessen their anonymity.
Female victims are objectified and glamorized chiefly by the color
of their hair, although it is odds-on certain that hair color had little
to do with their death.

Thus I found: "BLONDE TIED TO BED, STRANGLED" (July 6,
1971). She was reported to be someone's "estranged wife." And
two months later: "BRUNETTE, 26, FOUND SLAIN IN A VILLAGE FLAT"
(September 19, 1971). She was a shy, overweight clerk-typist who
lived down the street from her parents. Although the newspaper
did not report it this way, her rape and subsequent death by
suffocation was most probably an accidental by-product of a
routine "break-and-enter" burglary.

The occupation of a female victim is buried deep within the
story of a tabloid newspaper unless the occupation has a glamorous
connotation, however tenuous. Model, actress, stewardess, showgirl, go-go dancer, career girl, heiress and divorcee are the words to
conjure with. Women who can be fitted into these categories may
be catapulted in death to page one on a slow news day: "BLONDE EX-
SHOWGIRL SLAIN IN HOTEL SUITE" made page one of the *News* on
March 8, 1971.

"AIR STEWARDESS IS FOUND SLAIN" made page one on June 25,
1971, and again on June 26 with "HUNT SEX KILLER OF STEW-
ARDESS." The victim in this case, Cornelia Michelle Crilley, was
genuinely beautiful. She became New York City's big sex-killing
case for 1971. Her picture was plastered on the front pages of both
the *News* and the *Post*, and the *Post* kept her on the front page for

three days running. Her occupation and the neighborhood in which she lived, Manhattan's Upper East Side, offered rich material for tabloid feature writers. The News ran "COMB 'GIRL BELT' SWING SPOTS" and "EAST SIDE—THE MECCA FOR MAIDENS" with pictures of other "swinging singles." The Post countered with "CORNELIA'S TINSEL TOYLAND." (Cornelia Michelle Crilley was pushed off the front pages by Daniel Ellsberg and the Pentagon Papers. At this writing her murderer has not been found.)

The murder of a beautiful young woman is no more regrettable, no greater tragedy, than the murder of a plain one, except in a culture that values beauty in women above other qualities. By putting great store in the murder of a beauty, beauty acquires the seeds of its own destruction. The Daily News does not deliberately set out to create a myth of glamorous destruction, but its editorial policy performs that function by reporting the news of men-the-doers and spicing it with news of women as victims, with more space accorded to beautiful victims. Thus the myth that rape is a crime of passion touched off by female beauty is given great credence, and women are influenced to believe that to be raped, and even murdered, is a testament to beauty. *Beauty's beauty is confirmed by the Beast: we all may not be fair of face, but all of us can be victims.*

From January to December, 1971, a year in which Indira Gandhi won a landslide election victory and Golda Meir paid a visit to New York, all female-related front-page headlines in the Daily News were headlines of disaster, crime and rape-murder, with the one exception of Tricia Nixon's wedding. "MOTHER, BABY SLAIN IN QUEENS" . . . "FALL IN JAIL KILLS N.Y. HEIRESS" . . . "ALICE GUILTY IN 1ST DEGREE" . . . "MISSING GIRL, 8, FOUND SLAIN" . . . "KNIFED TO DEATH IN HER ELEVATOR" . . . "PROBE DIVORCEE MYSTERY DEATH." Meanwhile, men of strength and courage, alive and breathing, directed the reins of government, caught criminals, put out fires, ordered strikes and settled strikes, and went to the moon and came back victorious.

CONFESSIONS: "HE MADE ME DO IT!"

"BRUNETTE, 26, FOUND SLAIN IN VILLAGE FLAT" lived in my street, although I did not know her. We shared the corner candy store and newsstand, where I learned from the store's owner that she often browsed at the well-stocked rack of confession magazines. Kathy was her name, and from the second day's headline in the *Daily News* I also learned that the "SLAIN VILLAGE GIRL DIDN'T DRINK, DATE." But Kathy did read, and when one day in the course of my research I scooped up a month's supply of confession magazines from the corner newsstand, the thought crossed my mind that this was the stuff that Kathy devoured, that fed her fantasies and nourished her daydreams.

Who takes romance-confession magazines seriously? Certainly not the editors who edit them, and certainly not any literary critic or chronicler of the culture. Nor have the sociologists and psychologists shown interest, for that matter. Fredric Wertham's *Seduction of the Innocent*, the famous study of cultural violence and its effect on children, raised the comic book to serious and controversial status, but no one has examined the romance, confession and movie magazine industry for its cumulative effect on impressionable young women.* Who takes the magazines seriously? Only the several million girls and women who read them each month, women who are, for the most part, from the lower economic classes, with high-school educations or less, women who, statistics show, are the most frequent victims of forcible rape.

Between one dozen and fifteen confession magazines are carried on the newsstands, and each sells a minimum of one-quarter of a million copies. Confession-magazine addicts usually read more than one magazine a month and as many as nine readers may share one copy, passing it from hand to hand until it is in tatters. This multiple readership is generally acknowledged to be higher than for any other magazine genre. In the South and the Southwest, where the magazines have a wide audience, the readership is estimated to be 40 percent black. More than ten million girls and women form

---

* "Comic books," Dr. Wertham wrote in 1954, "create sex fears of all kinds. . . . A Western with a picture of Tom Mix on the cover has in one story no less than *sixteen consecutive* pictures of a girl tied up with ropes, her hands of course tied behind her back! She is shown in all kinds of poses, each more sexually suggestive than the other, and her facial expression shows that she seems to enjoy this treatment. Psychiatrically speaking, this is nothing but the masturbation fantasy of a sadist, and it has a corresponding effect on boys. For girls, and those boys who identify themselves with the girl, it may become the starting-point for masochistic fantasies."

the faithful market for the confessions but occasional readership may be twice that number. According to one sales survey, magazines with cover lines pertaining to brute force ("HE MADE ME DO IT!") sell best.*

The confession magazines I purchased during one expedition to my corner store were dated February or March, 1972. Each featured a tale of rape, a near-rape or a rape fantasy. Taken in toto they promulgated a philosophy of submission in which the female victim was often to blame, whereas the men in her life—husband, boyfriend or rapist—emerged as persons of complex emotion deserving of sympathy. In strict adherence to the confession formula, the rape functioned as a positive catalyst for the heroine in her never-ending quest for a new boyfriend or an improved relationship with a husband. Here are brief synopses.

"I WAS THE VICTIM OF A SEX GANG" (True Life Confessions, March). The blurb reads, "I was out for kicks and nobody was going to stop me! That's how I got caught by the toughest gang of guys around." Conceited Dory is bored by steady Perry, who tells her, "You talk too much. Guys don't like girls who are too quick with the wisecracks." On a dare Dory walks into the clubhouse of a gang of toughs and is nearly gang-raped. When she comes to after "blacking out," a stern policeman is bending over her. The gang is packed off to a reform school, but Dory confesses, "Actually I felt a little guilty." In the last paragraph Dory tells us, "I learned a lesson that I hope other girls will remember. When you ask for trouble—as I did—you can be sure you'll get it. And I'm grateful that I got out of it without being assaulted, that my sharp tongue and know-

---

* I speak from firsthand knowledge of the field, once having worked as an assistant editor for a group of confessions. The house I worked for also published a group of men's magazines, and we divided our editorial time accordingly. In contrast to the confessions—woeful tales of girls gone wrong—the men's magazines marketed a formula of blood and guts—superman triumphs over dangerous animals and luscious women. The cover art for both sets of magazines was revealing. The female confessions invariably pictured a young woman peeking out from a thicket of one-line blurbs implying guilt and/or distress. Covers for the men's magazines alternately depicted (a) an evil doctor, often in Nazi uniform, about to jab a hypodermic needle into a girl who was bound and gagged while a hero figure manfully strode to the rescue, or (b) a jungle animal, often a black panther, clawing at a prostrate, hysterical blonde while a white hunter in khakis rushed to the rescue. This cover, my boss informed me, was meant to symbolize interracial rape.

it-all attitude didn't wreck my life as it could so easily have done." Her virginity saved, she goes back to faithful Perry and "grows up."

"SEX CREEPS ALWAYS PICK ON GIRLS LIKE ME" (*Modern Love*, March). The blurb reads, "*It happens too often to be just accidental.*" Susan is disturbed by exhibitionists who expose themselves. She joins an encounter group and reveals her problem. The leader, a psychologist, suggests that Susan sends out signals to the men because deep down she is afraid of sex. Susan suddenly understands that unconsciously she had been staring at the men. She starts a new relationship with Chuck, one of the young men in her group.

"I THOUGHT NOBODY HAD RAPE DREAMS LIKE MINE" (*Real Confessions*, February). Betty Jo has daydreams of rape and coincidentally doesn't want to get pregnant. Husband Jack, a big guy, is a gentle lover. "I was disappointed by his tenderness," Betty Jo says. "I wanted to be overwhelmed by brute force." They consult a minister who tells them that Betty Jo's fantasies are normal. He recommends that they consult a doctor, who assures them, "Rape is a very common fantasy that women have, and that's why it turns up so often in movies and books. Most women who have these fantasies don't really want to be raped, not in the sense of being mistreated or hurt. They like being dominated and overwhelmed by a man." Thus reassured, Jack 'fesses up: "I have a few sex dreams of my own. Like—what it's like to make love to a woman whose [sic] fighting you every inch of the way. . . . The idea of forcing a woman turns me on. I don't mean beating her up, just showing her it's all gotta be my way, no matter what she wants." Betty Jo and Jack decide to practice "rape games" at home. The first time Jack tries, Betty Jo protests that she isn't wearing her diaphragm—she could get pregnant! Jack persists with "brute force." Betty Jo tells us, "I didn't have any choice. I had to submit and be overwhelmed by his absolute strength and masculinity. It left me free, somehow, in a way I never felt before, to experience all the thrills I could only dream about till then." In the last paragraph she reports they now have two kids.

"I MADE HIM DO IT . . . TO ME!" (*True Confessions*, February). The blurb reads, "*What kind of girl gets raped? What kind of man is a rapist? Right away you think you know the answers. But after you read this story, you may find you're wrong.*" Helen, a shy girl from Indiana, goes to a singles bar in New York where she meets Danny, an ex-marine "with a nice-looking face and large brown eyes." She is too prim and proper for Danny's tastes, and he ignores her. Crushed, she leaves the bar, "knowing that I should really take a taxi since no New York street is safe for a girl alone after dark." A few evenings later she returns to the bar, determined not to let Danny get away. She is very flirtatious and Danny accompanies her to her studio apartment for a cup of coffee. They kiss—but suddenly it gets more serious: "Danny, I—" "Shut up." Then, "A strangled sound broke from my throat as he forced himself upon me." Danny rapes her and leaves. Bleeding and in pain, Helen staggers to her feet and calls a girlfriend. The girlfriend wants to call the police, but Helen refuses. She will not go to a hospital, either. A young intern who lives in the friend's building is called in. He tells Helen she'll be "okay" after a few days of bed rest. Helen's friend still wants to call the police, but Helen is adamant. It is her fault! "What other girl would be such a fool? What other girl would invite a total stranger into her apartment in the middle of the night, let him start to make love to her and expect him to stop?" A few days later a remorseful Danny sends Helen $50 "for the doctor's bill." Next he calls her on the telephone, apologizes and says he has sworn off alcohol for good. Helen and Danny are dating now: "We seem to be helping each other through a bad time—a bad time that is slowly getting better."

"I GAVE UP THE MAN I LOVED TO KEEP A RAPIST'S CHILD" (*True Romance*, February). Karen is raped by an escapee from the state mental hospital. Her family is afraid the town "will jeer," so Karen's mother tells the newspapers that *she* was the victim. But Karen discovers she is pregnant. Despite a law that allows abortion, Karen decides to bear and keep the rapist's child, who is born retarded. Boyfriend Neal rejects her, but new boyfriend Mark steps into the breach. The blurb: *"Does a woman ever forget her help-less little first-born?"*

"RAPED WHILE PREGNANT!—AND I CAN'T TELL MY HUSBAND!" (*Personal Romances*, March). The blurb reads, *"It can only end in more terrible violence if I identify my attacker."* Cathy, a pregnant teacher's aide, is raped in her classroom. She miscarries that evening. Cathy decides not to tell the sheriff or husband Burt about the rape because the town will jeer and because Burt has always said he'd kill any man who attacked her. By coincidence, Cathy's friend Janice is also raped—and murdered—that same night in a neighboring county. The sheriff picks up a suspect for Janice's murder, but the suspect offers an unusual alibi. It was not Janice whom he raped, but Cathy. In this curious story, Cathy is finally convinced to admit her rape and identify her attacker *in order to save him* from the false and more serious charge of murdering Janice. There is much talk in this story about how "unmanned" Burt feels by Cathy's rape. Burt gets in a good sock at Cathy's rapist in the county jail, and the sheriff's wife says approvingly, "I'm glad he got to him, Cathy. It's the only way he could get some of that poison out and feel like a man again."

"DADDY, WHY DOES MOMMY CALL YOU A RAPIST?" (*True Love*, February). A child-rapist is at large and Midge's mother begins to suspect Midge's father because she has not slept with him for years and "it ain't natural for a man to go without . . ." Midge's mother is wrong about her husband, of course, and in the last paragraph it looks like the family sex life is beginning to improve.

I intended to limit my random sampling to one sweep of the magazine rack, but a few weeks later while I was buying my newspaper at the corner store I noticed that the March *Real Confessions* had just come in. I already had February in my possession, but a particularly provocative title caught my eye. The plot was the same story of an uppity girl getting her comeuppance from a gang of boys that I had read in the March *True Life Confessions*, "I WAS THE VICTIM OF A SEX GANG." The blurb on this new one, though, was a trifle more explicit: "*I knew I was partly to blame, too—because I tried too hard to change everybody's life.*" But the title spoke volumes! It read: "GANG-RAPED BY 7 BOYS—BECAUSE I LED THEIR GIRLS INTO A WOMEN'S LIB CLUB."

11

Victims:
The Crime

TESTIMONY: I am 73 years old and I was raped when I was 67. A young fellow followed me into the elevator of my apartment building. He was wearing a green uniform. He asked me if I knew the apartment number of a certain tenant but I told him that name was unfamiliar to me. I said, "Oh, are you the man from United Parcels? I'm expecting a package that hasn't arrived." He asked me my name and apartment number and told me he'd go down and check in the truck. A few minutes later my doorbell rang. I looked through the peephole and there was the young man with a package. Of course I opened the door right away. He had a wrench in one hand. He shoved me against the wall and started hitting my head. Later I had to have five stitches. He told me not to make a sound and he started walking through my apartment. I think he wanted to see if I was really alone, or he might have been looking for things to steal. When he came back to where I was he asked me where I hid the money. I told him I didn't have any money hidden, just what was in my pocketbook. He didn't seem to believe me. He told me to get on the bed. He pulled off my underthings and then he tore into me. When he was finished I watched him go through my dresser drawers. He took some jewelry and my portable TV. Finally he left, after warning me to keep quiet.

My neighbors and the police were very kind, but the police couldn't find him. The United Parcels Service said they didn't have any truck delivery route scheduled for my neighborhood that day and his description didn't match anyone they had working for them. It turned out my package had been delivered to the wrong apartment a few days earlier. It was sitting in the package room all the time.

Any female may become a victim of rape. Factors such as extreme youth, advanced age, physical homeliness and virginal life-style do not provide a foolproof deterrent or render a woman impervious to sexual assault.

A certain amount of risk is present whatever our attributes and demographic standing. Dr. Charles Hayman's five-year study conducted at D.C. General Hospital in Washington reported that victims of rape who were processed through the emergency ward ranged from a child of 15 months to a woman of 82. Results like Hayman's are confirmed by other studies.

TESTIMONY: I was eleven and my sister was seven. Looking back now I'm amazed I was so naive. I was coming home from the dentist with my sister at four in the afternoon, and I was aware that a man was behind me. He followed us into the building. We were scared. I said to my sister, "Julie, he's behind us, don't get into the elevator with him, run, let's run up the stairs." He caught us on the third floor stairwell and put a knife at my sister's throat. He said to me, "Pull up your dress and pull down your pants and I won't hurt the little one."

Statistical probability does matter. Just as there is a calculable "typical" rapist, there is also, to a lesser degree of certainty, a "typical" victim. While any woman is a natural target for a would-be rapist, the chances are that a rape victim will be of the same class and race as her attacker, at least between 70 and 90 percent of the time. More often than not, she also will be approximately the same age as her attacker, or slightly younger. Overall, the danger to women is greatest between the ages of 10 and 29. Teen-age girls, simply by being teen-age girls, run the greatest risk of any age group. In Menachem Amir's Philadelphia study, girls between the ages of 15 and 19 accounted for one-quarter of all reported victims of rape. In Brenda Brown's Memphis study, students comprised 27 percent of all rape victims and "made up the largest group having stated occupations."

Rape is usually an "ecologically bound" offense, to borrow a phrase from Amir. Not that rapists prefer their own class and kind (personal preference appears to be immaterial); it is simply that rape is a crime of opportunity and opportunity knocks most frequently in a familiar milieu. Women who live in urban lower-class neighborhoods of high crime and juvenile delinquency are subject to the greatest risk of any class. It follows then, and statistics bear it out, that the group of women who run the greatest risk of being assaulted, because of their proximity to those who are most quick to resort to forcible rape, are black, teen-age, urban lower-class girls.

TESTIMONY: Okay, I was 14 years old at the time. School had let out and I was walking home because I didn't have enough money for carfare. This guy saw me on the street or I saw him and he said, "Hey, are you looking for a job?" Wow, I thought to myself, how did he know I was looking for a job? So I said, "Yeah, why?" And he said, "Because I know someone, a friend of mine, who's looking for someone to work part-time in his office." So I said, "Where's your friend's office?" and he said, "I'm not doin' anything, I'll walk you over there right now." I told him my mother was expecting me home. I said, "Why don't you just tell me where it is?" He said it would be better if he went with me because he had the connections. He said, "Why don't you call your mother and tell her you'll be home later?" We walked to a phone booth and this guy gave me a dime. He actually gave me a dime to call my mother. I called and said, "Ma, I got a job. I'm going over there right now."

He walked me over to this building and then he told me to wait downstairs and he'd go up and see if his friend was in. I thought that was a little odd, I didn't see why I had to wait downstairs, but I waited around and in a while he came back and said we could go upstairs. We went into this place and there was nothing in it but a dirty mattress. The guy locked the door real quick and then I knew what was happening. I started to cry. I was a virgin. I pleaded with him not to touch me, but he did. It hurt. He hurt me. I was crying a lot.

Afterward he gave me 20 cents to get home. He had the nerve to ask for my phone number so he could call me again. He wanted me to ask my mother if he could date me. I gave him the wrong number and a phony name. All I could think of was that I had to go home and face my family, right? I had to go home, have dinner, smile and pretend nothing was wrong.

At dinner my ma kept asking, "What about your new job?" I said, "I don't want to talk about it, leave me alone. It didn't work out."

In recent years rape and other crimes of violence have been reported with increasing frequency at formerly protected citadels like the college campus. The publicized rape and sodomizing of two students at George Washington University in 1972 by an outsider who posed as a student and the son of a congressman is one such example. As it happens, the jury in this case refused to convict.

In 1971 the FBI added a new statistical chart to its *Uniform Crime Reports*, an index to the number of felonies committed at state universities (although not necessarily committed by students). Over the next three years, the University of California at Berkeley and Los Angeles, the University of Illinois, Southern Illinois at Edwardsville, the University of Indiana, Michigan State at East Lansing, the University of Kansas, and the University of Wisconsin at Madison and Milwaukee led the list. Eleven rapes were reported at Berkeley in one year, the highest ever recorded by a state university system. Many, if not most, of the rapes of college students occurred while hitchhiking.

TESTIMONY: I took a ride from a truck driver. I always thought truck drivers were good people to get rides from. My father used to drive trucks when he was young, and my cousin was a truck driver—they must be good people to take rides from, you know?

I got in the truck and he said to me, "Aren't you kind of young to be hitchhiking?" Right away I got scared. Then he told me that he'd have to pull off the highway and go to, I think it was Greenwich, or some other town. I thought, Oh God, he's going to pull off the highway and drive into the woods and rape me or stab me—because there had been a case I had just read about. I thought, My God, I have to jump out. I think he realized that this was on my mind because at that moment—we were on the highway—he started to attack me while he was driving. He started to beat me down and he started to rip off my blouse. He unzipped his pants and started to beat my mouth and head down on his penis.

In the meantime the truck is swerving back and forth. I said, "Well, we're both going to die now." I remember at one point I was thinking, Why don't I just take the wheel and just swerve the fucking truck off the highway and end it? That was the only way I could end it, but I didn't want to die. I don't know if this is what I imagine now, but I think there was some type of understanding between us that if I gave him all he wanted he would let me go.

According to the task force of the National Commission on the Causes and Prevention of Violence, half of all rape victims (53 percent) were total strangers to their attackers; another 30 percent were slightly acquainted. Seven percent had a family relationship to their rapists (daughter, sister, niece or cousin) and 3 percent were not related but had a previous close association. (As with most percentage distributions concerning crime, there is always a category called "unknown" or "other.") The task force concluded, "If a woman is attacked, then, considerable justification does appear to exist for the fear that the offender will be a stranger."

As I mentioned in Chapter 6, "The Police-Blotter Rapist," the statistical profile of rape falls midway between the profiles for assault and robbery. In keeping with this pattern, when interpersonal relationships in these three crimes of violence are compared side by side, we find that strangers commit 21 percent of all assaults, 53 percent of all rapes and 79 percent of all robberies.

> TESTIMONY: About five years ago when I lived in Chicago I awoke one night gagged with my hands pinned down by someone who was wearing leather gloves and holding a razor to my throat. I wasn't quite sure I was awake. I thought I must be in the middle of a nightmare that seemed much more realistic than usual and I couldn't break it up. I was trying to establish if there really was a person there. And then I did get my wrist cut slightly, so I realized it was real and that I was risking my life and that I'd better hold still and let the man have intercourse with me. He was very fast. He wasn't wearing any clothes on the bottom half of his body and he ran out the window in that position, just like Romeo on the balcony, onto the fire escape and down.
>
> I got up, turned on the lights and took a bath in alcohol. I was living alone. I had to get out of the apartment. I set off with my coat on and then I realized the man had gotten in my purse and left me without a penny. Apparently he had been in the apartment for some time before I woke up because I saw he had gagged me with my own dishtowel. It was then that I thought to call the police.

Stranger-rape has clearly been the preferred category from the point of view of the police precinct, the category most likely to win the determination of "founded." When a woman is raped by a total stranger, her status as victim is clean and untarnished in the station-house mentality. In Brenda Brown's 1973 Memphis study,

73 percent of all founded rapes were committed by strangers, and Brown reported, "The closeness of the relationship was a frequently used reason for categorizing cases as unfounded." According to the *Uniform Crime Reports*, unfounded cases are "frequently complicated by a prior relationship between victim and offender."

For this reason it remains difficult to assess the true percentage of rapes committed by strangers. As the women's movement continues to press a greater understanding of the crime of rape on the general public, women who have been assaulted by men they know will feel freer to report the crime and these reports will begin to be treated with the seriousness they deserve. At the present time, police precincts still operate from the assumption that a woman who has been raped by a man she knows is a woman "who changed her mind afterward."

TESTIMONY: I was raped when I was 17 by my fiancé the night before he was due to ship out with the Navy. Up to then I had tried to be everything he wanted according to the religious, social and moral codes by which both of us had been raised. I played the expected role throughout our engagement, deferring to him in judgment, in conversation, even in the way I dressed. I was sedate, demure, humble, submissive—and a virgin. He kept begging me to have intercourse and I kept saying, "No, not yet. It's not right." On our last date he pushed me in the back of his car and held me. I just gave up. After all, wasn't I supposed to defer to him in everything?

TESTIMONY: In psychiatric literature they always write that struggle is a component of the sex act. I think in college I must have met 15 men in my senior year who were really into that. The more you protested, the more determined they were to make love to you in the Sig Ep house parking lot. What do you do? Do you get out and run away at two o'clock in the morning? Yes, if you're smart. But a lot of girls can't.

TESTIMONY: I was 19, working in a bar as a waitress. I had a couple of dates with this guy who used to come into the bar. He was okay then, he never tried anything funny. Then he invited me to go out with him and two other couples on my day off.

There were two fellows already there when I got into the car, and we drove to places where we were supposed to pick up the other girls. But each time the fellows came back alone with some story about how the girls couldn't make it. We were way out in the country by this time. Then my date stopped the car and started messing around. So there I was, out in the middle of nowhere with three guys who all had their minds on one thing.

I kept struggling with my date and finally when he said, "If you don't let me, I'll put it in your mouth," I gave in. Then the other fellows took their turn. I wasn't screaming or fighting anymore. I just wanted to get it over with and not have anything worse happen to me. When they were all through they drove me home.

I tried to tell some older men in the bar about it a few days later. They asked me if I was hurt and when I said I wasn't they told me to forget about it.

When a potential victim and a potential offender are thrown together by the forces of fate, a complete process is inexorably set in motion. Each word, act and gesture on the part of the potential victim serves to either strengthen or lessen the resolve of the potential rapist, and hinder or help him commit his crime.

Victim precipitation is a new concept in criminology. It does not hold a victim responsible, but it seeks to define contributory behavior. Victim precipitation says, in effect, an unlawful act has been committed but had the victim behaved in a different fashion the crime in question *might have been avoided*. Part a priori guess-work and part armchair-detective fun and games, the study of victim precipitation is the least exact of the sociological methods, for it rests in the final analysis on a set of arbitrary standards.

TESTIMONY: We were living in Houston. My husband was at work and the children were at school. It must have been, oh, two o'clock in the afternoon. The doorbell rang and this young man asked if he could rake the leaves for a couple of dollars. I said, "Wonderful, how terrific." Well, he raked the leaves and then he came to the door and asked if he could have a glass of water. I was quite conscious of being alone in the house, but a glass of water did not seem like an unreasonable request. He finished the water and then asked for another glass. Of course I gave it to him. We were chatting about this and that and I wanted him out of my living room but I didn't know quite how to cut him off. I was also wondering if perhaps I was overreacting to be a little nervous. He was black and I had been very involved in the first stages of the civil rights movement, and after all, he was only asking for water. He must have had four glasses of water before he made his move. He broke my jaw in the process.

While most rational people might be able to agree on what constitutes rash, reckless or precipitant behavior leading to a homicide, in rape the parameters are indistinct and movable. Some men might consider a housewife who lets a strange man into her house for a glass of water guilty of precipitant behavior, and more men would consider a female hitchhiker who accepts a ride from an unknown male guilty of precipitant behavior. Rape-minded men would consider both actions tantamount to an open invitation. I, on the other hand, would consider the housewife and the hitchhiker insufficiently wary, but in no way would I consider their actions provocative or even mildly precipitant. Similarly, most men seem to consider a woman who engages in sex play but stops short of intercourse guilty not only of precipitant behavior, but of cruel, provocative behavior with no excuse, yet I and my sister feminists would argue that her actions are perfectly allowable and quite within the bounds of human decency and rational decisions.

Those who worked for the National Commission on the Causes and Prevention of Violence came up with their own definitions of victim precipitation, and because it is their statistics I am going to quote, it is their definitions that need to be expressed.

In criminal homicide: "Whenever the victim was the first to use physical force against his subsequent slayer."

In aggravated assault: "When the victim was the first to use either physical force or insinuating language, gestures, etc. against his attacker."

In forcible rape: "When the victim agreed to sexual relations but retracted before the actual act or when she clearly invited sexual relations through language, gestures, etc."

In armed and unarmed robbery: "Temptation-opportunity situations in which the victim clearly had not acted with reasonable self-protective behavior in handling money, jewelry, or other valuables . . . e.g., a robbery victim flashes a great deal of money at a bar and then walks home alone along a dark street late at night."

Armed with these working definitions, however vague, for its seventeen-city survey, the commission task force found that the

percentage of discernible victim precipitation in crimes of violence
looked like this:

Homicide	22.0%
Assault	14.4%
Rape	4.4%
Armed Robbery	10.7%
Unarmed Robbery	6.1%

Across the board, rape victims were responsible for less precipitant
behavior than victims of other kinds of violent crime.*

The behavior of women in a pre-rape situation is a critical area
that deserves more study. Equally critical is the behavior of women
within the actual act. Do women fight back, and can women fight
back successfully? According to the FBI's 1973 figures, more than
one-quarter of all reported rape offenses were not completed. They
were recorded on the precinct level as attempted rapes or as assaults with intent to commit rape.† Viewed from a positive angle,
this is rather an astonishing figure. Surely the would-be rapists had
a completed act in mind. What stopped them?

TESTIMONY: My child was sick and so was I, and I had to go to
the store to get some medicine. I suppose people would say it was
my own fault for doing such a dumb thing, but I took a short-cut

---

* The commission's staff was at pains to point out that these results differed
dramatically from the only other study of victim precipitation in rape, the
calculations of Menachem Amir in his 1958/1960 Philadelphia study. Amir
believed that a stunning 19 percent of all rape cases he examined had been
victim precipitated and he concluded that for the women in question, "The
contingencies of events may not make the victim solely responsible for what
becomes an unfortunate event; at least she is a complementary partner, and
victimization is not, then, a wholly and genuinely random affair." From my
reading of the Philadelphia study I gather that Amir's definition of precipitation was more generous to the rapists. He added "risky situations marred by
sexuality" and other, indefinite generalizations to his criterion.
† In the eyes of the law a completed rape does not require emission, only a
degree of penetration. One inch is the usual standard. Of course, evidence of
emission makes a stronger case in court, but sperm smears must be taken immediately since, according to the best medicolegal evidence, traces of sperm
may totally disappear within twenty-four to forty-eight hours. An attempted
rape falls short of penetration.

through the alley in back of my house. It was around dinner time and there he was, in the alley, waiting for me.

Initially, I think, he was after my purse. He knocked me down and we struggled. I wasn't scared. After all, I'm a black woman and you learn early when you're black and a woman. Anyway, this character wasn't all that impressive physically. He was about my size, a black man, tall and lean. Since he was dumb enough to jump me under the light he got scared and kept saying, "You seen me, you seen me!" Then I got mad and bit his hand. That made *him* mad, and he backed me up against the wall, tore down my jeans and tried to have intercourse. He kept trying but I figured as long as I'm fighting him standing up he couldn't do it.

I warned him the police would be going by. I tried to get up the back steps to my own house, but he kept tight hold, all the time telling me to lay down. But I knew if I did that, he'd finish the rape. I figured I had to do something to scare him, so I decided to act crazy. I started yelling my baby was right inside that house and she's sick and what he was doing was making me crazier and he'd better watch out. And that did it. He just took my money, about ten dollars, and then he beat it. So—I'd beaten off a would-be rapist.

TESTIMONY: I fought back. I kicked a guy in the lower extremity and put him in the hospital. I kicked that bastard's balls and at the time I was only 17. So we didn't have a rape case but we almost had manslaughter. That's what the police told me, if the guy died I'd be up for manslaughter. Can you imagine? I told the police I wanted to prosecute for attempted rape and they said, "Didn't you do enough already to the poor guy?" Their sympathy was with him. They told me I was a crazy, hostile hippie.

TESTIMONY: I awoke at 3 A.M. Someone had his hand over my mouth and a knife at my throat. He said, "If you move, I'll kill you." My first thought was it's a dream, wake up, but I felt the steel and a throat isn't a good place to get cut. I went into a computer mentality, totally cold. The Wylie-Hoffert case flashed through my head and I thought to myself, I don't want to be a *Daily News* headline. I also thought, this is like a Grade B movie. I got him talking, that's what I did, I stalled for time. I sat on the bed and talked. "Are you going to rape me?" I asked. "If you are, okay, but please put away the knife." To my surprise, he did. "I've been watching you for three weeks," he told me, "I watch you from the roof through the window." Where I got the courage to say this, I don't know, but I said, "If you watched me from the roof, someone may be watching right now. Why don't you check the window just to make sure." He went to the window and that's when I made a break for it. You see how I use that Hollywood language, "made a break for it," but I too had learned from the movies. I ran to the door, unlocked it, got it almost open. He grabbed my neck and I let out a scream that came from I don't know where. My next-door neighbor opened her door and he fled. I didn't beat him off or fight him, but I wasn't raped. I outwitted him, computer-cold and scared out of my wits.

Unfortunately no comparative study has ever been made on the behavior of victims of attempted rape versus the behavior of victims of a completed rape. Impotence may be responsible for some of the thwarted rapes, but strong resistance on the part of the woman seems the more logical possibility.

Menachem Amir attempted to measure victim resistance to rape on a statistical basis. Since he chose to limit his study from the outset to completed rapes, a valuable chance to do a comparative study of victim resistance in thwarted rapes was denied him.

Dealing only with police reports on victims of completed rapes—in other words, with victims who decisively *lost* in their encounters—Amir found that 55 percent had displayed what he termed submissive behavior, 27 percent had screamed and/or tried to escape, and another 18 percent fought back by kicking, hitting or throwing objects.*

Rapists brandishing weapons (ranging from guns and knives to sticks and rocks) accounted for one-fifth of all the Philadelphia cases and understandably these men elicited the highest percentage of submissive victims (71 percent). Rapists who displayed no weapons but choked or punched and kicked their victims (to achieve their goals but also as part of their raping pleasure) elicited a response that was far less submissive. Greater numbers of their victims screamed, fought and tried to escape. Often, Amir noted, a victim whose first reaction had been submissive began to resist "after [she] overcame her initial shock or when she realized what the offender was up to." Resistance, when it occurred, usually did

---

* Amir's overall figures included a high proportion of victimized children, who quite understandably proved to be the most submissive of any age group. Adolescent girls and adult women displayed submissive behavior in 51 percent of their cases; children were submissive in 66 percent of their cases.

not stop with the onset of the attack but continued throughout. When a victim understood that she was in for a rough, violent time beyond the act of rape, she screamed and fought back most gamely. The lowest percentage of submissive behavior (in the neighborhood of 30 percent) occurred in the category of "brutally beaten" rapes. Victims who were choked in the initial overture, however, responded with greater passivity than victims who were grabbed, punched and beaten. Overall, fewer victims fought back in gang rapes than in single-offender encounters. Victims of the same general age as their assailants showed the highest proportion of fighting behavior.

When the New York Radical Feminists held our first speakout on rape, a majority of the women who testified said that once the aggression had begun they were convinced they were going to die. "This wasn't an act of sex I was going through—I felt I was being murdered," one woman recalled. In later speak-outs this theme was repeated.

> TESTIMONY: Did you ever see a rabbit stuck in the glare of your headlights when you were going down a road at night? Transfixed— like it knew it was going to get it—that's what happened.

Two associates at Boston College, Ann Wolbert Burgess, associate professor of nursing, and Lynda Lytle Holmstrom, assistant professor of sociology, studied eighty rape victims who came to the emergency ward of Boston City Hospital. They reported their findings in the American Journal of Nursing. Burgess and Holmstrom found that half the women in their sample had been threatened with a weapon; another twenty-one reported being manhandled and twelve had succumbed to verbal threats alone. After lengthy interviews with the eighty women the Boston College professors stated unequivocally, "The primary reaction of almost all women to the rape was fear, that is, fear for their lives."

A quid pro quo—rape in exchange for life, or rape in exchange for a good-faith guarantee against hurtful or disfiguring physical damage—dominates the female mentality in rape. In situations involving dangerous weapons or groups of men, most women believe they are confronting the realistic possibility of death, or at least the probability of serious physical injury. They either gamble on the "fair exchange" of rape or they are terrorized into immobility, from shock or from a disbelief in their own capacity to successfully resist.

TESTIMONY: I was 19 and I was coming home from a Harvard weekend. I missed my bus connection so I decided to hitch. I had to get back to school for an 8 o'clock Monday class. I accepted a ride with a young man who seemed okay. We went for some coffee and doughnuts so that I could get an idea of who he was. There was nothing to get me alarmed. When we got back into the car he told me he had to stop and pick up some friends. I still didn't think anything was wrong. His friends got into the car and then they drove me to a deserted garage.

They told me I'd better cooperate or I'd be buried there and nobody would ever know. There were three of them and one of me. It was about one A.M. and no people were around. I decided to cooperate.

A weapon, unless one is familiar with weapons, is likely to produce a shock reaction in any person, male or female. Choking, unless one knows how to break the hold, can be even more effective, for nothing terrorizes faster than the inability to breathe. In addition to the normal reactive fear that is produced in women by the presence of an aggressing male intent on violence, the sheer physical presence of a number of potential assailants would serve to terrorize most females or convince them that resistance would be futile, unless, of course, they knew how to fight. But the reasoning process, even in one-to-one situations without the presence of a weapon or a threat of death, is not necessarily rational under stress.

TESTIMONY: When I think about it now, I'm sure I could have fought him off. He was smaller than I was. But at the time I blocked everything out, I mean, what was happening. All I could think of was my new dress, which I had just bought but hadn't paid for, and my stockings. I kept saying over and over, "Don't rip my nylon stockings."

TESTIMONY: This was on an arranged date, my mother had arranged it with his aunt. He was an intern at NYU Med School and he asked me if I wanted to see where he lived, where the interns lived, before we had dinner. We got to his room and he threw me on the bed and raped me, just like that. Afterwards he got up as if nothing had happened. I thought to myself, I wonder what happens now. I kept thinking about my mother, she'd never believe it. I'll tell you what happened next. We went out to have dinner. We proceeded along with the date as if nothing had happened. I was in such a state of shock I just went along with the rest of the date.

In the previous chapter I discussed how the *idea* of rape is mythified and glamorized in the culture not only for the rapist but also for the victim, but the actual act bears no relationship to storybook romance. Reality replaces myth with shocking swiftness. The female did not choose this battlefield, this method of warfare, this surprise contestant. Her position, at once, is unprepared and defensive. She cannot win; at best she can escape defeat.

Force, or the threat of force, is the method used against her, and a show of force is the prime requisite of masculine behavior that she, as a woman, has been trained from childhood to abjure. She is unfit for the contest. Femininity has trained her to lose.

According to the odds, she is three inches shorter and 24 pounds lighter than her male assailant. This works to her disadvantage psychologically as well as physically, but worse than the difference in size is the lifelong difference in mental attitude toward strength. He has been encouraged from childhood to build his muscles and toughen his fists. She has been encouraged to value soft skin, her slender wrist, her smooth, unmuscled thigh and leg. His clothing gives him maximum mobility. His shoes are sturdy; thick heels give him power. Her clothing hampers free movement by design, and fragile materials add to her vulnerability. One yank and her blouse is ripped. One stumble and her stockings are torn. Her skirt allows for easy access. One gesture, one motion and she is humiliatingly exposed. Her flimsy shoes have straps that break and heels that come loose. She cannot run.

Reviewing his own statistics, Amir wrote, "It seems that when confronted with a threat to her life or physical well-being, the victim was not willing to resist or fight." While this analysis has important legal ramifications—rape is the only crime of violence in which a victim is expected or required to resist—it raises another important question. Is submissive behavior in any way *helpful* to a victim of rape?

It would appear that the answer is negative. Acquiescent

cooperation by not screaming or struggling once the intent of the rapist is made manifest gives a victim no guarantee that she will be let off more easily. As I interpret Amir's sample, despite what a victim may have hoped (if her submissive behavior was to any degree a planned, rational response), her numb compliance or lack of resistance gave her no blanket insurance against gratuitous physical damage.

This point cannot be overstressed. A victim may choose to play by what she assumes are the rules, but a rapist does not necessarily respond with similar civility. Several of the Boston Strangler's victims (including Evelyn Corbin and Beverly Samans) who were initially terrorized by choking deliberately permitted themselves to be tied and raped, according to Albert DeSalvo's confessions. DeSalvo murdered them anyway; they had "won" no quid pro quo. In the 1966 case of Richard Speck, eight student nurses in Chicago under the threat of one man and one knife permitted themselves to be bound with strips of bedsheets and taken from the room one by one. The sole survivor of the massacre, Corazon Amurao, a 23-year-old Filipino, had suggested to the others that they band together to escape. The others told her not to panic and start something that might provoke him, for they all assumed that what was going on in the other room was "only rape." Corazon Amurao rolled under the bed and hid herself and Speck, in his glory, lost count. The rest went like lambs to their slaughter. The following morning eight bodies were found. Each had been slashed and strangled.

When a woman survives the physical trauma of rape, her emotional reaction may take many forms. She may cry, scream or tremble; she may be rigidly composed; she may smile inappropriately or tell the story with bursts of laughter. There is no uniform response to a rape, or a uniform time for recovery.

TESTIMONY: It was like a delayed terror reaction. Like, when I started thinking how easily he could have just killed me behind the building, I was shaking. I didn't want to tell my husband and I never did report it to the police. I just went into this whole terror thing. I was afraid to take that same way home again and I was afraid to go on the subway alone at night. I was just generally shaken.

TESTIMONY: For years afterward I felt it was my fault. I tried to figure out what had made him follow me. Was it the clothes I was wearing or was it my walk? It *had* to be my fault, you see? I was only a child—an innocent child, but I was ashamed for a long time.

TESTIMONY: I was raped in my elevator after he took my wallet. He had a knife. He told me to lie down and I lay down. It was over in two seconds, just like that. The sex was nothing at all. What do you want me to do? Be angry and hate all men? I just want to forget it. It's New York City life and I'm not going to let it destroy me.

TESTIMONY: I couldn't stay alone in that apartment anymore. I moved in with a friend. I didn't feel strong enough to live by myself for about a year, and when I did get a new place, it had to be a very secure building, not like my old tenement walk-up. I moved from a $75 a month apartment to one where I now pay $225, that's part of the price I had to pay. It wrecked me financially.

TESTIMONY: I kept thinking I saw him—on the street, in the elevator at work, on the bus. I was convinced he was still after me, that he'd get me for reporting it, that he'd come back to finish me off. Whenever the phone rang and the person hung up, I was sure it was him. I moved and got an unlisted number.

TESTIMONY: Somewhere along the line society had told me that if you're a woman and you stick your neck out by being conspicuous you're going to get it. The rape confirmed it. Before the rape I used to go all over the city with my cameras, I was never afraid for my safety. Afterwards I stopped taking pictures, or if I did go out into strange neighborhoods, I made sure that I had a male companion. But at some point you have to say that you're not going to be stopped by it. It's a war and you can't let them win. Otherwise you'd just have to stay indoors.

TESTIMONY: I was black and he was black. The encounter caused a tremendous change in my overall attitude toward men, and especially toward black men. For three months I was afraid to go out with a black man. I was afraid to be out on the streets alone at night. Until I met that man in the alley I thought I was really in control of my life. It taught me I wasn't.

TESTIMONY: I don't think I slept for a week. I lay on a cot in my sister's apartment with my clothes on. I thought of committing suicide. I had to quit my job—first of all I was a nervous wreck but also I was afraid he had spotted me going to and from work. I tried to stay still and make time move forward. I felt the course of my life had changed and nothing would ever be the same again. My being raped moved something in me so deeply that I could no longer not look at it: I'd had a fear of men all of my life.

TESTIMONY: We were what you'd call a middle-class black family, which means we were poor. I was 12 and all these strange things were happening to my body, I was sprouting here and there. It was very confusing and my parents kept saying, "Don't worry, it happens to all girls, you're developing." That was the word they used, developing. Then, after it happened to me, somehow in my head I tied it in with this developing.

TESTIMONY: I was raped when I was 14 in a home for delinquent boys and girls where my parents had left me because my father was having a nervous breakdown. I had just begun menstruation. I never menstruated again until I was 21.

TESTIMONY: For about nine months afterwards I was sure I was going to die of syphilis. I was also sure I was pregnant. Finally I went to a doctor in New York. He told me I was silly that I thought I had syphilis. To this day, even, I have a fear I have syphilis.

TESTIMONY: I was gang-raped when I was 17, after a party in Beverly Hills. My parents didn't prosecute because they were neighborhood boys. Instead they sent me into analysis. They came all over me, every which way. This may sound odd to you, but for two years afterward, no matter how much I washed, I couldn't get the smell of come out of my hair.

TESTIMONY: It's a terrible thing to be woken up at 3 in the morning with a knife at your throat. You never forget it and you're never the same. It did not affect my sexuality, I think, because that was always a strong area of my life, one that I was always pleased with, but what it affected was my career. I stopped taking chances, that's what it was. I wouldn't say that my experience caused my career problems, but it certainly aggravated them. It hits you where you're most vulnerable. Even though I had been very strong during my encounter, I felt more vulnerable in every way. About six months to a year later some of the vulnerability disappeared. It was replaced by rage. Oh, I wish now I had hit him. Or killed him.

TESTIMONY: After that, it was all downhill. None of the girls were allowed to have me in their homes, and the boys used to stare at me on the street when I walked to school. I was left with a reputation that followed me throughout high school.

TESTIMONY: People always say, you know, "time heals all wounds," "things get better with age," et cetera. *I hate that fucker more today than I did when it happened to me.*

TESTIMONY: I never told my mother to this very day. I wish she was here, maybe I could tell her now. I pushed it to the recesses of my mind. I never really dealt with it 'til a year ago—when my friend and I went to St. Thomas and she was raped. And then all the anguish and all the pain that all women have suffered all these years came out of me, and I was able for the first time to relate to another woman's pain.

"Forcible rape is one of the most falsely reported crimes," a California police manual, *Patrol Procedure*, begins its instruction. "The majority of 'second day reported' rapes are not legitimate." Chatty and chummy, *Patrol Procedure* warns the cop on the beat that rape calls often result when a husband leaves town on business and a wife takes the opportunity "to go out on the town," with later remorse. "These situations must be delicately handled," the manual advises.

TESTIMONY: I went to the police station and said, "I want to report a rape." They said, "Whose?" and I said, "Mine." The cop looked at me and said, "Aw, who'd want to rape you?"

TESTIMONY: When they let me go I ran down the street and found a milkman who told me where the police station was. I was calm and coherent. Too calm, I guess. I got disgusted with their questions and slow typing and asked to type my own version of the report. The policeman said, "You're so clear and detailed—what are you, a sociologist or something?"

When women in the feminist movement first got together to discuss the problems of rape, many testified that their complaints were met by insensitive, often hostile policemen. (In perfect frankness, some reported good experiences. For the most part, these were the older women, white children, those who went to the precinct with their husbands, and those who had professional, middle class occupations.)

TESTIMONY: They got more and more interested in the physical details. What did the man say to me? What did I say to him? Did he unzip his pants or take them off? How long did it take? In what position did he do it? Why did I help him? Did he have a climax? Did I? They made me tell the story over and over to different policemen, ostensibly to check the details. When I told them he had entered me from behind, they said that position was impossible. Had I been less frightened or demoralized, I might have pitied *them* for their unimaginative sex lives.

TESTIMONY: They rushed me down to the housing cops, who asked me questions like, "Was he your boyfriend? Did you know him?" Here I am, hysterical, I'm 12 years old, and I don't know these things even happen to people. Anyway, they took me to the precinct after that, and there, about four detectives got me in the room and asked me how long was his penis—like I was supposed to measure it. Actually they said, "How long was the *instrument*?" I thought they were referring to the knife—how was I supposed to know? *That* I could have told them 'cause I was sure enough lookin' at the knife.

In 1972 I was invited to address a seminar for police lieutenants training for promotion to captain at the New York Police Academy. I spoke about rape and was met with a chortle of hoots and laughter from the thirty assembled men. "Honey, you don't believe there *is* such a thing as rape, do you?" a lieutenant called out.

"Don't you?"

"Noooo" came the nearly unanimous response. Months after the seminar I paid a visit to my local precinct in Greenwich Village and asked a sergeant to show me some rape statistics. He politely obliged. That month there had been thirty-five rape complaints, an advance of ten over the same month for the previous year. The precinct had made two arrests.

"Not a very impressive record," I offered.

"Don't worry about it," the sergeant assured me. "You know what these complaints represent?"

"What do they represent?" I asked.

"Prostitutes who didn't get their money," he said firmly, closing the book.

Despite their knowledge of the law they are supposed to enforce, the male police mentality is often identical to the stereotypic views of rape that are shared by the rest of the male culture. The tragedy for the rape victim is that the police officer is the person who validates her victimization. A police officer who does not believe there is such a crime as rape can arrive at only one determination.

TESTIMONY: They finally told me they thought I was lying. They said I'd probably been having sex with my boyfriend and probably was afraid I was pregnant. They also theorized that my boyfriend had set me up for it. They wanted to know if he'd ever asked me to have relations with his friends.

When Brenda Brown did her Memphis study, she found that only 1.02 percent of all rape victims were prostitutes. In her report to her superiors she wrote, "This casts some doubt upon the persistent comforting myth that many rape victims are actually prostitutes who were unable to collect their fee." When New York City created a special Rape Analysis Squad commanded by policewomen, the female police officers found that only 2 percent of all rape complaints were false—about the same false-report rate that is usual for other kinds of felonies.

A lengthy analysis in the *University of Pennsylvania Law Review* attempted to measure the yardsticks that policemen use to "found" a rape. Rapes reported "within hours" and cases involving strangers, weapons and "positive violence" stood the highest chance of being believed. Rapes by strangers that took place in automobiles were considered more dubious than rapes by strangers that took place in the home or on the street. All dating rapes that occurred in automobiles were held unfounded by the police in this Pennsylvania study. Although the law does not mitigate the offense when the victim is judged to have been intoxicated, in practice the police "unfounded" 82 percent of these cases. Interestingly enough, the police seemed more ready to believe a complainant who claimed she had screamed than a complainant who said she had silently struggled. In the *Pennsylvania Law Review* study, black-on-black rapes were held unfounded by the police 22 percent of the time, whereas only 12 percent of the white-on-white rapes were unfounded. The authors wrote, "It appears impossible not to conclude that the differential . . . resulted primarily from lack of confidence in the veracity of black complainants and a belief in the myth of black promiscuity."

TESTIMONY: This was in Jacksonville, Florida, about 3 A.M., and I was traveling back to school, and here I am, in a bus station in an unfamiliar town. I was in Trailways and I had to make the connection to Greyhound, just one short block, they told me. A big, burly guy, he was black, was trying to talk to me, but I didn't want to be bothered. I went into the ladies' room to try and duck him, and then I took my little suitcase and went out fast through a side door. I was totally unfamiliar with this town, but I thought I had gotten rid of the guy.

As I was walking along the street he fell into step behind me. He pulled a gun on me and instructed me to continue walking. Just looking around, the lighting was very bad, there was nothing but warehouses all around, deserted warehouses, that sort of thing. We went into one of them and he told me to go upstairs. He told me to get undressed. I did everything he told me, and if I didn't do it fast enough, he would put his gun to my head. It was like dying a thousand deaths that night. I kept praying, lord, just let me live through this. I was just beginning to live, school was going well, and here was something else happening to me.

Afterwards he took $70 off me. He didn't even leave me a dime. I picked a quarter off the floor and he took that too. He threatened to make me walk down the street naked, but I guess he changed his mind. Eventually he left. I didn't know whether to get dressed or what. Finally I got my nerves up and I dressed sort of haphazardly and took off running for Trailways bus station. I got there, I went into the baggage room and demanded that the guy there call the cops.

They came 30 minutes or so later. I'm on the floor, completely paranoid and crying. They took me back to what they call the scene.

Eventually they said that the guy was my boyfriend and that everything was okay between us until he took my money. At that moment if I had had a gun I could have killed them all, I was angry enough.

After the questioning I left my number and name and address so as they could reach me. Nothing was ever done about it. Some time later, when I was back at school, I tried to contact them. They hung up on me.

In a depressing aside to the *University of Pennsylvania Law Review* study, the authors noted that most complainants were not informed that the offenses against them had been unfounded. Rape complaints deemed barely credible by the police at first hearing were classified merely as "investigation of persons." Occasionally police turned away a complainant without filing any report, or proceeded to close the case without conducting an investigation. Since these complaints had never been entered on the police blotter as "rape," the authors concluded that the overall number of unfounded cases was considerably higher than the official records might show. "Probably," they wrote, "at least 50 percent of the reported rapes are unfounded by the police."

Rape as it must be proved in an American court of law is

> the perpetration of an act of sexual intercourse with a female, not one's wife, against her will and consent, whether her will is overcome by force or fear resulting from the threat of force, or by drugs or intoxicants; or when, because of mental deficiency, she is incapable of exercising rational judgment; or when she is below an arbitrary "age of consent."

The jury deals with the same question that faced the police: Has a crime been committed? Unlike cases of murder, where the presence of a dead body points to the fact that there has been a crime, and unlike cases of robbery, where the physical goods, if recovered, are marked and tagged Exhibit A, and unlike cases of aggravated assault, where overt signs of physical damage are the main evidentiary proof, proof in a rape case is often intangible. The "perpetration of an act of sexual intercourse against a woman's will" leaves no *corpus delicti*, leaves no recoverable physical goods, and may leave no sign of physical damage.

What, then, does a jury start off with? The oath of a woman who says she was raped, and the oath of a man who denies it. There are a variety of criminal situations in which a jury must weigh "oath against oath," and juries, since juries have been in existence, have managed to convict or acquit based on whose oath they decided to trust. But rape is the only crime in which by law the victim is female and the offender is male. In a court of law, where the victim becomes the "complainant," or more harshly, "prosecutrix," and the offender becomes the "defendant," oath against oath at all times means the word of a woman against the word of a man.

Because of the male-against-female nature of rape, because rape is a deliberate distortion of the primal act of sexual inter-course—male joining with female in mutual consent—man's law has sought to measure such relative, qualitative and interrelated concepts as moral character, force, fear, consent, will and resistance to satisfy the overriding male concern that beyond the female's oath, her word, her testimony, there was not mutual intercourse and subsequent vindictiveness and wrath, but an objective, tangible crime.

Lord Chief Justice Matthew Hale, the famous seventeenth-century English jurist, assured himself of immortality when he wrote the words, "Rape is an accusation easily to be made and hard to be proved, and harder to be defended by the party accused, tho never so innocent."

"An old saw that has been quoted by virtually every legal writer who has discussed rape," as Camille E. LeGrand put it in the *California Law Review*, Hale's quaint homily has poorly stood the test of time despite its popularity. Since four out of five rapes go unreported, it is fair to say categorically that women do not find rape "an accusation easily to be made." Those who do report their rape soon find, however, that it is indeed "hard to be proved." As for the party accused, tho never so innocent or never so guilty, except for the tradition of Southern interracial cases, by and large a successful legal defense is nothing short of a cinch.

LeGrand pointed out that irrelevant as Hale's old saw might be to the twentieth-century American experience, it was included as late as 1973 in California's standard set of jury instructions for cases of rape, where it was followed by the admonition, "Therefore the law requires that you examine the testimony of the female person named in the information with caution."

That the testimony of the female person should be examined with caution is the bottom line in all rape cases from the moment they are reported to that rarer moment, if ever, when they are actually brought to trial. The issue goes deeper than "oath against oath." It is based on the cherished male assumption that female persons tend to lie.

Wigmore on *Evidence*, the American text defining evidentiary rules that is the unchallenged, esteemed and venerated classic treatise on the subject, asserts:

> Modern psychiatrists have amply studied the behavior of errant young girls and women coming before the courts in all sorts of cases. Their psychic complexes are multifarious, distorted partly by inherent defects, partly by diseased derangements or abnormal instincts, partly by bad social environment, partly by temporary physiological or emotional conditions. *One form taken by these complexes is that of contriving false charges of sexual offenses by men* [italics added].

Male fear of the false rape charge brought by a lying woman—the old syndrome of Potiphar's wife—is written into the rape laws of various states in the form of special rules of evidence that are conspicuously absent from evidentiary rules governing other kinds of violent crime. Unless these rules of evidence can be met, a prosecutor cannot bring a case into court, even though he knows, the victim knows, and the rapist knows that a crime has been committed.

> TESTIMONY: Anyway, I did not have any witnesses, it was his word against mine. My case was thrown out of court. One of the cops was in the courtroom and he tried to be consoling and sympathetic. He said, "Oh, look, honey, at least we kept him in jail overnight. That ought to make you happy."

One safeguard embodied in the law for the protection of defendants is the chastity, or unchastity standard, that is appended to statutory rape provisions governing assaults against females "below the age of consent." The principle of statutory rape holds that resistance is immaterial in the case of a child below a certain age since, as the saying goes, "the law resists for her." The age of consent itself has varied dramatically from state to state, from a low of 7 years in Delaware (changed to 16 years in 1973) to a high of 21, under certain conditions, in Tennessee. Most states set the age of consent somewhere between age 12 and age 16. States with a high age of consent usually employ the chastity standard for the upper-age limits. In some states the burden of proving prior chastity, that is, virginity, falls on the prosecutor; in others, the burden of proving prior unchastity falls on the defense. Previous unchastity on the part of a young victim means there can be no conviction for statutory rape.

> TESTIMONY: I was 11 years old. There was some kind of hearing but all I can remember about it is that the lawyer gave my father explicit instructions about the kind of clothes I should wear. I was told to wear a Peter Pan collar.

Evidentiary rules governing the trial of offenders who have raped adult women are more complex than those governing statutory rape. They, too, show marked inconsistencies from state to state. According to the *Yale Law Journal*, "Evidence of the complaining witness's consent to previous acts of coitus with the defendant may be admitted, via the theory of a 'continuing state of mind,' to prove her consent to the act in question. Also, evidence of her general moral character is usually admissible. Courts apparently reason that a reputation of 'loose moral character' probably has a basis in fact and that a girl with such a character is more likely than not to consent to intercourse in any given instance."

All jurisdictions allow testimony regarding previous acts of intercourse between offender and victim. In addition, many states allow testimony as to specific acts of intercourse between the victim *and other men at other times in her life* in an effort to prove her "loose moral character." Some states restrict admissible testimony to a general appraisal of her "reputation for chastity in the neighborhood in which she lives" from any number of witnesses, to be answered by "good" or "bad." Still other jurisdictions allow testimony concerning a woman's prior sexual history on the grounds that such information has a bearing on her "credibility."

> TESTIMONY: The suspect was arraigned but the grand jury refused to indict him. I think it was because they saw that my boyfriend was of another race. That made me a bad woman, right?

Either by statute law or by case law (judicial decisions that set a precedent), several jurisdictions in the nation have sought to protect the male defendant against the mere word of a woman in court by requiring independent corroborative proof in addition to her testimony. The burden of corroboration means that the prosecutor must prove, apart from the victim's word, that there was penetration (vaginal tears, bruises, sperm), that force was applied (body bruises, a weapon, torn clothing), or that the man on trial was the true offender (an eyewitness to some phase of the rape).

The sheer impossibility of providing total corroboration is best demonstrated by the sad history of New York City's conviction rate under the state's old corroboration statute. In 1971 there were 2,415 "founded" rape complaints in New York and the police managed to make 1,085 arrests. However, only 100 cases were ever presented to the grand jury, and these resulted in 34 indictments and only 18 convictions. Justice under the state's corroboration statute was an unbelievable, bizarre revolving door. In 1974 New York dropped its corroboration requirement, as did Connecticut and Iowa. But a corroboration requirement, which at this writing is clearly falling out of favor in judicial circles, is not the only bulwark against conviction. Surveys show that prosecutors seldom bring a rape case to trial without some form of corroborative proof because, regardless of the state's evidence rules, juries simply refuse to convict without corroboration.

> TESTIMONY: They trotted out my whole past life, made me go through all these changes, while he just sat at the defendant's table, mute, surrounded by his lawyers. Of course that was his right by law, but it looked like I was the one who was on trial.

While a woman's past sexual history may be trotted out for a jury's appraisal, a man's relevant sexual history, including prior charges and convictions for rape, may not be introduced in evidence if he does not take the witness stand. And so, a jury might see before them a sexually active woman and be told that her sexual activity reflects on her character and credibility, but the man may not be similarly examined or judged.

On the face of it, rape laws appear almost reasonable in the interrelated areas of force, resistance and consent. According to the *Yale Law Journal* in 1952, "Today most states hold that the amount of resistance must be proportional to the circumstances of the attack, such as the relative strength of the parties and the futility of persistence. Other states require only that degree of 'good faith' resistance which makes the woman's non-consent reasonably evident." Overt signs of physical damage, of course, may be introduced to prove force; and verbal threats of bodily harm or the presence of a weapon, courts have held, are also sufficient indicators of force.

But although evidentiary requirements on force and resistance may appear reasonable on paper, juries are influenced hardly at all by bruises and have the poorest understanding that the *threat* of violence might be sufficient to terrorize a woman into submission. While some defendants in a rape case claim that "some other guy did it," the standard defense is that there was no force and no resistance because the woman freely consented to the act. A jury's concept of "consent" is based almost exclusively on its interpretation of the events leading up to the rape, and its judgment of the victim's "moral character."

> TESTIMONY: I don't understand it. It was like I was the defendant and he was the plaintiff. I wasn't on trial. I don't see where I did anything wrong. I screamed. I struggled. How could they have decided that he was innocent, that I didn't resist?

"Despite the supposed emotional aspects of a rape trial," Judge Lawrence H. Cooke told a meeting of the New York Bar Association, "the defense rarely ever waives a jury trial knowing that the jury is an ally, not an enemy. Juries, which are often male-dominated, are extremely reluctant to convict."

Judge Cooke was speaking from personal observation. Of all kinds of criminal prosecutions, rape ranks second only to murder in the percentage of cases in which a defendant prefers to take his chances on a jury rather than elect to be tried by a judge alone. The defendants and their legal counsel are right. Juries are allies. Judges are made of sterner stuff. For one thing, a judge has a better grasp of criminal law; for another, he has seen many similar cases come before him and defense counsel gambits are no surprise. But juries are allies of male defendants and enemies of female complainants for reasons that run deeper than their poor grasp of the law or their predominantly male composition. They are composed of citizens who believe the many myths about rape, and they judge the female according to these cherished myths.

A vast, national study of the American jury system and how it functions was undertaken at the University of Chicago Law School by Harry Kalven and Hans Zeisel. Examining 106 cases of rape, and comparing the jury's decision to acquit or convict with a written statement from the judge on the case telling how he would have voted, Kalven and Zeisel uncovered major discrepancies between a jury's interpretation of law and fact and the judge's opinion.

The authors wrote, "The law recognizes only one issue in rape cases other than the fact of intercourse: whether there was consent at the moment of intercourse. The jury . . . does not limit itself to this one issue; it goes on to weigh the woman's conduct in the prior history of the affair. It closely, and often harshly, scrutinizes the female complainant and is moved to be lenient with the defendant whenever there are suggestions of contributory behavior on her part."

As Kalven and Zeisel saw it, juries in effect were rewriting the law. They were bootlegging concepts from tort law or civil actions such as "contributory negligence" and "assumption of risk" into a rape case. They "weighed the conduct of the victim in judging the guilt of the defendant."

The two professors found that juries preferred to acquit when there was no overt sign of physical force. "The jury's stance," they suggested, "is not so much that involuntary intercourse under these circumstances is no crime at all, but rather that it does not have the gravity of rape. . . . This rewriting of the law to accommodate the defendant when the female victim has taken a risk is on occasion carried to a cruel extreme."

Women who went drinking with the offender prior to the act, women who were "picked up," women who knew the offender previously and women whose past sexual history was alleged to be "promiscuous" were assessed by juries in this national study as having taken an undue risk and morally not worth a conviction for rape.

Kalven and Zeisel went on to separate out from their sample all cases in which there was evidence of "extrinsic violence," situations in which the defendant and victim were total strangers, and cases involving more than one assailant. The remaining cases, of which there were 42, they called for the purposes of their study "simple rape." In these 42 simple rapes, the judges reported they would have convicted in 22 of the cases. But the jury convicted in only three. "This result," wrote Kalven and Zeisel, "is startling."

12

Women Fight Back

On the fourteenth of November, 1642, a young *Virgine*, *daughter to Mr. Adam Fisher*, was hurrying along a country road in Devonshire *so darke that she could scarce discerne her hand* when the figure of a *Gentleman*, *Mr. Ralph Ashley*, a debased Cavalier, approached on horseback. Inspired by the *Devill* himself, this gentleman told the trusting maiden that he knew her father well and would be pleased to escort her home in safety, for there were lustful soldiers in those parts.

And then, Dear Reader, as if you didn't know what next, he galloped her off to a deserted spot and *went about to ravish her* while she fervently prayed, *Help, Lord, or I perish*.

Just then *a fearefull Comet burst out in the ayre and strucke* the rapacious Cavalier with *a streame of fire so that he fell downe staggering*.

According to some shepherds folding their flock who had witnessed the *Blazing Starre* from a distance, Mr. Ashley expired within the night, ranting and raving in terrible blasphemy about *that Roundheaded whore*. Adam Fisher's daughter, aroused from a graceful faint, found her Virginity intact and thanked her lucky starres and God Almighty.

The original text of this Puritan fable, a seventeenth-century propaganda pamphlet aimed at "those Cavaliers which esteem murder and rapine the chiefe Principalls of their religion," is housed today in the British Museum.

Three eventful centuries have passed since that fateful autumn night when Mr. Ralph Ashley attempted to ravish Mr. Adam Fisher's nameless daughter and was struck in his tracks by a bolt from the sky. Fewer of us these days, we would all agree, are young Virgines. The automobile has replaced the horse and blazing comets have proved fairly unpredictable after all. But the problem of rape, and how to deal with it, remains.

To a woman the definition of rape is fairly simple. A sexual invasion of the body by force, an incursion into the private, personal inner space without consent—in short, an internal assault from one of several avenues and by one of several methods—constitutes a deliberate violation of emotional, physical and rational integrity and is a hostile, degrading act of violence that deserves the name of rape.

Yet by tracing man's concept of rape as he defined it in his earliest laws, we now know with certainty that the criminal act he viewed with horror, and the deadly punishments he saw fit to apply, had little to do with an actual act of sexual violence that a woman's body might sustain. True, the law has come some distance since its beginnings when rape meant simply and conclusively the theft of a father's daughter's virginity, a specialized crime that damaged valuable goods before they could reach the matrimonial market, but modern legal perceptions of rape are rooted still in ancient male concepts of property.

From the earliest times, when men of one tribe freely raped women of another tribe to secure new wives, the laws of marriage and the laws of rape have been philosophically entwined, and even today it is largely impossible to separate them out. Man's historic desire to maintain sole, total and complete access to woman's vagina, as codified by his earliest laws of marriage, sprang from his need to be the sole physical instrument governing impregnation, progeny and inheritance rights. As man understood his male reality, it was perfectly lawful to capture and rape some other tribe's women, for what better way for his own tribe to increase? But it was unlawful, he felt, for the insult to be returned. The criminal act he viewed with horror and punished as rape was not sexual assault per se, but an act of unlawful possession, a trespass against his tribal right to control vaginal access to all women who belonged to him and his kin.

Since marriage, by law, was consummated in one manner only, by defloration of virginity with attendant ceremonial tokens, the act man came to construe as criminal rape was the illegal destruction of virginity outside a marriage contract of his making. Later, when he came to see his own definition as too narrow for the times, he broadened his criminal concept to cover the ruination of his wife's chastity as well, thus extending the law's concern to nonvirgins too. Although these legal origins have been buried in the morass of forgotten history, as the laws of rape continued to evolve they never shook free of their initial concept—that the violation was first and foremost a violation of male rights of possession, based on male requirements of virginity, chastity and consent to private access as the female bargain in the marriage contract (the underpinnings, as he enforced them, of man's economic estate).

To our modern way of thinking, these theoretical origins are peculiar and difficult to fully grasp. A huge disparity in thought—male logic versus female logic—affects perception of rape to this very day, confounding the analytic processes of some of the best legal minds. Today's young rapist has no thought of capturing a wife or securing an inheritance or estate. His is an act of impermanent conquest, not a practical approach to ownership and control. The economic advantage of rape is a forgotten concept. What remains is the basic male-female struggle, a hit-and-run attack, a brief expression of physical power, a conscious process of intimidation, a blunt, ugly sexual invasion with possible lasting psychological effects on all women.

When rape is placed where it truly belongs, within the context of modern criminal violence and not within the purview of ancient masculine codes, the crime retains its unique dimensions, falling midway between robbery and assault. It is, in one act, both a blow to the body and a blow to the mind, and a "taking" of sex through the use or threat of force. Yet the differences between rape and an assault or a robbery are as distinctive as the obvious similarities. In a prosecutable case of assault, bodily damage to the victim is clearly evident. In a case of rape, the threat of force does not secure a tangible commodity as we understand the term, although sex traditionally has been viewed by men as "the female treasure"; more precisely, in rape the threat of force obtains a highly valued sexual service through temporary access to the victim's intimate parts, and the intent is not merely to "take," but to humiliate and degrade.

This, then, is the modern reality of rape as it is defined by twentieth-century practice. It is not, however, the reality of rape as it is defined by twentieth-century law.

In order for a sexual assault to qualify as felonious rape in an American courtroom, there must be "forcible penetration of the vagina by the penis, however slight." In other words, rape is defined by law as a heterosexual offense that is characterized by genital copulation. It is with this hallowed, restrictive definition, the *sine qua non* of rape prosecutions, that our argument begins.

That forcible genital copulation is the "worst possible" sex assault a person can sustain, that it deserves by far the severest punishment, equated in some states with the penalties for murder, while all other manner of sexual assaults are lumped together under the label of sodomy and draw lesser penalties by law, can only be seen as an outdated masculine concept that no longer applies to modern crime.

Sexual assault in our day and age is hardly restricted to forced genital copulation, nor is it exclusively a male-on-female offense. Tradition and biologic opportunity have rendered vaginal rape a particular political crime with a particular political history, but the invasion may occur through the mouth or the rectum as well. And while the penis may remain the rapist's favorite weapon, his prime instrument of vengeance, his triumphant display of power, it is not in fact his only tool. Sticks, bottles and even fingers are often substituted for the "natural" thing. And as men may invade women through other orifices, so, too, do they invade other men. Who is to say that the sexual humiliation suffered through forced oral or rectal penetration is a lesser violation of the personal, private inner space, a lesser injury to mind, spirit and sense of self?

All acts of sex forced on unwilling victims deserve to be treated in concept as equally grave offenses in the eyes of the law, for the avenue of penetration is less significant than the intent to degrade. Similarly, the gravity of the offense ought not be bound by the victim's gender. That the law must move in this direction seems clear.

A gender-free, non-activity-specific law governing all manner of sexual assaults would be but the first step toward legal, reform.

The law must rid itself of other, outdated masculine concepts as well.

Since man first equated rape with the ruination of his wholly owned property, the theft of his private treasure, he reflected his concern most thunderously in the punishments that his law could impose. Today in many states of the Union, a conviction for first-degree felonious rape still draws a life sentence, and before the 1972 Supreme Court ruling that abolished capital punishment, a number of Southern states set the penalty at death. A modern perception of sexual assault that views the crime strictly as an injury to the victim's bodily integrity, and not as an injury to the purity or chastity of man's estate, must normalize the penalties for such an offense and bring them in line more realistically with the penalties for aggravated assault, the crime to which a sexual assault is most closely related.

Here the law must move from its view that "carnal knowledge" is the crux of the crime to an appreciation that the severity of the offense, and the corresponding severity of the penalty that may be imposed, might better be gauged by the severity of the objective physical injury sustained by the victim during the course of the attack. Another criterion that the law can reflect beyond objective physical injury in the imposition of penalties is the manner in which the assault was accomplished. As the current law distinguishes between the severity of an armed robbery versus an unarmed robbery, so must the law distinguish between the commission of a sexual assault with a deadly weapon—in which the threat against the victim's life is manifest and self-evident—and a sexual assault committed without a weapon. The participation of two or more offenders is another useful indicator of the severity of a sexual assault, since a number of assailants by their overwhelming presence constitutes a realistic threat of bodily harm.

Parenthetically I want to note at this point that I am one of those people who view a prison sentence as a just and lawful societal solution to the problem of criminal activity, the best solution we have at this time, as civilized retribution and as a deterrent against the commission of future crimes. Whether or not a term in jail is truly "rehabilitative" matters less, I think, than whether or not a guilty offender is given the penalty his crime deserves. It is important to be concerned with the treatment offenders receive in prison, but a greater priority, it would seem, is to ensure that offenders actually go to prison.*

Current feminist thinking on sexual assault legislation favors a system of sentencing that ranges from six months to twenty years, depending on the severity of the crime. This approach strikes me as sound, even generous, for with good behavior, a prisoner may be paroled after one-third of his sentence is served. (As it stands now, a convicted rapist who goes to jail serves an average of forty-four months; the problem, however, is that few rapists actually reach jail.) A sexual assault case in which the victim has suffered permanent physical damage or disfigurement, or lasting psychological damage, should subject the offender to additional charges and penalties for aggravated assault as well.

Rape, as the current law defines it, is the forcible perpetration of an act of sexual intercourse on the body of a woman *not one's wife.* The exemption from rape prosecutions granted to husbands who force their wives into acts of sexual union by physical means is as ancient as the original definition of criminal rape, which was synonymous with that quaint phrase of Biblical origin, "unlawful carnal knowledge." To our Biblical forefathers, any carnal knowledge outside the marriage contract was "unlawful." And any carnal knowledge within the marriage contract was, by definition, "lawful." Thus, as the law evolved, the idea that a husband could be prosecuted for raping his wife was unthinkable, for the law was conceived to protect *his* interests, not those of his wife. Sir Matthew Hale explained to his peers in the seventeenth century, "A husband cannot be guilty of rape upon his wife for by their mutual matrimonial consent and contract the wife hath given up herself in this kind to her husband, which she cannot retract." In other words, marriage implies consent to sexual intercourse at all times, and a husband has a lawful right to copulate with his wife against her will and by force according to the terms of their contract.

---

* Since "Castrate Rapists" has become a slogan in certain circles, I guess I should say on the record that I am not "for" castration any more than I am "for" cutting off the ear of an informer or cutting off the hand of a thief. As for retaliatory killing, of which there have been a few recent cases, I would go along with the law and say that the concept of justifiable homicide in self-defense is sound, but premeditated murder some time after the act can never be condoned.

The most famous marital rape in literature, occurring onstage in the popular television serial but offstage in the novel, is that of Irene by Soames in *The Forsyte Saga*. As Galsworthy presents the Soamesian logic, the logic of Everyhusband, although perhaps not of Galsworthy himself, the denied husband has "at last asserted his rights and acted like a man." In his morning-after solitude while he hears Irene still crying in the bedroom, Soames muses, "The incident was really of no great moment; women made a fuss about it in books; but in the cool judgment of right-thinking men, of men of the world, such as he recollected often received praise in the Divorce Court, he had but done his best to sustain the sanctity of marriage, to prevent her from abandoning her duty. . . . No, he did not regret it."

In the cool judgment of right-thinking women, compulsory sexual intercouse is not a husband's right in marriage, for such a "right" gives the lie to any concept of equality and human dignity. Consent is better arrived at by husband and wife afresh each time, for if women are to be what we believe we are—equal partners— then intercourse must be construed as an act of mutual desire and not as a wifely "duty," enforced by the permissible threat of bodily harm or of economic sanctions.

In cases of rape within a marriage, the law must take a philosophic leap of the greatest magnitude, for while the ancient concept of conjugal rights (female rights as well as male) might continue to have some validity in annulments and contested divorces—civil procedures conducted in courts of law—it must not be used as a shield to cover acts of force perpetrated by husbands on the bodies of their wives. There are those who believe that the current laws governing assault and battery are sufficient to deal with the cases of forcible rape in marriage, and those who take the more liberal stand that a sexual assault law might be applicable only to those men legally separated from their wives who return to "claim" their marital "right," but either of these solutions fails to come to grips with the basic violation.

Since the beginning of written history, criminal rape has been bound up with the common law of consent in marriage, and it is time, once and for all, to make a clean break. A sexual assault is an invasion of bodily integrity and a violation of freedom and self-determination wherever it happens to take place, in or out of the marriage bed. I recognize that it is easier to write these words than to draw up a workable legal provision, and I recognize the difficulties that juries will have in their deliberations when faced with a wife who accuses her husband of forcing her into copulation against her will, but the principle of bodily self-determination must be established without qualification, I think, if it is to become an inviolable principle on any level. And revolutionary as this principle may appear to the traditions of Anglo-American jurisprudence, it is accepted as a matter of course and human dignity in the criminal codes of Sweden and Denmark and in the codes of the U.S.S.R. and other countries in the Communist bloc as well, although how it works out in practice I cannot say. (Certain of these European countries, including Switzerland and Yugoslavia, also equate economic threats, such as the threatened loss of a job, with threats of physical force in cases of rape.)

The concept of consent rears its formidable head in the much debated laws of statutory rape, but here consent is construed in the opposite sense—not as something that cannot be retracted, as in marriage, but as something that cannot be given. Since the thirteenth-century Statutes of Westminster, the law has sought to fix an arbitrary age below which an act of sexual intercourse with a female, with or without the use of force, is deemed a criminal offense that deserves severe punishment because the female is too young to know her own mind. Coexistent with these statutory rape laws, and somewhat contradictory to them, have been the laws governing criminal incest, sexual victimization of a child by a blood relation, where the imposition of legal penalties has been charitably lenient, to say the least—yet another indication of the theoretical concept that the child "belongs" to the father's estate. Under current legislation, which is by no means uniform, a conviction for statutory rape may draw a life sentence in many jurisdictions, yet a conviction for incest rarely carries more than a ten-year sentence, approximately the same maximum penalty that is fixed by law for sodomy offenses.

If protection of the bodily integrity of all children is to be genuinely reflected in the law, and not simply the protection of patriarchal interests, then the current division of offenses (statutory rape for outsiders; incest for members of the victim's family) must be erased. Retaining a fixed age of consent seems a necessary and humane measure for the protection of young girls and young boys alike, although it must be understood that any arbitrary age limit is at best a judicious compromise since sexual maturity and wisdom are not automatically conferred with the passage of time. Feminists who have applied themselves to this difficult question are in agreement that all children below the age of twelve deserve unqualified protection by a statutory age provision in sexual assault legislation, since that age is reasonably linked with the onset of puberty and awareness of sex, its biologic functions and repercussions. In line with the tradition of current statutory rape legislation, offenses committed against children below the age of twelve should carry the maximum penalty, normalized to twenty years. Recognizing that young persons above twelve and below sixteen remain particularly vulnerable to sexual coercion by adults who use a position of authority, rather than physical force, to achieve their aim (within the household or within an institution or a medical facility, to give three all-too-common examples), the law ought to be flexible enough to allow prosecutorial discretion in the handling of these cases under a more limited concept of "statutory sexual assault," with corresponding lesser penalties as the outer age limits are reached.

"Consent" has yet another role to play in a case of sexual assault. In reviewing the act, in seeking to determine whether or not a crime was committed, the concept of consent that is debated in court hinges on whether or not the victim offered sufficient resistance to the attack, whether or not her will was truly overcome by the use of force or the threat of bodily harm. The peculiar nature of sexual crimes of violence, as much as man's peculiar historic perception of their meaning, has always clouded the law's perception of consent.

It is accepted without question that robbery victims need not prove they resisted the robber, and it is never inferred that by handing over their money, they "consented" to the act and therefore the act was no crime. Indeed, police usually advise law-abiding citizens not to resist a robbery, but rather to wait it out patiently, report the offense to the proper authorities, and put the entire matter in the hands of the law. As a matter of fact, successful resistance to a robbery these days is considered heroic.

In certain middle-class neighborhoods in New York City, people who must be out on the streets late at night, coming home from work, taking a trip to the deli, or walking the dog, have taken to carrying a ten-dollar bill as "mugger money" to satisfy the aims and rage of any robber who might accost them. Clearly, the feeling seems to be that the loss of a few bucks is a better bargain than the risk of physical violence. Handing over money at knife point, or dipping into one's wallet to assuage a weaponless but menacing figure on a dark, deserted street, may be financially painful or emotionally distressing, but it hardly compares to the massive insult to one's self-determination that is sustained during a sexual assault.

In a sexual assault physical harm is much more than a threat; it is a reality because violence is an integral part of the act. Body contact and physical intrusion are the purpose of the crime, not appropriation of a physically detached and removable item like money. Yet the nature of the crime as it is practiced does bear robbery a close resemblance, because the sexual goal for the rapist resembles the monetary goal of the robber (often both goals are accomplished during the course of one confrontation if the victim is a woman), and so, in a sex crime, a bargain between offender and victim may also be struck. In this respect, a sexual assault is closer in victim response to a robbery than it is to a simple case of assault, for an assaultive event may not have a specific goal beyond the physical contest, and furthermore, people who find themselves in an assaultive situation usually defend themselves by fighting back.

Under the rules of law, victims of robbery and assault are not required to prove they resisted, or that they didn't consent, or that the act was accomplished with sufficient force, or sufficient threat of force, to overcome their will, because the law presumes it highly unlikely that a person willingly gives away money, except to a charity or to a favorite cause, and the law presumes that no person willingly submits to a brutal beating and the infliction of bodily harm and permanent damage. But victims of rape and other forms of sexual assault do need to prove these evidentiary requirements—that they resisted, that they didn't consent, that their will was overcome by overwhelming force and fear—because the law has never been able to satisfactorily distinguish an act of mutually desired sexual union from an act of forced, criminal sexual aggression.

Admittedly, part of the law's confusion springs from the normal, biologic, male procedural activity in an act of unforced copulation, but insertion of the penis (a descriptive phrase less semantically loaded than penetration, I think) is not in itself, despite what many men think, an act of male dominance. The real reason for the law's everlasting confusion as to what constitutes an act of rape and what constitutes an act of mutual intercourse is the underlying cultural assumption that it is the natural masculine role to proceed aggressively toward the stated goal, while the natural feminine role is to "resist" or "submit." And so to protect male interests, the law seeks to gauge the victim's behavior during the offending act in the belief that force or the threat of force is not conclusive *in and of itself*.

According to Menachem Amir's study, the assailant actually displays a dangerous weapon in no more than one-fifth of all police-founded cases of rape. Clearly, these are the cases a jury would most likely believe. But most rapes are not accomplished by means of a knife, a gun, a lead pipe or whatever. The force that is employed more often consists of an initial stranglehold, manhandling, beating, shoving, tearing at clothes, a verbal threat of death or disfigurement, the sheer physical presence of two, three, four, five assailants, etc. Without doubt, any of these circumstances can and does produce immobilizing terror in a victim, terror sufficient to render her incapable of resistance or to make her believe that resistance would be futile.

Currently employed standards of resistance or consent vis-à-vis force or the threat of force have never been able to accurately gauge a victim's terror, since terror is a psychological reaction and not an objective standard that can be read on a behavior meter six months later in court, as jury acquittal rates plainly show. For this reason, feminists have argued that the special burden of proof that devolves on a rape victim, that she resisted "within reason," that her eventual compliance was no indication of tacit "consent," is patently unfair, since such standards are not applied in court to the behavior of victims in other kinds of violent crime. A jury should be permitted to weigh the word of a victimized complainant at face value, that is what it boils down to—no more or less a right than is granted to other victims under the law.

Not only is the victim's response during the act measured and weighed, her past sexual history is scrutinized under the theory that it relates to her "tendency to consent," or that it reflects on her credibility, her veracity, her predisposition to tell the truth or to lie. Or so the law says. As it works out in practice, juries presented with evidence concerning a woman's past sexual history make use of

386 | AGAINST OUR WILL

such information to form a moral judgment on her character, and here all the old myths of rape are brought into play, for the feeling persists that a virtuous woman either cannot get raped or does not get into situations that leave her open to assault. Thus the questions in the jury room become "Was she or wasn't she asking for it?"; "If she had been a decent woman, wouldn't she have fought to the death to defend her 'treasure'?"; and "Is this bimbo worth the ruination of a man's career and reputation?"

The crime of rape must be totally separated from all traditional concepts of chastity, for the very meaning of chastity presupposes that it is a woman's duty (but not a man's) to refrain from sex outside the matrimonial union. That sexual activity renders a woman "unchaste" is a totally male view of the female as his pure vessel. The phrase "prior chastity" as well as the concept must be stricken from the legal lexicon, along with "prosecutrix," as inflammatory and prejudicial to a complainant's case.

A history of sexual activity with many partners may be indicative of a female's healthy interest in sex, or it may be indicative of a chronic history of victimization and exploitation in which she could not assert her own inclinations; it may be indicative of a spirit of adventure, a spirit of rebellion, a spirit of curiosity, a spirit of joy or a spirit of defeat. Whatever the reasons, and there are many, prior consensual intercourse between a rape complainant and other partners of her choosing should not be scrutinized as an indicator of purity or impurity of mind or body, not in this day and age at any rate, and it has no place in jury room deliberation as to whether or not, in the specific instance in question, an act of forcible sex took place. Prior consensual intercourse between the complainant and the defendant does have some relevance, and such information probably should not be barred.

An overhaul of present laws and a fresh approach to sexual assault legislation must go hand in hand with a fresh approach to enforcing the law. The question of who interprets and who enforces the statutes is as important as the contents of the law itself. At present, female victims of sexual crimes of violence who seek legal justice must rely on a series of male authority figures whose masculine orientation, values and fears place them securely in the offender's camp.

The most bitter irony of rape, I think, has been the historic masculine fear of false accusation, a fear that has found expression in male folklore since the Biblical days of Joseph the Israelite and Potiphar's wife, that was given new life and meaning in the psychoanalytic doctrines of Sigmund Freud and his followers, and that has formed the crux of the legal defense against a rape charge, aided and abetted by that special set of evidentiary standards (consent, resistance, chastity, corroboration) designed with one collective purpose in mind: to protect the male against a scheming, lying, vindictive woman.

Fear of false accusation is not entirely without merit in any criminal case, as is the problem of misidentification, an honest mistake, but the irony, of course, is that while men successfully convinced each other and us that women cry rape with ease and glee, the reality of rape is that victimized women have always been reluctant to report the crime and seek legal justice—because of the shame of public exposure, because of that complex double standard that makes a female feel culpable, even responsible, for any act of sexual aggression committed against her, because of possible retribution from the assailant (once a woman has been raped, the threat of a return engagement understandably looms large), and because women have been presented with sufficient evidence to come to the realistic conclusion that their accounts are received with a harsh cynicism that forms the first line of male defense.

A decade ago the FBI's *Uniform Crime Reports* noted that 20 percent of all rapes reported to the police "were determined by investigation to be unfounded." By 1973 the figure had dropped to 15 percent, while rape remained, in the FBI's words, "the most under-reported crime." A 15 percent figure for false accusations is undeniably high, yet when New York City instituted a special sex crimes analysis squad and put policewomen (instead of men) in charge of interviewing complainants, the number of false charges in New York dropped dramatically to 2 percent, a figure that corresponded exactly to the rate of false reports for other violent crimes. The lesson in the mystery of the vanishing statistic is obvious. Women believe the word of other women. Men do not.

That women have been excluded by tradition and design from all significant areas of law enforcement, from the police precinct, from the prosecutor's office, from the jury box and from the judge's bench, up to and including the appellate and supreme court jurisdictions, has created a double handicap for rape victims seeking justice under the laws of man's devise. And so it is not enough that the face of the law be changed to reflect the reality; the faces of those charged with the awesome responsibility of enforcing the law and securing justice must change as well.

I am convinced that the battle to achieve parity with men in the critical area of law enforcement will be the ultimate testing ground on which full equality for women will be won or lost. Law enforcement means quite literally the use of force when necessary, to maintain the social order, and force since the days of the rudimentary *lex talionis* has been a male prerogative because of size, weight, strength, biologic construction and *deliberate training*, training from which women have been barred by custom as stern as the law itself.

If in the past women had no choice but to let men be our lawful protectors, leaving to them not only the law but its enforcement, it would now seem to be an urgent priority to correct the imbalance. For things have come full circle. The biologic possibility that allows the threat and use of rape still exists, but our social contract has reached a point of sophistication whereby brute force matters less to the maintenance of law and order, or so I believe. I am not unaware that members of the police force in various cities have shown considerable reluctance to admit that size and strength may not be the prime factor in the making of an effective police officer, and they may be temporarily pardoned for sticking to outdated male values. New studies show quite conclusively that women police officers are as effective as men in calming a disturbance and in making an arrest, and they accomplish their work in potentially violent situations without resorting to the unnecessary force that deserves its label, "police brutality."

I am not one to throw the word "revolutionary" around lightly, but full integration of our cities' police departments, and by full I mean fifty-fifty, no less, is a revolutionary goal of the utmost importance to women's rights. And if we are to continue to have armies, as I suspect we will for some time to come, then they, too, must be fully integrated, as well as our national guard, our state troopers, our local sheriffs' offices, our district attorneys' offices, our state prosecuting attorneys' offices—in short, the nation's entire lawful power structure (and I mean power in the physical sense) must be stripped of male dominance and control— if women are to cease being a colonized protectorate of men.

A system of criminal justice and forceful authority that genuinely works for the protection of women's rights, and most specifically the right not to be sexually assaulted by men, can become an efficient mechanism in the control of rape insofar as it brings offenders speedily to trial, presents the case for the complainant in the best possible light, and applies just penalties upon conviction. While I would not underestimate the beneficial effects of workable sex assault laws to "hold the line" and provide a positive deterrent, what feminists (and all right-thinking people) must look toward is the total eradication of rape, and not just an effective policy of containment.

A new approach to the law and to law enforcement can take us only part of the way. Turning over to women 50 percent of the power to enforce the law and maintain the order will be a major step toward eliminating machismo. However, the ideology of rape is aided by more than a system of lenient laws that serve to protect offenders and is abetted by more than the fiat of total male control over the lawful use of power. The ideology of rape is fueled by cultural values that are perpetuated at every level of our society, and nothing less than a frontal attack is needed to repel this cultural assault.

The theory of aggressive male domination over women as a natural right is so deeply embedded in our cultural value system that all recent attempts to expose it—in movies, television commercials or even in children's textbooks—have barely managed to scratch the surface. As I see it, the problem is not that polarized role playing (man as doer; woman as bystander) and exaggerated portrayals of the female body as passive sex object are simply "demeaning" to women's dignity and self-conception, or that such portrayals fail to provide positive role models for young girls, but that cultural sexism is a conscious form of female degradation designed to boost the male ego by offering "proof" of his native superiority (and of female inferiority) everywhere he looks.

Critics of the women's movement, when they are not faulting us for being slovenly, straggly-haired, construction-booted, whiny sore losers who refuse to accept our female responsibilities, often profess to see a certain inexplicable Victorian primness and antisexual prudery in our attitudes and responses. "Come on, gals," they say in essence, "don't you know that your battle for female liberation is part of our larger battle for sexual liberation? Free yourselves from all your old hang-ups! Stop pretending that you are actually offended by those four-letter words and animal noises we grunt in your direction on the street in appreciation of your womanly charms. When we plaster your faceless naked body on the cover of our slick magazines, which sell millions of copies, we do it in sensual obeisance to your timeless beauty—which, by our estimation, ceases to be timeless at age twenty or thereabouts. If we feel the need for a little fun and go out and rent the body of a prostitute for a half hour or so, we are merely engaging in a mutual act between two consenting adults, and what's it got to do with you? When we turn our movie theaters into showcases for pornographic films and convert our bookstores to outlets for mass-produced obscene smut, not only should you marvel at the wonders of our free-enterprise system, but you should applaud us for pushing back the barriers of repressive middle-class morality, and for our strenuous defense of all the civil liberties you hold so dear, because we have made obscenity the new frontier in defense of freedom of speech, that noble liberal tradition. And surely you're not against civil liberties and freedom of speech, now, are you?"

The case against pornography and the case against toleration of prostitution are central to the fight against rape, and if it angers a large part of the liberal population to be so informed, then I would question in turn the political understanding of such liberals and their true concern for the rights of women. Or to put it more gently, a feminist analysis approaches all prior assumptions, including those of the great, unquestioned liberal tradition, with a certain open-minded suspicion, for all prior traditions have worked against the cause of women and no set of values, including that of tolerant liberals, is above review or challenge. After all, the liberal *politik* has had less input from the feminist perspective than from any other modern source; it does not by its own considerable virtue embody a perfection of ideals, it has no special claim on goodness, rather, it is most receptive to those values to which it has been made sensitive by others.

The defense lawyer mentality had such a hold over the liberal tradition that when we in the women's movement first began to politicize rape back in 1971, and found ourselves on the side of the prosecutor's office in demanding that New York State's rape laws be changed to eliminate the requirement of corroborative proof, the liberal establishment as represented by the American Civil Liberties Union was up in arms. Two years later the ACLU had become sensitized to the plight of rape victims under the rules of law, thanks to the lobbying efforts of feminist lawyers, and once this new concern for rape victims was balanced against the ACLU's longstanding and just concern for the rights of all defendants, the civil-liberties organization withdrew its opposition to corroboration repeal. This, I believe, was a philosophic change of significant proportions, and perhaps it heralds major changes to come. In any event, those of us who know our history recall that when the women's liberation movement was birthed by the radical left, the first serious struggle we faced was to free ourselves from the structures, thought processes and priorities of what we came to call the *male* left—and so if we now find ourselves in philosophic disagreement with the thought processes and priorities of what has been no less of a male liberal tradition, we should not find it surprising.

Once we accept as basic truth that rape is not a crime of irrational, impulsive, uncontrollable lust, but is a deliberate, hostile, violent act of degradation and possession on the part of a would-be conqueror, designed to intimidate and inspire fear, we must look toward those elements in our culture that promote and propagandize these attitudes, which offer men, and in particular, impressionable, adolescent males, who form the potential raping population, the ideology and psychologic encouragement to commit their acts of aggression *without awareness, for the most part, that they have committed a punishable crime,* let alone a moral wrong. The myth of the heroic rapist that permeates false notions of masculinity, from the successful seducer to the man who "takes what he wants when he wants it," is inculcated in young boys from the time they first become aware that being a male means access to certain mysterious rites and privileges, including the right to buy a woman's body. When young men learn that females may be bought for a price, and that acts of sex command set prices, then how should they not also conclude that that which may be bought may also be taken without the civility of a monetary exchange?

That there *might* be a connection between prostitution and rape is certainly not a new idea. Operating from the old (and discredited) lust, drive and relief theory, men have occasionally put forward the notion that the way to control criminal rape is to ensure the ready accessibility of female bodies at a reasonable price through the legalization of prostitution, so that the male impulse might be satisfied with ease, efficiency and a minimum of bother.

Alas for these androcentric pragmatists, even Dr. Kinsey could unearth "no adequate data to prove the truth or falsity" of such a connection. Twenty years after Kinsey others of a similar mind were still trying, although the evidence still suggested that men who make frequent use of brothels are several years older than men who are usually charged with criminal rape. To my mind the experience of the American military in Vietnam, where brothels for GI's were officially sanctioned, even incorporated into the base-camp recreation areas, should prove conclusively that the availability of sex for a small price is no deterrent to the decision to rape, any more than the availability of a base-camp shooting range is a deterrent to the killing of unarmed civilians and children.

But my horror at the idea of legalized prostitution is not that it doesn't work as a rape deterrent, but that it institutionalizes the concept that it is man's monetary right, if not his divine right, to gain access to the female body, and that sex is a female service that should not be denied the civilized male. Perpetuation of the concept that the "powerful male impulse" must be satisfied with immediacy by a cooperative class of women, set aside and expressly licensed for this purpose, is part and parcel of the mass psychology of rape. Indeed, until the day is reached when prostitution is totally eliminated (a millennium that will not arrive until men, who create the demand, and not women who supply it, are fully prosecuted under the law), the false perception of sexual access as an adjunct of male power and privilege will continue to fuel the rapist mentality.

Pornography has been so thickly glossed over with the patina of chic these days in the name of verbal freedom and sophistication that important distinctions between freedom of political expression (a democratic necessity), honest sex education for children (a societal good) and ugly smut (the deliberate devaluation of the role of women through obscene, distorted depictions) have been hopelessly confused. Part of the problem is that those who traditionally have been the most vigorous opponents of porn are often those same people who shudder at the explicit mention of any sexual subject. Under their watchful, vigilante eyes, frank and free dissemination of educational materials relating to abortion, contraception, the act of birth, and female biology in general is also dangerous, subversive and dirty. (I am not unmindful that a frank and free discussion of rape, "the unspeakable crime," might well give these righteous vigilantes further cause to shudder.) Because the battle lines were falsely drawn a long time ago, before there was a vocal women's movement, the anti-pornography forces appear to be, for the most part, religious, Southern, conservative and right-wing, while the pro-porn forces are identified as Eastern, atheistic and liberal.

But a woman's perspective demands a totally new alignment, or at least a fresh appraisal. The majority report of the President's Commission on Obscenity and Pornography (1970), a report that argued strongly for the removal of all legal restrictions on pornography, soft and hard, made plain that 90 percent of all pornographic material is geared to the male heterosexual market (the other 10 percent is geared to the male homosexual taste), that buyers of porn are "predominantly white, middle-class, middle-aged married males" and that the graphic depictions, the meat and potatoes of porn, are of the naked female body and of the multiplicity of acts done to that body.

Discussing the content of stag films, "a familiar and firmly established part of the American scene," the commission report dutifully, if foggily, explained, "Because pornography historically has been thought to be primarily a masculine interest, the emphasis in stag films seems to represent the preferences of the middle-class American male. Thus male homosexuality and bestiality are relatively rare, while lesbianism is rather common."

The commissioners in this instance had merely verified what purveyors of porn have always known: hard-core pornography is not a celebration of sexual freedom; it is a cynical exploitation of female sexual activity through the device of making all such activity, and consequently all females, "dirty." Heterosexual male consumers of pornography are frankly turned on by watching lesbians in action (although never in the final scenes, but always as a curtain raiser); they are turned off with the sudden swiftness of a water faucet by watching naked men act upon each other. One study quoted in the commission report came to the unastounding conclusion that "seeing a stag film in the presence of male peers bolsters masculine esteem." Indeed. The men in groups who watch the films, it is important to note, are *not* naked.

When male response to pornography is compared to female response, a pronounced difference in attitude emerges. According to the commission, "Males report being more highly aroused by depictions of nude females, and show more interest in depictions of nude females than [do] females." Quoting the figures of Alfred Kinsey, the commission noted that a majority of males (77 percent) were "aroused" by visual depictions of explicit sex while a majority of females (68 percent) were not aroused. Further, "females more often than males reported 'disgust' and 'offense.'"

From whence comes this female disgust and offense? Are females sexually backward or more conservative by nature? The gut distaste that a majority of women feel when we look at pornography, a distaste that, incredibly, it is no longer fashionable to admit, comes, I think, from the gut knowledge that we and our bodies are being stripped, exposed and contorted for the purpose of ridicule to bolster that "masculine esteem" which gets its kick and sense of power from viewing females as anonymous, panting playthings, adult toys, dehumanized objects to be used, abused, broken and discarded.

This, of course, is also the philosophy of rape. It is no accident (for what else could be its purpose?) that females in the pornographic genre are depicted in two cleanly delineated roles: as virgins who are caught and "banged" or as nymphomaniacs who are never sated. The most popular and prevalent pornographic fantasy combines the two: an innocent, untutored female is raped and "subjected to unnatural practices" that turn her into a raving, slobbering nymphomaniac, a dependent sexual slave who can never get enough of the big, male cock.

There can be no "equality" in porn, no female equivalent, no turning of the tables in the name of bawdy fun. Pornography, like rape, is a male invention, designed to dehumanize women, to reduce the female to an object of sexual access, not to free sensuality from moralistic or parental inhibition. The staple of porn will always be the naked female body, breasts and genitals exposed, because as man devised it, her naked body is the female's "shame," her private parts the private property of man, while his are the ancient, holy, universal, patriarchal instrument of his power, his rule by force over her.

Pornography is the undiluted essence of anti-female propaganda. Yet the very same liberals who were so quick to understand the method and purpose behind the mighty propaganda machine of Hitler's Third Reich, the consciously spewed-out anti-Semitic caricatures and obscenities that gave an ideological base to the

Holocaust and the Final Solution, the very same liberals who, enlightened by blacks, searched their own conscience and came to understand that their tolerance of "nigger" jokes and portrayals of shuffling, rolling-eyed servants in movies perpetuated the degrading myths of black inferiority and gave an ideological base to the continuation of black oppression—these very same liberals now fervidly maintain that the hatred and contempt for women that find expression in four-letter words used as expletives and in what are quaintly called "adult" or "erotic" books and movies are a valid extension of freedom of speech that must be preserved as a Constitutional right.

To defend the right of a lone, crazed American Nazi to grind out propaganda calling for the extermination of all Jews, as the ACLU has done in the name of free speech, is, after all, a self-righteous and not particularly courageous stand, for American Jewry is not currently threatened by storm troopers, concentration camps and imminent extermination, but I wonder if the ACLU's position might change if, come tomorrow morning, the bookstores and movie theaters lining Forty-second Street in New York City were devoted not to the humiliation of women by rape and torture, as they currently are, but to a systematized, commercially successful propaganda machine depicting the sadistic pleasures of gassing Jews or lynching blacks?

Is this analogy extreme? Not if you are a woman who is conscious of the ever-present threat of rape and the proliferation of a cultural ideology that makes it sound like "liberated" fun. The majority report of the President's Commission on Obscenity and Pornography tried to pooh-pooh the opinion of law enforcement agencies around the country that claimed their own concrete experience with offenders who were caught with the stuff led them to conclude that pornographic material is a causative factor in crimes of sexual violence. The commission maintained that it was not possible at this time to scientifically prove or disprove such a connection.

But does one need scientific methodology in order to conclude that the anti-female propaganda that permeates our nation's cultural output promotes a climate in which acts of sexual hostility directed against women are not only tolerated but ideologically encouraged? A similar debate has raged for many years over whether or not the extensive glorification of violence (the gangster as hero; the loving treatment accorded bloody shoot-'em-ups in movies, books and on TV) has a causal effect, a direct relationship to the rising rate of crime, particularly among youth. Interestingly enough, in this area—nonsexual and not specifically related to abuses against women—public opinion seems to be swinging to the position that explicit violence in the entertainment media does have a deleterious effect; it makes violence commonplace, numbingly routine and no longer morally shocking.

More to the point, those who call for a curtailment of scenes of violence in movies and on television in the name of sensitivity, good taste and what's best for our children are not accused of being pro-censorship or against freedom of speech. Similarly, minority group organizations, black, Hispanic, Japanese, Italian, Jewish, or American Indian, that campaign against ethnic slurs and demeaning portrayals in movies, on television shows and in commercials are perceived as waging a just political fight, for if a minority group claims to be offended by a specific portrayal, be it Little Black Sambo or the Frito Bandido, and relates it to a history of ridicule and oppression, few liberals would dare to trot out a Constitutional argument in theoretical opposition, not if they wish to maintain their liberal credentials. Yet when it comes to the treatment of women, the liberal consciousness remains fiercely obdurate, refusing to be budged, for the sin of appearing square or prissy in the age of the so-called sexual revolution has become the worst offense of all.

A law that reflects the female reality and a social system that no longer shuts women out of its enforcement and does not promote a masculine ideology of rape will go a long way toward the elimination of crimes of sexual violence, but the last line of defense shall always be our female bodies and our female minds. In making rape a *speakable* crime, not a matter of shame, the women's movement has already fired the first retaliatory shots in a war as ancient as civilization. When, just a few years ago, we began to hold our speak-outs on rape, our conferences, borrowing a church meeting hall for an afternoon, renting a high-school auditorium and some classrooms for a weekend of workshops and discussion, the world out there, the world outside of radical feminism, thought it was all very funny.

"You're talking about *rape*? Incredible! A *political* crime against women? How is a sex crime political? You're actually having women give testimony about their own rapes and what happened to them afterwards, the police, the hospitals, the courts? Far out!" And then the nervous giggles that betray confusion, fear and shame disappeared and in their place was the dim recognition that in daring to speak the unspoken, women had uncovered yet another part of our oppression, perhaps the central key: historic physical repression, a conscious process of intimidation, guilt and fear.

Within two years the world out there had stopped laughing, and the movement had progressed beyond the organizational forms of speak-outs and conferences, our internal consciousness-raising, to community outreach programs that were imaginative, original and unprecedented: rape crisis centers with a telephone hot line staffed twenty-four hours a day to provide counseling, procedural information and sisterly solidarity to recent rape victims and even to those whose assault had taken place years ago but who never had the chance to talk it out with other women and release their suppressed rage; rape legislation study groups to work up model codes based on a fresh approach to the law and to work with legislators to get new laws adopted; anti-rape projects in conjunction with the emergency ward of a city hospital, in close association with policewomen staffing newly formed sex crime analysis squads and investigative units. With pamphlets, newsletters, bumper stickers, "Wanted" posters, combative slogans—"STOP RAPE"; "WAR— WOMEN AGAINST RAPE"; "SMASH SEXISM, DISARM RAPISTS!"—and with classes in self-defense, women turned around and seized the offensive.

The wonder of all this female activity, decentralized grassroots organizations and programs that sprung up independently in places like Seattle, Indianapolis, Ann Arbor, Toronto, and Boulder, Colorado, is that none of it had been predicted, encouraged, or faintly suggested by men anywhere in their stern rules of caution, their friendly advice, their fatherly solicitude in more than five thousand years of written history. That women should organize to combat rape was a women's movement invention.

Men are not unmindful of the rape problem. To the contrary, their paternalistic codes reserved the harshest penalties for a violation of their property. But given an approach to rape that saw the crime as an illegal encroachment by an unlicensed intruder, a stranger come into their midst, the advice they gave (and still try to give) was all of one piece: a set of rules and regulations designed to keep their property penned in, much as a sheepherder might try to keep his flock protected from an outlaw rustler by taking precautions against their straying too far from the fold. By seeing the rapist always as a stranger, never as one of their own, and by viewing the female as a careless, dumb creature with an unfortunate tendency to stray, they exhorted, admonished and warned the female to hide herself from male eyes as much as possible. In short, they told her not to claim the privileges they reserved for themselves. Such advice—well intentioned, solicitous and genuinely concerned—succeeded only in further aggravating the problem, for the message they gave was to live a life of fear, and to it they appended the dire warning that the woman who did not follow the rules must be held responsible for her own violation.

Clinton Duffy, the famous warden of San Quentin, couldn't understand why women didn't imprison themselves under maximum security conditions for their own protection. He wrote, "Many break the most elementary rules of caution every day. The particularly flagrant violators, those who go to barrooms alone, or accept pickups from strangers, or wear unusually tight sweaters and skirts, or make a habit of teasing, become rape bait by their actions alone. When it happens they have nobody to blame but themselves."

Duffy heaped scorn on women who "regularly break common-sense rules of caution" by neglecting to draw the shades or put out the light while undressing, by forgetting to lock all doors and windows, by failing "to report telephone callers who hang up when they answer, or suspicious-looking loiterers," by letting a lone male stranger into the house, by walking home alone late at night. "If it's impossible for a woman to keep off lonely streets at night," he instructed, "she should walk near the curb with her head up and her eyes straight forward, move rapidly and keep going. . . . Women in these situations should carry a police whistle in the palm of their hand until they are out of the danger area. Ridiculous as it may sound," he concluded, "women should be careful to hang underwear out to dry in the least conspicuous places on the line. If a woman lives alone she shouldn't hang it outside at all."

A fairly decent article on rape in the March, 1974, issue of *The Reader's Digest* was written by two men who felt obliged to warn,

Don't broadcast the fact that you live alone or with another woman. List only your last name and initial on the mailbox and in the phone book. Before entering your car, check to see if anyone is hiding on the rear seat or on the rear floor. If you're alone in a car, keep the doors locked and the windows rolled up. If you think someone is following you . . . do not go directly home if there is no adult male there. Possible weapons are a hatpin, corkscrew, pen, keys, umbrella. If no weapons are available, fight back physically only if you feel you can do so with telling effect.

What immediately pops into mind after reading the advice of Warden Duffy and *The Reader's Digest* is the old-time stand-up comedian's favorite figure of ridicule, the hysterical old maid armed with hatpin and umbrella who looks under the bed each night before retiring. Long a laughable stereotype of sexual repression, it now appears that the crazy old lady was a pioneer of sound mind after all.

But the negative value of this sort of advice, I'm afraid, far outweighs the positive. What it tells us, implicitly and explicitly, is:

1. A woman alone probably won't be able to defend herself. Another woman who might possibly come to her aid will be of no use whatsoever.

2. Despite the fact that it is men who are the rapists, a woman's ultimate security lies in being accompanied by men at all times.

3. A woman who claims to value her sexual integrity cannot expect the same amount of freedom and independence that men routinely enjoy. Even a small pleasure like taking a spin in an automobile with the windows open is dangerous, reckless behavior.

4. In the exercise of rational caution, a woman should engage in an amazing amount of pretense. She should pretend she has a male protector even if she hasn't. She should deny or obscure her personal identity, life-style and independence, and function on a sustained level of suspicion that approaches a clinical definition of paranoia.

Of course I think all people, female and male, child and adult, must be alert and on guard against the warning signs of criminal violence and should take care in potentially hazardous situations, such as a dark, unfamiliar street at night, or an unexpected knock on the door, but to impose a special burden of caution on women is no solution at all. There can be no private solutions to the problem of rape. A woman who follows this sort of special cautionary advice to the letter and thinks she is acting in society's interest—or even in her own personal interest—is deluding herself rather sadly. While the risk to one potential victim might be slightly diminished (and I even doubt this, since I have known of nuns who were raped within walled convents), not only does the number of potential rapists on the loose remain constant, but the ultimate effect of rape upon the woman's mental and emotional health has been accomplished *even without the act.* For to accept a special burden of self-protection is to reinforce the concept that women must live and move about in fear and can never expect to achieve the personal freedom, independence and self-assurance of men.

That's what rape is all about, isn't it? And a possible deepdown reason why even the best of our concerned, well-meaning men run to stereotypic warnings when they seek to grapple with the problem of rape deterrence is that they *prefer* to see rape as a woman's problem, rather than as a societal problem resulting from a distorted masculine philosophy of aggression. For when men raise the spectre of the unknown rapist, they refuse to take psychologic responsibility for the nature of his act.

We know, or at least the statistics tell us, that no more than half of all reported rapes are the work of strangers, and in the hidden statistics, those four out of five rapes that go unreported, the percent committed by total strangers is probably lower. The man who jumps out of the alley or crawls through the window is the man who, if caught, will be called "the rapist" by his fellow men. But the known man who presses his advantage, who uses his position of authority, who forces his attentions (fine Victorian phrase), who will not take "No" for an answer, who assumes that sexual access is his right-of-way and physical aggression his right-on expression of masculinity, conquest and power is no less of a rapist—yet the chance that this man will be brought to justice, even under the best of circumstances, is comparatively small.

I am of the opinion that the most perfect rape laws in the land, strictly enforced by the best concerned citizens, will not be enough to stop rape. Obvious offenders will be punished, and that in itself will be a significant change, but the huge gray area of sexual exploitation, of women who are psychologically coerced into acts of intercourse they do not desire because they do not have the wherewithal to physically, or even psychologically, resist, will remain a problem beyond any possible solution of criminal justice. It would be deceitful to claim that the murky gray area of male sexual aggression and female passivity and submission can ever be made amenable to legal divination—nor should it be, in the final analysis. Nor should a feminist advocate to her sisters that the best option in a threatening, unpleasant situation is to endure the insult and later take her case to the courts.

Unfortunately for strict constructionists and those with neat, orderly minds, the male-female sexual dynamic at this stage in our human development lends itself poorly to objective arbitration. A case of rape and a case of unpleasant but not quite criminal sexual extortion in which a passive, egoless woman succumbs because it never occurred to her that she might, with effort, repel the advance (and afterward quite justifiably feels "had") flow from the same oppressive male ideology, and the demarcation line between the two is far from clear. But these latter cases, of which there are many, reflect not only the male ideology of rape but a female paralysis of will, the result of a deliberate, powerful and destructive "feminine" conditioning.

The psychologic edge men hold in a situation characterized by sexual aggression is far more critical to the final outcome than their larger size and heavier weight. They know they know how to fight, for they have been trained and encouraged to use their bodies aggressively and competitively since early childhood. Young girls, on the other hand, are taught to disdain physical combat, healthy sports competition, and winning, because such activities dangerously threaten the conventional societal view of what is appropriate, ladylike, feminine behavior. The case for a strong mind in a strong body as a necessary step in the battle for equality (which Susan B. Anthony argued for vehemently in the earliest issues of her feminist newspaper, *The Revolution*) is being dramatically and effectively argued each day by our professional female athletes—who at long last are becoming female stars—and by recent struggles to integrate the Little League and to equalize expenditures for female sports programs in grade schools, high schools and colleges.

This sudden upsurge of interest in female athletics is more than a matter of giving girls who like sports a chance to fully explore their potential. It is based on a new female recognition (something men have always known) that there are important lessons to be learned from sports competition, among them that winning is the result of hard, sustained and serious training, cool, clever strategy that includes the use of tricks and bluffs, and a positive mind-set that puts all reflex systems on "go." This knowledge, and the chance to put it in practice, is precisely what women have been conditioned to abjure.

It is no wonder, then, that most women confronted by physical aggression fall apart at the seams and suffer a paralysis of will. We have been trained to cry, to wheedle, to plead, to look for a male protector, but we have never been trained to fight and win.

Prohibitions against a fighting female go back to the Bible. In one of the more curious passages in Deuteronomy it is instructed that when two men are fighting and the wife of one seeks to come to his aid and "drag her husband clear of his opponent, if she puts out her hand and catches hold of the man's genitals, you shall cut off her hand and show her no mercy." When the patriarchs wrote the law, it would seem, they were painfully cognizant of woman's one natural advantage in combat and were determined to erase it from her memory.

Man's written law evolved from a rudimentary system of retaliatory force, a system to which women were not particularly well adapted to begin with, and from which women were deliberately excluded, ostensibly for our own protection, as time went by. Combat has been such a traditional, exclusionary province of man that the very idea of a fighting woman often brings laughter, distaste or disbelief and the opinion that it must be "unnatural." In a confusion partially of their own making, local police precincts put out contradictory messages: they "unfound" a rape case because, by the rule of their own male logic, the woman did not show normal resistance; they report on an especially brutal rape case and announce to the press that the multiple stab wounds were the work of an assailant who was enraged because the woman resisted.

Unthinkingly cruel, because it is deceptive, is the confidential advice given from men to women (it appears in The Reader's Digest article), or even from women to women in some feminist literature, that a sharp kick to the groin or a thumb in the eye will work miracles. Such advice is often accompanied by a diagram in which the vulnerable points of the human anatomy are clearly marked—as if the mere knowledge of these pressure spots can translate itself into devastating action. It is true that this knowledge has been deliberately obscured or withheld from us in the past, but mere knowledge is not enough. What women need is systematic training in self-defense that begins in childhood, so that the inhibition resulting from the prohibition may be overcome.

It would be decidedly less than honest if at this juncture I did not admit that my researches for this book included a three-month training program in jujitsu and karate, three nights a week, two and a half hours a night, that ended summarily one evening when I crashed to the mat and broke my collarbone. I lost one month of writing and the perfect symmetry of my clavicular structure, but I gained a new identification with the New York Mets' injury list, a recognition that age thirty-eight is not the most propitious time in life to begin to learn how to kick and hit and break a stranglehold, and a new and totally surprising awareness of my body's potential to inflict real damage. I learned I had natural weapons that I didn't know I possessed, like elbows and knees. I learned how to kick backward as well as forward. I learned how to fight dirty, and I learned that I loved it.

Most surprising to me, I think, was the recognition that these basic aggressive movements, the sudden twists, jabs and punches that were so foreign to my experience and ladylike existence, were the stuff that all little boys grow up learning, that boy kids are applauded for mastering while girl kids are put in fresh white pinafores and patent-leather Mary Janes and told not to muss them up. And did that early difference in rearing ever raise its draconic head! At the start of our lessons our Japanese instructor freely invited all the women in the class, one by one, to punch him in the chest. It was not a foolhardy invitation, for we discovered that the inhibition against hitting was so strong in each of us that on the first try none of us could make physical contact. Indeed, the inhibition against striking out proved to be a greater hindrance to our becoming fighting women than our pathetic underdeveloped muscles. (Improvement in both departments was amazingly swift.)

Not surprisingly, the men in our class did not share our inhibitions in the slightest. Aggressive physical grappling was part of their heritage, not ours. And yet, and yet . . . we women discovered in wonderment that as we learned to place our kicks and jabs with precision we were actually able to inspire fear in the men.

We *could* hurt them, we learned to our astonishment, and hurt them hard at the core of their sexual being—if we broke that Biblical injunction.

Is it possible that there is some sort of metaphysical justice in the anatomical fact that the male sex organ, which has been misused from time immemorial as a weapon of terror against women, should have at its root an awkward place of painful vulnerability? Acutely conscious of their susceptibility to damage, men have protected their testicles throughout history with armor, supports and forbidding codes of "clean," above-the-belt fighting. A gentleman's agreement is understandable—among gentlemen. When women are threatened, as I learned in my self-defense class, "Kick him in the balls, it's your best maneuver." How strange it was to hear for the first time in my life that women could fight back, *should* fight back and make full use of a natural advantage; that it is *in our interest* to know how to do it. How strange it was to understand with the full force of unexpected revelation that male allusions to psychological defeat, particularly at the hands of a woman, were couched in phrases like emasculation, castration and ball-breaking because of that very special physical vulnerability.

Fighting back. On a multiplicity of levels, that is the activity we must engage in, together, if we—women—are to redress the imbalance and rid ourselves and men of the ideology of rape.

Rape can be eradicated, not merely controlled or avoided on an individual basis, but the approach must be long-range and cooperative, and must have the understanding and good will of many men as well as women.

My purpose in this book has been to give rape its history. Now we must deny it a future.

ACKNOWLEDGMENTS

In the four years from the day I made the firm decision to write a book about rape to the day I turned the manuscript in to my publisher, I incurred many debts: ideological, emotional and financial. These categories did not remain separate and distinct; they crisscrossed and overlapped in friendship and support.

An ideological debt is something that only another movement person can truly understand. I was there when we in the women's movement first began to explore the many aspects of rape, and I listened to those (Diane Crothers, Sara Pines, Lilia Melani) who understood the issues far better than I. The movement also made my book possible by its courage and imagination, and by its contribution of personal testimony that opened up the subject of rape from a woman's point of view for the first time in history. Three events deserve specific mention, and I am proud that they were organized by a group to which, I am fond of saying, "I gave my life's blood." These were: The New York Radical Feminist Speak-Out on Rape, January 24, 1971; The New York Radical Feminist Conference on Rape, April 17, 1971; and the joint New York Radical Feminist–National Black Feminist Organization Speak-Out on Rape and Sexual Abuse, August 25, 1974.

To piece together the current picture and at the same time to try to reconstruct rape's history required a vast intake of research materials. People who knew me casually and people who knew me well didn't wait to be asked. They supplied leads, sources, citations and newspaper clippings that I never could have amassed on my own. At one point I drew up a list of what I had begun to think of as my private journalists-and-feminists rape network. Among my contributors were: Ann Lane, Louise

Thompson, Doris O'Donnell, Gloria Steinem, Betsy Steuart, Ben Bradlee, Bill Leonard, Waltraut Eschenbach, Ann Blackman, Mary Anne Krupsak, David Gurin, Jackie Bernard, Vivien Leone, Kay Schurr, James Aronson, Minda Bikman, Alix Kates Shulman, Lucy Komisar, Shelley Clayman, Kirsten Grimstad, Susan Rennie, Roslyn Fliegel, Elizabeth Evans, Irene Mahoney, Ruth Gross, Noemie Emery, Barbara Mehrhof, Pam Kearon, Mary Orovan, Holly Forsman, Letty Cottin Pogrebin, Sue Davis, Helene Silverstein, Evan Morley, Howard Meyer, Mary-Helen Mautner, Karen Kollias, Allan M. Siegal, Al McCullough, Ann Pollon, Joan Goulianos, Jane Jacobs, Marta Vivas, Grace Lichtenstein, Len Sandler, Nora Ephron, Fran Goldin, Jonathan Goldberg, Signe Hammer, Barbara Janes, Jo Roman, Arthur Rubine, Vicky Schultz, Linda Farin.

Several libraries proved essential. A field trip to the New York State Library in Albany introduced me to abstracts and indexes I didn't know existed. The month I camped out at the A. A. Brill Collection of the New York Psychoanalytic Institute gave me access to the best collection of Freudian literature in the nation, and a chance to read it in a most pleasant setting. The days and nights that turned into weeks when I roamed the subterranean stacks of the NYU Law Library as a "nonstudent with special privileges" made me indeed feel privileged. Columbia University's International Law Library and the National Archives in Washington held documents unavailable elsewhere.

But how can I adequately thank that great institution, the New York Public Library, that became my work space and psychologic home for most of the writing of this book? More than anything else, my book is a product of the research collections of the New York Public Library. During the three years I daily walked its marble halls, became acquainted with its awesome facilities and leaned on the expertise of the librarians in the special collections (most particularly, American History and the Jewish Division), got to know the guards, clerks and book retrievers and ate lunch in the employees' cafeteria, my identification with "The New York Public" became so complete that if someone asked me what I did for a living I'd absent-mindedly answer, "I work in the Forty-second Street library," which was literally true.

My book was written inside the library in a very special place called the Frederick Lewis Allen Room, where I was given a desk for my typewriter and a shelf for my books. I was also given the companionship of a score of writers who became my own private seminar in how to get the job done. The interrelationship of my Allen Room friends and me is too complex to detail; suffice it to say that each of us struggled together, respectful of one another's progress, in a supportive environment dedicated to hard work and accomplishment, a writer's Utopia or close to it.

Early on it became apparent that money, or lack of money, was a problem that had to be faced. Eden Lipson, John J. Simon and Nancy Milford were among those whose advice I solicited and followed. Grants from the Alicia Patterson Foundation and the Louis M. Rabinowitz Foundation supported me for two full years. Richard H. Nolte, Jane Hartwig and Victor Rabinowitz deserve special thanks for rooting for me with few questions asked, and a debt of gratitude is owed all the good people who wrote those enthusiastic letters of recommendation.

To sustain a relationship with me over the long haul, all friends had to become involved with my sole obsession, "the book." That they did attests more to their character than to the rewards of listening to my one subject of conversation. Four people bore the major brunt, and each contributed so much input that I am at a loss to adequately define their roles. Alison Owings, in Washington and New York, had an unerring way of always being a half step ahead of wherever I happened to be in a chapter; her perceptions were uncanny, her contributions were always on target. Florence Rush patiently worked out many philosophic and technical problems in animated, late-night discussions that only two people who shared the same specific interest could have. Jan Goodman loyally read the work in progress whenever I thrust it at her, and used her incisive legal mind to tell me forthrightly what should be cut and what was unclear. She argued intrepidly when argument was necessary and boosted me in a hundred ways when I needed concrete aid. It was the lot of Kevin Cooney to live with the book as he lived with me: research gathering, stylistic impasses, failures of nerve—all mine—dominated our life and Kevin bore them with an even-handed stoicism that extended itself to the three-o'clock-in-the-morning tremors when everything seemed too diffuse and complicated to ever get done. It seems clear to me now, as I write this, that with the support I got from those close and dear to me, of course the work got done.

SOURCE NOTES

1. The Mass Psychology of Rape: An Introduction

(11) rapists as degenerate, imbecilic men: Richard von Krafft-Ebing, *Psychopathia Sexualis* (1886), trans. from the Latin by Harry E. Wedeck, New York: Putnam, 1965, p. 435.

(12) Bebel on rape: August Bebel, *Women Under Socialism* (1883), trans. from the German by Daniel DeLeon, New York: Labor News Press, 1904, p. 27. See also pp. 29, 56–58.

(12) "masculine ideology of rape": Wilhelm Reich, *The Sexual Revolution* (1945), trans. from the German by Theodore P. Wolfe, New York: Farrar, Straus, 1969, p. 27.

(13) Goodall on chimpanzees: Jane van Lawick-Goodall, *In the Shadow of Man*, New York: Dell, 1972, pp. 193–194.

(13) "The male monkey": Leonard Williams, *Man and Monkey*, London: Deutsch, 1967, p. 157. See also pp. 80, 88.

2. In the Beginning Was the Law

(17) Forcible seizure perfectly acceptable: William Blackstone, *Commentaries on the Laws of England*, 10th ed., London, 1787, Vol. IV, p. 208.

(17) terror of being "rapt": Amy Kelly, *Eleanor of Aquitaine and the Four Kings*, New York: Random House Vintage ed., 1959, p. 4.

(17) Bride capture, Tasadays: John Noble Wilford, "Stone-Age Tribe in Philippines Is Imperiled," *New York Times*, Oct. 17, 1971.

(17) Bride capture, Sicily: Peter Kayser, "Situationer—Women," Reuter, Rome, Aug. 7, 1973: "In Sicily another sex ritual was recently acted out when a shepherd, Guiseppe Ilardo, 30, kidnapped 18-year-old Anna Puccia, raped her and then fled hoping she would marry him to clear her name. Following the traditional Sicilian scenario, he then

asked for the girl's hand through some friends but Anna refused, clearing the way for police to arrest Ilardo and jail him on rape charges. Her action went strongly against all tradition . . ."

(17) "Those whom we marry": Robert A. LeVine, "Gusii Sex Offenses: A Study in Social Control," *American Anthropologist*, Vol. 61 (Dec. 1959), p. 966.

(18) Code of Hammurabi: Chilperic Edwards, *The Hammurabi Code*, London: Watts, 1921, pp. 27–31.

(19) "let him first cast a stone": John 8:7.

(19) Hebrew social order: Deuteronomy 22:13–29.

(20) *lex talionis*, Assyrians: Louis M. Epstein, *Sex Laws and Customs in Judaism*, New York: Bloch Pub. Co., 1948, p. 180.

(20) Dinah: Genesis 34.

(21) Levite, Benjamites and the daughters of Shiloh: Judges 19–21.

(22) Potiphar's wife: Genesis 39.

(22) a staple in many cultures, etc.: H. R. Hays, *The Dangerous Sex* (1964), New York: Pocket books, 1972, p. 109.

(23) "she herself became a litigant": Epstein, p. 188.

(23) Under Talmudic interpretation: Epstein, pp. 183–191. I am also indebted to Epstein for his interpretation of Biblical legislation, pp. 179–182, and for his brilliant concept of "theft of virginity," which I have shamelessly appropriated.

(23) Maimonides on monetary compensation: Epstein, p. 188 n.

(23) *Footnote*, Maimonides' sex manual: Moses Maimonides, "On Sexual Intercourse," *Medical Historical Studies of Medieval Jewish Medical Works*, Brooklyn: Rambash Pub. Co., 1961, Vol. 1.

(24) Before the Norman Conquest: Blackstone, IV p. 211.

(24) "the lands passing": G. G. Coulton, *Medieval Panorama*, Cambridge, Eng.: The University Press, 1938, pp. 48–49.

(24) "trading in marriages": *Ibid.*

(24) Henry VII rules heiress-stealing a felony: Blackstone, IV, p. 208.

(24) rule of King Athelstan: Samuel E. Thorne, trans. and ed., *Bracton on the Laws and Customs of England*, Cambridge, Mass.: Belknap Press of Harvard, 1968, Vol. II, p. 418.

(25) accept her ravisher in marriage: *Ibid.*

(25) Punishment reduced by William the Conqueror: Blackstone, IV, p. 211.

(25) "woman's . . . inability to fight": Frederick Pollock and Frederic William Maitland, *The History of English Law Before the Time of Edward I* (1895), Cambridge, Eng.: The University Press, 1968, Vol. I, p. 485.

(25) "Let him lose his eyes": Bracton, II, pp. 414–415.

(26) only suits a woman could bring: Bracton, II, p. 419.

(26) "She must go at once": Bracton, II, p. 415.

(26) "that he had her as his concubine": Bracton, II, pp. 416–417.

(27) "a common person": Bracton, II, p. 417.

(27) "As a rule": Sidney Painter, *A History of the Middle Ages*, New York: Knopf, 1960, p. 120.

(27) savage wife beating, etc.: *Ibid.*

(28) *jus primae noctis*: For an interesting discussion, see August Bebel, *Woman Under Socialism* (1883), trans. from the German by Daniel DeLeon, New York: Labor News Press, 1904, pp. 56–58.

(28) Lord Baltimore and Sarah Woodcock: *The Trial of Frederick Calvert Esq., the baron of Baltimore in the kingdom of Ireland, for a Rape on the Body of Sarah Woodcock,* held at the Kingston Assizes for the County of Surry, taken in shorthand by Joseph Gurney, London: W. Owen, 1768.

(28) justice for "matrons, nuns, widows, concubines and even prostitutes": *Bracton,* II, p. 415.

(28) "Concerning these matters": Pollock and Maitland, Vol. II, pp. 490–492.

(29) Statutes of Westminster: These statutes are recorded in full, with annotations, in Edward Coke, *The Second Part of the Institutes of the Laws of England* (2 vols.), London: W. Clarke, 1809. Westminster I, Cap. 13, enacted in the third year of the reign of Edward I (1275), appears in Vol. 1, pp. 179–181. Westminster II, Cap. 34, enacted in the thirteenth year of Edward's reign (1285), appears in Vol. 2, pp. 432–436. The historic importance of the Westminster rape statutes is confirmed by Pollock and Maitland, among others.

(29) statutory rape derived from these statutes: *American Journal of Legal History,* Vol. 7, 1963, pp. 162–163. See also *South Carolina Law Review,* Vol. 18, 1966, p. 254.

(29) Within marriage no such crime as rape by a husband: Matthew Hale, *History of the Pleas of the Crown,* Philadelphia: R. H. Small, 1847, Vol. I, p. 628.

(30) "If she be of evil fame": Blackstone, IV, p. 213.

3. WAR

(31) "I then told him": George S. Patton, Jr., *War As I Knew It,* Boston: Houghton Mifflin, 1947, p. 23.

(31) knights and pilgrims, First Crusade: Colin Wilson, *A Casebook of Murder,* London: Leslie Frewin, 1969, p. 27.

(31) George Washington's papers: John C. Fitzpatrick, ed., *The Writings of George Washington from the Original Manuscript Sources, 1745–1799,* Washington: U.S. Government Printing Office, 1937, Vol. 19, p. 224.

(32) Rape got out of hand "regrettably": Kasturi Rangan, "Bhutto Regrets 'Crimes' in Bangladesh," *New York Times,* June 29, 1974.

(33) status of women captured in war: Deuteronomy 20:14; 21:10–14.

(34) Augustine on Sabines: Augustine, *City of God* (414), II, 17 (trans. by Henry Bettenson; ed. by David Knowles; Middlesex, Eng.: Penguin, 1972, pp. 66–67).

(34) Totila the Ostrogoth: Thomas A. Walker, *A History of the Law of Nations,* Cambridge, Eng.: The University Press, 1899, Vol. I, p. 65.

(34) Richard II's Articles of War: William Winthrop, *Military Law and Precedents,* Boston: Little, Brown, 1896, Vol. II, p. 1412.

(34) Grotius: Walker, I, p. 316.

(35) "Booty and beauty": For an interesting discussion of this phrase, and how it was pinned on the British, or even on Jackson, see Robin Reilly, *The British at the Gates: The New Orleans Campaign in the War of 1812,* New York: Putnam, 1974, pp. 265–266.

(36) "It so happened": *Memoires de Claude Haton*, Vol. I, pp. 501–502, Paris: 1857. Passage translated for me by Irene Mahoney.

(37) Hundred Years' War: Sidney Painter, *French Chivalry*, Baltimore: Johns Hopkins Press, 1940, pp. 141–146.

(37) *Footnote*, An exception to this rule: See *We Charge Genocide*, New York: Civil Rights Congress, 1951, pp. 124–125; Herbert Aptheker, *History and Reality*, New York: Cameron Associates, 1955, pp. 254–278; and David Breasted, "Two Black GI's on Rape Rap Seek Justice," New York *Daily News*, June 9, 1971.

(38) story of Culloden: John Prebble, *Culloden*, London: Secker & Warburg, 1961, pp. 123, 208, 210, 216, 222, 224, 225, 323.

WORLD WAR I

(41) Toynbee on Germany Army atrocities: See throughout, Arnold Joseph Toynbee, *The German Terror in Belgium*, New York: George H. Doran, 1917; and Arnold Joseph Toynbee, *The German Terror in France*, London: Hodder & Stoughton, 1917.

(42) "Outrages upon the honour of women": J. H. Morgan, *German Atrocities: An Official Investigation*, New York: Dutton, 1916, pp. 81–83. Also quoted in Toynbee, *France*, pp. 210–211.

(43) "not been due to the immobility of the fronts": Toynbee, *Belgium*, p. 16.

(44) "use an atrocity": Harold D. Lasswell, *Propaganda Technique in the World War*, New York: Knopf, 1927, pp. 81–82.

(44) Hillis propaganda: Newell Dwight Hillis, *German Atrocities: Their Nature and Philosophy*, New York: Fleming H. Revell, 1918, pp. 25–26, 54–56.

(47) witty dismissal of rape: James M. Read, *Atrocity Propaganda, 1914–1919*, New Haven: Yale University Press, 1941, pp. 80, 153.

WORLD WAR II

(48) Goebbels himself: Eva Figes, *Patriarchal Attitudes*, New York: Stein and Day, 1970, pp. 133–134.

(48) "Man should be trained": Friedrich Nietzsche, *Thus Spake Zarathustra* (1883), Part One, 18 (*The Philosophy of Nietzsche*, New York: Modern Library, 1927, p. 69).

(49) "Hitler always said": Albert Speer interview, *Playboy*, June 1971, p. 76.

(49) Eva Figes and Kate Millett: See Figes, pp. 121–134. See also Kate Millett, *Sexual Politics*, New York: Doubleday, 1970, pp. 159–168.

(49) Reports of mob rape during *Kristallnacht*: Raul Hilberg, *Destruction of the European Jews*, Chicago: Quadrangle, 1961, p. 28; William L. Shirer, *The Rise and Fall of the Third Reich*, New York: Simon and Schuster, 1960, pp. 430–431.

(50) pattern of first-phase violence: See *The Black Book: The Nazi Crime Against the Jewish People*, New York: The Jewish Black Book Committee, 1946, pp. 301, 329, 340, 342, 366, 436.

(50) "Before the war I lived in Minsk": Sophia Glushkina deposition, *The Black Book*, pp. 342–343.

(51) "race defilement": Hilberg, p. 28; Shirer, p. 431; Nora Levin, *The Holocaust*, New York: Thomas Y. Crowell, 1968, p. 150.

(51) "I was in a small office": Sala Pawlowicz with Kevin Klose, *I Will Survive*, New York: Norton, 1962, p. 41.

(52) "Their actions shamed me": Pawlowicz, p. 54.

(52) Warsaw ghetto: Jacob Apenszlak, ed., *The Black Book of Polish Jewry*, New York: The American Federation for Polish Jews, 1943, pp. 25–29.

(53) Captured German documents (SS in Poland): Hilberg, pp. 126–127.

(53) rabbi from Kovno: Harry Gersh, *The Sacred Books of the Jews*, New York: Stein and Day, 1968, pp. 181–183.

(55) "The Molotov Note": Dated Jan. 6, 1942, and read into evidence at the Nuremburg war-crimes tribunal on Feb. 14, 1946. *Trial of the Major War Criminals before the International Military Tribunal* (42 vols.), Nuremberg, 1947, Vol. 7, pp. 456–457.

(56) reprisals against Maquis: Testimony of Jan. 31 1946, Nuremberg war-crimes tribunal, Vol. 6, pp. 404–407.

(57) "A few uninvestigated cases": *Life*, Jan. 10, 1938, p. 51.

(58) "Among the injured females": Nanking International Relief Committee, *War Damage in the Nanking Area*, Shanghai: The Mercury Press, 1938, p. 8.

(58) "Rape! Rape! Rape!": *International Military Tribunal for the Far East*, Tokyo, 1946 (typed transcripts), p. 4467.

(58) Mrs. Shui Fang Tsen at Ginling: Tokyo tribunal (typed transcripts), pp. 4464–4466.

(59) similar stories, etc.: Tokyo tribunal (typed transcripts), pp. 3904–3943, 4459, 4476, 4479, 4526–4536, 4544, etc.

(59) A statement from Mrs. Chang Kia Sze: Tokyo tribunal (typed transcripts), pp. 4506–4507.

(59) Wong Pan Sze's affidavit: Tokyo tribunal (typed transcripts), p. 4501.

(60) Items 12 and 13: Tokyo tribunal (typed transcripts), p. 4515.

(61) "approximately 20,000 cases": *Judgment of the International Military Tribunal for the Far East* (2 vols.), Tokyo, 1948, p. 1012.

(61) "Death was a frequent penalty": *Judgment*, pp. 1012–1019.

(61) Matsui had crowed: *Judgment*, p. 707.

(61) "secretly ordered or willfully committed": *Judgment*, p. 1001.

(61) "rumors . . . perhaps in fun": Tokyo tribunal (typed transcripts), p. 33869.

(61) "I am not directly responsible": Tokyo tribunal (typed transcripts), p. 33874.

(61) Nakayama, "I hope that such incidents": Tokyo tribunal (typed transcripts), p. 21944.

(62) top-secret instructions: *Judgment*, p. 1023.

(63) "The guard hesitated": Agnes Newton Keith, *Three Came Home*, Boston: Atlantic–Little, Brown, 1947, p. 150.

(63) Vatican archives: Paul Hoffman, "Pius Knew in 1941 of Drive on Jews," *New York Times*, Apr. 27, 1974. This exchange of correspondence, including reports of denials by the Slovak government, is contained in *The Holy See and the War Victims, January 1941–December 1942*, Libreria Editrice Vaticana, 1974, pp. 470, 475, 504, 543–544.

(63) Enjoyment Duty: Ka-Tzetnik, *House of Dolls*, New York: Simon and Schuster, 1955.

(64) Auschwitz brothel of Aryans: R. J. Minney, *I Shall Fear No Evil; The Story of Dr. Alina Brewda*, London: William Kimber, 1966, pp. 141 ff.

(64) Tulchin: *The Black Book: The Nazi Crime Against the Jewish People*, p. 164.

(64) Vught: *New York Times*, Nov. 13, 1944, p. 1.

(64) Smolensk: "The Molotov Note," *loc. cit.*

(64) Kweilin, in Kwangsi Province: *Judgment*, p. 1022.

(65) "These filthy lechers": Ilya Ehrenburg, *Russia at War*, London: Hamish Hamilton, 1943, pp. 116–117.

(66) "To gain an hour": Ehrenburg, p. 254.

(66) "screams": Hildegard Knef, *The Gift Horse*, trans. from the German by David Anthony Palastanga, New York: Dell, 1972, p. 77. See also p. 70.

(66) "Russian soldiers not rape!": Knef, p. 98.

(66) rape during the fall of Berlin: Cornelius Ryan, *The Last Battle*, New York: Simon and Schuster, 1966, pp. 26–33, 484–493.

(68) committee of anti-Communist scholars: Theodor Schieder, ed., *Documents on the Expulsion of the Germans from Eastern-Central Europe* (4 vols.), Bonn, 1953–1960. Vol. I, *The Expulsion of the German Population from the Territories East of the Oder-Neisse Line*, throughout.

(69) "When we were lying in bed": Schieder, I, p. 257.

(69) "Where could one lodge a complaint?": Schieder, I, p. 244.

(70) "The raping of German women": Schieder, I, p. 49.

(70) Ehrenburg incited: *Ibid.*

(70) "Kill! Kill!": Karl Doenitz, *Memoirs: Ten Years and Twenty Days*, Cleveland: World Pub. Co., 1959, p. 431.

(70) "safety valve to the ravening troops": Karl Bednarik, *The Male in Crisis*, New York: Knopf, 1970, p. 69.

(71) Ryan's researches in Moscow: Ryan, p. 493 n.

(71) Djilas on rape, Stalin: Milovan Djilas, *Conversations with Stalin*, New York: Harcourt, Brace, 1962, pp. 89, 95.

(72) Solzhenitsyn on rape: Aleksandr I. Solzhenitsyn, *The Gulag Archipelago, 1918–1956*, trans. from the Russian by Thomas P. Whitney, New York: Harper, 1973, p. 21.

(72) *Footnote*, Chalidze: Harrison E. Salisbury, "Struggling Now for Human Rights: A Talk with Valery Chalidze," *New York Times Magazine*, Mar. 4, 1973, p. 60.

(73) Patton on rape: Patton, pp. 23, 71.

(74) Stuttgart subway incident and Normandy peninsula: *U.S. Congressional Record*, Senate, June 29, 1945, Vol. 91, Part 5, pp. 6995–6996; "Eastland's Charges Hit, SHAEF Has No Knowledge of Offenses Laid to Negroes," *New York Times*, July 3, 1945, p. 4; "Rape Story Unsupported, 6th Army Group Says Stuttgart Inquiry Finds No Basis For It," *New York Times*, July 7, 1945, p. 4; "Rape Story Dispute Grows in Stuttgart," *New York Times*, Aug. 11, 1945, p. 10.

(74) *Footnote*, Red Ball Express: John D. Silvera, *The Negro in World War II*, Passaic, N.J.: The Military Press, Inc., 1946.

(75) "Italian women would perform": Robert H. Adleman and George

Walton, *Rome Fell Today*. Boston: Little, Brown, 1968, p. 184. See also pp. 259, 268.

(75) "You should have seen": Danilo Dolci, *Report from Palermo*, trans. from the Italian by P. D. Cummins, New York: Orion Press, 1959, p. 68.

(76) "Rape has nothing to do": Author's conversation with Abraham Nemrow, Chief Clerk, U.S. Army Court of Military Review (JAG), Washington, Feb. 2, 1973. Rape conviction figures for World War II and further opinions of the Clerk of the Court were obtained during this interview.

BANGLADESH

(78) first account: William Drummond, "Raped Bengalis Called 'Heroes,'" *New York Post*, Dec. 22, 1971.

(79) "A stream of victims": Joseph Fried, "Women Back in Jessore as Terror Lifts," *New York Daily News*, Dec. 27, 1971.

(79) press conference in Geneva: Associated Press, Jan. 17, 1972; United Press International, Jan. 17, 1972; *New York Times*, Jan. 18, 1972.

(80) "It is unthinkable": Shelley Steinberg *et al.*, "To the Editor" (Jan. 24, 1972), *New York Times*, Feb. 9, 1972.

(80) International aid from Planned Parenthood: Jill Tweedie, "The Rape of Bangladesh," *The Guardian*, London, Mar. 6, 1972; Robert Trumbull, "Dacca Raising the Status of Women While Aiding Rape Victims," *New York Times*, May 12, 1972.

(80) Bengal was a state: Accurate statistics concerning the Bangladesh war are impossible to come by. What is incontrovertible, or at least impartially confirmed by all sources, is the original population estimate, the length of the Pakistani repression, and the period of India's armed intervention. Body counts of the dead, the refugee population, and the number of raped women fluctuated wildly from newspaper report to newspaper report as the full horror of Bangladesh became known. For example, some reports maintained that "tens of thousands" may have lost their lives and "tens of thousands" may have fled across the border. As for the statistic of most concern to us here, the number of raped women, AP and UPI used the 200,000 figure on Jan. 17, 1972, the *New York Times* of Mar. 5, 1972, reported 50,000, and the *New York Times Magazine* of Jan. 21, 1973, p. 22, used the 400,000 figure. Intermediate figures popped up on other occasions.

(80) Eighty percent were Moslems: Bérengère d'Aragon, photo captions and research material for Black Star, March 1972.

(80) purdah: Rounaq Jahan, Dacca University, "Women in Bangladesh," paper presented at the IX International Congress of Anthropological and Ethnological Sciences, Chicago, Aug. 28–Sept. 8, 1973 (mimeo); also in Ruby Rohrlich Leavitt, ed., *Women Cross-Culturally: Change and Challenge*, The Hague: Mouton Publications, 1975.

(80) racial difference: Bérengère d'Aragon.

(81) rape by Mukti Bahini and Bihari razakars: *Ibid.*

(81) Aubrey Menen reconstructed: Aubrey Menen, "The Rapes of Bangladesh," *New York Times Magazine*, July 23, 1972, pp. 11 ff.

(82) Girls of eight, grandmothers of seventy-five: Bérengère d'Aragon.

(82) military barracks, women kept naked: Jill Tweedie. See also *New York Times*, Mar. 5, 1972.

(82) pornographic movies: Jill Tweedie, quoting Indian writer Dr. Mulk Raj Anand.

(83) Khadiga, Kamala Begum: Bérengère d'Aragon.

(83) ill-starred campaign: Robert Trumbull.

(83) demands of the men, attitudes of the women: *Ibid.*

(84) venereal disease: *Ibid.*

(84) 25,000 pregnancies: "Killing of Babies Feared in Bengal" (AP), *New York Times*, Mar. 5, 1972.

(84) would never be accepted: *Ibid*; also Bérengère d'Aragon.

(84) suicide, infanticide, indigenous abortion: Robert Trumbull.

(84) Mother Theresa's: Menen; d'Aragon.

(84) abortion clinics: Trumbull; d'Aragon; Jane E. Brody, "Physicians Throughout the World Are Studying New, Simple Techniques for Terminating Pregnancies," *New York Times*, Dec. 20, 1973.

(84) a woman doctor: Bérengère d'Aragon.

(85) Women social workers: *Ibid.*

(85) "An earning woman": Khushwant Singh, "Bangladesh, after the first year: Will it ever be a workable country?" *New York Times Magazine*, Jan. 21, 1973, p. 22.

(85) ". . . landed in brothels": *Ibid.*

(85) "a campaign of terror": Aubrey Menen.

(85) ". . . to create a new race": Jill Tweedie.

VIETNAM

(86) Lansdale mission: *The Pentagon Papers* as published by *The New York Times*, New York: Bantam, 1971, p. 55.

(87) Peter Arnett: All quotations and comments attributed to AP's special correspondent were obtained by the author in interviews conducted in New York City on Dec. 11, 1972, Dec. 19, 1972, and Jan. 22, 1973.

(88) American Civil War, low rape: This phenomenon was first suggested to me by *Harper's Magazine* editor John Fischer, a Civil War buff, who wrote to me on Jan. 18, 1973, "I have never run across any mention of rape in my fairly extensive reading in memoirs about the Civil War. For example, of Sherman's march from Atlanta to the sea they are full of outrage about the behavior of the Northern troops, mentioning every teaspoon stolen and every barn burned—but in none of them did I ever see any accusation of rape, or even of serious discourtesy." Fischer's observation was confirmed for me by historian James Shenton of Columbia University, and others. Although historians of other wars also tended to dismiss the incidence of rape when I spoke with them, books they directed me to, or books I found on my own, gave me ample evidence with little difficulty. My exploratory readings into the American Civil War, unlike the American Revolution or any other war I looked into, drew a blank. I found fear of rape as Sherman's army advanced, for example, in Mary Boykin Chestnut's *Diary from Dixie*, and in a few other sources, but nothing concrete. The lack of documentation in the personal

memoirs, I think, is significant, but I stand ready to be corrected by some later historian.

(88) South Vietnamese rape in Cambodia: Henry Kamm, "Big Rubber Tract in Cambodia Falls to Saigon Troops," New York Times, May 25, 1970, pp. 1, 6.

(89) Sihanouk to Fallaci: New York Times Magazine, Aug. 12, 1973, p. 31.

(90) "Horror stories abound": "Thieu's Political Prisoners of War," Time, Dec. 25, 1972, p. 18.

(90) French paratroopers, Algeria: Henri Alleg, The Question, New York: Braziller, 1958, p. 42.

(90) Argentina: Juan de Onis, "The Political Torture of a Woman Shakes Argentina," New York Times, May 25, 1972, p. 3.

(90) Brazil: "Amnesty Group Accuses Brazil of Torturing Political Prisoners," New York Times, Sept. 7, 1972, p. 10.

(90) Angola and Mozambique: "Torture Is Reported" (Reuter), New York Times, Mar. 26, 1973, p. 11.

(90) Chile: David Binder, "Chile Accused of Torture By OAS Investigators," New York Times, Dec. 10, 1974, p. 8.

(91) Footnote, ". . . not even a needle or thread": Agnes Smedley, The Great Road: The Life and Times of Chu Teh (1956), New York: Monthly Review Press, 1972, p. 229. See also p. 301.

(91) Footnote, Rather remained unaware: Author's interview with Dan Rather, New York City, Feb. 24, 1975.

(92) Webb, "Everybody wants to know": Judy Klemesrud, "Prisoner of the Vietcong for 23 Days, She Calls the Experience Rewarding," New York Times, Aug. 8, 1972, p. 38.

(92) Nelson, "This is a question": Vietnam Veterans Against the War, The Winter Soldier Investigation: An Inquiry into American War Crimes, Boston: Beacon Press, 1972, p. 133.

(92) Patton and military brothels: Bernard Fall, Street Without Joy, New York: Schocken, 1972, p. 133.

(93) French mobile field brothels: Fall, pp. 132–134.

(93) Committee for the Defense, etc.: Andrew Borowiec, Associated Press Special Report, Saigon, July 8, 1966.

(94) U.S. military brothels within perimeter of base camps: For further information, see Charles Winick and Paul M. Kinsie, The Lively Commerce, Chicago: Quadrangle, 1971, pp. 245–267. See also Stuart H. Loory, Defeated: Inside America's Military Machine, New York: Random House, 1973, pp. 214–234.

(95) Army brothels in Vietnam existed by the grace, etc.: Throughout the war, existence of the brothels remained a touchy subject that reporters chose to handle by avoidance. For a rare newspaper treatment, see "U.S. Army Retreats, Allows Prostitutes on Vietnam Base" (UPI), Washington Post, Jan. 24, 1972.

(96) In 1969 GIs contracted venereal disease: Winick and Kinsie, p. 266.

(97) ". . . not being able to live without sex": Time, Feb. 26, 1973, p. 14.

(97) no comparable training against rape: The Army had four anti-VD training films in circulation in Vietnam, and an additional three for its medical personnel, but no anti-rape film was ever made or circulated,

according to author's telephone conversation with Lynn Gunn-Smith, Army Information Office, Washington, D.C., Aug. 23, 1974.

(97) particularly bad reputations for atrocity: Arnett interviews.

(98) U.S. Army court-martial statistics, Vietnam: Obtained from Abraham Nemrow, U.S. Army Court of Military Review (JAG), in Washington, Feb. 2, 1973; confirmed and supplemented by V. M. McElroy, U.S. Army Court of Military Review (JAG), by telephone to Washington, Sept. 20, 1974.

(99) U.S. Army court-martial statistics, Korea: Nemrow interview.

(99) peak troop strength, Korea, Vietnam: By telephone from Col. Audrey Thomas, press officer, Department of Defense, Washington, Sept. 16, 1974.

(99) ". . . some people will say the Army": By telephone from V. M. McElroy, Sept. 1, 1974.

(100) Air Force court-martial statistics, Vietnam and world-wide: By telephone from Col. Audrey Thomas, DOD, Sept. 10, 1974.

(100) Footnote, discussion of Articles in UCMJ: Definitions and table of maximum punishments are contained in Manual for Courts-Martial, United States, U.S. Government Printing Office, 1969, Chap. 25, pp. 13–15. Decline of court-martial rate is discussed in Task Force on Administration of Military Justice in the Armed Forces, U.S. Government Printing Office, 1972, Vol. I, pp. 9–11. Catchall use of Article 134 is discussed in Task Force, I, p. 26.

(101) Navy and Marine Corps court-martial statistics: By telephone from Lt. Steve Becker, Navy Information Office, Washington, Sept. 18, 1974.

(101) ". . . we didn't live there": Ibid.

(101) one specific incident: Daniel Lang, Casualties of War, New York: McGraw-Hill, 1969, throughout. Lang's piece originally appeared in The New Yorker, Oct. 18, 1969.

(103) My Lai: Seymour M. Hersh, My Lai 4: A Report on the Massacre and Its Aftermath, New York: Random House, 1970, pp. 18, 34, 47, 67, 72, 83, 85, 87, 147, 185. See also Joseph Lelyveld, "The Story of a Soldier Who Refused to Fire at Song My," New York Times Magazine, Dec. 14, 1969.

(103) Army's Criminal Investigation Division settled on 347: W. R. Peers, Report of the Department of the Army Review of the Preliminary Investigations into the My Lai Incident, Washington: U.S. Government Printing Office, Mar. 14, 1970, Vol. 1 (released Nov. 13, 1974), p. 6/18.

(105) Although the Army confirmed: Peers Report, pp. 2/3, 6/8, 6/10, 6/20, 12/2, 12/33. The last citation, regarding 2nd Lieutenant Steven K. Brooks (Deceased), reads as follows: "Although he knew that a number of his men habitually raped Vietnamese women in villages during operations, on 16 March 1968, he observed, did not prevent, and failed to report several rapes by members of his platoon while in My Lai (4)."

(105) charges were quietly dropped: Seymour M. Hersh "Army Issues My Lai Cover-Up Report," New York Times, Nov. 14, 1974, p. 16.

(105) Chu Lai, "a serious incident": U.S. Army, Office of the Judge Advocate General, Court of Military Review, CM 419652, United States v. Specialist Four William C. Ficke, Jr., Apr. 25, 1969; U.S.

Army, Office of the Judge Advocate General, Court of Military Review, CM 420332, United States v. Captain Leonard Goldman, Dec. 4, 1970. Supplementary material from Maurine Beasley, "Court Clears Captain of Hiding Viet Atrocity," Washington Post, July 31, 1971, p. A-3.

(107) "They only do it": Lucy Komisar, "The Machismo Factor," work in progress.

(107) "Me and one of the buck sergeants": Roger Neville Williams, The New Exiles: American War Resisters in Canada, New York: Liveright, 1971, p. 276.

(108) From vet to vet: Winter Soldier Investigation, pp. 13, 28, 29, 44, 46, 53, 67, 94, 118.

4. RIOTS, POGROMS AND REVOLUTIONS

THE AMERICAN REVOLUTION

(115) As early as 1768: Oliver Morton Dickerson, comp., Boston Under Military Rule, 1768–1769, as revealed in A Journal of the Times, Boston: Chapman and Grimes, 1936. Background material I use is contained in Dickerson's introduction, pp. vii–xii. Specific quotations from the Journal appear on pp. 21, 29, 34, 93, 100, 114. See also pp. 71, 79, 90, 99, 108, 118.

(117) cavalier view from Rawdon: Henry Steele Commager and Richard B. Morris, eds., The Spirit of 'Seventy-Six, Indianapolis: Bobbs-Merrill, 1958, p. 424.

(117) "The enemy make great devastation": Col. George Measam to Gen. Anthony Wayne, Albany, Jan. 11, 1777, Anthony Wayne Correspondence, New York Public Library.

(117) British and Hessian campaigns notorious: Commager and Morris, p. 524.

(117) "Since I wrote to you this morning": New Jersey Historical Society Archives, Series 2, Vol. 1, Trenton: 1901, pp. 245–246.

(118) "The Damages Done by these Plunderings": Varnum Lansing Collins, ed., A Brief Narrative of the Ravages of the British and Hessians at Princeton in 1776–77, Princeton: The University Library, 1906, pp. 14–15.

(119) Gen. Washington's special order: Commager and Morris, p. 525.

(119) Continental Congress, committee report: Commager and Morris, pp. 525–527.

(120) Congress ordered the printing: Elizabeth Evans, Weathering the Storm: Women in the American Revolution, New York: Scribner's, 1975, p. 26.

(120) six affidavits in a two-day period: Papers of the Continental Congress, Item 53: Papers and Affidavits Relating to the Plundering, Burnings and Ravages Committed by the British, 1775–84, folios 29–40. These handwritten affidavits are now in the Center for the Documentary Study of the American Revolution, The National Archives, Washington, D.C. I wish to thank George C. Chalou, Archivist, for providing me with photocopies of the originals.

POGROMS

(121) Chmelnitzky pogroms: Ronald Sanders, *The Downtown Jews*, New York: Harper & Row, 1969, p. 17.
(121) replications in the Ukraine: Ande Manners, *Poor Cousins*, New York: Coward, McCann, 1972, pp. 37–39.
(121) ". . . amateurish quality": *Ibid.*
(122) wave that began in 1919: Documentation and eyewitness accounts of this pogrom in *Massacres and Other Atrocities Committed Against the Jews in Southern Russia*, New York: American Jewish Congress, pamphlet, 1920.
(123) "The tired and oppressed Jews": *Ibid.*
(123) Periodic rape sorely taxed the rabbinical concept: Louis M. Epstein, *Sex Laws and Customs in Judaism*, New York: Bloch Pub. Co., 1948, pp. 191–192, 215.
(124) ". . . 'a beautiful Jewess' ": Jean-Paul Sartre, *Anti-Semite and Jew* (1946), trans. from the French by George J. Becker, New York: Schocken, 1965, pp. 48–49.

THE MORMON PERSECUTIONS

(125) Mormon persecutions: Herman C. Smith, "Mormon Torubles in Missouri," *Missouri Historical Review*, Vol. IV, No. 4 (July 1910), pp. 238–251.
(126) "The mob was now let loose": Elder B. H. Roberts, *The Missouri Persecutions*, Salt Lake City: George Q. Cannon & Sons, 1900.
(126) ". . . boasted of raping virtuous wives": *Ibid.*

MOB VIOLENCE AGAINST BLACKS: THE KKK

(126) Memphis Riot: Jack D. L. Holmes, "The Underlying Causes of the Memphis Race Riot of 1866," *Tennessee Historical Quarterly*, Vol. 17, No. 3 (Sept. 1958), pp. 195–221.
(126) several black women spoke of rape: Testimony of Frances Thompson, Lucy Smith, Lucy Tibbs and Cynthia Townsend before the Congressional Investigating Committee appears in Gerda Lerner, ed., *Black Women in White America: A Documentary History*, New York: Pantheon, 1972, pp. 174–177.
(128) origins of the Ku Klux Klan: Thomas B. Alexander, "Kukluxism in Tennessee, 1865–1869," *Tennessee Historical Quarterly*, Vol. 8, No. 3 (Sept. 1949), pp. 195–219. See also Stanley F. Horn, *Invisible Empire*, Cos Cob: Edwards, 1969.
(129) a joint Congressional committee: Testimony of Harriet Simril and Ellen Parton in Lerner, pp. 183–186. Testimony of Hannah Tutson in Herbert Aptheker, *A Documentary History of the Negro People in the United States* (1951), New York: Citadel, 1968, Vol. 2, pp. 579–585.
(131) ". . . no records of the rape . . . of white women": Lerner, p. 180.
(131) Under the guise of punishing immorality: See Irving Leibowitz, *My Indiana*, New York: Prentice-Hall, 1964, for his account of the whipping of white women, and of the Stephenson trial.

MOB VIOLENCE AGAINST WHITES: THE CONGO

(132) Pro-Lumumba papers in England: New Statesman, July 23, 1960, pp. 107–108.

(132) "what the black savages": National Review, Aug. 27, 1960, p. 101.

(132) "Wherever its operations have ranged": E. D. Morel, The Future of the Congo, London: Smith, Elder & Co., 1909, pp. 34–35. A history of the Force Publique may also be found in Colin Legum, Congo Disaster, London: Penguin, 1961.

(133) mutiny at Thysville, etc.: Catherine Hoskyns, The Congo Since Independence. London: Oxford University Press, 1965, p. 89.

(133) "The attacks on European women": Helen Kitchen, ed., Footnotes to the Congo Story: An "Africa Report" Anthology, New York: Walker & Co., 1967, pp. 21–23.

(133) Belgian white paper: Edwin S. Munger, "Conflict in the Congo, Part III: An Inquiry into Rape Charges" (Sept. 1960), African Field Reports, American Universities Field Staff, 1961.

(138) Philippa Schuyler's reporting: Philippa Schuyler, Who Killed the Congo?, New York: Devin-Adair, 1962, pp. 185–190.

(138) "It would be interesting to know": New Statesman, July 23, 1960, p. 108.

5. Two Studies in American History

INDIANS

(141) "I have been in the midst": The Narrative of the Captivity and Restoration of Mrs. Mary Rowlandson (1682), Boston: Houghton Mifflin, 1930, p. 71.

(141) Isabella McCoy: Frederick Drimmer, ed., Scalps and Tomahawks: Narratives of Indian Captivity, New York: Coward-McCann, 1961, p. 13.

(141) "I don't remember": Ibid.

(141) "Anyone reading": Drimmer, p. 12.

(141) Iroquois matrilineal: Peter Farb, Man's Rise to Civilization as Shown by the Indians of North America from Primeval Times to the Coming of the Industrial State, New York: Avon/Discus, 1971, pp. 130–131.

(142) experience of Mary Jemison: James Seaver, A Narrative of the Life of Mary Jemison (1824), American Scenic and Historic Preservation Society, 1932.

(142) Female captives were closely scrutinized: William B. Rice, "The Captivity of Olive Oatman," California Historical Society Quarterly, June 1941, p. 97.

(142) "Some women who had been delivered up": Drimmer, p. 14.

(142) "From all history and tradition": Mix commentary in Seaver, p. 421.

(143) "I told her she had better": Abbie Gardner-Sharp, History of the Spirit Lake Massacre and Captivity of Miss Abbie Gardner, Des Moines: Iowa Printing Co., 1902, p. 217.

(144) narrative of Fanny Kelly: Drimmer, pp. 330–369.

(144) different version: Stanley Vestal, Sitting Bull, Champion of the Sioux, Boston: Houghton Mifflin, 1932, pp. 65–69.

(144) "Women when captured": J. P. Dunn, *Massacres of the Mountains, A History of the Indian Wars of the Far West 1815–1875* (1886), New York: Archer House, 1958, p. 319.

(144) ". . . meting to a man in his own measure": Dunn, p. 367.

(145) *Footnote*, "We were recons": Lucy Komisar, "The Machismo Factor," work in progress.

(145) Ewbanks, "He forced me": Dunn, p. 368.

(145) appended to Evans' apologia: See "Reply of Governor Evans of the Territory of Colorado to that part referring to him of the Report of the Committee on the Conduct of the War, headed 'Massacre of Cheyenne Indians,' " Denver, 1865 (Eames Indian Collection, New York Public Library), p. 6 and Appendix. Mrs. Ewbanks' statement was also printed in several newspapers of the day.

(145) most famous captivity rape of the West: To retell the story of Josie Meeker, Arvilla Meeker and Flora Ellen Price, I have drawn heavily on Marshall Sprague, *Massacre: The Tragedy at White River*, Boston: Little, Brown, 1957. Political overview of the White River Massacre, and the government's efforts to remove the Utes from Colorado, may be found in Dee Brown, *Bury My Heart at Wounded Knee*, New York: Holt, Rinehart, 1970, pp. 367–389. Verbatim testimony of the three women appears in "White River Ute Commission Investigation," House of Representatives, 46th Congress, 2nd Session, 1880, Ex. Doc. 83, pp. 13–19, 21–27, 40–50. Comment of Chief Ouray re "oath of a woman," Ex. Doc. 83, pp. 12–13.

(151) "Only occasionally was the voice": Brown, p. xv.

(151) Camp Grant massacre: Dunn, pp. 621–623.

(151) Sand Creek massacre: Dunn, pp. 342–382.

(152) Miksch, ". . . these men pulled out the bodies of the squaws": Stan Hoig, *The Sand Creek Massacre*, Norman: University of Oklahoma Press, 1961, p. 186.

(152) Connor, "In going over the battleground": Brown, p. 328.

(152) "ghastly, unprintable disclosures": L. V. McWhorter, *Hear Me, My Chiefs*, Caldwell, Idaho: Caxton, 1952, p. 116.

(152) "A Nez Percé woman": McWhorter p. 121.

(153) Chief Joseph, "On the way we captured": "An Indian's Views of Indian Affairs," *North American Review*, Vol. 128 (Apr. 1879), p. 427.

SLAVERY

(154) "Sexually as well as in every other way": Winthrop D. Jordan, *White Over Black: American Attitudes Toward the Negro, 1550–1812*, Chapel Hill: University of North Carolina Press, 1968, p. 141.

(154) "Lawdy, them was tribbolashuns": Gerda Lerner, ed., *Black Women in White America: A Documentary History*, New York: Pantheon, 1972, pp. 47–48.

(154) In-country breeding was crucial: Frederic Bancroft, *Slave Trading in the Old South* (1931) New York: Ungar, 1959, p. 67.

(154) small industry, reliably profitable: Bancroft, pp. 68–69.

(154) In colonial Massachusetts: Bancroft, p. 79.

(154) state of Virginia exported: Bancroft, p. 71.

(155) "It has always (perhaps erroneously)": Theodore Weld, ed., *Ameri-*

can *Slavery As It Is: Testimony of a Thousand Witnesses* (1839), New York: Arno Press & *The New York Times*, 1968, p. 182.

(155) "One day the owner ordered": Weld, p. 15.

(156) "The women who visited me": Frances Anne Kemble, *Journal of a Residence on a Georgian Plantation in 1838–1839* (1863), John A. Scott edn., London: Jonathan Cape, 1961, p. 222.

(156) "proven" commanded higher price: Bancroft, pp. 77 n, 81–82.

(156) "Negroes for Sale": Weld, p. 175.

(156) It mattered little who did the impregnating: Bancroft, p. 85.

(156) Paternity was seldom entered: The delicious speculation by Fawn Brodie and others on the liaison between Thomas Jefferson and Sally Hemings, his slave, hinges on just this fact.

(156) female arbitrarily assigned a partner, ordered to mate: Bancroft, p. 84. See also Kenneth M. Stampp, *The Peculiar Institution*, New York: Knopf, 1956, p. 341.

(156) "I wish the three girls you purchest": Ulrich B. Phillips, *Life and Labor in the Old South*, Boston: Little, Brown, 1929, p. 278.

(157) "Having to submit": Stampp, p. 335.

(157) "We don't care what they do": Phillips, p. 204.

(157) "Flogged Joe Goodwyn": Stampp, p. 342.

(157) slave woman forced to live: Charles Ball, *Fifty Years in Chains* H. Dayton 1859, pp. 122, 197.

(157) used by her white owner: Stampp, p. 355.

(157) "I believe it is the custom": Lydia Maria Child, comp., *The Patriarchal Institution as Described by Members of its own Family*, New York: The American Anti-Slavery Society, 1860, p. 28.

(157) young sons eager for initiation: Stampp, p. 355.

(157) ". . . I have not humped": James Thomas Flexner, *George Washington and the New Nation (1783–1793)*, Boston: Little, Brown, 1970, p. 24.

(158) privilege filtered down: Stampp, p. 354.

(158) "This same planter": Weld, p. 15.

(158) "Patsey was slim and straight": "Twelve Years a Slave, the Narrative of Solomon Northup" (1853), Gilbert Osofsky, ed., *Puttin' On Ole Massa*, New York: Harper Torchbooks, 1969, pp. 327–328, 333–334, 350–351, 367–369.

(160) "The female slave": Child, p. 28.

(160) "White mothers and daughters": *Ibid.*

(161) "Will not the natural impulses": Child, p. 34.

(161) "A Negress was hung this year": Frederick Law Olmsted, *A Journey in the Seaboard Slave States* (1856), New York: Negro Universities Press, 1968, p. 601.

(161) Footnote, ". . . white women apparently believed": Stampp, p. 356.

(161) "The day I arrived": Weld, p. 157.

(162) Lucy and Frank: Ball, p. 295.

(162) Peggy and Patrick: James H. Johnston, *Race Relations in Virginia and Miscegenation in the South, 1776–1860* (1937), Amherst: University of Massachusetts Press, 1970, p. 307.

(162) concept of raping a slave did not exist: Ulrich Phillips has written, ". . . although the wilful killing of slaves was generally held to be murder, the violation of their women was without criminal penalty." He also cites a rule that one plantation owner imposed on his over-

seers: "Having connection with any of my female servants will most certainly be visited with a dismissal from my employment, and no excuse can or will be taken." (Ulrich B. Phillips, *American Negro Slavery* [1918], Baton Rouge: Louisiana State University Press, 1969, pp. 500, 273–274.) See also Jordan, p. 157.

(163) *Footnote*, advertisement for runaway: Ulrich B. Phillips, ed., *Plantation and Frontier* (*A Documentary History of American Industrial Society*, Vol. II), Cleveland: Arthur H. Clark, 1910, p. 122.

(163) "Slaves are bound": Jordan, p. 160.

(163) Statutory prohibitions: Jordan, p. 139; Johnston, pp. 172–175.

(164) Even in South Carolina: Jordan, p. 140.

(164) divorce suits and bastardy charges: Jordan, p. 139; Johnston, pp. 175–179, 250–257.

(164) "The slave is undoubtedly subject": Helen T. Catterall, ed., *Judicial Cases Concerning American Slavery and the Negro* (1932), New York: Octagon, 1968, Vol. 3, p. 316.

(165) slaveholder wills: Johnston, pp. 218–236.

(165) "We forbear to lift the veil": Child, p. 29.

(165) "The character of the white ladies": Gerda Lerner, *The Grimké Sisters from South Carolina*, Boston: Houghton Mifflin, 1967, p. 179.

(166) "Of this woman's life": Frances Anne Kemble, *Journal of a Residence on a Georgian Plantation in 1838–1839*, New York: Harper & Brothers, 1863, pp. 140–141 n. By comparing this edition with the Scott edition published by Cape (*op. cit.*), I have been able to fill in some names that a fearful Kemble chose to identify by an initial in her original work.

(166) "Before reaching the house": Kemble, 1863 edn., p. 232.

(167) "Almost beyond my patience": Kemble, 1863 edn., p. 228.

(168) Kemble privately circulated: See editor's introduction, Scott edn., for a reliable short history of the *Journal*'s fortunes. See also Kemble, *Records of a Later Life*, New York: Holt, 1882, p. 324, for a reference to the role played by Lydia Maria Child. See *Mr. Butler's Statement*, Philadelphia: J. C. Clark, 1850, pp. 15–18, for the role played by Butler in the *Journal*'s suppression and the role played by the *Journal* in the Kemble-Butler divorce.

(168) Traders openly sold their prettiest: Bancroft, pp. 329–338.

(168) "Every slaveholder is the legalized keeper": Frederick Douglass, *Lectures on American Slavery*, Buffalo: G. Reese, 1851, "Lecture No. 2, December 8, 1850." Also in Herbert Aptheker, ed., *A Documentary History of the Negro People in the United States*, New York: Citadel, 1951, Vol. 1, p. 313.

(169) ". . . largest market for 'fancy girls' ": Bancroft, p. 329.

(169) ". . . great profit": *Ibid.*

(169) ". . . luxurious ideal": *Ibid.*

ADDENDUM: THE CLIOMETRICIANS

(170) cliometricians argue: Robert William Fogel and Stanley L. Engerman, *Time on the Cross: The Economics of American Negro Slavery*, Boston: Little, Brown, 1974, Vol. I, pp. 130–138, 143–144; Vol. II, pp. 24–25, 106, 114–115, 169.

(172) age of first menstrual period declining: H. Katchadourian and

D. T. Lunde, *Fundamentals of Human Sexuality*, New York: Holt, Rinehart, 1972, p. 86.

(173) fertility in the first few years: Ashley Montagu, *Sex, Man & Society*, New York: Tower Publications, 1969, pp. 115–128 (Chap. 14, "Adolescent Sterility"); Clellan S. Ford and Frank A. Beach, *Patterns of Sexual Behavior*, New York: Harper Colophon, 1972, pp. 172–173. Ford and Beach, professors at Yale, say succinctly, "Relatively few girls are capable of reproduction before fifteen years of age, and even then their reproductive capacity is not as great as it will be later. The average age for full reproductive maturity in women has been estimated at approximately twenty-three years. This means that coitus is less likely to result in conception in the postpuberal girl than in the mature woman."

6. The Police-Blotter Rapist

(175) "one of the most under-reported crimes": Federal Bureau of Investigation, *Uniform Crime Reports*, 1973, p. 15.

(175) one in five or one in twenty: Menachem Amir, *Patterns in Forcible Rape*, Chicago: University of Chicago Press, 1971, pp. 27–28.

(175) a provable bias: See my Chapter 11, "Victims: The Crime."

(175) On a national average: *UCR*, p. 15.

(175) In some locales: Speech by Leslie Snyder, Assistant Manhattan District Attorney, before the Bar Association of the City of New York, Jan. 16, 1974. Snyder's computation was for New York County, based on the number of arrests for rape in 1972. She offered the following rates for other locales: Chicago, 17%; Boston, 11.5%; San Francisco, 28%.

(175) In 1973 the FBI reported: *UCR*, p. 14.

(175) comparative statistics, murder, assault, robbery: *UCR*, pp. 6, 11, 15.

(176) comparative clearance rates: *UCR*, pp. 10, 11, 16.

(176) police-blotter rapists, statistical description: *UCR*, p. 15.

(176) Connell's protagonist: Evan S. Connell, Jr., *The Diary of a Rapist*, New York: Simon and Schuster, 1966, throughout.

(177) "Philosophically a sex offense": Manfred S. Guttmacher, *Sex Offenses*, New York: Norton, 1951, p. 15.

(178) "Moral opprobrium": Benjamin Karpman, *The Sexual Offender and His Offenses*, New York: Julian Press, 1954, p. 477.

(178) ". . . defies the biological goal": Karpman, p. 372.

(178) Freudian definition: Karpman, pp. 347, 479, 482.

(178) ". . . sexually well-adjusted youths": Guttmacher, p. 50.

(178) two clinical studies: Guttmacher, pp. 81–86.

(179) "The conclusions reached were that the wives": David Abrahamsen, *The Psychology of Crime*, New York: Columbia University Press, 1960, p. 165.

(179) Footnote, a missing link: Paul H. Gebhard et al., *Sex Offenders* (1965), New York: Bantam, 1967, pp. 9–10, 16, 178, 205.

(180) "Social class looms large": Marvin E. Wolfgang, ed., *Studies in Homicide*, New York: Harper & Row, 1967, p. 5.

(181) "demonstration of masculinity and toughness": Marvin E. Wolfgang

and Franco Ferracuti, *The Subculture of Violence*, London: Tavistock, 1967, p. 154.

(181) rapist within the subculture of violence: Amir, pp. 314–331.
(182) Philadelphia police files, 1958, 1960: Amir, p. 334.
(182) 43 percent, pairs or groups: Amir, p. 337.
(182) age: Amir, p. 52.
(182) not married: Amir, p. 65.
(182) *Footnote*, Amir's raw material versus FBI's: See *UCR*, pp. 13–14; Amir, pp. 34, 37, 39.
(182) "lower part of the occupational scale": Amir, p. 339.
(182) prior arrest record: Amir, pp. 112–114.
(182) the Philadelphia rapist generally lived: Amir, pp. 89–94.
(182) percentage black: Amir, p. 43.
(182) *Footnote*, FBI's "Careers in Crime" file: Donald J. Mulvihill *et al.*, *Crimes of Violence*, a staff report to the National Commission on the Causes and Prevention of Violence, Washington: U.S. Government Printing Office, 1969, Vol. 12, pp. 532, 533, 544.
(183) "Rape was found": Amir, p. 336.
(183) "Contrary to past impression": Amir, p. 341.
(183) planning: Amir, pp. 140–143, 213–214.
(183) "no previous idea": Amir, pp. 141–142.
(183) Further observations: Amir, p. 339.
(184) some form of physical force: Amir, pp. 154–156.
(185) rape capitals of the nation: The cities I mention are those whose rate of reported rapes exceeds or approaches 50 cases per 100,000 inhabitants, "Table 5, Index of Crime, 1973, Standard Metropolitan Statistical Areas," *UCR*, 1973, pp. 77 ff.
(185) populations in excess: *UCR*, p. 13.
(185) Southwestern states: *UCR*, pp. 6, 11, 13.
(185) traditions of violence: This point is explored in *Crimes of Violence*, Vol. 11, pp. 75–80.
(185) Memphis study: Brenda A. Brown, "Crime Against Women Alone," a System Analysis of the Memphis Police Department Sex Crime Squad's 1973 Rape Investigations, May 18, 1974 (mimeo), pp. 7–8.
(186) 17-city survey: *Crimes of Violence*, Vol. 11, p. 221.
(186) Philadelphia study: Amir, pp. 145, 138–139.
(186) comparison study: Stephen Schafer and Gilbert Geis, "Forcible Rape: A Comparative Study of Offenses Known to the Police in Boston and Los Angeles, 1967," presented to the American Sociological Association meeting in San Francisco, 1969 (mimeo).

PAIRS, GROUPS AND GANGS

(187) Toronto survey: By J. W. Mohr as quoted in John M. MacDonald, *Rape Offenders and Their Victims*, Springfield: Charles C. Thomas, 1971, p. 160.
(187) Washington, D.C., study: Charles R. Hayman *et al.*, "Rape in the District of Columbia," presented to the 99th Annual Meeting, American Public Health Association, Minneapolis, Oct. 12, 1971 (mimeo).
(187) ". . . these results are amazing": Amir, p. 200.

(187) "silence": *Ibid.*
(188) gangs and pairs: Amir, p. 200.
(188) A California group psychologist: W. H. Blanchard, "The Group Process in Gang Rape," *Journal of Social Psychology*, 1959, No. 49, pp. 259–266.

"GRATUITOUS ACTS, EXTRAVAGANT DEFILEMENTS"

(195) "they slapped her a few times": Hubert Selby, *Last Exit to Brooklyn*, New York: Grove, 1965, p. 116.
(195) police department m.o. sheets: Forms in author's possession.
(195) A law professor: G. D. Woods, "Some Aspects of Pack Rape in Sydney," *Australian & New Zealand Journal of Criminology* (1969), Vol. 2, No. 2, pp. 105–119.
(196) "sexual humiliation": Amir, pp. 158–161, 222–225.
(196) ". . . not the acts of an 'impotent' ": Amir, p. 160.
(196) "Taking repeated turns": Amir, p. 222.
(197) few showed interest in cunnilingus, etc.: Amir, p. 159 (Table 56).

RAPE-MURDER

(197) "In New York City last year": Robert Daley, "Police Report on the TV Cop Shows," *New York Times Magazine*, Nov. 19, 1972.
(197) New York City rape-murders: By telephone from Police Officer Ann Gallagher, NYPD Sex Crimes Analysis Squad, Sept. 24, 1974.
(197) Memphis rape-murders: Brown, p. 10 n.
(197) Washington rape-murders: By telephone from Lt. William Caldwell, D.C. Homicide Squad, Sept. 24, 1974.
(197) Homicide statistics as they relate to the sexes: *Crimes of Violence*, Vol. 11, pp. 209–210, 216–218.
(198) Aggravated assault statistics: *Crimes of Violence*, Vol. 11, pp. 209, 211, 217–219.
(199) few advance to become rape-murderers: This is apparent from a reading of Table 19, *Crimes of Violence*, Vol. 12, p. 544.
(199) Kitty Genovese case: *Time*, June 26, 1964, pp. 21–22.
(200) addendum to Moseley's story: *Time*, Nov. 20, 1972, p. 74.
(200) Albert DeSalvo: To retell this incredible case I have drawn heavily on Gerold Frank, *The Boston Strangler*, New York: NAL Signet, 1967, throughout. Individual citations follow.
(200) indicted for child molestation: Frank, pp. 347–349.
(201) "I just put my hand on them": Frank, pp. 335–336.
(201) "breaking and entering": Frank, p. 256.
(202) wine bottle or broomstick: Frank, pp. 257, 258, 296, 323.
(203) "I didn't touch her": Frank, p. 353.
(203) psychiatric profile: Frank, pp. 165–172.
(203) *Footnote*, Attitudes of women assistants, struggle of woman reporter: Frank, pp. 178–179, 58–61.
(204) rage against his brutal father: Frank, pp. 329, 345.
(204) "Attractiveness has nothing to do with it": Frank, p. 300.
(204) ". . . my rights as a husband": Frank, p. 276.
(205) ". . . made me feel powerful": Frank, pp. 338–339.
(205) ". . . like any other normal guy": Frank, p. 327.
(205) "Tall, very tall": Frank, pp. 302–303.

(205) Hurkos profile: Frank, pp. 106–108.
(206) DeSalvo was murdered: John Kifner, "DeSalvo, Confessed 'Boston Strangler,' Found Stabbed to Death in Prison Cell," *New York Times*, Nov. 27, 1973.
(206) "The only problem we had with Albert": *Ibid.*
(206) *Footnote*, Massachusetts law permitting women jurors to be barred from sex cases still on the books: Confirmed by Edward Perlman, Deputy Assistant Attorney General, Massachusetts State Attorney General's Office, by telephone, Sept. 24, 1974.
(207) serves less than four years: U.S. Department of Justice, *National Prisoner Statistics: Prisoners Released from State and Federal Institutions*, 1960, Figure B, Figure C.
(207) twice as likely to insist on innocence: Karpman, p. 72.
(207) Sing Sing study: Bernard Glueck, "Final Report, Research Project for the Study and Treatment of Persons Convicted of Crimes Involving Sexual Aberrations," submitted to the Governor of the State of New York, 1956, p. 303.
(207) New York City report: Karpman, p. 72.
(207) Canadian study: R. J. McCaldon, "Rape," *Canadian Journal of Corrections*, Vol. 9, No. 1 (Jan. 1967), pp. 37–59.
(207) "In two-thirds of the cases": McCaldon, p. 47.
(208) warden of San Quentin: Clinton T. Duffy with Al Hirshsberg, *Sex and Crime*, New York: Doubleday, 1965, throughout.
(208) "I'm no rapo": Duffy, p. 58.
(208) 'three-page rap sheet": *Ibid.*
(208) "Rape is often so difficult to prove": Duffy, p. 57.
(208) "Rapists are usually all-round offenders": Duffy, p. 132.
(208) ". . . may cut some ice": Duffy, p. 58.

7. A QUESTION OF RACE

(211) wrote a long piece: Susan Brownmiller, "Rashomon in Maryland," *Esquire*, May 1968, pp. 130 ff.
(213) According to the FBI: Federal Bureau of Investigation, *Uniform Crime Reports*, 1973, pp. 15, 10, 19.
(213) black population, 1970 census: Figure obtained from U.S. Bureau of Census by telephone, Nov. 1, 1974.
(214) 17-city survey, interracial rape: Donald J. Mulvihill et. al., *Crimes of Violence*, a staff report to the National Commission on the Causes and Prevention of Violence, Washington: U.S. Government Printing Office, 1969, Vol. 11, pp. 209, 212.
(214) "Because white males": *Crimes of Violence*, Vol. 11, p. 245.
(214) *Footnote*, 17-city survey, interracial robbery: *Crimes of Violence*, Vol. 11, pp. 208, 214.
(214) Memphis study: Brenda A. Brown, "Crime Against Women Alone," a System Analysis of the Memphis Police Department Sex Crime Squad's 1973 Rape Investigations, May 18, 1974 (mimeo), pp. 10–11.
(214) Philadelphia study: Menachem Amir, *Patterns in Forcible Rape*, Chicago: University of Chicago Press, 1971, p. 44.
(214) Washington study: Charles R. Hayman et al., "Rape in the District

of Columbia," presented to the 99th Annual Meeting, American Public Health Association, Minneapolis, Oct. 12, 1971 (mimeo), pp. 6–7.

(215) "In contrast to Amir": Charles R. Hayman, "Comment," *Sexual Behavior*, Vol. 1, No. 8 (Nov. 1971), p. 33.

(215) Wolfgang-Amsterdam study: James Q. Wilson, "The Death Penalty," *New York Times Magazine*, Oct. 28, 1973, pp. 34, 36.

(215) Wolfgang on comparative patterns: Marvin E. Wolfgang and Bernard Cohen, *Crime and Race*, New York: Institute of Human Relations Press, 1970, p. 81.

(215) Justice Department statistics, executions: U.S. Department of Justice, *National Prisoner Statistics Bulletin No. 46: Capital Punishment* (Aug. 1971), Table 1.

(216) Baltimore study: "Negroes Accuse Maryland Bench: Double Standard Is Charged in Report on Rape Cases," *New York Times*, Sept. 18, 1967, p. 33.

(217) "The entire Negro population": Winthrop D. Jordan, *White Over Black*, Chapel Hill: University of North Carolina Press, 1968, p. 153.

(217) "After confessing the conspiracy": *Ibid.*

(217) no evidence that rape played a part: Herbert Aptheker, *American Negro Slave Revolts*, New York: Columbia University Press, 1943, p. 224 n.

(217) "Infuriating sexual slander": John Henrik Clarke, ed., *William Styron's Nat Turner: Ten Black Writers Respond*, Boston: Beacon Press, 1968, p. 85.

(217) Genovese suggested: Eugene D. Genovese, *In Red and Black: Marxian Explorations in Southern and Afro-American History*, New York: Pantheon, 1971, pp. 211–212.

(217) "The slaves destroyed tirelessly": C. L. R. James, *The Black Jacobins: Toussaint L'Ouverture and the San Domingo Revolution* (1938), New York: Vintage Books, 1963, p. 88.

(218) state of Virginia's records: Ulrich B. Phillips, *American Negro Slavery* (1918), Baton Rouge: Louisiana State University Press, 1969, p. 458.

(218) "That no slave women were mentioned": *Ibid.*

(218) Footnote, During the same time span: Phillips, pp. 457–458.

(218) penalty of castration: Jordan, p. 157.

(218) Jefferson, "The principle of retaliation": Jordan, p. 463.

(219) The 1860 Code of Virginia: Donald H. Partington, "The Incidence of the Death Penalty for Rape in Virginia," *Washington and Lee Law Review*, Vol. 22 (1965), p. 50.

(219) Mississippi newspaper on Judge Lynch: Phillips, pp. 460–461.

(219) "chief slave of the harem": Harriet Martineau, *Society in America* (3 vols.) London: 1837, Vol. 2, p. 328. This quote is blind in Martineau's text but I have seen it attributed to Dolley Madison.

(220) Colonial legislation in North Carolina, etc.: James H. Johnston, *Race Relations in Virginia and Miscegenation in the South* (1937), Amherst: University of Massachusetts Press, 1970, pp. 172–180.

(220) A colonial Pennsylvania court: Johnston, p. 179. The black man in this case, apparently a slave, was ordered merely "never more to meddle with white women on paine of his life," for he had sworn to the court that "she inticed him."

(220) During a forty-four-year period in Virginia: Johnston, pp. 257–263.

(220) "The said Patsy Hooker": Johnston, p. 261.

(221) case of Tasco Thompson: Johnston, pp. 262–263.

(222) *Birth of a Nation* caused near-riots: Milton MacKaye, "The Birth of a Nation," *Scribner's*, Nov. 1937, p. 46.

(222) Cash on Southern "rape complex": W. J. Cash, *The Mind of the South*, New York: Knopf, 1941, pp. 115–117.

(223) NAACP lynch statistics: *Thirty Years of Lynching in the United States, 1889–1918*, New York: National Association for the Advancement of Colored People, 1919.

(223) Footnote, terse report, black female lynch victim: *Notes on Lynching in the United States, compiled from The Crisis*, New York: NAACP, 1912, p. 3.

(224) "It may be fairly pointed out": *Thirty Years of Lynching*, p. 10.

(224) "We declare lynching is an indefensible crime": *A New Public Opinion on Lynching*, Atlanta: Association of Southern Women for the Prevention of Lynching, Bulletin No. 5, 1935.

(225) Jessie Ames later credited female suffrage: Jessie Daniel Ames, *Toward Lynchless America*, Washington: American Council on Public Affairs, 1941, p. 5.

(225) "Lowndes County, Miss.": *Are the Courts to Blame?*, Atlanta: Association of Southern Women for the Prevention of Lynching, Bulletin No. 3, 1934, p. 7.

(225) "Whatever else may be said about Southern women": Ames, p. 5.

(226) the Southern women began naming names: Reports cited from *Feeling Is Tense*, Atlanta: Association of Southern Women for the Prevention of Lynching, Bulletin No. 8, 1938, p. 7.

(226) "Where Were the Peace Officers?": *Feeling Is Tense*, p. 8.

(227) International Publishers laid down the party line: Harry Haywood and Milton Howard, *Lynching, A Weapon of National Oppression*, New York: International Publishers, International Pamphlet No. 25, 1932.

(227) Du Bois, White, Darrow, "dastardly evasion": Haywood and Howard, p. 5.

(227) "Lynchings defend profits!": Haywood and Howard, p. 7.

(227) "Lynching is the ultimate threat": *To Secure These Rights*, Report of The President's Committee on Civil Rights, Washington: U.S. Government Printing Office; New York: Simon and Schuster, 1947, p. 24.

(227) "The 'Rape' Lie": Haywood and Howard, pp. 7–8.

(228) Wigmore on *Evidence*: See my page 370 for Wigmore's views on the veracity of female rape complainants.

(228) To Communists, feminism was always a dirty word: See Clara Zetkin, *Lenin on the Woman Question*, New York: International Publishers, 1934, pp. 6–7, 15; Ella Reeve Bloor, *We Are Many*, New York: International Publishers, 1940, pp. 92–104.

(229) Deutsch found "marked sexual attraction to Negro men" etc.: John Dollard, *Caste and Class in a Southern Town* (1937), New York: Doubleday Anchor Books, 1957, pp. 169–170 n.

(229) ". . . innocent men accused of rape by hysterical women": Helene Deutsch, *The Psychology of Women*, New York: Grune & Stratton, 1944, Vol. I, p. 254.

(230) the name of that case was Scottsboro: To retell the Scottsboro story
I have relied most heavily on Arthur Garfield Hays, *Trial by Prejudice*,
New York: Covici, Friede, 1933 pp. 25–150. Additional sources that
proved useful were: Mary Heaton Vorse, "How Scottsboro Happened," *The New Republic*, May 10, 1933, pp. 356–358; "Report on
the Scottsboro, Ala. Case made by Miss Hollace Ransdell representing the American Civil Liberties Union," New York, May 27, 1931
(mimeo); "Opinion of Judge James E. Horton of the Alabama Circuit Court granting a motion for a new trial in the Scottsboro Case,"
reproduced by the ACLU, July 1933 (mimeo); appellant briefs for
Haywood Patterson and Clarence Norris, argued before the Supreme
Court of the State of Alabama by Osmond K. Fraenkel and Samuel S.
Leibowitz, 1934, 1937; Quentin Reynolds, *Courtroom: the Story
of Samuel S. Leibowitz*, New York: Farrar, Straus, 1950, pp. 248–
314; Haywood Patterson and Earl Conrad, *Scottsboro Boy*, New
York: Doubleday, 1950; Allan K. Chalmers, *They Shall Be Free*,
New York: Doubleday, 1951. Specific quotes taken from the text of
these sources and references for certain critical facts are cited below.

(231) "Dearest Earl," she began: Hays, pp. 115–116.

(232) some of the black defendants swore in court they had seen the others
do the raping: Hays, pp. 61–64.

(232) many a pamphlet charged that Victoria Price was a prostitute: For
one example, see Guy Endore, *The Crime at Scottsboro*, Hollywood:
Hollywood Scottsboro Committee, 1938, pp. 11–12. For an example
of the way this unsupported charge has become a "fact," see Elias M.
Schwarzbart, "The Scottsboro Case," *New York Times*, Jan. 25,
1975, p. 27.

(232) Women did not win the right to sit on Alabama juries until 1966: By
telephone from William McQueen, Assistant Attorney General,
Montgomery, Ala., Sept. 10, 1974.

(233) "tossed out of the precinct": Reynolds, p. 305.

(233) corralled by a posse of white men: Hays, p. 35; Chalmers, p. 19.

(233) ". . . when the two girls were taken from the train": Ransdell to the
ACLU, p. 3.

(234) ". . . fearing a vagrancy charge": Vorse, *The New Republic*, p. 357.

(234) cost Horton his judicial career: See "J. E. Horton Dies; Scottsboro
Judge," *New York Times*, Mar. 30, 1973, p. 42.

(234) "History, sacred and profane": Horton opinion, ACLU mimeo,
p. 15; also quoted by Hays, Reynolds and Patterson.

(234) Louisiana study: Oakley C. Johnson, "Is the Punishment of Rape
Equally Administered to Negroes and Whites in the State of
Louisiana?" (1950), *We Charge Genocide* (1951), New York:
International Publishers, 1970, Appendix, Document B.

(234) Virginia study: Donald H. Partington, "The Incidence of the Death
Penalty for Rape in Virginia," *Washington and Lee Law Review*,
Vol. 22 (1965), pp. 43, 68–70. Partington was able to ascertain that
in half of these cases the victim had been white. In one case the victim
had been black. Information on race of victim was not available for
the rest of the cases (most of those before 1930).

(236) "The attack on Mrs. Taylor was an attack on all women": Earl Conrad and Eugene Gordon, *Equal Justice Under the Law*, New York:
Committee for Equal Justice for Mrs. Recy Taylor, 1945, pp. 9–10.

(237) "The conspiracy has made potent use of the spurious charge": *We Charge Genocide*, p. 149.

(238) "Why did she change her story": Mel Fiske, "The Story of the Martinsville Frameup," *Daily Worker*, Feb. 4 and 5, 1951.

(239) And then there was Willie McGee: To retell the McGee case I have drawn on the following sources: Carl T. Rowan, *South of Freedom*, New York: Knopf, 1952, pp. 174–192; *New York Times*, May 8, 1951, p. 1; *Time*, May 14, 1951, p. 26; *Life*, May 21, 1951, p. 44; and several articles that appeared in the *Daily Worker* from March to May, 1951. Individual citations follow.

(240) No white man had ever been executed for rape in Mississippi: *Time*, May 14, 1951, p. 26; *Life*, May 21, 1951, p. 44.

(240) Her husband was no drunken intruder: *Daily Worker*, Mar. 12, 1951, p. 4.

(240) "Down South you tell a woman like that": *Ibid.*

(240) ". . . she'll say she was raped": *Ibid.*

(240) The Worker called Willametta Hawkins a Potiphar's wife, etc.: *Daily Worker*, Mar. 15, 1951, p. 6.

(241) "I've always been skeptical": *Daily Worker*, Mar. 19, 1951, p. 2.

(241) ". . . almost impossible to rape a woman": *Ibid.*

(241) ". . . known to the entire community": *Daily Worker*, Mar. 27, 1951, p. 1.

(241) ". . . it was Mrs. Hawkins who raped my husband": *Daily Worker*, Apr. 25, 1951, p. 1.

(241) among those who watched: Rowan, p. 190; *New York Times*, May 8, 1951, p. 1.

(241) "Willie McGee was murdered because the white woman": *Daily Worker*, May 9, 1951, p. 1.

(241) "something very unfortunate happened to Willie": *Life*, May 21, 1951, p. 44.

(241) "He was never in the Armed Services": *Ibid.*

(242) ". . . utterly no evidence of such a relationship": *Time*, May 14, 1951, p. 26.

(242) Footnote, One exception: *The Nation*, May 5, 1951, p. 421.

(242) That year Carl Rowan: Rowan, pp. 174–192.

(242) As a teen-ager in McMinnville: Rowan, pp. 32–33.

(243) to Congresswoman Bella Abzug: Author's interview with Bella Abzug, New York City, Dec. 27, 1973. All of Abzug's remarks were obtained during this interview.

(245) the "wolf-whistle" murder of Emmett Till I have drawn on the following sources: Carl T. Rowan, *Go South to Sorrow*, New York: Random House, 1957, pp. 38–56; "Emmett Till's Day in Court," *Life*, Oct. 3, 1955; William Bradford Huie, "The Shocking Story of Approved Killing in Mississippi," *Look*, Jan. 24, 1956; William Bradford Huie, "What's Happened to the Emmett Till Killers?" *Look*, Jan. 22, 1957. Individual citations follow.

(246) "While the Delta Negroes peered, in delicious awe": Huie, *Look*, Jan. 22, 1957, p. 63.

(246) women were excluded by law from Mississippi juries until 1968: By telephone from Mary Libby Payne, Assistant Attorney General, Jackson, Miss., Sept. 10, 1974.

(246) a courtroom tableau: *Life*, Oct. 3, 1955, pp. 36–37.

(246) Mack Charles Parker: *Life*, May 4, 1959, p. 44; *Look*, Jan. 19, 1960, p. 82.

(247) "He showed me the white gal's picture!": Huie, *Look*, Jan. 22, 1957, p. 63.

(248) "While looking at the picture": Eldridge Cleaver, *Soul on Ice*, New York: Dell-Delta/Ramparts, 1968, p. 11.

(248) ". . . against white women in particular": *Ibid*.

(248) ". . . as a matter of principle": Cleaver, p. 13.

(248) "I became a rapist": Cleaver, p. 14.

(249) "Come up, black dada nihilismus": *Ibid*.

(249) ". . . the funky facts of life": Cleaver, p. 15.

(249) "I am well aware": Calvin C. Hernton, *Sex and Racism in America*, New York: Grove Press, 1966, pp. 67–68.

(249) "Any oppressed group": Hernton, p. 79.

(249) ". . . to comply with the white woman's fantasies": Hernton, p. 45.

(250) "Whoever says rape says Negro": Frantz Fanon, *Black Skin, White Masks* (1952), trans. from the French by Charles Lam Markmann, New York: Grove Press, 1967, p. 166.

(250) "When a woman lives the fantasy of rape": Fanon, p. 179.

(250) ". . . fear of rape . . . cry out for rape": Fanon, p. 156.

(250) ". . . I know nothing about her": Fanon, pp. 179–180.

(250) Footnote, "Impotence in an Algerian following the rape of his wife": Frantz Fanon, *The Wretched of the Earth* (1961), trans. from the French by Constance Farrington, New York: Grove Press, 1968, pp. 254–259.

(251) ". . . practicing on black girls in the ghetto": Cleaver, p. 14.

(251) ". . . when I considered myself smooth enough": *Ibid*.

(251) "Rape was an insurrectionary act": *Ibid*.

(251) ". . . lost my self-respect": Cleaver, p. 15.

(251) ". . . a combination of business and pleasure": Cleaver interview in *Playboy*, December 1968, as quoted in John M. MacDonald, *Rape Offenders and Their Victims*, Springfield: Charles C. Thomas, 1971, p. 53.

(251) "It takes a certain boldness": Geismar intro to Cleaver, p. xii.

(252) "Aren't any black people guilty": Tad Szulc, "George Jackson Radicalizes the Brothers in Soledad and San Quentin," *New York Times Magazine*, Aug. 1, 1971, p. 10.

(252) "like a carrot on a stick": Cleaver, p. 10.

(253) Boston and Washington study: Sandra Sutherland and Donald J. Scherl, "Patterns of Response Among Victims of Rape," *American Journal of Orthopsychiatry*, Vol. 40, No. 3 (Apr. 1970), pp. 503–511.

(253) "I just cant' throw off history": *New York Post*, June 8, 1973, p. 39.

(253) "Locking up individual rapists": *Sister*, Vol. 4, No. 12 (Mar. 1974), p. 3.

(254) fight against capital punishment: When the U.S. Supreme Court overturned the death penalty on June 29, 1972, on the grounds of "cruel and unusual" punishment, two of the three cases under review (*Jackson v. Georgia, Branch v. Texas*) were cases of black men sentenced to death for raping white women. *Furman v. Georgia*, the case that topped the list, concerned a robbery-murder. (Information

from Jack Himmelstein, NAACP Legal Defense and Educational Fund. See also *New York Times*, June 30, 1972, pp. 1, 14.)

(254) ". . . cowboy-and-Indian movies": Paul L. Montgomery, "New Drive on to Make Rape Convictions Easier," *New York Times*, Nov. 13, 1973, p. 47.

8. POWER: INSTITUTION AND AUTHORITY

PRISON RAPE: THE HOMOSEXUAL EXPERIENCE

(258) homosexuals segregated in New York prison for their own protection: Ted Morgan, "Entombed," *New York Times Magazine*, Feb. 17, 1974, p. 19.

(258) Robert A. Martin press conference: Jared Stout, "Quaker Tells of Rape in D.C. Jail," *Washington Star-News*, Aug. 25, 1973; David L. Aiken, "Ex-Sailor Charges Jail Rape, Stirs Up Storm," *The Advocate* ("Newspaper of America's Homophile Community"), Sept. 26, 1973, p. 5.

(260) Nine inmates at Sumter: Reuter file, June 9, 1973.

(260) Two inmates at Raiford: "Florida's Rape Law Held No Protection for Males," *New York Times*, Jan. 13, 1974.

(260) county judge in upstate New York: "Judge Releases a Homosexual Rather Than Send Him to Attica," *New York Times*, Nov. 13, 1972.

(260) Two bright young Nixon aides: "Panel Offers Dean Limited Immunity," *New York Daily News*, May 9, 1973, p. 2; Edward B. Fiske, "Trying to Explain to a Young Son Why His Father Must Go to Jail" *New York Times*, Feb. 4, 1974, p. 25 (Égil Krogh).

(260) straightforward account of the hierarchic sex code: Haywood Patterson and Earl Conrad, *Scottsboro Boy*, New York: Doubleday, 1950, pp. 79–85.

(261) "a raped child": Jean-Paul Sartre, *Saint Genet*, trans. from the French by Bernard Frechtman, New York: Braziller, 1963, p. 79.

(262) ". . . an iron embrace has made him a woman": *Ibid.*

(262) Genet was subjected to repeated assaults: Jean Genet, *Miracle of the Rose* (1951), trans. from the French by Bernard Frechtman, London: Anthony Blond, 1965, throughout.

(262) tube of Vaseline: Jean Genet, *The Thief's Journal* (1949), trans. from the French by Bernard Frechtman, New York: Grove Press, 1964, pp. 21–22.

(262) Winter's "pretty mug": *Miracle of the Rose*, p. 248.

(262) Bulkaen's gang spitting: *Miracle of the Rose*, pp. 266–268.

(262) anal compliments: *Miracle of the Rose*, pp. 180–181, 199.

(262) His adoration of the muscular thighs, etc.: This runs as a theme in all his writings; his attraction to Nazis is most pronounced in *Funeral Rites*.

(263) "a male that fucks another male": Jean Genet, *Our Lady of the Flowers* (1943), trans. from the French by Bernard Frechtman, New York: Grove Press, 1963, p. 253.

(263) ". . . the Saint who lets herself be raped": Sartre, p. 367.

(263) *Footnote*, Lytton Strachey at the Hampstead Tribunal: Michael Holroyd, *Lytton Strachey*, London: Penguin, 1971, pp. 628–629.

(263) "the rump is the secret femininity of males": Sartre, p. 457.

(264) T. E. Lawrence's gang rape: T. E. Lawrence, Seven Pillars of Wisdom, New York: Doubleday, 1935, p. 443; Anthony Nutting, Lawrence of Arabia, London: Hollis & Carter, 1961, pp. 112–116, 244–247.

(264) ". . . seduction . . . gone wrong": John H. Gagnon and William Simon, Sexual Conduct, Chicago: Aldine Pub. Co., 1973, p. 250.

(264) Philadelphia study: Alan J. Davis, "Sexual Assaults in the Philadelphia Prison System," Gagnon and Simon, eds., The Sexual Scene, Chicago: Transaction/Aldine, 1970, pp. 107–124.

(267) periodic exposés: See Wayne King, "Killing of Carolina Jailer, Charged to a Woman, Raises Question of Abuse of Inmates," New York Times, Dec. 1, 1974. In this story it was reported that one month earlier the U.S. Attorney General had been alerted to "serious evidence that hundreds of women, both black and white, have been subjected to illegal and immoral sexual assaults by jailers and jail trusties where they were confined" in North Carolina penal institutions. See also "2 Mental Patients Raped by Prisoners," Washington Post, Jan. 12, 1972, p. B-3; "31 in Ohio Charged with Mistreating Asylum Inmates," New York Times, Nov. 25, 1971, p. 42; Jerry M. Flint, "31 Ex-Employees at Ohio Hospital Appear in Court," New York Times, Nov. 27, 1971, p. 24; Grace Lichtenstein, "Allegation of Staff Violence Tainting Rome State School," New York Times, May 5, 1973; "Legislator Asserts Crime Rose at Willowbrook School in 1973," New York Times, Feb. 14, 1974. All of these stories mention sexual assault within an institutional setting.

(267) inmate hierarchy in a women's prison: See Rose Giallombardo, Society of Women: A Study of a Women's Prison, New York: John Wiley, 1966, Chaps. 8, 9 and 10.

(268) lesbian rape of an inmate: Frances Farmer, Will There Really Be a Morning? New York: Dell, 1973, pp. 145–152.

(268) newspaper exposé of Children's Center: Murray Schumach, "Gangs of Girls Terrorize Staff and the Retarded at Children's Unit Here," New York Times, Sept. 8, 1974, p. 1; Murray Schumach, "Teen-Aged Girls to Leave Center," New York Times, Sept. 12, 1974, p. 1.

POLICE RAPE

(268) In October 1972, officer Farley was suspended: "City Patrolman, Accused of Raping Girl, Suspended," New York Times, Oct. 8, 1972.

(269) Farley sentenced to fifteen years: "Former City Detective Given 15-Year Sentence for Rape," New York Times, Feb. 5, 1974.

(269) twelve-year sentence in another jurisdiction, Suffolk case still pending: Ibid.

(269) entire raping career while member of NYPD: Verification from Assistant District Attorney Leslie Snyder, who prosecuted the Manhattan cases, by telephone, Sept. 13, 1974.

(269) New York newspaper monitoring, one new case per year: "Cop Guilty in Queens Sex Case," New York Post, June 29, 1971 (Brooklyn patrolman, 31, convicted of statutory rape and sexual abuse of a 15-year-old girl in a Woodside, Queens, motel); "Patrolman Held in Sex Attacks on Two Women in Forest Hills," New

York Times, June 4, 1972 (Queens patrolman, 24, assigned to duty in Manhattan, suspended from force and arrested and charged with rape, sodomy and unlawful imprisonment for two separate attacks at gunpoint, one on a 44-year-old woman); "TPF Cop Is Accused of Rape," *New York Post*, Feb. 24, 1973 (Tactical Patrol Force officer, 26, arrested and arraigned in Queens criminal court on charges of rape and sodomy on a 29-year-old woman in the hallway of her home; promptly suspended from force).

(269) Washington, Cleveland, Houston: "Policeman Charged in Second Rape," *Washington Post*, Nov. 12, 1971; "2nd Girl Says Patrolmen Raped Her," Cleveland *Plain Dealer*, Feb. 25, 1972; "City civil service commissioners have suspended two policemen for insubordination stemming from the controversy over whether they beat and raped a prostitute," United Press International, Houston, Mar. 23 ,1974.

(269) Detroit: Michael Graham, "Officers Accused of Sex Crimes, Three Suspended After Investigation," Detroit *Free Press*, Nov. 22, 1973, p. 1. See also United Press International, Detroit, "Police," Nov. 22, 1973.

(269) dismissed from force after departmental hearing, etc.: By telephone from Sgt. James Jackson, Detroit Police Department press officer, Sept. 13, 1974.

(270) "Two young Negro women": *We Charge Genocide* ("The historic petition to the United Nations for relief from a crime of the United States government against the Negro People," 1951), New York: International Publishers, 1970, p. 82.

(271) women's folklore of rape: See Ann Landers' column, *New York Daily News*, Sept. 16, 1974, for results of an informal poll taken among her readers regarding sexual advances made by doctors, dentists, clergymen and divorce lawyers.

THE SEXUAL ABUSE OF CHILDREN

(271) "Dear Abby": *New York Post*, Feb. 11, 1972.

(272) in prison child molester lowest of the low: Clinton T. Duffy with Al Hirshberg, *Sex and Crime*, New York: Doubleday, 1965, p. 58. This was the theme of Miguel Pinero's play *Short Eyes*.

(272) Seen as a confused, conflicted man with a "morality" problem or bad judgment: Paul H. Gebhard *et al.*, *Sex Offenders* (1965), New York: Bantam, 1967, pp. 81–82.

(272) Washington study: Charles R. Hayman *et al.*, "Rape in the District of Columbia," presented to the 99th Annual Meeting, American Public Health Association, Minneapolis, Oct. 12, 1971 (mimeo), pp. 5–6.

(272) Memphis study: Brenda A. Brown, "Crime Against Women Alone," a System Analysis of the Memphis Police Department Sex Crime Squad's 1973 Rape Investigations, May 18, 1974 (mimeo), Appendix, K-1.

(273) Philadelphia study: Menachem Amir, *Patterns in Forcible Rape*, Chicago: University of Chicago Press, 1971, p. 52.

(273) molestation of Virginia Woolf: Quentin Bell, *Virginia Woolf*, New York: Harcourt, Brace, 1972, pp. 42–44, 61, 78, 95–96.

(273) rape of Billie Holiday: Billie Holiday with William Dufty, *Lady Sings the Blues* (1956), New York: Lancer, 1972, pp. 15–17.

(273) molestation of Viva: Viva, *Superstar*, New York: Putnam, 1970, pp. 25–28.

(273) rape of Maya Angelou: Maya Angelou, *I Know Why the Caged Bird Sings*, New York: Bantam, 1971, pp. 57–73.

(275) Freud on female patients: Sigmund Freud, *New Introductory Lectures on Psychoanalysis* (1933), No. 33, "Femininity." (New York: Norton, 1965, p. 120.) Freud made this point on other occasions as well, and it was clearly the inspiration for the attitudes of Helene Deutsch and others.

(276) "unusually attractive and charming personalities": Lauretta Bender and Abram Blau, "The Reaction of Children to Sexual Relations with Adults," *American Journal of Orthopsychiatry*, 1937, pp. 500–518.

(276) ". . . highly probable that the child had used his charm": Lauretta Bender and Alvin E. Grugett, "A Follow-Up Report on Children Who Had Atypical Sexual Experience," *American Journal of Orthopsychiatry*, 1952, pp. 825–837.

(276) chastised mothers: See Yvonne M. Tormes, *Child Victims of Incest*, Denver: American Humane Association, Children's Division, 1968 (pamphlet); see also John M. MacDonald, *Rape Offenders and Their Victims*, Springfield: Charles C. Thomas, 1971, pp. 201–202.

(276) "A problem which deserves noting": Alfred C. Kinsey et al., *Sexual Behavior in the Human Male*, Philadelphia: W. B. Saunders, 1948, pp. 237–238.

(276) One in four women interviewed: Alfred C. Kinsey et al., *Sexual Behavior in the Human Female*, Philadelphia: W. B. Saunders, 1953, pp. 117–118.

(276) "It is difficult to understand": Kinsey, *Female*, p. 121.

(277) "With the usual male arrogance": Florence Rush, "The Sexual Abuse of Children: A Feminist Point of View," paper presented to the New York Radical Feminist Conference on Rape, Apr. 17, 1971 (mimeo); also in Cassandra Wilson and Noreen Connell, eds., *Rape: The First Sourcebook for Women*, New York: NAL Plume, 1974.

(277) Brooklyn-Bronx study: Vincent DeFrancis, *Protecting the Child Victim of Sex Crimes Committed By Adults*, Denver: American Humane Association, Children's Division, 1969. Individual citations follow.

(277) Association's definition of a sex crime: DeFrancis, pp. 25–26.

(277) core sample represented a fraction: DeFrancis, p. 37.

(277) actual incidence probably twice reported incidence: *Ibid*.

(278) major findings: DeFrancis, pp. vii, 66.

(278) specific findings: DeFrancis, pp. vii, 68–69.

(278) arrests and prosecutions: DeFrancis, p. xi.

(278) *Footnote*, New York State legislature kept corroborative requirement for cases of assaults against children: David A. Andelman, "Assembly Votes to Drop Rape Corroboration Rule," *New York Times*, Jan. 15, 1974.

(279) emotional damage to child victim: DeFrancis, pp. x, 152–179.

(279) ". . . some parents projected blame on the child": DeFrancis, p. 160.

(279) four-year-old played similar "game": DeFrancis, pp. 160–161.

(279) careened into promiscuity: DeFrancis, p. 162.

(279) 29 became pregnant: DeFrancis, p. x.

(279) profile of the adult offender: DeFrancis, pp. 66–70.

(279) Amir showed median age of twenty-three: Amir, p. 52.

(279) *Footnote*, case studies of prostitutes unearth accounts of childhood rape: Jacob and Rosamond Goldberg, *Girls on City Streets*, New York: American Social Hygiene Association, 1935, pp. 56, 58, 103, 112, 136; John M. Murtagh and Sara Harris, *Cast the First Stone*, New York: McGraw-Hill, 1957, p. 21; Charles Winick and Paul M. Kinsie, *The Lively Commerce*, Chicago: Quadrangle, 1971, pp. 52, 54–55; Harold Greenwald, *The Call Girl*, New York: Ballantine, 1958, pp. 33, 110–111, 112, 192, 194, 201, 203, 225.

(279) *Footnote*, pimp: "The majority of girls I've gotten": "New York: White Slavery, 1972," *Time*, June 5, 1972, p. 24.

(279) *Footnote*, Pimps understand rape as method to "turn out" likely teen-age candidate: See Martin Arnold, "13 Accused Here of Torturing Girls to Force Them into Prostitution," *New York Times*, Apr. 6, 1971.

(280) Brooklyn-Bronx study, only 10 percent involved more than one offender: DeFrancis, p. 66.

(280) ". . . more than one member of a household": *Ibid.*

(281) Gebhard on father rapists: Gebhard, pp. 248, 270.

(281) Washington State Supreme Court decision: *Time*, Dec. 25, 1972, p. 41.

9. THE MYTH OF THE HEROIC RAPIST

(283) Greek myths: I have relied on H. J. Rose, *A Handbook of Greek Mythology*, New York: Dutton paperback, 1959.

(284) "A shudder in the loins": W. B. Yeats, "Leda and The Swan." (*Collected Poems of W. B. Yeats*, New York: Macmillan, 1954, pp. 211–212.)

(284) Graves has suggested: Robert Graves, *The Greek Myths*, New York: Braziller, 1957, p. 56 n.

(284) others have elaborated: See Ludwig Eidelberg, *The Dark Urge*, New York: Pyramid, 1961, p. 147.

(284) "Of rape the Arapesh know nothing": Margaret Mead, *Sex and Temperament in Three Primitive Societies* (1935), New York: Dell, 1968, p. 110.

(284) Among the violent Mundugumor: Mead, p. 219.

(284) Iatmul headhunters: Margaret Mead, *Male and Female*, New York: Morrow, 1949, p. 52.

(285) Plains Indians: Margaret Mead, *The Changing Culture of an Indian Tribe* (1932), New York: Capricorn, 1966, pp. 91–92.

(285) Mundurucú: Robert F. Murphy, "Social Structure and Sex Antagonism," *Southwestern Journal of Anthropology*, Vol. 15 (1959), pp. 89–98.

(286) Tapirapé rape observed by Wagley: Murphy, p. 94.

(286) "The Yanomamö themselves": Napoleon A. Chagnon, Yanomamö, The Fierce People, New York: Holt, Rinehart, 1968, p. 123.

(287) anthropological study of rape among the Gusii: Robert A. LeVine, "Gusii Sex Offenses: A Study in Social Control," American Anthropologist, Vol. 61, No. 6 (Dec. 1959), pp. 965–990.

(288) rape and abduction of Sicilian women: Peter Kayser, "Situationer—Women," Reuter, Rome, Aug. 7, 1973.

(288) current rape rate for certain American cities actually exceeds the Gusii's: See Table 5, Uniform Crime Reports, 1973, pp. 77 ff. For a more complete listing of these cities, see my p. 185 and corresponding source note.

(288) condottieri in Renaissance Italy: G. Rattray Taylor, Sex in History, New York: Vanguard, 1954, p. 138.

(288) Malatesta raped the Duchess: J. R. Hale, ed., Renaissance Venice, Totowa, N. J.: Rowman & Littlefield, 1973, p. 133.

(288) samurai in modern Japanese pornography: Richard Halloran, "Picasso's 'Erotic' Prints Exhibited in Tokyo, After a Little Censorship," New York Times, June 20, 1973, p. 2.

(288) "The ravages of the Bold Bucks": Christopher Hibbert, The Roots of Evil, London: Weidenfeld & Nicolson, 1963, p. 45.

(289) "One of them was complaining about the number of female writers": Nathanael West, Miss Lonelyhearts (1933), New York: New Directions, pp. 33–34.

(290) ". . . tang of rape": Ian Fleming, Casino Royale (1953), New York: NAL Signet, 1960, p. 127.

(290) "A man's highest job in life": As quoted in Harold D. Lasswell, Power and Personality, New York: Norton, 1948, p. 43.

(290) "When you find a convenient place": Andreas Capellanus, The Art of Courtly Love (1186), trans. from the Latin by John Jay Parry, New York: Norton, 1969, p. 150.

(291) Chrétien, "If a knight found a damsel": As quoted in Robert Briffault, The Mothers, New York: Macmillan, 1927, Vol. 3, p. 404.

(291) Sir Gawain ravished Gran de Lis: Ibid.

(291) "To judge from contemporary poems": Ibid (quoting Traill and Mann).

(291) rapacious knight and screaming lady: Thomas Malory, Le Morte d'Arthur, III, 5 (Eugene Vinaver, ed., The Works of Sir Thomas Malory, Oxford: Clarendon, 1967, Vol. 1, p. 103).

(291) Malory's rape charge discovered: Edward Hicks, Sir Thomas Malory: His Turbulent Career, Cambridge: Harvard University Press, 1928, pp. 25–26, 96, 105.

(292) ". . . double charge of rape was manifestly absurd": Kittredge introduction to Hicks, p. viii.

(292) convinced that Malory had been a faithful husband: Hicks, p. 56.

(292) "piling on the agony": Hicks, p. 53.

(292) ". . . Joan Smyth . . . Potiphar's Wife": Hicks, p. 57.

(292) Gilles de Rais: Thomas Wilson, Blue-Beard, New York: Putnam, 1899; A. L. Vincent and Clare Binns, Gilles de Rais: The Original Bluebeard, London: Philpot, 1926.

(292) confessed to influence of Caligula, who "sported with children": Vincent and Binns, p. 42.

(292) Role of Charles Perrault: Wilson, p. xiii. Perrault's Mother Goose stories, based on folk material, were published in 1697.

(293) Gilles de Rais and Dean Allen Corll: "The Mind of the Mass Murderer," *Time*, Aug. 27, 1973, p. 56.

(293) scenes in which men "do it" to men *verboten* in heterosexual pornography: Frankly, I learned this from some acquaintances, down on their luck, who briefly turned out the stuff for money, but for those who prefer a more proper citation: *The Report of The Commission on Obscenity and Pornography*, Washington. U.S. Government Printing Office, Sept. 1970, p. 115.

(294) Annan on Ripper as "hero of horror": *New York Review of Books*, Dec. 17, 1970, p. 39.

(294) McCabe on Ripper, "that great hero," etc.: San Francisco *Chronicle*, Oct. 7, 1971, p. 43.

(295) Wilson on Ripper: Colin Wilson, *A Casebook of Murder*, London: Leslie Frewin, 1969, pp. 133–148.

(295) Wilson disgusted by lesbian murder: Wilson, pp. 223–225.

(295) ". . . sexual act has a close affinity with murder": Wilson, p. 220.

(295) newspaper feature writers rehashed the story: See Kermit Jaediker, "Was DeSalvo the Boston Strangler?" New York *Sunday News*, Jan. 6, 1974, Leisure, pp. 20–21.

(296) "Keith Richard sways": Don Heckman, "As Cynthia Sagittarius Says—'Feeling . . . I mean, isn't this what the Rolling Stones are all about?' " *New York Times Magazine*, July 16, 1972, p. 38.

(296) "Well, you heard about The Boston—": "Midnight Rambler," words and music by Mick Jagger and Keith Richard. © 1969 ABKCO Music, Inc. Reprinted by permission. All rights reserved.

(297) tragedy at Altamont: For a good print account, with pictures, see Ralph J. Gleason, "Aquarius Wept," *Esquire*, Aug. 1970, pp. 84 ff.

(297) Amboy Dukes: The rock group as advertised in *Rolling Stone*, May 27, 1971, p. 64; the book: Irving Shulman, *The Amboy Dukes*, New York: Doubleday, 1947.

(298) Thompson's first defense of the Angels: Hunter S. Thompson, "The Motorcycle Gangs: Losers and Outsiders," *The Nation*, May 17, 1965, pp. 522–526.

(298) continued mythologizing: Hunter S. Thompson, *Hell's Angels*, New York: Random House, 1967, throughout; quoted material appears on pp. 190–196.

(299) ". . . got picked up on a phony rape charge": J. Anthony Lukas, "The Prince of Gonzo" (*More*), a journalism review, Nov. 1972, p. 7. Another version, which has Thompson in jail on the phony rape charge, appears in Timothy Crouse, *The Boys on the Bus*, New York: Ballantine, 1974, p. 334.

(299) Dick Turpin who "raped an occasional servant girl": Wilson, p. 60.

(300) "After the Sack—the Saturnalia": Edgcumb Pinchon, *Viva Villa!*, New York: Harcourt, Brace, 1933, p. 131.

(300) ". . . I believe in rape": Barbara Gelb, *So Short a Time*, New York: Norton, 1973, p. 66. Interestingly, Reed's mentor, Lincoln Steffens, seemed to have a different view of rape. Commenting on President Wilson's decision to send the marines to Vera Cruz, Steffens reflected, "We Americans can't seem to get it that you can't commit

rape a little." (Justin Kaplan, *Lincoln Steffens*, New York: Simon and Schuster, 1974, p. 211.)

(300) rape of Villa's sister and blood vengeance: For four different versions of this legend see Pinchon: Haldeen Braddy, *Cock of the Walk*; Louis Stevens, *Here Comes Pancho Villa*; and John Reed, *Insurgent Mexico*. Reed alone discounts the rape of Villa's sister as probable fiction; he also discounts Villa's own rapes as well.

(300) Abe Reles: Burton B. Turkus and Sid Feder, *Murder, Inc., The Story of "the Syndicate,"* New York: Farrar, Straus, 1951, pp. 111–112; *New York Times*, Nov. 13, 1941, p. 29.

(301) Tijerina story: "Policemen Accused in Gang Rape," *Washington Post*, Oct. 24, 1971, p. A-30. See also *El Grito del Norte* (Espanola, N.M.) special issue, Oct. 28, 1971, which bears the front-page headline, "They put me in prison, they called me a 'danger to the community' and then they raped my wife!" Page 11 of this same issue retells the Villa story under the headline, "An Old Tactic." See also *El Grito del Norte*, Dec. 6, 1971, p. 2, for more of the same.

(301) "If I'm old enough to kill": Harold Robbins, *The Adventurers*, New York: Pocket Books, 1966, pp. 39, 49.

(302) "At its most profound level": Paul D. Zimmerman, "Kubrick's Brilliant Vision," *Newsweek*, Jan. 3, 1972, pp. 28–31.

(302) "Alex symbolizes man": Bernard Weinraub, "Kubrick Tells What Makes 'Clockwork Orange' Tick," *New York Times*, Jan. 4, 1972.

(302) *Footnote*, "As a child I dreamed": Carlos Fuentes, "The Discreet Charm of Luis Buñuel," *New York Times Magazine*, Mar. 11, 1973, p. 87.

(303) "psychopathic rapists": Victoria Sullivan, "Does 'Frenzy' Degrade Women?" *New York Times*, July 30, 1972.

(303) "Hitchcock's graphic": Paul D. Zimmerman, "Return of the Master," *Newsweek*, June 26, 1972, p. 83.

(303) ". . . raped my picture": *Time*, Dec. 27, 1971, p. 49.

(303) twenty rape scenes in two years: Aljean Harmetz, "Rape—an Ugly Movie Trend," *New York Times*, Sept. 30, 1973.

(304) *Deliverance* metaphor for rape of the environment: *Newsweek's* Paul D. Zimmerman identified with neither rapists nor victims and didn't like the movie at all (*Newsweek*, Aug. 7, 1972, p. 61). *Time's* reviewer dwelt on the enviromental aspects and foggily concluded, "It is nature in all its untamable forces that finally rapes man." (*Time*, Aug. 7, 1972, p. 75.)

(305) *Footnote*, rape sequence in *The Godfather*: Mario Puzo, *The Godfather*, New York: Fawcett Crest, 1969, pp. 29–33.

(306) Eleanor Perry and *Cat Dancing*: Harmetz, *loc. cit.*

(306) "On top of you this morning": Morty Sklar, "Rape," *New York Quarterly*, No. 11 (Summer 1972), p. 86.

(306) Mailer on aggressive sperm: See Norman Mailer, *The Prisoner of Sex*, Boston: Little, Brown, 1971.

(306) "a little bit of rape": *Time*, Nov. 6, 1972, p. 70.

(307) rape as buffoonery: Ed Bullins, *The Reluctant Rapist*, New York: Harper & Row, 1973. Quotations I use appear on pp. 70–72, 82.

(308) A skyjacker is analyzed: David G. Hubbard, *The Skyjacker*, New York: Collier Books, 1973, Chap. 13.

(308) police records of two other skyjackers: *Newsweek*, Nov. 20, 1972, p. 35.

(308) Four armed men: Pranay Gupte, "Governess is Raped by One of 4 Robbers in Greenwich Home," *New York Times*, Aug. 31, 1973, p. 29.

(308) Two Bronx teen-agers: "Youth Sentenced for Raping Victim in Spouse's Presence," *New York Times*, May 18, 1974, p. 63.

(308) Three convicts escape: "3 Convicts in Killing Wave Flee into Forest in Texas," *New York Times*, Aug. 26, 1974, p. 60; "3 Convicts Are Sighted in Texas as Hundreds of Police Close In," *New York Times*, Aug. 27, 1974, p. 1; "2 Convicts Boast to Police of Crime Wave in Texas," *New York Times*, Aug. 28, 1974, p. 15.

10. Victims: The Setting

(310) Mae West, "Funny, every man I meet": *My Little Chickadee*, 1940.

(312) "You can't thread a moving needle": Balzac, "The Maid of Portillon" or "How the Portillon Beauty Scored Over the Magistrate" (Honoré de Balzac, *Droll Stories*, trans. from the French by Alec Brown, London: The Folio Society, 1961, pp. 357–362).

(313) ". . . as a raped woman might struggle": John Updike, *Couples*, New York: Knopf, 1968, p. 415.

(313) ". . . a woman who changed her mind afterward": John Updike, *Rabbit Redux*, New York: Knopf, 1971, p. 37.

(314) "It was an act that could be performed": Ayn Rand, *The Fountainhead* (1943), Indianapolis: Bobbs-Merrill, 1968, p. 220.

(314) "I've been raped": Rand, p. 223.

(315) Freud on female masochism: Sigmund Freud, "The Economic Problem in Masochism" (1924), *Collected Papers*, London: Hogarth Press, 1948, Vol. 2, pp. 255–268.

(315) Deutsch on female masochism, rape: Helene Deutsch, *The Psychology of Women*, New York: Grune & Stratton, 1944, 1945, Vol. I, pp. 219–278 (Chap. 6, "Feminine Passivity"; Chap. 7, "Feminine Masochism"), Vol. II, pp. 77–105 (Chap. 4, "The Psychology of the Sexual Act"). Individual citations follow.

(316) "service to the species": Deutsch, II, p. 77.

(317) clitoris and vagina an "overendowment": Deutsch, II, p. 78.

(317) "physiologically determined": Deutsch, II, p. 80.

(317) "transfer . . . never completely successful": Deutsch, II, p. 78.

(317) "The 'undiscovered' vagina": Deutsch, II, pp. 79–80.

(317) "completely passive vagina": Deutsch, I, p. 230.

(317) male organ does the awakening: Deutsch, I, p. 233.

(317) ". . . feminine need to be overpowered": Deutsch, II, p. 82.

(317) ". . . frequent fear of coitus": Deutsch, II, p. 92.

(317) "Woman's entire psychologic preparation": Deutsch, I, p. 277.

(317) she flees, must be won or overpowered: Deutsch, I, p. 221.

(318) "It is no exaggeration to say": Deutsch, I, p. 222.

(318) "Every time I see": *Ibid.*

(318) copulation originally an act of male violence: *Ibid.*

(318) "The powerful embrace": Deutsch, I, p. 223.

(318) analysis of Leda and Zeus: *Ibid.*

(319) tokens of virginity required in Hebrew marriage contract: Deuteronomy 22:13–21.

(319) "passive-masochistic attitude": Deutsch, I, p. 254.

(320) "In dreams the rape is symbolic": Deutsch, I, p. 255.

(321) Horney argued that female masochism was culturally, not biologically, induced: Karen Horney, "The Problem of Feminine Masochism" (1935), *Feminine Psychology*, New York: Norton, 1967, pp. 214–233; Karen Horney, *The Neurotic Personality of Our Time*, New York: Norton, 1937, p. 280; Karen Horney, *New Ways in Psycho-analysis*, New York: Norton, 1939, pp. 113–117.

(321) Horney on young girls' "instinctive" rape dreams: Karen Horney, "The Denial of the Vagina" (1933), *Feminine Psychology*, pp. 154–155.

(321) "In other words we must assume": *Ibid.*

THE CONSCIOUS RAPE FANTASY

(324) "The conscious masochistic rape fantasies": Deutsch, I, p. 225.

(325) *Footnote*, Horney, "The possibility of rape": *Feminine Psychology*, pp. 230–233.

(326) "I was naked, strapped": Viva, *Superstar*, New York: Putnam, 1970, p. 27.

(326) "My self, woman, womb": Gunther Stuhlmann, ed., *The Diary of Anaïs Nin*, Vol. 2, 1934–1939, New York: Harcourt, Brace, 1967, p. 184.

(326) "Sometimes in the street": *Nin*, p. 209.

(327) "mastered, wanted to lose": *Nin*, p. 7.

(327) poems of Sylvia Plath: "Lady Lazarus" and "Daddy" appear in Sylvia Plath, *Ariel*, New York: Harper & Row, 1966, pp. 6–9, 49–51.

(327) Deutsch, "certain amount of masochism": Deutsch, I, p. 276.

(328) Augustine on Lucretia, rape and suicide: Augustine, *City of God* (414), Book I, Chaps. 16–19 (trans. by Henry Bettenson; ed. by David Knowles; Middlesex, Eng.: Penguin, 1972, pp. 26–31).

(329) Aquinas on rape: Thomas Aquinas, *Summa Theologiae* (1266–1273), 2, 2, Question 154, Article 12 (New York: Blackfriars–McGraw-Hill, 1968, Vol. 43, p. 249).

(330) virgin martyrs: John Coulson, ed., *The Saints*, New York: Hawthorn Books, 1958; Thurston and Attwater, eds., *Butler's Lives of the Saints*, New York: J. J. Kennedy & Sons, 1956.

(330) Maria Goretti: In addition to Coulson and Thurston and Attwater, I have drawn on the following sources: Maria Cecilia Buehrle, *Saint Maria Goretti*, Milwaukee: Bruce Pub. Co., 1950; Alfred MacConastair, *Lily of the Marshes*, New York: Macmillan, 1951; Pietro DiDonato, *The Penitent*, New York: Hawthorn Books, 1962. Individual citations follow.

(330) cause of Bavarian victim displaced: DiDonato, pp. 147–148.

(331) newspaper account of Serenelli at Maria's beatification: "Slayer Attends Girl's Beatification 45 Years After He Murdered Her," *New York Times*, Apr. 28, 1947, p. 25.

(331) denial of Serenelli's attendance: DiDonato, p. 159.

(331) speech of Pope Pius at beatification: Thurston and Attwater, Vol. III, pp. 28–29. See also *New York Times*, June 25, 1950, p. 9, for similar speech by Pius at Maria's canonization.

(331) speediest canonization and largest crowd: Buehrle, p. 158; Thurston and Attwater, *loc. cit.*

(331) sturdy, robust little peasant girl: DiDonato, p. 185.

(331) iconographic idealization: *L'Art Sacre* (Paris), May–June 1951, p. 14.

(332) "exceptionally beautiful": Coulson, p. 323.

(332) "beautiful Jewish girls" in Chmelnitzky pogroms: S. M. Dubnow, *History of the Jews in Russia and Poland*, trans. from the Russian by I. Friedlander, Philadelphia: Jewish Publication Society of America, 1916, Vol. I, p. 147.

(332) Soviet propaganda: Genia Demianova, *Comrade Genia*, preface by Ronald Scarfe, London: Nicholson & Watson, 1941.

(332) suicide poem from ninety-three girls: *The Reconstructionist* (New York), Mar. 5, 1943, p. 23.

(332) *Footnote*, Agostina Pietrantoni: "Pope Paul Beatifies Nun Who Was Slain in Attempted Rape," *New York Times*, Nov. 12, 1972.

THE BEAUTIFUL VICTIM

(334) *"This is the oppressor's language"*: Adrienne Rich "The Burning of Paper Instead of Children," *The Will to Change*, New York: Norton, 1971.

(334) pudenda, meaning "parts of shame": Augustine, *City of God*, Book 14, Chap. 17.

(334) *Footnote*, *Love Story* heralded as "Return to Romance": *Time*, Jan. 11, 1971, cover, pp. 40 ff.

CONFESSIONS: "HE MADE ME DO IT!"

(342) confession-magazine statistics: Author's interview with Johanna Roman Smith, Editor, *Personal Romances*, New York City Mar. 1972.

(342) *Footnote*, "Comic books create sex fears": Fredric Wertham, *Seduction of the Innocent*, New York: Rinehart & Co., 1954, p. 185.

11. VICTIMS: THE CRIME

Note: Testimony from rape victims that is interspersed throughout this chapter comes from the following sources: New York Radical Feminist Speak-Out on Rape, St. Clement's Episcopal Church, New York City, Jan. 24, 1971; New York Radical Feminist Conference on Rape, Washington Irving High School, New York City, Apr. 17, 1971; New York Radical Feminist–National Black Feminist Organization Speak-Out on Rape and Sexual Abuse, Junior High School 104, New York City, Aug. 25, 1974. Additional testimony supplied by rape victims interviewed by the author, and from the following printed sources: *Women: A Journal of Liberation*, Baltimore, Vol. 3, No. 1, p. 18; Nancy Gager Clinch and Cathleen Schurr, "Rape," *The Washingtonian*, June 1973; transcript of "The Rape Tape," produced by the Under One Roof Women's Videotape Collective, in Noreen Connell and Cassandra Wilson, eds., *Rape: The First Sourcebook for Women*, New York: New American Library Plume Book, 1974, pp. 46–53; Karlyn Barker, "She Felt Like a Defendant: Rape Victim Calls Jury Verdict 'Preposterous,' " *Washington Post*, Dec. 2, 1972, p. E-1.

(348) age of victims in Washington study: Charles R. Hayman et al., "Rape in the District of Columbia," presented to the 99th Annual Meeting, American Public Health Association, Minneapolis, Oct. 12, 1971 (mimeo), p. 5.

(348) age of victims in Philadelphia study: Menachem Amir, *Patterns in Forcible Rape*, Chicago: University of Chicago Press, 1971, pp. 51–52.

(348) students comprise largest victim group in Memphis: Brenda A. Brown, "Crime Against Women Alone," a System Analysis of the Memphis Police Department Sex Crime Squad's 1973 Rape Investigations, May 18, 1974 (mimeo), p. 9.

(348) "ecologically bound" offense: Amir, pp. 87–94.

(350) George Washington University case: Barker, "She Felt Like a Defendant," Washington *Post*, Dec. 2, 1972, p. E-1.

(350) Eleven rapes reported at Berkeley: Federal Bureau of Investigation, *Uniform Crime Reports* ,1972, p. 257.

(351) relationship of victims to rapists: Donald J. Mulvihill et. al., *Crimes of Violence*, a staff report to the National Commission on the Causes and Prevention of Violence, Washington: U.S. Government Printing Office, 1969, Vol. 11, p. 217.

(351) "If a woman is attacked": Crimes of Violence, Vol. 11, p. 219.

(351) percentage of strangers committing other violent crimes: Crimes of Violence, Vol. 11, p. 217.

(352) percentage of "founded" rapes committed by strangers in Memphis: Brown, p. 10.

(352) "The closeness of the relationship": Ibid.

(352) "frequently complicated by a prior relationship": UCR, 1973, p. 15.

(354) definitions of victim precipitation: Crimes of Violence, Vol. 11, pp. 224–229.

(355) comparative percentages of victim precipitation: Crimes of Violence, Vol. 11, p. 226.

(355) one-quarter of all reported rapes not completed: UCR, 1973, .p. 13.

(355) *Footnote*, difference in interpretation between commission's staff report and Amir study: Crimes of Violence, Vol. 11, p. 228; Amir, pp. 260, 266.

(355) *Footnote*, traces of sperm may disappear: Frederick P. Bornstein, M.D., "Investigation of Rape: Medicolegal Problems," *Medical Trial Technique Quarterly*, 1963, p. 233.

(357) Amir on victim resistance: Amir, pp. 166–171, 226.

(358) Boston City Hospital study: Ann Wolbert Burgess and Lynda Lytle Holmstrom, "The Rape Victim in the Emergency Ward," *American Journal of Nursing*, Oct. 1973, pp. 1740–1745.

(360) "It seems that when confronted": Amir, p. 169.

(361) Boston Strangler's victims: Gerold Frank, *The Boston Strangler*, New York: NAL Signet, 1967, pp. 272, 355.

(361) case of Richard Speck and eight student nurses: Colin Wilson, *A Casebook of Murder*, London: Leslie Frewin, 1969, pp. 243–247.

(364) "Forcible rape is one of the most falsely reported": George T. Payton, *Patrol Procedure*, Los Angeles: Legal Book Corp., 1967, p. 312.

(366) Memphis study, prostitutes: Brown, pp. 9–10.

(366) NYC Rape Analysis Squad found only 2 percent of complaints were false: "Remarks of Lawrence H. Cooke, Appellate Division Justice,

Before the Association of the Bar of the City of New York," Jan. 16, 1974 (mimeo), p. 6.

(366) same false-report rate that is usual for other felonies: *Ibid*.

(366) yardsticks that policemen use to "found" a rape: "Police Discretion and the Judgment That a Crime Has Been Committed—Rape in Philadelphia," *University of Pennsylvania Law Review*, Vol. 117 (Dec. 1968), pp. 277–322.

(367) "It appears impossible not to conclude": "Police Discretion," p. 304.

(368) ". . . at least 50 percent of the reported rapes are unfounded": "Police Discretion," p. 279 n.

(369) ". . . an accusation easily to be made": Matthew Hale, *History of the Pleas of the Crown*, Philadelphia: R. H. Small, 1847, Vol. I, p. 634.

(369) "An old saw": Camille E. LeGrand, "Rape and Rape Laws: Sexism in Society and Law," *California Law Review*, Vol. 61 (1973), p. 932.

(369) California's jury instructions: *Ibid*.

(370) "Modern psychiatrists have amply studied": John Henry Wigmore *Evidence in Trials at Common Law* (1940), revised by James H. Chadbourn, Boston: Little, Brown, 1970, Vol. 3A, p. 736 (§924a). It is significant that this paragraph did not appear in Wigmore's 1923 edition, published before the popularization of psychoanalytic theories. Wigmore concludes (1940), "No judge should ever let a sex offense charge go to the jury unless the female complainant's social history and mental makeup have been examined and testified to by a qualified physician." In 1937–1938, he records, the American Bar Association's Committee on the Improvement of the Law of Evidence passed a similar resolution.

(370) chastity standard in statutory rape: Earle G. Prevost "Statutory Rape: A Growing Liberalization," *South Carolina Law Review*, Vol. 18 (1966), pp. 254–266; "Forcible and Statutory Rape: An Exploration of the Operation and Objectives of the Consent Standard," *Yale Law Journal*, Vol. 62 (Dec. 1952), pp. 55–83; Isabel Drummond, *The Sex Paradox: An Analytic Survey of Sex and the Law in the United States Today*, New York: Putnam, 1953, pp. 101–103; Samuel G. Kling, *Sexual Behavior and the Law*, New York: Bernard Geis, 1965, pp. 216–218.

(370) age of consent changed in Delaware from 7 to 16: By telephone from John Denney, Deputy Attorney General, Wilmington, Feb. 18, 1975.

(371) "Evidence of the complaining witness's consent": *Yale Law Journal*, Vol. 62 (Dec. 1952), p. 59.

(371) corroboration: "The Rape Corroboration Requirement," *Yale Law Journal*, Vol. 81 (June 1972), pp. 1365–1391.

(372) results of corroboration requirement in New York City: "Remarks of Lawrence H. Cooke," pp. 1–2.

(372) corroboration requirement dropped: David A. Andelman, "New Law on Rape Signed by Wilson, Corroboration No Longer to be Needed," *New York Times*, Feb. 20, 1974; Conn.: "Meskill Signs a Rape-Corroboration Act Repealer," *New York Times*, May 7, 1974; Iowa: confirmation by telephone from Roxanne Conlin, Assistant Attorney General, Des Moines, Feb. 18, 1975.

(372) prosecutors seldom bring a rape case to trial without some form of corroboration: "The Rape Corroboration Requirement," pp. 1382–1383.

(372) "Today most states hold": *Yale Law Journal*, Vol. 62 (Dec. 1952), pp. 56–57.

(373) ". . . the jury is an ally": "Remarks of Lawrence H. Cooke," p. 10.

(373) rape ranks second to murder in defendant preference for jury trial: Harry Kalven and Hans Zeisel, *The American Jury*, Boston: Little, Brown, 1966, p. 26.

(374) "The law recognizes only one issue": Kalven and Zeisel, p. 249.

(374) bootlegging concepts: Kalven and Zeisel, p. 243.

(374) "The jury's stance": Kalven and Zeisel, pp. 250–251.

(374) verdict pattern for "simple rape": Kalven and Zeisel, pp. 252–254.

12. WOMEN FIGHT BACK

Note: Suggestions for changing the laws on rape that appear in this chapter reflect my own thinking; however, model codes and legislative proposals that originated elsewhere helped to clarify my views and provided me with new insights: Lee Cross et al., "Report of the District of Columbia Task Force on Rape," submitted to the D.C. City Council, Washington: July 9, 1973 (mimeo); Jan BenDor et al., "Background Material for a Proposal for Criminal Code Reform to Respond to Michigan's Rape Crisis" and other material relating to Senate Bill 1207, Ann Arbor: Michigan Women's Task Force on Rape, 1974 (mimeo).

(375) "a young Virgine, daughter to Mr. Adam Fisher": *A Blazing Starre Seene in the West*, London: Jonas Wright, 1642 (Joseph Arnold Foster, ed., *Reprints of English Books, 1475–1700*, Ingram, Pa.: 1939, No. 20).

(380) convicted rapists serve an average of forty-four months: U.S. Department of Justice, *National Prisoner Statistics: Prisoners Released from State and Federal Institutions*, 1960, Figure B.

(380) "A husband cannot be guilty": Matthew Hale, *History of the Pleas of the Crown*, Philadelphia: R. H. Small, 1847, Vol. I, p. 628.

(381) "The incident was really of no great moment": John Galsworthy, *The Forsyte Saga*, New York: Scribner's, 1922, pp. 245–246.

(382) marital rape in criminal codes of Sweden, Denmark, etc.: Ernst Livneh, "On Rape and the Sanctity of Matrimony," *Israel Law Review*, Vol. 2, No. 3 (July 1967), pp. 415–422.

(382) certain countries equate economic threats with physical threats: Richard C. Donnelly, "The New Yugoslav Criminal Code," *Yale Law Journal*, Vol. 61 (Apr. 1952), pp. 527–528.

(382) penalties for statutory rape, incest and sodomy: Isabel Drummond, *The Sex Paradox: An Analytic Survey of Sex and the Law in the United States Today*, New York: Putnam, 1953, pp. 347–351.

(385) assailant displays a weapon in one-fifth of police-founded cases: Menachem Amir, *Patterns in Forcible Rape*, Chicago: University of Chicago Press, 1971, p. 153.

(388) women police officers as effective as men: "Women Effective on

Police Patrol, Men Differ Little on Job, Capital Survey Shows," *New York Times*, May 21, 1974, p. 38.

(388) women police officers do not resort to unnecessary force: "The Women in Blue," *Time*, May 1, 1972, p. 60.

(392) "no adequate data to prove the truth or falsity": Alfred C. Kinsey et al., *Sexual Behavior in the Human Male*, Philadelphia: W. B. Saunders, 1948, p. 608.

(392) others still trying although evidence still suggested: See R. N. Barber, "Prostitution and the Increasing Number of Convictions for Rape in Queensland," *Australian and New Zealand Journal of Criminology*, Vol. 2, No. 3 (1969), pp. 169–174; Charles Winick and Paul M. Kinsie, *The Lively Commerce: Prostitution in the United States*, Chicago: Quadrangle, 1971, p. 224.

(393) pornography geared to male heterosexual market: *The Report of The Commission on Obscenity and Pornography*, Washington: U.S. Government Printing Office, Sept. 1970, pp. 15–16.

(393) "predominantly white, middle-class": *The Report of The Commission*, p. 21.

(393) "familiar and firmly established": *The Report of The Commission*, p. 114.

(393) "Because pornography historically": *The Report of The Commission*, p. 115.

(393) ". . . bolsters masculine esteem": *The Report of The Commission*, p. 201.

(393) "Males report being more highly aroused": *The Report of The Commission*, p. 175.

(394) Kinsey on arousal and disgust: *The Report of The Commission*, p. 167.

(395) majority report on relationship between pornography and rape: *The Report of The Commission*, pp. 217–242. For minority report, see pp. 562–582.

(398) "Many break the most elementary rules": Clinton T. Duffy with Al Hirshberg, *Sex and Crime*, New York: Doubleday, 1965, pp. 128–130.

(399) "Don't broadcast the fact": Carl T. Rowan and David M. Mazie, "The Terrible Trauma of Rape," *The Reader's Digest*, Mar. 1974, p. 204.

(400) Nun raped in convent: "Man Convicted of Raping Nun, 63," *New York Times*, Feb. 1, 1975, p. 31.

(401) case for a strong mind in a strong body argued by Susan B. Anthony: *The Revolution* (New York), Vol. 1, No. 2 (Jan. 15, 1868), p. 17; Vol. 1, No. 13 (Apr. 2, 1868), p. 194.

(402) ". . . you shall cut off her hand": Deuteronomy 25:11–12.

INDEX

More about Penguins
and Pelicans

Some Books on World Affairs
and Current Events
published by Penguin Books

Some Books on World Affairs
and Current Events
published by Penguin Books

Some Books on Sociology
and Anthropology
published by Penguin Books

Some Books on Sociology
and Anthropology
published by Penguin Books

Some Books on Sociology
and Anthropology
published by Penguin Books

Some Books on Sociology
and Anthropology
published by Penguin Books